Gender, Generation and Poverty

Gender, Generation and Poverty

Exploring the 'Feminisation of Poverty' in Africa, Asia and Latin America

Sylvia Chant

Professor of Development Geography, London School of Economics, UK

Edward Elgar

Cheltenham, UK • Northampton, MA, USA

Published by
Edward Elgar Publishing Limited
Glensanda House
Montpellier Parade
Cheltenham
Glos GL50 1UA
UK

Edward Elgar Publishing, Inc.
William Pratt House
9 Dewey Court
Northampton
Massachusetts 01060
USA

A catalogue record for this book
is available from the British Library

Library of Congress Cataloguing in Publication Data

Chant, Sylvia H.
    Gender, generation and poverty: exploring the 'feminisation of poverty' in Africa, Asia and Latin America/Sylvia Chant.
        p.   cm.
    Includes bibliographical references and index.
    1. Women in development—Developing countries. 2. Poor women—Developing countries. 3. Poverty—Developing countries. I. Title.
HQ1240.5.D44C533   2007
305.48'96942091724—dc22

                                                            2006101242

ISBN 978 1 84376 992 7 (cased)
ISBN 978 1 84376 993 4 (paperback)

Printed and bound in Great Britain by MPG Books Ltd, Bodmin, Cornwall

Contents

Figures

Tables

Boxes

Preface and acknowledgements

This book is the fruit of three years work supported by a Major Research Fellowship from the Leverhulme Trust (Award no. F07004R). The award provided for 80 per cent alleviation of my teaching load at the London School of Economics between 2003 and 2006, and financial contributions towards fieldwork in my three case study countries – The Gambia, the Philippines and Costa Rica I am grateful to the Trust for providing me with this unique opportunity, as well as to my colleagues and students for tolerating long stretches of absence overseas.

In respect of the fieldwork in The Gambia, thanks go to Baba Njie for his help with focus group collaboration and translation, as well as to Tracey Martin of Voluntary Service Overseas, and Kebba Barrow of the Association of Non-Governmental Organisations for their particularly dedicated efforts to facilitate contacts. Suelle Nachif, Dodou Faal, Maebou Njie and Dodou Ceesay also deserve special mention for their fascinating insights on Gambian culture, and on the Wolof language, which I am still struggling to master! In the Philippines, I am grateful to Tessie Sato, Jose Chan and Fe Largado of the Office of Population Studies, University of San Carlos, Cebu for energetic field assistance, and to their colleagues Delia Carbo, Jojo Avila and Tita Lorna Perez for ancillary help. The efforts of Jaime Glomar and Nica Bertulfo of the NORFIL Foundation, Gwen Ngolaban and Sheila Capaban of FORGE (Fellowship for Organising Endeavours Inc.), and Tessie Fernandez of Lihok Pilipina, Cebu for help in organising and/or facilitating focus group discussions in Metro Cebu are also much appreciated, as are those of Emmeline Verzosa, Executive Director of the National Council on the Role of Filipino Women in (re-)opening so many doors for me in Metro Manila after more than a decade away. In Costa Rica, heartfelt gratitude goes to my expert field team – Enid Jaén Hernández, Luis Castellón Zelaya, and Roberto Rojas of the Universidad de Costa Rica, Sede Regional de Guanacaste – for focus group facilitation and transcription and for assistance with individual interviews in Liberia, Santa Cruz, Villareal, Filadelfia and Nicoya. Thanks are also owed for their huge support, academically and otherwise, to Polly De Fraene, Wagner Moreno, Eugenia Rodríguez, Carolyn Hall and Ana María Trejos.

In the UK, my gratitude extends to several people for their diverse and enriching inputs into this volume, ranging from practical, technical and statistical assistance, to translation, to discussion and feedback on findings and ideas. In strictly alphabetical order these are: Nicola Anyamene, Sarah Bradshaw, Javier Fernández Peña, Susana Franco, John Fyson, Ros Gill, Mercedes González de la Rocha, Edward Hart, Michaela Hendricks, Katya Jassey, Hazel Johnstone, Gareth Jones, Ralph Kinnear, Stephan Klasen, Cathy McIlwaine, Mina Moshkeri, Maxine Molyneux, Eric Neumayer, Jane Parpart, Diane Perrons and Silvia Posocco.

Thanks are also due to the dedicated and highly professional efforts of the team at Edward Elgar – Caroline Cornish, Alexandra O'Connell, Catherine Elgar and Felicity Plester – for making this publishing experience so seamless and enjoyable.

Last but not least, I would like to thank my husband Chris Mogridge for his willingness to visit me on the bulk of my trips, for joining in with some of the fieldwork, and for helping me out in other ways too numerous to mention.

Sylvia Chant
February 2007

Abbreviations

ADB	Asian Development Bank
AEU	Adult Equivalent Unit
AfDB	African Development Bank
AFTA	ASEAN Free Trade Area
AIDS	Acquired Immune Deficiency Syndrome
APEC	Asia-Pacific Economic Cooperation
APIS	Annual Poverty Indicator Survey (Philippines)
APRC	Alliance for Patriotic Reorientation and Construction (The Gambia)
APWW	Asia-Pacific Women's Watch
ARMM	Autonomous Region of Muslim Mindanao (Philippines)
ARV	Annual Rate of Variation
ASEAN	Association of South East Asian Nations
AVAWACA	Anti-Violence Against Women and Children Act (Philippines)
AWIR	Abuse of Women in Intimate Relationships (Philippines)
BAFROW	Foundation for Research on Women's Health, Productivity and Development (The Gambia)
BANVHI	Banco Hipotecario de la Vivienda (Costa Rica)
BCC-KMC	Banjul City Council-Kanifing Municipal Council
BFV	Bono Familiar de Vivienda (Costa Rica)
BLES	Bureau of Labour and Employment Statistics (Philippines)
BNCR	Banco Nacional de Costa Rica
BOI	Board of Investments (Philippines)
BOP	Balance of Payments
BPFA	Beijing Platform for Action
BPO	*Barangay* Protection Order (Philippines)
BSP	Banko Sentral ng Pilipinas (Philippines)
BWIs	Bretton Woods Institutions
BWS	Battered Woman Syndrome
BWYW	Bureau of Women and Young Workers (Philippines)
CAFTA	Central American Free Trade Agreement

CARICOM	The Caribbean Community
CARP	Comprehensive Agrarian Reform Programme (Philippines)
CBO	Community-based Organisation
CCSS	Caja Costarricense de Seguro Social
CCUP	City Commission for the Urban Poor (Philippines)
CDD	Community-driven Development
CDM	Colectiva por el Derecho de la Mujer (Costa Rica)
CEDAW	Convention on the Elimination of All Forms of Discrimination Against Women
CEFEMINA	Centro Feminista de Información y Acción (Costa Rica)
CEN/CINAI	Centros Integrales de Atención Infantil (Costa Rica)
CHED	Commission on Higher Education (Philippines)
CIDA	Canadian International Development Agency
CIDSS	Comprehensive and Integrated Delivery of Social Services (Philippines)
CLHNS	Cebu Longitudinal Health and Nutrition Survey (Philippines)
CMF	Centro Nacional para el Desarrollo de la Mujer y de la Familia (Costa Rica)
CMP	Community Mortgage Programme (Philippines)
CNS	Consejo Nacional de Salarios (Costa Rica)
COFIs	Community-Oriented Financial Intermediaries System (Philippines)
CONAPAM	Consejo Nacional para el Adulto Mayor (Costa Rica)
COSORE	Consejo Social Regional (Costa Rica)
CPA	Child Protection Alliance (The Gambia)
CPDH	Centro Pro-Derechos Humanos (Costa Rica)
CPM	Capability Poverty Measure
CPP	Communist Party of the Philippines
CRC	Convention on the Rights of the Child
CSIP	Community Skills Improvement Programme (The Gambia)
CSO	Civil Society Organisation
CWC	Council for the Welfare of Children (Philippines)
DAC	Development Assistance Committee (of the OECD)
DECS	Department of Education, Culture and Sports (Philippines)
DepEd	Department of Education (Philippines)
DFID	Department for International Development
DILG	Department of the Interior and Local Government (Philippines)

DIWATA	Development Initiatives for Women and Transformative Action, Inc. (Philippines)
DMC	Developing Member Country (of Asian Development Bank)
DOH	Department of Health (Philippines)
DOLE	Department of Labour and Employment (Philippines)
DOSE	Department of State for Education (The Gambia)
DOSH	Department of State for Health (The Gambia)
DOSFEA	Department of State for Financial and Economic Affairs (The Gambia)
DOSSW	Department of State for Social Welfare (The Gambia)
DRF	Drug Revolving Fund (The Gambia)
DSWD	Department of Social Welfare and Development (Philippines)
DTI	Department of Trade and Industry (Philippines)
DWUP	Division for the Welfare of the Urban Poor (Philippines)
EBAIS	Equipos Básicos de Atención Integral en Salud (Costa Rica)
ECD	Early Childhood Development
ECLAC	Economic Commission for Latin America and the Caribbean
ECOWAS	Economic Organisation of West African States
EFA-FTI	Education for All – Fast-Track Initiative
EHPM	Encuesta de Hogares de Propósitos Múltiples (Costa Rica)
ENH	Encuesta Nacional de Hogares (Costa Rica)
EO	Executive Order (Philippines)
EOI	Export-oriented Industrialisation
EPZ	Export Processing Zone
ERPAT	Empowerment and Reaffirmation of Paternal Abilities Programme (Philippines)
EU	European Union
FASE	Fight Against Social Exclusion
FAWEGAM	Forum for African Women Educationalists – The Gambia
FDI	Foreign Direct Investment
FFS	Filipino Family Survey
FGM	Female Genital Mutilation
FHH	Female-headed Household
FIES	Family Income and Expenditure Survey (Philippines)
FLOL	Fixed Level of Living Line (Philippines)
FODESAF	Fondo de Desarrollo Social y Asignaciones Familiares (Costa Rica)

FONAES	Fondo Nacional de Apoyo a Empresas Sociales (Mexico)
FPW	Framework Plan for Women (Philippines)
FTAA	Free Trade Area of the Americas
FTZ	Free Trade Zone
GAA	General Appropriations Act (Philippines)
GABRIELA	General Assembly Binding Women for Reform, Integrity, Empowerment, Leadership and Action (Philippines)
GAD	Gender and Development
GAMCOTRAP	The Gambia Committee on Traditional Practices Affecting the Health of Women and Children
GBA	Greater Banjul Area (The Gambia)
GBI	Gender Budget Initiative
GCAP	Global Call to Action Against Poverty
GCR	Gobierno de Costa Rica
GDA	Gender Disparity Adjusted Human Development Index
GDI	Gender-Related Development Index
GDP	Gross Domestic Product
GEM	Gender Empowerment Measure
GENDERNET	Network on Gender Equality (of DAC)
GER	Gross Enrolment Ratio
GEWEF	Gender Equality and Women's Empowerment Framework
GNP	Gross National Product
GNYSS	Gambia National Youth Service Scheme
GOCC	Government Owned and Controlled Corporation (Philippines)
GOTG	Government of The Gambia
GPI	Gendered Poverty Index
GPP	Gambian People's Party
GRC	GAD Resource Centre (Philippines)
GRN	Gender Resource Network (Philippines)
GSIS	Government Service Insurance System (Philippines)
GSP	Generalised System of Preferences (EU)
GTTI	Gambia Technical Training Institute
HDI	Human Development Index
HIPC	Heavily Indebted Poor Country
HIV	Human Immunodeficiency Virus
HPI	Human Poverty Index
ICESR	International Covenant on Economic, Social and Cultural Rights

ICPD	International Conference on Population and Development
ICT	Information and Communications Technology
ICT	Instituto Costarricense de Turismo (only Chapter 6 on Costa Rica)
IDA	Instituto de Desarrollo Agrario (Costa Rica)
IDESPO	Instituto de Estudios Sociales en Población (Costa Rica)
IDH	Indice de Desarrollo Humano (Costa Rica)
IDS	Indice de Desarrollo Social (Costa Rica)
IFAD	International Fund for Agricultural Development
IFI	International Financial Institution
IFMIS	Integrated Financial Management Information System
IFPRI	International Food Policy Research Institute
IHPS	Integrated Household Poverty Survey (The Gambia)
II	Isis International
ILO	International Labour Organisation
IMAS	Instituto Mixto de Ayuda Social (Costa Rica)
IMF	International Monetary Fund
INAMU	Instituto Nacional de las Mujeres (Costa Rica)
INEC	Instituto Nacional de Estadísticas y Censos (Costa Rica)
INCIENSA	Instituto Costarricense de Investigación y Enseñanza en Nutrición y Salud (Costa Rica)
IPC	International Poverty Centre
IPEC	International Programme on the Elimination of Child Labour
IPPF	International Planned Parenthood Federation
ISI	Import Substitution Industrialisation
IT	Information Technology
ITC	International Trade Centre
KALAHI	*Kapit Bisig Laban sa Kahirapan* (Linking Arms to Fight Poverty) (Philippines)
KMC	Kanifing Municipal Authority (The Gambia)
LABAN	Laban ng Demokratikong Pilipino (Philippines)
Lakas	Lakas ng Edsa – National Union of Christian Democrats (Philippines)
LCW	Local Commission on Women (Philippines)
LDC	Less Developed Country
LGC	Local Government Code (Philippines)
LGU	Local Government Unit (Philippines)
LPIMS	Local Poverty Indicator Monitoring System (Philippines)

LPRAO	Local Poverty Reduction Action Officer (Philippines)
LPRAP	Local Poverty Reduction Action Plan (Philippines)
MBN	Minimum Basic Needs
MCH	Maternal and Child Health
MDG	Millennium Development Goal
MDGR	Millennium Development Goal Report
MDI	Management Development Institute (The Gambia)
MEP	Ministerio de Educación Pública (Costa Rica)
MEPZ	Mactan Export Processing Zone
MFA	Multi-Fibre Agreement
MFC	Movimiento Familiar Cristiano (Christian Family Movement)
MFI	Micro-finance Institution
MILF	Moro Islamic Liberation Front (Philippines)
MIVAH	Ministerio de Vivienda y Asentamientos Humanos (Costa Rica)
ML	Partido Movimiento Libertario (Costa Rica)
MNLF	Moro National Liberation Front (Philippines)
MT	Ministerio de Trabajo (Costa Rica)
MTPDP	Medium-Term Philippine Development Plan
MWSS	Manila Water and Sanitation Service (Philippines)
NADD	National Alliance for Democracy and Development (The Gambia)
NAPC	National Anti-Poverty Commission (Philippines)
NAPS	National Anti-Poverty Strategy (Philippines)
NAWEC	National Water and Electricity Company (The Gambia)
NCP	National Convention Party (The Gambia)
NCR	National Capital Region (Philippines)
NCRFW	National Commission on the Role of Filipino Women
NCW	National Commission on Women (Philippines)
NCWP	National Wages and Productivity Commission (Philippines)
NDAM	National Democratic Action Movement (The Gambia)
NEDA	National Economic and Development Authority (Philippines)
NGO	Non-governmental Organisation
NHA	National Housing Authority (Philippines)
NHPS	National Household Poverty Survey (The Gambia)
NPACL	National Programme Against Child Labour (Philippines)
NPAGW	National Policy for the Advancement of Gambian Women

NPC	Nationalist People's Coalition (Philippines)
NRP	National Reconciliation Party (The Gambia)
NSCB	National Statistical and Coordination Board (Philippines)
NSO	National Statistics Office (Philippines)
NWB	National Women's Bureau (The Gambia)
NWC	National Women's Council (The Gambia)
NWPC	National Wages and Productivity Commission (Philippines)
OCW	Overseas contract work (Philippines)
ODA	Official Development Assistance
OECD	Organisation for Economic Co-operation and Development
OFI	Overseas Filipino Investor
OFIM	Oficina de la Mujer (Costa Rica)
OFW	Overseas Filipino Worker
OHSC	Occupational Safety and Health Centre (Philippines)
OIJ	Organismo de Investigación Judicial (Costa Rica)
OPA	Overseas Performing Artist (Philippines)
OPD	Oficina de la Primera Dama (Costa Rica)
OSCA	Office of Senior Citizens' Action (Philippines)
PAC	Partido Acción Ciudadana (Costa Rica)
PAE	Programa de Ajuste Estructural (Costa Rica)
PCFC	People's Credit Finance Corporation (Philippines)
PDOIS	People's Democratic Organisation for Independence and Socialism (The Gambia)
PDPW	Philippine Development Plan for Women
PDTF	People's Development Trust Fund (Philippines)
PER	Public Expenditure Review
PES	Parent Effectiveness Service (Philippines)
PEZA	Philippine Economic Zone Authority
PHC	Primary Health Care
PIN	Partido Integración Nacional (Costa Rica)
PLANOVI	Plan Nacional para la Atencion y Prevención de la Violencia Intrafamiliar (Costa Rica)
PLDT	Philippine Long Distance Telephone Company
PLN	Partido Liberación Nacional (Costa Rica)
PLWHA	People Living With HIV/AIDS
PNAC	Philippines National AIDS Council
PNCP	Plan Nacional de Combate a la Pobreza (Costa Rica)
PnM	Puwersa ng Masa (Philippines)
PNP	Philippine National Police

PNS	Plan Nacional de la Solidaridad (Costa Rica)
POEA	Philippine Overseas Employment Administration
POLO	Philippine Overseas Labour Officer
POPCOM	Population Commission (Philippines)
PPA	Participatory Poverty Assessment
PPC	People's Power Coalition (Philippines)
PPC	Partido del Pueblo Costarricense (Costa Rica)
PPGD	Philippine Plan for Gender-Responsive Development
PPMP	Philippine Population Management Programme
PPP	Purchasing Power Parity
PPP	People's Progressive Party (The Gambia)
PRA	Participatory Rural Appraisal
PRC	Partido Renovación Cristiana (Costa Rica)
PRGF	Poverty Reduction and Growth Facility
PROPAG	Pro-Poor Advocacy Group
PRS	Poverty Reduction Strategy
PRSP	Poverty Reduction Strategy Paper
PSCB	Productivity Skills Capability Building for Disadvantaged Women (Philippines)
PSS	Philippine Statistical System
PTBP	Philippine Time-Bound Programme
PUSC	Partido Unidad Social Cristiana (Costa Rica)
PVN	Plan Vida Nueva (Costa Rica)
RA	Republic Act (Philippines)
RKCG	Regional KALAHI Convergence Group (Philippines)
RP	Republic of the Philippines
SAP	Structural Adjustment Programme
SCC	Senior Citizens' Centre (Philippines)
SDF	Social Development Fund
SIPO	Sistema de Información de la Población Objetivo (Costa Rica)
SISBEN	Sistema de Selección de Beneficiarios para Programas Sociales (Costa Rica)
SJMA	San José Metropolitan Area (Costa Rica)
SMEs	Small and Medium-sized Enterprises (Costa Rica)
SNA	System of National Accounts
SONA	State of the Nation Address (Philippines)
SPA	Strategy for Poverty Alleviation (The Gambia)
SPACO	Strategy for Poverty Alleviation Coordinating Office (The Gambia)
SRA	Social Reform Agenda (Philippines)
SRC	Social Reform Council (Philippines)

SRP	Self-rated Poverty
SSS	Social Security System (Philippines)
STI	Sexually Transmitted Infection
SUC	State University and College (Philippines)
SWS	Social Weather Stations (Philippines)
TANGO	The Association of Non-Governmental Organisations (The Gambia)
TBA	Traditional Birth Attendant
TCP	Training Cum Production (Philippines)
TESDA	Technical Education and Skills Development Authority (Philippines)
TFEE	Task Force on Economic Empowerment (Philippines)
TFEGE	Task Force on Education and Gender Equality
TFR	Total Fertility Rate
TNC	Transnational Corporation
UCW	Unpaid Care Work
UDP	United Democratic Party (The Gambia)
UN	United Nations
UNDP	United Nations Development Programme
UNESCO	United Nations Educational, Scientific, and Cultural Organisation
UNFPA	United Nations Fund for Population Activities
UNICEF	United Nations Children's Fund
UNIFEM	United Nations Development Fund for Women
UNMP	United Nations Millennium Project
UNSD	United Nations Statistics Division
VAW	Violence Against Women
VAWC	Violence Against Women and Children
VAWCC	Violence Against Women Coordinating Committee (Philippines)
VHW	Village Health Worker
VSO	Voluntary Service Overseas
WAND	Women's Action Network for Development (Philippines)
WB	World Bank
WEDO	Women's Environment and Development Organisation
WEDPRO	Women's Education, Development and Productivity Organisation (Philippines)
WEED	Women Workers' Employment and Entrepreneurship Development (Philippines)
WEF	World Economic Forum

WHO	World Health Organisation
WID	Women in Development
WINT	Women in New Trades (Philippines)
WTO	World Trade Organisation

1. Introduction

The 'feminisation of poverty' has become common currency in the development lexicon in recent years.[1] This is especially so since the Fourth United Nations World Conference on Women in 1995 when eradicating the 'persistent and increasing burden of poverty on women' was adopted as one of the twelve arms of the Beijing Platform for Action (BPFA).[2] Although there are varied perspectives on the meanings of this 'pithy and polyvalent phrase' (Molyneux, 2006a; see also Box 1.1), the most popularised tenets are three-fold. The first is that women are the majority of the world's poor. The second is that their disproportionate share of poverty is rising relative to men's. The third is that the 'feminisation of poverty' is linked with the 'feminisation of household headship', as manifested in the widely cited epithet that women-headed households are the 'poorest of the poor' (see Box 1.2).[3]

BOX 1.1 COMMON CHARACTERISATIONS OF THE 'FEMINISATION OF POVERTY'

- Women experience a higher incidence of poverty than men.
- Women experience greater depth/severity of poverty than men (i.e. more women are likely to suffer 'extreme' poverty than men).
- Women are prone to suffer more persistent/longer-term poverty than men.
- Women's disproportionate burden of poverty is rising relative to men.
- Women face more barriers to lifting themselves out of poverty.
- The 'feminisation of poverty' is linked with the 'feminisation' of household headship.
- Women-headed households are the 'poorest of the poor'.
- Female household headship transmits poverty to children ('inter-generational transmission of disadvantage').

Sources: Baden (1999); Cagatay (1998); Chant (1997b; 2003a; 2003b); Davids and van Driel (2001; 2005); Medeiros and Costa (2006); Moghadam (1997; 2005); Wennerholm (2002).

BOX 1.2   ASSERTIONS ABOUT FEMALE-HEADED HOUSEHOLDS AS THE 'POOREST OF THE POOR'

'The global economic downturn has pressed most heavily on women-headed households, which are everywhere in the world, the poorest of the poor' (Tinker, 1990: 5).

'Women-headed households are over-represented among the poor in rural and urban, developing and industrial societies' (Bullock, 1994: 17–18).

'One continuing concern of both the developing and advanced capitalist economies is the increasing amount of women's poverty worldwide, associated with the rise of female-headed households' (Acosta-Belén and Bose, 1995: 25).

'What is clear is that in many countries women tend to be over-represented in the ranks of the 'old' or structural poor, and female-headed households tend to be among the most vulnerable of social groups' (Graham, 1996: 3).

'The number of female-headed households among the poor and the poorer sections of society is increasing and . . . they, as a group – whether heterogeneous or not – are more vulnerable and face more discrimination because they are poor and also because they are man-less women on their own' (Bibars, 2001: 67).

'Households headed by females with dependent children experience the worst afflictions of poverty . . . Female-headed households are the poorest' (Finne, 2001: 8).

'Households headed by women are particularly vulnerable. Disproportionate numbers of women among the poor pose serious constraints to human development because children raised in poor households are more likely to repeat cycles of poverty and disadvantage' (Asian Development Bank, 2003: 11).

Source: Chant (2006: 5).

Table 1.1   Trends in poverty: developing world regions, 1990–2015

	Millions			%		
	1990	1999	2015	1990	1999	2015
People living on less than $1 a day						
East Asia and Pacific	486	279	80	30.5	15.6	3.9
Excluding China	110	57	7	24.2	10.6	1.1
Europe and Central Asia	6	24	7	1.4	5.1	1.4
Latin America and Caribbean	48	57	47	11.0	11.1	7.5
Middle East and North Africa	5	6	8	2.1	2.2	2.1
South Asia	506	488	264	45.0	36.6	15.7
Sub-Saharan Africa	241	315	404	47.4	49.0	46.0
Total	1292	1169	809	29.6	23.2	13.3
Excluding China	917	945	735	28.5	25.0	15.7
People living on less than $2 a day						
East Asia and Pacific	1114	897	339	69.7	50.1	16.6
Excluding China	295	269	120	64.9	50.2	18.4
Europe and Central Asia	31	97	45	6.8	20.3	9.3
Latin America and Caribbean	121	132	117	27.6	26.0	18.9
Middle East and North Africa	50	68	62	21.0	23.3	16.0
South Asia	1010	1128	1139	89.8	84.8	68.0
Sub-Saharan Africa	386	480	618	76.0	74.7	70.4
Total	2712	2802	2320	62.1	55.6	38.1
Excluding China	1892	2173	2101	58.7	57.5	44.7

Notes: The projections for 2015 assume an average annual growth rate in per capita GDP of 3.4 per cent. The number of people in developing countries living on less than $2 a day is projected to fall by 593 million between 2000 and 2015, with most of this occurring in East Asia and the Pacific.

Source: World Bank data, http://www.developmentgoals.org/Poverty.htm#percapita, accessed June 2004.

While these notions will be explored (and challenged) in the current book, the value of determining trends in the gendered burdens of poverty remains paramount. Although the proportion of the world's population living in poverty has declined since the early 1990s, absolute numbers in many parts of the South are rising (see Table 1.1), and 'unless drastic measures are taken', this may well continue (Middleton et al., 2001: 2). This is important since although headcount ratios (the percentage of the poor within the population), satisfy a 'Likelihood Principle' (the probability of being poor), they do not, unlike aggregate headcounts (the total absolute number of the poor), uphold a 'Constituency Principle' whereby poverty has an intrinsic importance to those it afflicts (see Subramanian, 2005). Moreover, current trends suggest that inequalities in income distribution will undergo further polarisation. Although income inequalities are rarely deemed as 'politically sensitive' as poverty per se, they may be particularly important for women since they concern power relations, with women's lack of power arguably being among the most fundamental reasons why poverty is feminising (see Johnson, 2005: 57).

While defining poverty, let alone which individuals or groups are the 'poorest', is both highly complex and contested, one of the main connotations in prevailing constructions of the 'feminisation of poverty' is that women suffer a greater incidence of income poverty than men (Chant, 2006). Notwithstanding that collecting data on incomes can be extremely problematic and prone to error, many argue that 'money-metric' poverty is the easiest to identify and enumerate. Indeed, the 'Copenhagen measure' whereby the (extremely) poor are classified as all those persons living on less than one US dollar a day, is the only indicator which is accepted internationally (Johnsson-Latham, 2004b: 28).[4] Yet while we know more or less how many people this applies to (around 1.5 billion as of 2005, or one-sixth of the world's population), we are unable to pinpoint its gender dimensions with any precision in the absence of a globally comprehensive database on women's poverty relative to men's (see UNIFEM, 2002: 60). On top of this, although 'feminisation' implies a trend for gender gaps in poverty to be widening over time, the possibilities for empirical verification are virtually non-existent (Nauckhoff, 2004: 65). As summarised by Johnsson-Latham (2004b: 18):

> In spite of the suggestion that the majority of the poor are women, there are neither firm data to confirm this – nor the suggestion that there is a trend of 'feminisation of poverty'. This is due to the fact that few efforts have been made to estimate the scope and magnitude of female poverty. (See also later)

With the exception of Latin America, where the regional United Nations Economic Commission (Economic Commission for Latin America and the Caribbean – ECLAC) has produced headcounts of females and males who fall below national poverty lines (see CEPAL, 2002; also Chapter 3 in this volume), data in developing areas are usually collected at the household level and, as noted by Klasen (2004: 2), which makes it 'conceptually and practically difficult to "assign" households [*sic*] incomes or assets to individuals of different gender *within* households' (emphasis added). As echoed by Baden (1999: 10): 'the lack of systematic data which disaggregates expenditure or consumption by gender means that such broad statements are often based on questionable assumptions'. Yet a continued dearth of comprehensive sex-disaggregated data[5] has done little to dissuade major development organisations from asserting that between 60 and 70 per cent of the world's poor are female, and that poverty increasingly has a 'woman's face' (UNDP, 1995: 4; see also DFID, 2000: 13; UN, 1996: 6; UNIFEM, 1995: 4, cited in Marcoux, 1997; also ADB, 2000: 16).[6] Indeed, the assumption that poverty afflicts women more than men has become so engrained in international development discourse that this seems to have obviated the need for substantiating the hypothesis. As stated by Davids and van Driel (2005: 5), women's impoverishment has become a 'global orthodoxy that is not questioned anymore'.

Yet for all the problems weakly substantiated pronouncements of a 'feminisation of poverty' might entail, that they draw attention to women's privation represents a significant breakthrough given that until recently most discussions have dealt with 'sexless averages' (Johnsson-Latham, 2004b: 18), and '(P)overty programmes have not ordinarily incorporated gender as an important dimension' (UNDP, 2000b: 3).

Testifying to the growing prominence of gender in poverty analysis and strategy is ECLAC's (2004b: 82) claim that one of its main priorities for Latin America and the Caribbean is to 'identify the characteristics of female poverty and its associated causes'. This is also a major concern for the Asian Development Bank (ADB) (2002: 135), who argue that the 'overarching goal of poverty reduction is closely linked to improving the status of women, since equity – especially gender equity – is now recognised as an essential factor in transforming growth to development and reducing poverty'. With something of a 'win–win formula' having emerged from the conjectured synergies between greater gender equity, economic growth and effective poverty reduction (Rodenberg, 2004: iv), it is no surprise that popularisation of the 'feminisation of poverty' seems to have led to a 'feminisation' of anti-poverty programmes. The latter is evidenced in initiatives to increase women's literacy, education and vocational skills, to facilitate their access to micro-credit, to recruit them as volunteers in community solidarity and self-help schemes, and/or to provide targeted support to female heads of household (see Chant, 1999; 2003a; Kabeer, 1997; Mayoux, 2002; 2006; Molyneux, 2006a; 2006b; Pankhurst, 2002; UNDAW, 2000: 3 and 9; Yates, 1997). Growing acknowledgement of the strategic importance of gender in combatting poverty has also propelled it into the macro-level domain of Poverty Reduction Strategy Papers (PRSPs) and the Millennium Development Goals (MDGs).

THE IMPACTS OF THE 'FEMINISATION OF POVERTY' ON MACRO-LEVEL POVERTY REDUCTION INITIATIVES

Gender in PRSPs

Poverty Reduction Strategy Papers aim to alleviate poverty and have been devised by an increasing number of the world's poorest countries in order to attain debt relief.[7] Gender has become identified in these as a 'cross-cutting' issue, requiring, *inter alia*, that women should be a vital con-stituency in consultation and that proposals should 'mainstream gender' (see Bradshaw and Linneker, 2003; Whitehead, 2003). These provisos are driven by what Zuckerman (2003) identifies as three compelling reasons to 'en-gender' PRSPs. The first is the 'poverty reduction case' which asserts the centrality of gender to reducing poverty. The second is the 'business–World Bank case' which focuses on the costs of gender inequality to development. The third is the 'human rights case' which regards gender equality as inte-gral to full and equal human rights for all. In turn, Rodenberg (2004: v) claims that two of the most positive outcomes of the purported 'en-gendering' of PRSPs are that 'an array of entry points are identified for alleviating and discriminating against women in the community and the market', and that strategic concerns such as improving women's legal posi-tion and preventing domestic violence are making an increasing appear-ance in policy documents.

This said, what happens in practice is often a far cry from rhetoric, and from the BPFA, which, as Johnsson-Latham (2004b: 34) argues, remains the 'most far-reaching political agreement in defining female poverty and deprivation', addressing, as it does, core issues in women's disadvantage such as land and inheritance rights (see also Painter, 2004: 41).

Shortcomings in the 'en-gendering' of PRSPs highlighted by Bradshaw and Linneker (2003) include the lack of a minimum gender threshold, no clear guidance from the international financial institutions (IFIs) on how and which groups of women (or men) should be included in the policy development process, that the gender guidelines issued by the World Bank tend to focus on economic growth, productivity and efficiency rather than equity, and that insufficient time or opportunity is given to consultation with women's organisations. Other qualifications pointed up by Rodenberg (2004) are that women and gender tend to feature in traditionally 'female' sectors such as health and education at the expense of 'gender-neutral' fields such as trade and development financing, that PRSPs rarely take into account women's vast amount of unpaid labour in reproduction and sub-sistence at domestic and community levels, and that under the heading of gender 'girls' and 'mothers' are mentioned to a much greater extent than 'men' and 'boys', with 'fathers' seldom mentioned, if ever (ibid.: 25 and 37; also de Vylder, 2004; UNRISD, 2005). It has also been asserted that 'Because cross-cutting issues are supposed to be everyone's business, they tend to become the responsibility of no-one' (UNMP/TFEGE, 2005: 23). Given these wide-ranging contradictions, and that 'business' and 'efficiency' considerations tend to have overridden those of 'human rights', it is no surprise to find allegations that: 'Only a handful of PRSPs can be said to have taken women's poverty seriously' (Whitehead, 2003: 35), or that 'PRSPs do not at present appear to be a fruitful avenue for women's empowerment' (UNRISD, 2005: 56). Indeed, if anything, PRSPs could actually be exacerbating women's poverty, with women's organisations in Latin America noting that they constitute:

> little more than a rerun of the old structural adjustment programmes of the 1980s which led to a 'feminisation of poverty' as a result of the privatisation of basic services and cuts in public social services. They [women] now fear that their governments may use the participation procedure as a means of co-opting them i.e. of using their active participation to legitimise and formulate disguised growth-oriented structural adjustment programmes instead of encouraging them to participate actively in implementing socio-political change. (Rodenberg, 2004: 38)

Gender and the MDGs

Criticisms around the gender shortfalls in PRSPs are in many ways similar to those levelled at the MDGs. Issued in the spirit of the Millennium Declaration by 191 United Nations (UN) member states in 2000, the MDGs are described as 'time-bound and measurable goals and targets for combatting poverty, hunger, disease, illiteracy, environmental degradation and discrimination against women', with the halving of extreme poverty by 2015 being the first and overriding objective (Barton, 2004: 3; Rodenberg, 2004: i; see also Box 1.3).

The MDGs arguably reflect a human rights agenda, drawing as they do from various world conferences of the 1990s built, in turn, on earlier treaties such as the International Covenant on Economic, Social and Cultural Rights (ICESR) and the Convention on the Elimination of All Forms of Discrimination Against Women (CEDAW) (Abeyesekera, 2004; Painter, 2004: 5). The purported centrality of gender equality and women's human rights in the MDGs not only implies making connections between the MDGs and global agreements such as CEDAW, the BPFA and so on, but also 'requires a commitment from donors to finance women's empowerment' (Heyzer, 2005: 11). As articulated by UNMP/TFEGE (2005: 1):

BOX 1.3 THE UNITED NATIONS MILLENNIUM DECLARATION AND THE MILLENNIUM DEVELOPMENT GOALS

UN Millennium Declaration, September 2000
'We will spare no effort to free our fellow men, women and children from the abject and dehumanising conditions of extreme poverty, to which more than a billion of them are currently subjected.'

Goals and targets	Indicators

GOAL 1: Eradicate extreme poverty and hunger

Target 1: Halve the proportion of people on less than US$1 per day between 1990 and 2015	1. Proportion of population below US$1 per day 2. Poverty gap ratio (incidence × depth of poverty) 3. Share of poorest quintile in national consumption
Target 2: Halve the proportion of people who suffer from hunger between 1990 and 2015	4. Prevalence of underweight children (under 5 years of age) 5. Proportion of population below minimum level of dietary energy consumption

GOAL 2: Achieve universal primary education

Target 3: By 2015, ensure that all children complete full primary education	6. Net enrolment ratio in primary education 7. Proportion of pupils starting grade 1 who reach grade 5 8. Literacy rate of 15–24-year-olds

GOAL 3: Promote gender equality and empower women

Target 4: Eliminate gender disparity in primary and secondary education preferably by 2005, and at all levels of education by 2015	9. Ratio of girls to boys in primary, secondary and tertiary education 10. Ratio of literate females to males in 15–24-year age group

11. Share of women in wage employment in the non-agricultural sector
12. Proportion of seats in parliament held by women

GOAL 4: Reduce child mortality

Target 5: Reduce by two-thirds the under-5 mortality rate between 1990 and 2015

13. Under-5 mortality rate
14. Infant mortality rate
15. Proportion of 1-year-old children immunised against measles

GOAL 5: Improve maternal health

Target 6: Reduce maternal mortality ratio by three-quarters between 1990 and 2015

16. Maternal mortality ratio
17. Proportion of births attended by skilled personnel

GOAL 6: Combat HIV/AIDS, malaria and other diseases

Target 7: Halt and begin to reverse spread of HIV/AIDS by 2015

18. HIV prevalence among 15–24-year-old pregnant women
19. Contraceptive prevalence rate
20. Number of children orphaned by HIV/AIDS

Target 8: Halt and begin to reverse the incidence of malaria and other major diseases by 2015

21. Prevalence and death rates associated with malaria
22. Proportion of population in malaria risk areas using effective malaria prevention and treatment measures
23. Prevalence and death rates associated with tuber-culosis
24. Proportion of TB cases detected and cured under Directly Observed Treatment Short Course (DOTS)

GOAL 7: Ensure environmental sustainability*

Target 9: Integrate the principles of sustainable development into country policies and programmes and reverse the loss of environmental resources

25. Proportion of land area covered by forest
26. Land area protected to maintain biological diversity
27. Gross domestic product (GDP) per unit of energy (as proxy for energy efficiency)
28. Carbon dioxide emissions per capita (plus two figures of global atmospheric pollution: ozone depletion and the accumulation of global warming gases)

Target 10: Halve by 2015 the proportion of people without sustainable access to safe drinking water

29. Proportion of population with sustainable access to an improved water source.
30. Proportion of people with access to improved sanitation

Target 11: Achieve a significant improvement in the lives of at least 100 million slum-dwellers by 2020

31. Proportion of people with access to secure tenure

GOAL 8: Develop a global partnership for development

Target 12: Develop further an open, rule-based predictable, non-discriminatory trading and financial system
Includes a commitment to good governance, development and poverty reduction – both nationally and internationally

Official development assistance (ODA)

Target 13: Address the special needs of the Least Developed Countries

32. Net ODA as percentage of DAC donors' GNP (targets of 0.7 per cent in total and 0.15 per cent for LDCs)

Includes tariff and quota free access for LDC exports; enhanced programme of debt relief for HIPC and cancellation of official bilateral debt, and more generous ODA

33. Proportion of ODA to basic social services (education, primary healthcare, nutrition, safe water and sanitation)
34. Proportion of ODA which is untied
35. Proportion of ODA for environment in small island developing states
36. Proportion of ODA for transport sector in land-locked countries
Market access
37. Proportion of exports by value (excluding arms), admitted free of duties and quotas

Target 14: Address the Special Needs of landlocked countries and small island developing states (through Barbados Programme and 22nd General Assembly provisions)

38. Average tariffs and quotas on agricultural products, and textiles and clothing
39. Domestic and export agricultural subsidies in OECD countries
40. Proportion of ODA provided to help build trade capacity
Debt sustainability
41. Proportion of official bilateral heavily indebted poor country (HIPC) debt cancelled

Target 15: Deal comprehensively with the debt problems of developing countries through national and international measures in order to make debt sustainable in the long term

42. Debt service as a percentage of exports of goods and services
43. Proportion of ODA provided as debt relief
44. Number of countries reaching HIPC decision and completion points

Target 16: In cooperation with developing countries develop and implement strategies for decent and productive work for youth	45. Unemployment rate of 15–24-year-olds
Target 17: In cooperation with pharmaceutical companies, provide access to affordable, essential drugs in developing countries	46. Proportion of population with access to affordable essential drugs on a sustainable basis
Target 18: In cooperation with the private sector, make available the benefits of new technologies, especially information and communications	47. Telephone lines per 1000 people 48. Personal computers per 1000 people

Note:　* The selection of indicators for Goals 7 and 8 is subject to further revision. Also, some of the indicators for Goal 8 will be monitored separately for the Least Developed Countries, Africa, landlocked countries and small island developing states.

Source:　Millennium Development Goals website, http://www.developmentgoals.org/, accessed June 2005.

'The inclusion of gender equality and women's empowerment in the third Millennium Development Goal is a reminder that many promises have not been met, while simultaneously offering yet another international opportunity to implement them.'

That there is a separate goal – MDG 3 – which calls for 'promotion of gender equality and the empowerment of women', is viewed by some as 'a powerful symbol of the success of the international feminist movement on international politics and development' (Sweetman, 2005: 3; also Hayes, 2005: 67). Moreover, that MDG 3 is not only 'explicitly valued as an end in itself' (Kabeer, 2005: 13), but is deemed fundamental to realising all the objectives set out in the Millennium Declaration, is also construed as signalling genuine commitment to 'mainstreaming' gender (see also Satterthwaite, 2003; World Bank GDG, 2003). The inclusion of MDG 5 – to improve maternal health – is also promising on grounds that this is often regarded as a 'litmus test' of women's status, not only due to fairly consistent links between poverty and maternal mortality levels (Graham, 2004: 6; WHO, 2005a),[8] but because early and dangerously frequent pregnancies often stem from male control over female sexuality (see Fraser, 2005;

UNDP, 2005: 33). As summarised by Isis International/Asia-Pacific Women's Watch (II/APWW) (2004: 10): 'Maternal death is the result of social injustice and a violation of women's rights to life.'

That the MDG process requires regular country reports (Millennium Development Goal Reports [MDGRs]) is also seen to constitute 'a new opportunity for gender advocates to enlarge the space for dialogue and build a broad national commitment to women's rights and gender equality' (UNDP, 2003b: 2). Indeed, with the MDGs having become 'the overarching framework for national development and the reference for pro-people and pro-poor policy-making', such reporting can potentially 'catalyse gender-responsive policy-making and programming', and 'facilitate more optimal resource allocation' (UNDP, 2005: 3).

Yet aside from some undoubted potential to advance gender equality, many feminists have criticised the relatively limited grounds on which gender is included in the MDGs (Johnsson-Latham, 2004b; World Bank GDG, 2003). Barton (2005: 25), for example, observes that: 'When the MDGs emerged from the UN Secretariat, women's groups were dismayed that gender equality as an issue in its own right was limited to one quite limited Goal, and that the issue of reproductive rights was not explicit.' The idea that Goal 3 might be achieved without guarantees of sexual and reproductive rights is widely deemed untenable given that these are fundamental to women 'being able to expand their capabilities, to access economic and political opportunities and have any level of determination over their own lives' (UNMP/TFEGE, 2005: 6). Another concern is that preoccupation with male–female ratios, as in education, may detract from the fact that:

> the empowerment of women does not just depend on the elimination of numerical gender disparities. It is possible to equalise the enrolment of boys and girls in school at a low level for both, a situation that empowers neither. Equality in deprivation does not represent a genuine fulfilment of Goal 3. (UNIFEM, 2002: 6)

Qualms about numbers have also been expressed with respect to poverty, with Johnsson-Latham (2004b: 27) claiming that owing to an overemphasis on measurable data 'efforts to capture power-related dimensions of poverty appear almost to have come to a halt' (see also Painter, 2004: 22). Lack of time frames set for women's political and economic empowerment are also worrying (Rodenberg, 2004: iii). In light of these caveats, and because the MDGs are argued to divert attention not just from the Beijing but from other UN Platforms for Action such as Cairo (Population, 1994), Vienna (Human Rights, 1993), Copenhagen (Social Development, 1997), and Istanbul (Habitat, 1996), Antrobus (2004; 2005) has gone as far to use the acronym 'MDG' to refer to 'Major Distracting Gimmick'.

Inasmuch as the MDGs themselves may be limited in respect of their gender objectives, the monitoring and reporting process to date is also wanting. Despite lofty rhetoric about the significance of MDG 3 to all the other goals, for example, a 2003 UNDP review of the status of gender concerns in 13 MDGRs found that not one identified gender as a 'cross-cutting' issue – MDG 3 being the only goal in which gender had been systematically addressed in all countries. Even if gender and/or women often got a mention in relation to MDG 5 and MDG 1 (Box 1.3), the latter asserted by the UNDP (2003b: 6) as being 'particularly critical for women', of the nine reports which mentioned gender and/or women in relation to poverty, only five specifically referred to gender inequality as a source of poverty and/or identified gender-related interventions as part of poverty plans (ibid.: 8). This led the UNDP to highlight a notable 'ghettoisation' of gender issues within women-specific sectors, along with a persistent portrayal of women 'in terms of their vulnerabilities, and cast in their traditional roles as mothers or victims rather than actors in development' (ibid.: 22). Although some progress had been made by 2005, when 78 MDGRs were reviewed by UNDP, only a handful of countries had gone 'outside the MDG box', with most concentrating only on the minimum indicators (UNDP, 2005: 53).

In order to rectify these shortcomings the UN Millennium Project Task Force on Education and Gender Equality (UNMP/TFEGE) has been working on improving indicators and strategies. Aside from advocating the inclusion of gender-equality targets in every MDG, the Task Force has recommended that MDG 3 might include strategic priorities aligned with CEDAW and BPFA encompassing guaranteed sexual and reproductive rights, and an end to violence against women and girls (Hayes, 2005: 68–9; also Box 1.4). Even if it has been cautioned that fewer indicators may work better, and that 'adding to the basket' may pose impossible demands on national capacities and workloads (see World Bank GDG, 2003), the menu of specific indicators proposed for MDG 3 by the Task Force would undoubtedly help to make more meaningful changes in women's lives (see Box 1.5).

Moreover, it is important that efforts are made to follow-through the Task Force calls for particular attention to poor women on the grounds that gender inequalities are greatest among the poor, especially in respect of capabilities and opportunities, that increasing numbers of poor households are headed and/or maintained by women, and that the 'well-being and survival of poor households depend on the productive and reproductive contributions of their female members' (UNMP/TFEGE, 2005: 3–4). This would also complement the efforts of women's groups to integrate gender equality as a critical element of poverty eradication in the MDGs since the

---

BOX 1.4   STRATEGIC PRIORITIES FOR GENDER EQUALITY: SUGGESTED AMENDMENTS TO MDG 3

- Strengthen opportunities for post-primary education for girls while simultaneously meeting commitments to universal primary education.
- Guarantee sexual and reproductive health and rights.
- Invest in infrastructure to reduce women's and girls' time burden.
- Guarantee women's and girls' property and inheritance rights.
- Eliminate gender inequality in employment by decreasing women's reliance on informal employment, closing gender gaps in earnings and reducing occupational segregation.
- Increase women's share of seats in national parliaments and local government bodies.
- Combat violence against girls and women.

Sources: UNDP (2005); UNMP/TFEGE (2005).

---

launch of the Global Call to Action Against Poverty (GCAP) at the World Social Forum in Brazil in January 2005 (see Barton, 2005: 31). Yet whether a focus on poor women, let alone MDG targets more generally, are attainable without a major reorientation of current neoliberal macroeconomic growth strategies is doubtful (Mbilinyi, 2004; Williams, 2004). As Painter (2004: 5) argues: 'The MDGs have not un-seated the predominance of a neoliberal, economic growth-driven model of development that relies on women as instruments as opposed to agents of development.' This is particularly serious for countries whose burdens of debt service preclude their making the necessary investments in health, education and infrastructure to enable them to attain their goals (ibid.: 19; see also Reddy and Heuty, 2005a; 2005b). As such, many feminists advocate primary allegiance to the BPFA:

> Given that the MDGs are weak on the goal of gender equality and that the gender dimensions of the other MDGs are almost invisible, those committed to the advancement of women's equality and empowerment need to consider putting their efforts into developing strategies for monitoring and measuring progress toward the achievement of the Beijing Platform for Action. After all,

BOX 1.5 MENU OF INDICATORS FOR MDG 3 PROPOSED BY THE TASK FORCE ON EDUCATION AND GENDER EQUALITY

Education

- Ratio of female to male gross enrolment in primary, secondary and tertiary education.
- Ratio of female to male completion rate in primary, secondary and tertiary education.

Sexual and reproductive health and rights

- Proportion of contraceptive demand satisfied.
- Adolescent fertility rate.

Infrastructure

- Hours per day (or year) spent by women and men in fetching water and collecting fuel.

Property rights

- Land ownership by women, men or jointly held.
- Housing title, disaggregated by women, men or jointly held.

Employment

- Share of women in employment (wage and self-employment), by type.
- Gender gaps in earnings in wage and self-employment.

Participation in national parliaments and local government bodies

- Percentage of seats held by women in national parliament.
- Percentage of seats held by women in local government bodies.

Violence against women

- Prevalence of domestic violence.

Sources: UNDP (2005: 53); UNMP/TFEGE (2005: box 1).

the BPFA is theoretically consistent (which the MDGs are not); it includes all of the MDGs; and it already has a constituency of support. Work will have to be done to make links between the MDGs and BPFA in terms of Targets and Indicators, and new Indicators, such as violence and time use, may have to be added. (Antrobus, 2004: 16; see also Pietila, 2004)

Gender Budgets

While the 'en-gendering' of PRSPs and the MDGs may leave a lot to be desired, another more promising breakthrough, taking place in national contexts, but inspired by global feminist interchange, is that of 'gender budgets', which have undergone experimentation in around 40 countries so far. Gender budgets seek to advance gender equality through changing the ways in which public revenue is raised and expended, and as pointed-up by Kabeer (2003: 220) can 'potentially promote greater transparency and accountability in policy processes', as well as help to 'match policy intent with resource allocation'. As echoed by UNRISD (2005: 60):

> Budget audits can be used to review and analyse national budgets and expenditures to determine which groups benefit from fiscal policies, and whether there are inbuilt biases against women, especially from low-income families . . . Gender budget audits can also examine the likely feedback effects of public expenditures on unpaid work. For example, health care expenditures may be found to rebound on women's unpaid labour time. The implementation of user fees for essential goods such as water and electricity may have similar effects. (See also Borges Sugiyama, 2002; BRIDGE, 2003; Budlender, 2000; Budlender and Hewitt, 2002; Elson, 1998; 1999b; 2004; Mbilinyi, 2004).

With gender budgets in particular, there has undoubtedly been some political expediency to the idea that poverty is feminising. By the same token, it could also be levelled that insufficient analysis, substantiation and nuancing of the 'feminisation of poverty' has not led to the most effective policy initiatives. One untoward outcome, for example, is a palpable merger of poverty alleviation and Gender and Development (GAD) interventions despite the fact that gender and poverty are distinct, albeit overlapping, forms of disadvantage (Jackson, 1996; 1998; Jackson and Palmer-Jones, 1999; Kabeer, 2003). In turn, differences in the theoretical and political goals of gender stakeholders on the one hand, and poverty stakeholders on the other, may not make for the most productive alliances. As pointed up by de Vylder (2004: 85), the pursuit of gender equality has usually been regarded within the GAD community as an end in itself and from a human rights perspective, yet pursuing gender equality as a means to achieve poverty reduction is of a more instrumentalist nature and grounded in efficiency considerations (see also Mayoux, 2006).

KEY CONCERNS AND QUESTIONS ABOUT THE 'FEMINISATION OF POVERTY'

In light of the above, I feel it is important to go back to basics and, in particular, to think about the utility of the 'feminisation of poverty' in depicting trends in women's poverty across developing countries, how appropriately it defines and accounts for poverty, and how effectively it contributes to framing responses to female disadvantage. This needs to take into account a number of concerns already aired in the feminist literature, such as the problems attached to the formulaic nomenclature of the 'feminisation of poverty' insofar as it links poverty with women (rather than gender relations), and leads to a focus on the 'victims' of unequal development as the catalyst for transformation. Another is the tendency to privilege income privation which may downplay matters such as 'overwork', 'time deficiency', 'powerlessness', and 'vulnerability' which can be as, if not more, relevant to women's perceptions of disadvantage, and to the 'trade-offs' they make (or are able to negotiate) between different aspects of poverty (Blanc-Szanton, 1990; Chant, 1997b; Fonseca, 1991; Fukuda-Parr, 1999; Kabeer, 1997; Sen, G., 1999; Whitehead and Lockwood, 1999). In short, grassroots subjective experiences of poverty are often eclipsed by quantitative 'objective' measures which portray affected parties as 'passive victims' on the basis of narrow externally imposed criteria. In addition to this, given the relative dearth of basic sex-disaggregated headcount panel data, even for income poverty, how do we know whether there is actually any trend at all for women to be bearing more poverty over time? Indeed, it is somewhat strange that while women were supposed to be 70 per cent of the world's poor in 1995, more than a decade on, the figure seems not to have shifted (Chant, 2006).

How Legitimate is the Term 'Feminisation of Poverty'?

Leading on from the above, one of my own most abiding concerns is that while 'feminisation' implies dynamism, one of the central tenets of the 'feminisation of poverty' – namely that women feature disproportionately among the world's poor – is inherently static. A pattern of poverty which indicates a female bias may not actually be an outcome of a *trend* for more women to become poor relative to men. Indeed, women in poverty could still outnumber men at a global scale even if poverty was 'masculinising' over a given time period (see Chant, 2006). As Medeiros and Costa (2006: 3) summarise:

> In spite of its multiple meanings, the feminisation of poverty should not be confused with the existence of higher levels of poverty among women or

female-headed households . . . The term 'feminisation' relates to the way poverty changes over time, whereas 'higher levels' of poverty (which include the so-called 'over-representation'), focuses on a view of poverty at a given moment. Feminisation is a process, 'higher poverty' is a state.

Even if we accept what tenuous evidence there is that women in general are becoming poorer than men, the terms of this tendency, such as how far and in which ways gender gaps are widening, and which age groups in the population are most affected, remain inadequately specified and elaborated, as do their causal mechanisms (see Johnsson-Latham, 2004b). For example, is it the incidence of poverty among women and men which is the main issue, or the depth or severity of women's poverty compared with men?[9] And is the trend to 'feminisation' something which is simply occurring over time, or does it relate to a widening of gendered poverty gaps across generations? To date, generational differences among women have tended to be glossed over, even though they may be highly illuminating in respect of the reasons for growth in women's poverty relative to men's. For example, demographic ageing combined with women's greater life expectancy, may well be leading to clusters of disadvantaged women among senior citizens, especially as older women are more likely to be widowed, to suffer greater social and economic discrimination than their male counterparts, and to lack access to benefits such as work-related pensions (Ofstedal et al., 2004: 166–7; also ECLAC, 2004b: 45–6; UNMP/TFEGE, 2005: 13). Indeed, even in Latin America where investments in human resources have a longer history than some other regions of the South, gender gaps in education and literacy are still greater among older than younger populations (CELADE, 2002: 17). This is arguably significant given that 60 per cent of the population aged 60 and above in Latin America and the Caribbean are female (PAHO/MIAH, 2004: 1).

Alternatively, is it that gender disparities in income and resource exchange are becoming more uneven in younger age groups? If so, how does this square with the wide-ranging interventions that different countries in the South have made to redress gender inequalities following the UN Decade for Women (see Longwe, 1995: 18), or indeed the widely documented efforts undertaken by women at the grassroots to overcome their disadvantage? Even if 'progress towards gender equality is not necessarily permanent or stable', and 'gains can be tenuous' (UNRISD, 2005: 56), the signs are in many places that gender disparities in earnings, assets and human capital are lessening rather than intensifying, especially among youth (Chant and McIlwaine, 1998; Quisumbing, 2003; UNIFEM, 2002). As noted by Moghadam (1997: 3): 'The feminisation of poverty would . . . appear to refute the idea that economic development and growth are generally accompanied by a trend towards the diminution of patriarchal gender relations and an advancement in the status of women through improvements in women's capabilities.'

Does the 'Feminisation of Poverty' Imply a 'Masculinisation' of Wealth and Privilege?

Leading on from this, if we are to accept that poverty is becoming increasingly feminised, does this mean that there is counterpart 'masculinisation' of power, privilege and asset accumulation? If so, how is this explained when there is so much talk of a 'crisis of masculinity' and mounting evidence that men in some countries are beginning to fall behind women in respect of educational attainment and access to employment (see Chant, 2006; also Chapter 2 in this volume). Indeed, it has also been argued that a progressive narrowing of gender pay gaps may owe more to driving down of male wages than to improvements in women's earnings (Elson, 1999). The latter is noted for some Latin American countries which, in the context of an on-going 'feminisation of labour',[10] are 'witnessing "equality by impoverishment" as a result of the increased precariousness of men's employment' (ECLAC, 2004b: 7). Yet while some men may be disadvantaged, and this is exerting costs such as higher suicide rates and stress- and alcohol-related health risks, it may well be the case in more general terms, as UNRISD (2005: 12) claims, that 'Male underachievement has not led to parallel underachievements in wealth and politics'. Indeed, globally, for example, women's earnings are still only an average of 75 per cent of men's (Rodenberg, 2004: ii). Without any investigation of men in the context of discussions of the 'feminisation of poverty', however, real and perceived gender gaps remain hard to determine, let alone to track over time.

Is the 'Feminisation of Poverty' Linked with the 'Feminisation' of Household Headship?

Another issue which needs serious consideration is whether the feminisation of poverty is intrinsically linked with the mounting incidence of households headed by women which presently constitute an estimated 13 per cent of households the Middle East and North Africa, 16 per cent in Asia, 22 per cent in sub-Saharan Africa, and 24 per cent in Latin America (Bongaarts, 2001: 14). As noted by Wennerholm (2002: 10), from the 1970s onwards 'the existence and vulnerability of female-headed households has . . . alarmed researchers and advocates', with the 'feminisation of poverty' during and since the 1980s and 1990s, being 'used and linked to the debate about the vulnerability of female-headed households'. Asgary and Pagán

(2004: 97) go as far to say that 'the feminisation of poverty is the process whereby poverty becomes more concentrated among individuals living in female-headed households' (see also Box 1.2).

Whether this association has come about because female household heads are commonly a proxy for 'women' in poverty statistics, or because synergies are suggested by parallel rises in the 'feminisation of poverty' and the 'feminisation of household headship', or because no other criterion of differentiation among women has been applied, the two phenomena have become so firmly wedded to one another that, as Davids and van Driel (2001: 162) assert: 'the feminisation of poverty focuses on female-headed households as an expression of that same feminisation of poverty'. In turn, because lone mothers are often the biggest sub-group of female heads,[11] the 'culture of single motherhood' has often been designated as the 'New Poverty Paradigm' (Thomas, 1994, cited in Budowski et al., 2002: 301). This carries with it the idea that female headship is not just a problem for women, but for their children, with the contention that female heads cannot 'properly support their families or ensure their well-being' (Mehra et al., 2000: 7), having translated into the concept of an 'inter-generational transmission of disadvantage' whereby the conjectured privations experienced by 'fatherless' children impinge upon their short- and longer-term well-being. Such negative perspectives are perhaps no surprise given Jassey's (2002: 1) observation that:

> women have predominantly been presented as *victims*, and sometimes as *culprits*, and themselves responsible for whatever happens to them due, for example, to their 'backwardness', illiteracy, isolation or cultural habits. Seldom are they presented as actors and strategists . . . This *homogenisation* of women does not only turn its back on the diversity of contexts we live in, but it also denies our individual differences and agency, resting instead on perceptions and connotations of all women as weak and dependent. (Emphasis in original; see also Angeles, 2000b)

Yet while not denying that in most societies women lag behind men in respect of access to the resources necessary for survival and self-determination, given that feminist research has highlighted the fact that women's poverty is often strongly linked with unequal gender relations within as well as beyond the home, the question arises as to why it has been so rarely articulated that assuming household headship may be a medium through which they are actually able to enhance their own and their children's well-being. Since economic development has provided some opportunities for women which, in principle, expand their choices and allow them to establish their own households (see Safa, 1995; van Vuuren, 2003), it is entirely possible that: 'this may represent a positive choice, so that the connotations of powerlessness and victimhood are inappropriate' (Baden, 1999: 13). Indeed, studies conducted in a range of contexts indicate that children in female-headed households may actually be better off than their counterparts in male-headed units in terms of educational attainment, nutrition and health (Blumberg, 1995; Chant, 1997a; Engle, 1995; Moore and Vaughan, 1994; Oppong, 1997).

Another very basic qualification is that it is extremely difficult to find macro- or micro-level data which show any consistent relationship between female headship and poverty (see CEPAL, 2001; Chant, 1997b; Fuwa, 2000; Moghadam, 1997; Quisumbing et al., 1995; Wartenburg, 1999). Following on from the idea that 'variations in the correlation between female headship and poverty within and between countries indicate the need for context-specific research' (Nauckhoff, 2004: 66; see Moghadam, 1997: 43), dismantling the a priori associations between women's (income) poverty and female household headship in the context of detailed research is essential if we are to take the 'feminisation of poverty' beyond a loosely deployed term, to a more clearly defined and robust concept or, indeed, 'thesis'. Additionally, if we are to continue talking about the 'feminisation of poverty' as a trend, then we need to have some handle on how things are changing for women and men across generations, and, given that 'global' is so often prefixed to the term, to establish whether the incidence of poverty among women is systematically rising relative to men in the majority of countries.

In interrogating evidence for a 'feminisation of poverty' it is also arguably critical to be more precise about which particular dimensions of poverty we are referring to, and to scrutinise more closely what makes some women poorer than some men in different developing contexts. The paramount importance of determining *which* women are most affected also needs to be determined not only with reference to objective measures (where these exist in an appropriate sex-disaggregated form), but to women's and men's own perceptions of their relative privation, and with due regard for differentiation within as well as between the two groups. As articulated by Nauckhoff (2004: 49–50) in relation to PRSPs:

> People cannot be described by only using two categories of men and women, even if these are necessary. Obviously men and women are not the same all over the world. Difference and variation in terms such as age, socio-economic and ethnic group and geographical location have to be introduced to make groups and categories fully visible and their situation comprehensible.

More holistic analysis of this nature may help us pin down a concept that can be more readily substantiated and have greater explanatory power, as well make for more gender-responsive poverty reduction strategies. Otherwise, as cautioned by the UNDP (2003b: 22) in relation to its earlier-mentioned review of 13 MDGRs, when statements about the 'feminisation of poverty' 'are not backed up by data or policy commitments', these are of 'little value either as entry-points for refocusing the direction of poverty policy or as benchmarks for tracking change' (see also Marcoux, 1998a; 1998b).

KEY ENQUIRIES INTO THE 'FEMINISATION OF POVERTY' IN THE PRESENT BOOK

With the above in mind, this book interrogates the 'feminisation of poverty' on the basis of dedicated case study research in three countries with diverse economic and cultural characteristics – The Gambia, the Philippines, and Costa Rica. Drawing on consultations with a total of 223 low-income women and men from different age cohorts, with representatives from 40 state organisations, non-governmental organisations (NGOs) and in-country offices of international agencies, and on statistical and documentary evidence, I aim to establish the extent to which income- (and other types of) poverty are, and are *perceived* to be, feminised and/or subject to ongoing feminisation. While taking into account quantitative macro-level data on trends in development and poverty, particular attention is paid to subjective views on the intersection of poverty with generational changes in women's and men's activities, capabilities and entitlements, and household transitions. The principal objectives are to establish whether poverty differences between women and men are growing over time and/or across generations, the extent to which household circumstances act to offset or exacerbate women's disadvantage, and the significance of domestic versus broader societal factors in perpetuating gender gaps.

Without wishing to overstate the significance of the research, it is distinctive from most previous analyses of the gender and poverty in three crucial respects. First, it combines original case study material with analysis of secondary bibliographical and statistical sources in three countries drawn from three major regions in the South and with differing levels of poverty and human development. Second, it follows a gender relations approach which includes men as well as women. Third, it is inclusive of different generations of women and men, which I believe helps in illuminating how gendered poverty is changing over time. While I do not pretend to endorse or refute the 'feminisation of poverty' on the basis of small-scale localised research in only three countries, I feel that debate on the subject as far as the Global South is concerned can only be furthered by more primary, micro-level, and comparative exploration of this nature.

WHY THE GAMBIA, THE PHILIPPINES AND COSTA RICA?

My choice of The Gambia, the Philippines and Costa Rica as case studies is grounded mainly in pragmatic considerations insofar as I had already worked in all three countries (ranging from the late 1980s in Costa Rica, to the early 1990s in the Philippines, to the early twenty-first century in The Gambia).[12] Earlier fieldwork in these contexts had not only contributed to my knowledge of their differing histories, cultures and economies, but also facilitated access to, and progressive 'trust-building' with, institutional personnel and individuals at the grassroots.

Among other important reasons for comparing these three countries is that each is located within a different region of the Global South which yields interesting contrasts for comparative research on gender and poverty. Not only do the three countries sit within three different UNDP categories of 'human development' (Costa Rica being classified as having 'high' human development, the Philippines, 'medium', and The Gambia 'low'), but they differ substantially in respect of economic structure, orientation and privation (see Tables 1.2–1.4), cultural and social organisation, and gender- and poverty-related variables such as female education, household headship, and labour force participation. While cultural variations in particular clearly make it difficult to isolate the impacts of specific features of national development on changes in gendered dimensions of poverty, they do highlight the importance of diversity in gendered experiences of privation, and how interventions to tackle gendered disadvantage should arguably desist from the 'one size fits all' formula often promulgated by international financial and development institutions.

METHODOLOGY

As intimated above, my main methodology for setting the scene for each case study country involved examining statistics on regional and national demographic, economic and social trends, existing indicators of poverty and well-being, and bibliographic and policy documentation on poverty, gender, family, youth and the elderly. Yet unevenness in the availability and quality of longitudinal data on gendered poverty between the three countries – ranging from substantial in Costa Rica to virtually non-existent in The Gambia – meant that my principal comparative information was garnered through first-hand fieldwork with personnel from relevant policy-making and planning bodies (in gender and/or poverty alleviation), and with poor women and men at the grassroots, the latter providing an

Table 1.2   The Gambia, Philippines and Costa Rica: selected information on population, human development and poverty

	The Gambia	Philippines	Costa Rica
Population (millions), 2002	1.4	78.6	4.1
Annual population growth rate (%), 1975–2002	3.4	2.3	2.6
Total fertility rate (TFR) (per woman)			
1970–1975	6.5	6.0	4.3
2000–2005	4.7	3.2	2.3
Life expectancy at birth (years) 2000–2005	54.1	69.8	78.1
Urban population (as % of total population)			
1975	17.0	35.6	42.5
2002	31.2	60.2	60.1
GDP per capita (PPP US$), 2002	1690	4170	8840
Human Development Index (HDI) value, 2002[a,b]	0.452	0.753	0.834
HDI rank, 2002[c]	155	83	45
Human Poverty Index (HPI-1) Value (%)[d]	45.8	14.8	4.4
Human Poverty Index (HPI-1) Rank[e]	81	28	4
Population below income poverty line ($1 a day), (%) 1990–2002[f]	59.3	14.6	2.0

Notes:
a. The HDI is an aggregate index comprising information on life expectancy at birth, adult literacy among the population aged 15 years or more, the combined primary, secondary and tertiary gross enrolment ratio, and GDP per capita (expressed in US$ Purchasing Power Parity [PPP]). Information pertaining to education and literacy is provided in Table 4.4 in this volume.
b. The highest value of the HDI in 2002 was 0.956 (Norway) and the lowest, 0.273 (Sierra Leone).
c. Rank out of 177 countries.
d. The Human Poverty Index comprises four indicators: probability at birth of not surviving to the age of 40 years; adult illiteracy rate; population without sustainable access to an improved water source, and children under weight for age. The lower the value, the lower the incidence of poverty (for example, Barbados, with the lowest HPI-1 out of 95 developing countries has a value of 2.5 per cent, whereas the highest HPI-1 is for Burkina Faso, with a value of 65.5 per cent – UNDP, 2004: 147–9).
e. Rank out of 95 developing countries.
f. Equivalent to $1.08 a day.

Source: UNDP (2004: tables 1, 3, 5 and 8).

Table 1.3　*Comparisons of monetary and capability poverty: The Gambia, Philippines and Costa Rica*[a]

	Percentage of population in poverty		
	HPI-1[b]	International Monetary Poverty, 1990–2001[c]	National poverty line, 1987–2000
The Gambia	45.8	59.3	–
Philippines	14.8	14.6	36.8
Costa Rica	4.4	6.9	–

Notes:
a.　The format for this table is based on table 1 in Ruggeri Laderchi et al. (2003).
b.　Human Poverty Index = geometric average of the percentage of people who have a probability at birth of not surviving to the age of 40 years; adult illiteracy rate; population without sustainable access to an improved water source, and children under weight for age.
c.　Monetary poverty = percentage of population living on less than one dollar a day ($1.08), valued at PPP (Purchasing Power Parity).
–　　= No data.

Source:　UNDP (2003a: table 3).

Table 1.4　*Estimates of poverty for The Gambia, Philippines and Costa Rica based on three international poverty lines*

	Percentage of poor			Number of poor (millions)		
	World Bank[a]	IPC1[b]	IPC2[c]	World Bank	IPC1	IPC2
The Gambia	21.97	34.09				26.39
	0.29	0.46		0.35		
Philippines	15.04	29.20	20.14	11.58	22.49	15.51
Costa Rica	2.02	4.46				2.76
	0.08	0.17		0.11		

Notes:
a.　World Bank estimates based on 1993 PPP US$1.08 per day.
b.　IPC1 = International Poverty Centre estimates based on typical poverty line among low-income countries in the late 1990s.
c.　IPC2 = International Poverty Centre estimates based on minimum nutritional requirements.

Source:　IPC (2004c).

essential medium for examining how poverty is experienced, and perceived to arise by different age stakeholders.

The grassroots samples were split broadly between women and men in different age bands as indicated in Table 1.5, with slight variations arising

Table 1.5   Breakdown of grassroots survey populations: The Gambia, Philippines and Costa Rica

	Youth (10–29 years)	Middle adults (30–49 years)	Senior adults (50 years plus)	Total
The Gambia				
Female	16	14	11	41
Male	17	6	9	32
Total	33	20	20	73
Philippines				
Female	9	20	21	50
Male	11	7	9	27
Total	20	27	30	77
Costa Rica				
Female	13	24	10	47
Male	10	6	10	26
Total	23	30	20	73
Total	76	77	70	223

by default, such as where participants in focus groups (often organised through local NGOs) did not turn up.[13] Drawing a line between different generations was clearly difficult given differences in characteristics such as age at first birth, life expectancy and so on between the countries. While I decided to interview three main cohorts, defined as 'young people' (13–29 years), 'middle adults' (30–49 years) and 'senior/elderly adults' (50 years plus), within any one age band there can clearly be individuals with very different experiences and perceptions of their stage in the life course. Technically, for example, although quite seldom in practice, men or women may be grandparents by the age of 30 and no longer see themselves as 'young'. Similarly, while it might seem premature for people aged 50 years or over to be defined as 'elderly', when taking into consideration differences in life expectancy across countries, this decision had to be made to take into account the situation in The Gambia where average life expectancy is only 54.1 (see Table 1.5).[14]

In comparing three countries with such different histories and contemporary social and economic characteristics, 'standardisation' of samples was clearly difficult. In respect of choosing case study localities, for example, this was primarily influenced by pre-existing contacts in specific communities, which led me to focus on the capital region in The Gambia (Greater Banjul Area), on Metro Cebu, the second largest conurbation in the Philippines, and in Costa Rica, in urban areas in Guanacaste province, one of the poorest parts of an otherwise relatively wealthy country. However, while there were differences in size of the communities in which I worked, and in respect of position in their national urban hierarchies, one thread in common was that all had been affected by tourism development which had led to some similarities in respect of labour market characteristics, including in-migration and a preponderance of service jobs. Selection of informants was made either on the basis of previous acquaintance or through contacts in local NGOs.

ORGANISATION OF THE BOOK

Having set out the key objectives and rationale for the book, and the reasons for my choice of case study countries, the following two chapters establish the general theoretical and empirical anataomy of the 'feminisation of poverty'. Chapter 2 reviews the 'en-gendering' of poverty analysis and measurement over time, while Chapter 3 examines key assumptions underpinning the 'feminisation of poverty' and supporting evidence in the Global South, particularly in relation to trends in income poverty and the 'feminisation' of household headship. In Chapters 4 to 6 discussion turns to The Gambia, the Philippines and Costa Rica with the principal aim of establishing actual and perceived trends in gendered poverty burdens and their causal mechanisms. In Chapter 7, I summarise and comment on the case study explorations, drawing out comparative dimensions along with major theoretical, methodological and policy implications. This entails revisiting – and some re-casting – of the 'feminisation of poverty' such that it better reflects patterns and trends in gendered disadvantage in the Global South.

NOTES

1. The term first appears to have been coined by Pearce (1978) in relation to the USA, as discussed further in Chapter 3.
2. All items adopted in UN Global Platforms for Action nominally require the special attention of governments. A total of 189 countries in 1995 declared their intention to 'advance the goals of equality, development and peace for all women everywhere in the interests of all humanity' (WEDO, 2005: 10).
3. In most national and international data sources 'female household headship' refers to situations where an adult woman (usually with children) resides without a male partner (or, in some cases, another adult male such as a father or brother) (Chant, 1997a: 5 et seq; also Wartenburg, 1999: 77). Despite the difficulties of standardised definitions when headship is not a politically neutral concept, when it is subject to diverse interpretations at the grassroots, and when male-bias leads to the under-reporting of female household headship (see Buvinic and Gupta, 1997: 260; Feijoó, 1999: 162; Folbre, 1991; Harris,

1981; van Vuuren, 2003), women are estimated to head between 20 and 25 per cent of households worldwide (Delamonica et al., 2004; Varley, 2002).

4. In actuality, 'one dollar a day', which converts one US dollar to local currency using PPP (Purchasing Power Parity) exchange rates, is US$1.08 a day. Known as the 'Copenhagen measure' because it was established at the World Summit for Social Development in Copenhagen in 1995, this did not become widely deployed until the *World Development Report 2000/2001: Attacking Poverty* (see World Bank, 2000), and its adoption by the UN Millennium Summit as the benchmark for monitoring reduction in extreme poverty worldwide. The measure has been criticised on a number of grounds including its arbitrariness and the fact that it only records material aspects of poverty (Johnsson-Latham, 2004b: 28), that the line is too low and should instead be based on the local cost of an adequate diet (Kakwani, 2004b), that PPP conversion factors are inappropriate and/or grounded in weak evidence (Reddy and Heuty, 2005b), and that since poverty is multidimensional it is difficult to convert into a meaningful uniform measure (Karshenas, 2003; Reddy, 2004; Srinivasan, 2004; Virola, 2002). This said, Lipton (2001: 41) asserts that: 'The simple "Copenhagen measure" of dollar-poverty is practical, comparable and monitorable', and 'overrides the genuine, if contestable, case for more complex measures' (see also Ravallion, 2004a; and Chapter 2 in this volume).

5. Corner (2003: 2) argues that 'gender statistics' are better described as 'disaggregated by sex' rather than 'disaggregated by gender', since they involve disaggregation by biological sex, rather than 'gender' which is a contextually specific and socially constructed entity.

6. 'Assertion' is used advisedly here. Aside from lack of robust empirical evidence, Marcoux (1998a; 1998b) points up that the 70 per cent share of poverty assigned to women in 1995 is untenable in light of the age distribution of the global population and its household characteristics. Even assuming a priori that being female places persons at a greater risk of being poor, given that the sex of children under 15 is unlikely to have more than a negligible impact on gender differentials in household poverty, only single-person and lone-parent units could be responsible for the excess of female poverty. Yet there are simply not enough households of this type to give rise to the purported 70/30 ratio of poor women and girls to poor men and boys (see also Klasen, 2004).

7. The PRSP initiative was launched in 1999 by the Bretton Woods Institutions following the establishment of the Enhanced Heavily Indebted Poor Countries Initiative (HIPC II) at the World Economic Summit in Cologne (Rodenberg, 2004: 31). The core aim of the HIPC initiative was to reduce debt by at least two-thirds in the world's poorest and most debt-burdened countries and so liberate resources to combat poverty. This required the drawing up by client countries of PRSPs designed to marry structural macroeconomic reforms, such as market-led growth and stabilisation, with policies to reduce poverty, such as the promotion of education and employment. Nominally PRSPs require broad-based stakeholder participation, and are processual in nature, whereby a series of rolling, 'multi-phase' plans are shaped by successive poverty analyses, implementation, monitoring, evaluation, and reformulation. As of 2004, an overall total of 33 and 48 interim PRSPs had been designed (ibid.). Although the form and recommendations of poverty reduction strategies are widely alleged to display pronounced similarities with their forebear, structural adjustment programmes (SAPs), Nauckhoff (2004: 51–2) points-up three major differences. First in PRSPs, poverty reduction is a specific goal; second, participation is signalled as a *sine qua non* in their design and implementation, and third, the PRSP process is expected to result in better coherence among donors.

8. Poor women are not more prone to obstetric complications, but are less likely to receive adequate medical treatment before, during or after childbirth (Graham, 2004: 7).

9. The incidence of poverty measures the proportion of the poor in a given population and is the most commonly used indicator when assessing poverty differentials between women and men, or between female- and male-headed households. The intensity of (income) poverty is measured by the aggregated difference between the observed income of poor populations and the poverty line, while the severity of poverty refers to 'some combination of the incidence and intensity of poverty and inequality among the poor' (Medeiros and Costa, 2006: 20n).

10.   The term 'feminisation of labour' is not only used to describe an increasing female pres-
      ence in the workforce, but a process whereby more people (male and female alike) have
      come to be occupied in jobs marked by conditions normally associated with female
      labour (precarious, underpaid, lacking in social benefits, protection by labour legislation,
      and so on) (see Standing, 1999).
11.   Female-headed households are often equated with 'lone-mother households' consisting
      solely of mothers and children. Although in many contexts these predominate, in a sub-
      stantial number of cases they may be extended in composition. Other types of female-
      headed households include grandmother-headed, women-only, and lone-female
      households (see Chant, 1991b; 1997a: ch. 1; also Folbre, 1991). Moreover, despite
      common assumptions that the bulk of 'lone mothers' are 'unmarried', the majority are
      often separated, divorced and/or widowed (Chant, 1997a: ch. 6; see also Marenco et al.,
      1998: 8).
12.   In respect of the dedicated fieldwork for the present book, this was conducted in The
      Gambia in 2003 and 2004, in the Philippines in 2004, and in Costa Rica in 2005.
13.   There were important gender dimensions here. For example, in one focus group con-
      vened through a parent–teacher association in Costa Rica, only mothers turned up.
14.   Many older individuals in The Gambia, the bulk of whom were illiterate, did not possess
      knowledge of their exact age, and had no birth certificate (see also van der Sande et al.,
      2001). This was especially the case among older women (50 plus), some of whom
      declared that they were 20–30 years older than they actually were. While this was possi-
      bly an indication of *feeling* older than their years, and important in itself, I also wanted
      to try to establish their numerical ages, and attempted to do so by asking when they had
      got married and either at what age they had their first child, or how old their first sur-
      viving child was now. Even then, some women did not know the exact ages of their chil-
      dren, simply saying that the first had been born immediately prior to or soon after
      marriage, and thereafter, 'every 2–3 years'. As such, some ages in the Gambian case study
      must be taken as approximate.

2. Analysing poverty from a gender perspective

To set the scene for detailed discussion of the 'feminisation of poverty' in Chapter 3, my aim here is to review approaches to the conceptualisation and measurement of poverty, and their interrelations with gender analysis.

As flagged up in Chapter 1, poverty has long been open to different definitions, tools of measurement, and modes of representation. In the last three decades, however, momentum has gathered in support of more 'holistic' views of poverty which expand on a rather narrow and static focus on incomes and consumption and embrace poverty as multidimensional and dynamic. In addition to aspects of 'physical deprivation', poverty is increasingly acknowledged as encompassing factors pertaining to 'social deprivation' such as self-esteem, respect, and power. This requires moving beyond poverty as an 'objective' money-metric entity, 'collected' and presented in a quantitative form, to taking on board subjective experiences of poverty via more qualitative and participatory methods.[1]

Gender considerations have been integral to more holistic approaches to poverty, not only forging increased awareness that women's experiences of poverty are often different to those of men (Kabeer, 1997: 1), but bringing poverty assessment closer to GAD analysis which has 'always focused on voice, participation and legal and structural reforms needed for advancing the status of women' (Johnsson-Latham, 2004b: 20). As articulated by ECLAC (2004b: 19):

> Analysing poverty from a gender perspective makes it possible to connect with other forms of domination (e.g. ethnic and racial) that structure social relations, and to understand it as a result of power relationships that affect access to, and control of, goods and services, as well as other material and symbolic resources.

Even if it has been asserted that 'neither the poverty discourse nor the discourse on gender and development have ever put a *main* focus on female poverty' (Johnsson-Latham, 2004b: 20, emphasis in original), and mainstream poverty frameworks remain wanting in gender-sensitivity, as summarised by Johnsson-Latham (2004b: 20):

The value of integrating poverty and gender and development has been increasingly acknowledged both within UN agencies such as the UNFPA and UNIFEM, among bilateral development agencies, and in the research communities in the North and South. Thus today more coherent efforts are made to better understand poverty by applying a gender perspective.

Given the importance of nearly 40 years of dedicated feminist research in developing regions in 'en-gendering' methodological and conceptual frameworks for poverty, the first section of this chapter highlights the principal bodies of feminist literature which have had direct and/or indirect influences in this regard. In the second section I draw out the main impacts of feminist research for the conceptualisation and measurement of poverty. In the third section I identify some of the main outstanding barriers to the gender-responsiveness of poverty analysis.

STEPPING STONES TO THE 'EN-GENDERING' OF POVERTY ANALYSIS

Early Research on Women and Development: The UN Decade (1975–85)

The UN Decade for Women (1975–85) spawned unprecedented efforts to investigate how development was affecting women, with one major set of implications for the 'en-gendering' of poverty analysis being the attention drawn to gender gaps in income. Given prevailing concerns with economic growth, a major focus was on gender disparities in earnings, and the factors underlying these such as inequalities in literacy and education, unequal domestic divisions of labour, and discrimination in the workplace.

A second set of perspectives on poverty emanating from this early feminist research centred on the difficulties of gleaning meaningful data on *any* aspect of women's lives (whether economic or otherwise) from macro-level statistics. This called into question how data that were not sensitive to, nor disaggregated by, sex could provide an effective basis for gender-aware policy interventions. Such lacunae gave weight to CEDAW's exhortations for the production of sex-disaggregated data, and indicators which measured changes between women and men over time (see Corner, 2003; Gaudart, 2002).

A third feature of early gender research with relevance for poverty analysis was growing recognition not only of the diversity of household arrangements in different parts of the world – many of which diverged from the Western idealised/'naturalised' norm comprising a husband, wife and children – but of their internal differentiation and dynamics. Research indicated, for example, that in directing development projects to male household heads, women either missed out as heads of household in their own right, or as spouses in male-headed units. Since enhancing access to resources on the part of men did not automatically confer benefits to women and children this raised questions about the relevance of 'the household' as a unitary entity, and, *ipso facto*, as either an appropriate tool in poverty measurement, or as a target of development interventions (see also later).

Fourth, early gender research flagged up the disparities between women's often considerable inputs to household survival and the limited social recognition accorded to their contributions, either within the context of their families, communities or society at large. The frequent 'invisibility' of women drew attention to the fact that there was more than a material dimension to gendered hardship and subordination, and, in turn, provided an important impetus for more multidimensional analyses of poverty.

Gender and Structural Adjustment

A second spate of gender research with implications for poverty analysis came with the 'Lost Decade' of the 1980s.[2] Explorations of the grassroots impacts of structural adjustment in different parts of the South demonstrated how women were harder hit by debt crisis and neoliberal reform than their male counterparts, particularly in respect of accumulating greater burdens of both 'productive' and 'reproductive' labour (see Elson, 1989; Moser, 1989; Safa and Antrobus, 1992).

Several studies drew attention to how cutbacks in state services and subsidies (in relation to basic foodstuffs, public health care, housing and infrastructure and so on), transferred considerable costs to the private sector, with women being the ones who largely 'footed the bill' (Kanji, 1991). While the declining purchasing power of wages not only required greater effort from women in domestic and community provisioning, but more involvement in income-generating activities (see Benería, 1991; Brydon and Legge, 1996; González de la Rocha, 1988a; Weekes-Vagliani, 1992), there was little evidence for a corresponding rise in the range and intensity of men's inputs to household survival (Chant, 1994; Langer et al., 1991; Moser, 1996; UNICEF, 1997). This underlined the impossibility of analysing the impacts of structural adjustment without acknowledging gender, and further endorsed the need to question prevailing notions of a 'unitary household'.

Female-Headed Households and the 'Feminisation of Poverty'

Leading on from the above, another significant strand of early feminist research was investigation into growing numbers of women-headed households both during and after the 'Lost Decade', much of which placed emphasis on their disadvantage relative to male-headed units. As noted in Chapter 1, rising numbers of women-headed households were linked with the concept of a 'global feminisation of poverty', and became almost unilaterally typecast as the 'poorest of the poor' (Boxes 1.1 and 1.2). While this categorical association helped to put gender on the policy agenda, subsequent debates around the validity and verification of its underlying premises (as discussed further in Chapter 3) have had productive impacts on poverty research in their own right. For example, the debates have provoked momentum for examining gender differences in poverty and their domestic as well as extra-domestic causes, not to mention reinforcing calls both to disaggregate households in poverty evaluations, and to consider poverty from a broader optic than levels of earned income (see Cagatay, 1998; Fukuda-Parr, 1999; Whitehead and Lockwood, 1999). Debates on female household headship and poverty have also brought issues of 'power' and 'empowerment' to the fore in so far as they have stressed how women's capacity to *command* and *allocate* resources can be as, if not more, important than the actual resource base in their households, and that the relationship between women's access to material resources and female empowerment is by no means straightforward.

Women's 'Empowerment'

'Empowerment', in turn, has constituted a fourth major body of gender research with relevance for poverty, and the stated aim of an increasing number of policy interventions has been to 'empower women'.

Although definitions of empowerment remain contested, as do the implications of empowerment, both for women themselves, and for their relationships with others (Oxaal, 1997; Parpart, 2002; Rowlands, 1996; UNIFEM, 2000), analytically, empowerment is often regarded as comprising three main dimensions: resources (preconditions), agency (process), and achievements (outcomes) (Kabeer, 1999). These criteria are necessarily interrelated since, as articulated by UNDP (2005: 19): 'To be empowered, women must gain equal capabilities and equal opportunities, as well as agency to use their rights, capabilities and opportunities to control their own lives and destinies.' Despite the difficulties of exerting agency when there are few real or perceived alternatives (Kabeer, 2005: 14), and especially where women are subject to violence or coercion (UNDP, 2005: 19), important 'lessons' emanating from discussions of empowerment include: (1) the idea that empowerment is a process, rather than an end-state, (2) that empowerment cannot be 'given' but has to come 'from within', (3) that empowerment works at different scales (the personal, the interpersonal, the collective, the local, the global), and (4) that 'measuring' empowerment requires tools which are sensitive to the perceptions of stakeholders at the grassroots, and to the different meanings and manifestations of empowerment in different cultural contexts (see Kabeer, 1999; Parpart, 2002; Rowlands, 1996).

These insights on empowerment have, in turn, enjoyed particular cross-fertilisation with poverty discourses in respect of emphasising that poverty is not a static but a dynamic phenomenon, that the alleviation or eradication of poverty cannot be answered by 'top-down', 'one-off', non-participatory approaches, and that Women in Development (WID) approaches which tend to focus on women only, and frequently as a homogeneous constituency, need to be replaced by GAD approaches which conceptualise gender as a dynamic social construct, and require consideration not only of women, but men and gender relations. Another vitally important contribution is the acknowledgement that poverty is unlikely to be effectively addressed by a unilateral focus on incomes. As articulated by Sweetman (2005: 6):

> money alone does not make for empowerment. Other resources needed include less tangible goods. These include self-confidence and pride in one's own worth, and knowledge and skills acquired through formal and informal means. Very importantly, resources also include the time and freedom to form strong relationships with other women, which can form a counterpart to the traditional power of the family and marriage in women's lives.

Despite these theoretical developments, in practical terms a less auspicious scenario has often resulted. For example, micro-finance has been one of the main thrusts of empowerment interventions to date, especially since the Micro-Credit Summit Campaign of 1997 established its second official goal as 'reaching and empowering women' (after its first goal – reducing poverty). Yet since different understandings and goals relating to female empowerment may exist in 'uneasy tension and with continually contested degrees of dominance' (Mayoux, 2006: 7), only one out of three main paradigms guiding micro-finance identified by Mayoux (2006), notably the 'feminist empowerment paradigm' (see Table 2.1) prioritises a radical and rounded transformation in women's lives and status. As for the other two paradigms – 'poverty alleviation' and 'financial self-sustainability' – 'despite the rhetoric of "empowerment", gender policy risks "evaporation" into merely using women's time and resources for programme efficiency or community development' (ibid.: 2). In this light it is no surprise that concerns are expressed about the way in which:

> the use of apparently similar terminology of empowerment, participation and sustainability conceals radical differences in policy priorities. Although women's

Table 2.1 Mayoux's classification of paradigms guiding micro-finance programmes

	Feminist empowerment paradigm	Poverty alleviation paradigm	Financial self-sustainability paradigm
Main policy focus	Microfinance as an entry point for women's economic, social and political empowerment	Microfinance as part of an integrated programme for poverty reduction for the poorest households	Financially self-sustainable micro-finance programmes which increase access to micro-finance services for large numbers of poor people
Target group	Poor women, alternative role models	The poorest	The entrepreneurial poor
Reason for targeting women	Gender equality and human rights	Higher levels of female poverty Women's responsibility for household well-being	Efficiency because of high female repayment rates Contribution of women's economic activity to economic growth
Underlying paradigm	Structuralist and socialist feminist critique of capitalism	Interventionist poverty alleviation and community development	Neoliberal market growth
Main policy instruments	Gender awareness and feminist organisation	The importance of small savings and loan provision Group formation for community development Methodologies for poverty targeting and/or operating in remote areas	Setting of interest rates to cover costs Separation of micro-finance from other interventions for separate accounting Programme expansion to increase outreach and economies of scale *Ways of using groups to*

Table 2.1 (continued)

	Feminist empowerment paradigm	Poverty alleviation paradigm	Financial self-sustainability paradigm
			decrease costs of delivery
Main focus of gender policy	Gender awareness and feminist organisation	Increasing women's participation in self-help groups	Providing the framework for equal access for women
Definition of empowerment	Transformation of power relations throughout society	Increased well-being, community development and self-sufficiency	Economic empowerment, expansion of individual choice and capacities for self-reliance

Source: Mayoux (2006: 4).

empowerment may be a stated aim in the rhetoric of official gender policy and programme promotion, in practice it becomes subsumed in and marginalised by concerns of financial sustainability and/or poverty alleviation. (Mayoux, 2006: 7)

HOW HAS GENDER ANALYSIS CONTRIBUTED TO SHIFTS IN THE DEFINITION AND CONCEPTUALISATION OF POVERTY?

Notwithstanding a more general tendency for feminist research to get 'lost in translation' in policy design and outcomes, it is undeniable that it has made a significant mark on defining and conceptualising poverty. Three contributions which stand out are first, the stress on poverty's multidimensional and dynamic nature, second, the significance of household disaggregation, and third, the importance of power, agency and subjectivity.

Embracing Poverty as a Multidimensional and Dynamic Entity

Emphasis on poverty as a multidimensional and dynamic concept responds to the limitations of income and consumption figures to convey the complexity of poor women's and men's lives. As summarised by Johnsson-Latham (2004b: 19):

Multidimensional definitions of poverty provide for a discourse which acknowl-
edges that well-being is not only a question of material assets . . . and help us
address broad issues like gender-based asymmetrical distribution, both in terms
of access to resources and voice. They also point to the need of addressing both
economic aspects of poverty and other crucial aspects of well-being such as self-
respect, dignity, empowerment, belonging and participation – and awareness of
the right not to be discriminated against.

That people's material well-being is influenced by factors beyond their work
in the paid economy has been central to the evolution of 'livelihoods'
approaches to poverty analysis, which draw theoretically on concepts such as
'entitlements' and 'capabilities' (Sen, 1981; 1985; 1987a), 'vulnerability', and
'poverty as process' (Chambers, 1983; 1989; also Haddad, 1991). Although
wages clearly are a 'trigger for other activities', and a 'motor of reproduction' (González de la Rocha, 2003a: 21), livelihoods perspectives emphasise
the importance of a range of activities undertaken by different household
members (such as domestic work and subsistence production), alongside
access to public services and infrastructure. For instance, even if people have
limited income, this may be offset by the public provision of medical care,
safe water supplies and sanitary infrastructure, and social protection and
benefits such as subsidised housing. In addition, there may be other important components of household 'asset bases' which help to temper poverty
such as 'human capital' (education, skills and so on), and 'social capital',
encompassing kin and friendship networks and support from community
organisations (see Cagatay, 1998; Chambers, 1995; McIlwaine, 1997; Moser,
1996; 1998; Moser and McIlwaine, 1997; Rakodi, 1999; Rakodi with Lloyd-
Jones, 2002; UNFPA, 2002; Wratten, 1995; also Box 2.1).

The assets and capabilities possessed by households, which can be stored,
accumulated, exchanged, and/or mobilised to generate income or other
benefits, influence vulnerability to poverty in the short- and long-term, with
May (2004: 10) noting that: 'Focusing on the likelihood of being poor
rather than on observed levels of poverty permits a richer understanding of
changes in well-being.' Moreover, while most households faced with precarious existences: 'aim at a livelihood which has high resilience and low
sensitivity to shocks and stresses' (Rakodi, 1999: 318), this can take many
forms, and a detailed focus on what different people in different contexts
aspire to, what they have, and how they make use of it, allows for a much
more comprehensive, culturally grounded, and person-oriented appreciation of how survival is negotiated (Moser, 1998). As summarised by
Enríquez Rosas (2002: 82), this represents: 'a movement from an understanding of poverty centred on individual shortcomings of the poor, to a
perspective that pays attention primarily to the resources and responses
developed by the poor in order to face their condition'.

BOX 2.1   CAPITAL ASSETS OF THE POOR

Human capital

- – vocational skills, knowledge, labour (access to/command over), health.

Social capital

- – relationships of trust, reciprocity and exchanges that facilitate cooperation, and may provide for informal safety nets among the poor (*Note*: there can also be 'negative' social capital in the form of violence, mistrust and so on).

Natural capital

- – natural resource stocks, for example trees, land, biodiversity.

Physical capital

- – basic infrastructure and producer goods such as transport, shelter, water supply and sanitation, energy, and communications.

Financial capital

- – savings (whether in cash, livestock, jewellery), and inflows of money, including earned income, pensions, remittances, and state transfers.

Source: Rakodi (1999).

Yet notwithstanding the value of a livelihoods perspective in helping to (re)instate the agency, ingenuity and energy of poor people, some caution is necessary. A cumulative erosion of income during protracted periods of neoliberal economic restructuring, for example (see González de la Rocha, 2001; 2003a), may rob people of capacity to use whatever other assets are nominally available to them. As noted by May (2004: 10) in the context of 'poverty traps' in South Africa:

> Financial constraints limit the ability of poor people to utilise effectively the productive assets and endowments they do possess. Moreover, the burden of meeting basic needs like water and fuelwood creates 'time poverty' which further

constrains a household's ability to employ the resources at its disposal . . . People remain poor because they cannot borrow against future earnings to invest in inputs or accumulate assets for production, including education. They are unable or unwilling to engage in entrepreneurial activities because the costs of failure are too high. They cannot insure themselves against risks and lack information about market opportunities. And they are deprived of many public goods such as property rights, public safety and infrastructure, thereby incurring high direct and time costs when trying to obtain them . . .

Qualifying the scope for agency in livelihoods approaches is especially relevant when it comes to gender, with the resources on which women may draw often being: 'circumscribed by rules, norms and practices which limit their market engagement . . . These include legal or other restrictions on occupations in which women may work, prevailing ideas about appropriate gender divisions of labour, or husbands' prohibitions on wives' working' (Baden, 1999: 12; see also Lavinas and Nicoll, 2006). Other constraints include lack of access to land and property, and may extend to public goods and services such as education and health (UNDP, 2005: 6). As further pointed out by ECLAC (2004b: 22): 'Women's dependency, or lack of autonomy within the household, though not synonymous with income poverty, affects their economic self-sufficiency and decision-making capacity' (see also Box 2.2).

That women may be able to exert less agency than men over livelihood strategies has added weight to exhortations to open-up households 'so as to assess how resources are generated and used, how they are converted into assets, and how the returns from these assets are distributed among household members' (González de la Rocha and Grinspun, 2001: 59–60). This, in turn, has fed into a second major impact of gender research: the need for household disaggregation.

The Importance of Household Disaggregation

Two sets of arguments relating to household disaggregation have had particular impacts on poverty analysis. The first is that total household incomes are inappropriate for comparing households when, *inter alia*, households vary in size. This is especially pertinent to female-headed households which tend to be smaller than male-headed units, and may thus *appear* poorer though in actuality are as well off or better off (Chant, 1997b; Kabeer, 1996: 14; Kennedy, 1994; Paolisso and Gammage, 1996: 21; Shanthi, 1994: 23). While there are clearly some provisos with per capita incomes in so far as the consumption needs of household members tend to vary according to age (Lloyd and Gage-Brandon, 1993: 121),[3] and larger households may benefit from economies of scale in respect of 'household

BOX 2.2 SELECTED INTRA-HOUSEHOLD INEQUALITIES

- Differential valuation of individuals.
- Non-recognition and/or non-valuation of work of female members, especially in respect of domestic and non-market work.
- Lack of female control over property and income (including male appropriation of women's earnings).
- Confinement of women to childbearing and childrearing.
- Less schooling for girls than boys.
- Lack of participation by girls in parental decisions regarding marriage and choice of spouse.
- Male decision-making over household expenditures, investments and migration.
- Lack of female control over family formation, size, duration and dissolution.
- Domestic violence.
- Male-bias in provision of nutrition and healthcare.
- Female foeticide.

Note: Some of these manifestations are clearly more common and/or geographically widespread than others.

Source: Moghadam (1997: 11–12).

establishment costs' relating to property and consumer goods (Buvinic, 1990, cited in Baden, 1997), they are likely to provide a somewhat closer approximation of the resources individuals potentially have at their disposal (see Chant, 1997b; González de la Rocha, 1994b).

A second, and possibly even more compelling reason to disaggregate households, however, is that taking household incomes, or even assets, in aggregate assumes an equality which may well not exist (Razavi, 1999: 412; also Klasen, 2004). While not denying that cross-cutting axes of difference such as age, birth order, relationship to the household head and so on are important in influencing domestic inequalities (see Bolt and Bird, 2003: 9), Lampietti and Stalker (2000: 4) highlight two main reasons for unequal treatment on grounds of gender in resource-constrained households. The first is on grounds of 'efficiency', with households investing less in women because the perceived returns to investments are lower. The second is 'cultural bias' in favour of men. The latter in particular is supported by a vast body of empirical work which highlights that women (and girls) are often at the mercy of 'secondary poverty' in male-headed households on account of son-preference, and because fathers may retain varying proportions of their income for discretionary personal expenditure (see Benería and Roldan, 1987: 114; Dwyer and Bruce, 1988; Kabeer, 2003: 165 et seq.; Young, 1992: 152). While part may go on routine expenses such as transport and food, a larger share may be channelled to 'non-merit' goods oriented to self-aggrandisement or gratification such as alcohol, drugs, tobacco and extramarital liaisons. These not only deprive other household members of income in the short term, but can exact financial, social and psychological costs down the line (Appleton, 1991; Chant, 1997a; Hoddinott and Haddad, 1991; Kabeer, 1994: 104). For example, where men become ill or unable to work through 'risk-taking' behaviour, others in their households may be forced into assuming greater labour burdens attached to looking after them, or bearing the costs of pharmaceuticals and formal medical attention (see Chant, 1997a). As identified in the context of HIV/AIDS affected households in Sierra Leone by Delamonica et al. (2004: 23):

> A parent's protracted illness and death will have a psychological impact on other family members, especially children. A sick husband or partner exerts various economic pressures on the household: financial resources dwindle with the loss of a wage earner and rising healthcare expenses; other family members must work extra hours to compensate for lost labour; and extra hours are spent caring for a sick or dying husband. The family may also lose property as items are sold to pay for healthcare or supplement household income. Pressures continue after the husband or partner has died: there are funeral expenses, and debts left by the deceased husband. The loss of a provider is sometimes compounded by loss of property or land access as the husband's family takes over. Social stigma and blame can result in discrimination against the surviving widow, further impoverishing her household. Sometimes widows and their children are absorbed into other families, but this is not always the case. Finally, widows may have been infected by their husbands, so that the children risk the loss of their surviving parent. (See also UNDP, 2005: 9 and 39)

While not denying that expenditure on extra-domestic pursuits may form a critical element of masculine identities in various parts of the world, and even enhance men's access to the labour market (through social networks and the like), for women and children in poverty the implications can clearly be disastrous (see Tasies Castro, 1996).

These observations have contributed to a major theoretical shift from 'unitary' to 'collective' household models which has had repercussions well beyond gender circles (see Bolt and Bird, 2003: 11 *et seq.*; also

Quisumbing and Maluccio, 2003). Kanbur (2003: 3), for example, claims that the bringing home to economists that the ' "unitary" model of the household simply could not capture or explain the evidence on deprivation among females in developing economies', has constituted a leading example of 'conceptual ferment' on distributional issues in economics and development economics in the last 20 years.

Notions of the 'unitary' household, as emphasised in 'New Household Economics', centred on the belief that households were not subject to the same competitive processes as markets. Instead they were naturally cohesive, consensus-based entities in which inequalities were tolerated by members on account of a 'joint utility function' whereby household interests prevailed over individual concerns. This tended to legitimise (and essentialise) 'maternal altruism' and to deny the need for microeconomic research at the sub-domestic level (see Kabeer, 1994: ch. 5). 'Collective' models of the household associated with 'New Institutional Economics' by contrast, emphasised that households were as much an 'institution' as states or markets, and were more readily characterised as 'social arenas' marked by gender- (and age-) differentiated struggles for individual and collective interests (Enriquez Rosas, 2002: 82; see also Dwyer and Bruce, 1988; Young, 1992).

Collective models encompass a variety of frameworks, one being 'cooperative models' which view decision-making in the context of 'bargaining power' processes whereby although individuals attempt to achieve their preferences, they compromise with a 'fall-back' position determined by the relative costs and consequences of household break-up (Bolt and Bird, 2003). A major and perhaps most widely known variant is the 'cooperative conflict model' devised by Amartya Sen (1987b; 1990) which emphasises, *inter alia*, how prevailing notions of roles and obligations within households place women under greater pressure than men to subordinate their own needs to those of others (Bolt and Bird, 2003: 12). The main impact of these different perspectives on poverty analysis is their underlining of the need to scrutinise what goes on *inside* households rather than leaving them as irreducible 'blank boxes' governed by 'natural' proclivities to benevolence, consensus and joint welfare maximisation (see also Baden, 1997; Cagatay, 1998; González de la Rocha, 2003a; Hart, 1997; Kabeer, 1994: ch. 5; Molyneux, 2001: ch. 4; Muthwa, 1993).

Power, Agency and Subjectivity: The Concept of 'Trade-Offs'

Leading on from the above, a third major contribution of feminist research to poverty analysis has been its role in highlighting 'power'. As articulated by ECLAC (2004b: 17):

although poverty may be defined concisely as a critical lack of income, it is a multidimensional phenomenon, and thus, an analysis of it must include an examination of other power relationships – in the case of women, focusing particularly on those associated with unpaid work, reproductive rights, violence against women, and individuals' use of time.

As echoed by Sweetman (2005: 3), poverty 'is as much about agency compromised by abuse, stress, fatigue and voicelessness, as it is about lack of resources'.

Although women are often victims of unequal power relations and limited agency, emphasis on subjectivity has brought about recognition that this can also drive women to make choices for themselves and their dependants which reduce access to some types of resource, but enhance their prospects of others, as encapsulated in the concept of 'trade-offs' (see Chant, 1997b; Kabeer, 1997; 1999). The relevance of 'trade-offs' has perhaps been best underlined by research on female household headship, where decisions to avoid co-residence with men, or, more usually, to remain unpartnered following break-up or bereavement, can be highly tactical (and beneficial) within a constrained range of livelihood options. Women may well be poorer in income terms on their own than as wives or partners in male-headed households, for example, but can *feel* better off and, importantly, be less vulnerable, on account of having more autonomy, more control, and/or greater personal security (Chant, 1997b: 41; see also Chapter 3 in this volume).

HOW HAVE GENDER PERSPECTIVES ENRICHED THE MEASUREMENT AND ASSESSMENT OF POVERTY?

The stress placed by gender research on moving beyond the 'household' as the unit of assessment in poverty analysis has made a valuable contribution not only to conceptualising poverty, but how to measure it. Even if the use of per capita incomes has not yet displaced reliance on aggregate household incomes in many countries, at a macro-level there have been important shifts towards broadening the range of indicators used in poverty measurement, as well as to make poverty assessments more participatory.

Broadening the Indicators used in Macro-Level Poverty Assessments

As far as quantitative macro-level assessments are concerned, an important step towards the diversification of indicators has been made through a range of aggregate indices devised by the United Nations Development

Programme (UNDP), one of particular relevance for poverty being the Human Poverty Index (HPI) which came into being in 1997.[4] The HPI evolved out of the 'Capability Poverty Measure' (CPM) developed on the basis of Amartya Sen's ideas about how income and commodities are important only in so far as they contribute to people's capabilities to achieve the lives they want, namely, 'functioning achievements' (see Sen, 1985; 1999; also Kabeer, 2003: 84; Ruggeri Laderchi et al., 2003: 16).[5]

Consonant with the concept of human development as a process of 'widening people's choices and the level of well-being they achieve' (UNDP, 1997: 13), the HPI identifies the proportion of people who lack essential human capabilities – notably health, reproduction and education – which, as summarised by UNFPA (2002) are 'ends in themselves and are needed to lift one from income poverty and to sustain strong human development'. For example, poor health can be as much a *cause* as well an *effect* of income poverty in so far as it 'diminishes personal capacity, lowers productivity and reduces earnings' (ibid.; see also Bergés, 2005: 4; Fukuda-Parr, 1999; May, 2001; UNDP, 2002: 13).

Recognition of gender disparities in well-being has been critical in the development of the UNDP's Gender-Related Development Index (GDI), and the Gender Empowerment Measure (GEM) (see Bardhan and Klasen, 1999; also Dijkstra and Hanmer, 2000; Klasen, 2006; UNFPA, 2002). Originating in 1995, and subject to successive review and revision, the GDI adjusts the HDI for gender disparities in the three main indicators making up the Human Development Index (HDI) (see note 4), namely:

1. 'longevity' (female and male life expectancy at birth),
2. 'knowledge' (female and male literacy rates, and female and male combined primary, secondary and tertiary enrolment ratios), and
3. 'decent standard of living' (estimated female and male earned income, to reflect gender-differentiated command over resources).

Notwithstanding variations in the degree and kind of inequalities within as well as between nations (see Tables 2.2–2.4), and that the GDI score is heavily influenced by the HDI, it is eminently apparent from this index that 'women have markedly less chance to lead their lives in dignity and prosperity' (Rodenberg, 2004: ii; see also Johnson, 2005: 58; UN/UNIFEM, 2003: 20).

While the GDI focuses on the impact of gender inequality on human development, the GEM is concerned with the relationship between gender and opportunity, and measures equity in *agency* – in other words, the extent to which women are actually able to achieve equality with men (Bardhan and Klasen, 1999; Cueva Beteta, 2006; Rodenberg, 2004: ii).

Table 2.2 Gender-Related Development Index (GDI): Latin American countries

	Gender-Related Development Index (GDI) 2001–02		Life expectancy at birth (years) 2002		Adult literacy rate (% aged 15 years or more) 2002		Combined primary, secondary and tertiary gross enrolment ratio (%) 2001–02		Estimated earned income (PPP US$)² 2002		HDI rank minus GDI rank 2001–02
	Rank¹	Value	Female	Male	Female	Male	Female	Male	Female	Male	
Argentina	36	0.841	77.6	70.5	97.0	97.0	98	90	5 662	15 431	–3
Bolivia	92	0.674	65.8	61.6	80.7	93.1	82	89	1 559	3 463	0
Brazil	60	0.768	72.5	63.0	86.5	86.2	94	90	4 594	10 897	–1
Chile	40	0.830	78.9	72.9	95.6	95.8	79	80	5 442	14 256	0
Colombia	59	0.770	75.2	69.0	92.2	92.1	70	67	4 429	8 420	1
Costa Rica	44	0.823	80.5	75.7	95.9	95.7	66	67	4 609	12 577	–2
Cuba	–	–	78.6	74.7	96.3	94.6	77	72	–	–	–
Dominican Republic	78	0.728	69.2	64.4	84.4	84.3	81	73	3 491	9 694	0
Ecuador	79	0.721	73.4	68.2	89.7	92.3	71	73	1 656	5 491	1
El Salvador	84	0.709	73.6	67.6	77.1	82.4	65	66	2 602	7 269	–2
Guatemala	98	0.635	68.7	62.8	62.5	77.3	52	59	2 007	6 092	1
Honduras	95	0.662	71.4	66.5	80.2	79.8	61	64	1 402	3 792	–2
Mexico	50	0.792	76.3	70.3	88.7	92.6	74	73	4 915	12 967	–3
Nicaragua	97	0.660	71.8	67.1	76.6	76.8	66	63	1 520	3 436	2
Panama	53	0.785	77.3	72.2	91.7	92.9	75	71	3 958	7 847	–1
Paraguay	75	0.736	73.0	68.5	90.2	93.1	72	72	2 175	6 641	–2
Peru	74	0.736	72.3	67.2	80.3	91.3	88	88	2 105	7 875	–3

| Uruguay | 41 | 0.829 | 78.8 | 71.5 | 98.1 | 97.3 | 90 | 81 | 5 367 | 10 304 | 2 |
| Venezuela | 58 | 0.770 | 76.6 | 70.8 | 92.7 | 93.5 | 66 | 64 | 3 125 | 7 550 | −2 |

Notes:
1. Rank out of 144 countries; top = Norway (0.955); bottom = Niger (0.278).
2. See Anand and Sen (2000).
– = No data.

Source: UNDP (2004: table 24).

Table 2.3   *Gender-Related Development Index (GDI): South-East Asian countries*

	Gender-Related Development Index (GDI) 2001–02		Life expectancy at birth (years) 2002		Adult literacy rate (% aged 15 years or more) 2002		Combined primary, secondary and tertiary gross enrolment ratio (%) 2002		Estimated earned income (PPP US$) 2002		HDI rank minus GDI rank 2001–02
	Rank[1]	Value	Female	Male	Female	Male	Female	Male	Female	Male	
Brunei Darussalam	–	–	78.7	74	88.1	94.6	84	81	–	–	–
Cambodia	105	0.557	59.2	55.2	59.3	80.8	53	64	1 622	2 117	–1
China	71	0.741	73.2	68.8	86.5	95.1	64	69	3 571	5 435	5
Hong Kong, China (SAR)	23	0.898	82.7	77.2	89.6	96.9	70	73	18 805	34 776	0
Indonesia	90	0.685	71.4	66.7	86.9	93.9	61	67	1 888	2 723	3
Korea, Rep. of	29	0.882	79.2	71.7	96.6	99.2	85	98	10 747	23 226	–1
Lao PDR	107	0.528	55.6	53.1	55.5	77.4	53	65	1 358	2 082	0
Malaysia	52	0.786	75.6	70.7	85.4	92.0	72	69	5 219	13 157	–1
Mongolia	94	0.664	65.7	61.7	97.5	98.0	76	64	1 316	1 955	1
Myanmar	–	–	60.1	54.5	81.4	89.2	48	47	–	–	–
Papua New Guinea	106	0.536	58.5	56.6	57.7	71.1	40	42	1 566	2 748	0
Philippines	66	0.751	71.9	67.9	92.7	92.5	82	81	3 144	5 326	3
Singapore	28	0.884	80.2	75.8	88.6	96.6	75	76	15 822	31 927	–3
Thailand	61	0.766	73.4	65.2	90.5	94.9	72	74	5 284	8 664	1
Vietnam	87	0.689	71.4	66.7	86.9	93.9	61	67	1 888	2 723	3

Notes:
1. Rank out of 144 countries.
– = No data.

Source: UNDP (2004: table 24).

Table 2.4 Gender-Related Development Index (GDI): sub-Saharan African countries

	Gender-Related Development Index (GDI) 2001–02		Life expectancy at birth (years) 2002		Adult literacy rate (% aged 15 years or more) 2002		Combined primary, secondary and tertiary gross enrolment ratio (%) 2002		Estimated earned income (PPP US$) 2002		HDI rank minus GDI rank 2001–02
	Rank[1]	Value	Female	Male	Female	Male	Female	Male	Female	Male	
Angola	–	–	41.5	38.8	–	–	27	32	1627	2626	–
Benin	130	0.406	53.1	48.5	25.5	54.8	41	64	876	1268	0
Botswana	102	0.581	42.3	40.4	81.5	76.1	70	70	5353	10550	0
Burkina Faso	143	0.291	46.3	45.1	8.1	18.5	18	26	855	1215	0
Burundi	140	0.337	41.3	40.2	43.6	57.7	29	38	561	794	0
Cameroon	111	0.491	48.1	45.6	59.8	77.0	51	61	1235	2787	2
Cape Verde	83	0.709	72.7	66.9	68.0	85.4	72	73	3229	7034	1
Central Africa	138	0.345	41.0	38.7	33.5	64.7	24	38	889	1469	–1
Chad	135	0.368	45.7	43.6	37.5	54.5	25	44	760	1284	0
Comoros	108	0.510	62.0	59.2	49.1	63.5	41	50	950	1669	0
Congo, Dem. Rep. of the	136	0.355	42.4	40.4	51.8	74.2	24	30	467	846	0
Congo Rep.	112	0.488	49.9	46.6	77.1	88.9	44	52	707	1273	4
Côte d'Ivoire	132	0.379	41.5	40.9	38.4	60.3	31	46	818	2222	0
Equatorial Guinea	86	0.691	50.5	47.7	76.0	92.8	49	68	16852	42304	2
Eritrea	127	0.431	54.2	51.1	45.6	68.2	29	38	654	1266	0
Ethiopia	137	0.346	46.4	44.6	33.8	49.2	27	41	516	1008	1
Gabon	–	–	57.6	55.7	–	–	81	85	4937	8351	–
Gambia, The	125	0.446	55.4	52.5	30.9	45.0	43	51	1263	2127	1
Ghana	104	0.564	59.3	56.4	65.9	81.9	42	49	1802	2419	0

Table 2.4 (continued)

	Gender-Related Development Index (GDI) 2001–02		Life expectancy at birth (years) 2002		Adult literacy rate (% aged 15 years or more) 2002		Combined primary, secondary and tertiary gross enrolment ratio (%) 2002		Estimated earned income (PPP US$) 2002		HDI rank minus GDI rank 2001–02
	Rank[1]	Value	Female	Male	Female	Male	Female	Male	Female	Male	
Guinea	–	–	49.3	48.6	–	–	26	41	1 569	2 317	–
Guinea-Bissau	141	0.329	46.8	43.7	24.7	55.2	34	52	465	959	–1
Kenya	114	0.486	46.4	44.0	78.5	90.0	52	53	962	1 067	6
Lesotho	117	0.483	39.0	33.3	90.3	73.7	65	61	1 357	3 578	0
Liberia	–	–	–	–	–	–	–	–	–	–	–
Madagascar	121	0.462	54.6	52.3	60.6	74.2	43	45	534	906	1
Malawi	134	0.374	38.2	37.5	48.7	75.5	70	74	427	626	0
Mali	142	0.309	49.0	47.9	11.9	26.7	26	38	635	1 044	0
Mauritius	55	0.775	75.7	68.3	80.5	88.2	68	70	5 827	15 897	–1
Mozambique	139	0.339	40.0	36.9	31.4	62.3	32	42	840	1 265	0
Namibia	101	0.602	46.3	43.8	82.8	83.8	75	72	4 833	9 511	0
Niger	144	0.278	46.3	45.7	9.3	25.1	14	21	575	1 005	0
Nigeria	122	0.458	52.0	51.2	59.4	74.4	41	49	562	1 322	1
Rwanda	129	0.423	39.4	38.4	63.4	75.3	51	52	968	1 570	0
São Tomé and Principe	–	–	72.7	66.9	–	–	–	–	–	–	–
Senegal	128	0.429	54.9	50.6	29.7	49.0	34	41	1 140	2 074	0
Sierra Leone	–	–	35.6	33.1	–	–	44	57	337	815	–
Somalia	–	–	–	–	–	–	–	–	–	–	–
South Africa	96	0.661	51.9	46.0	85.3	86.7	77	78	6 371	14 202	1
Sudan	115	0.485	57.0	54.1	49.1	70.8	32	36	867	2 752	–4

Swaziland	109	0.505	36.9	34.4	80.0	82.0	75	78	2259	7227	0
Tanzania	131	0.401	44.4	42.7	69.2	85.2	31	31	467	660	0
Togo	119	0.477	51.4	48.3	45.4	74.3	53	80	941	2004	–4
Uganda	113	0.487	46.4	44.9	59.2	78.8	66	75	1088	1651	5
Zambia	133	0.375	32.5	32.9	73.8	86.3	43	47	571	1041	0
Zimbabwe	118	0.482	33.5	34.3	86.3	93.8	58	62	1757	3059	1

Notes:
1. Rank out of 144 countries.
– = No data.

Source: UNDP (2004: table 24).

More specifically, the GEM aims to assess gender inequality in economic and political opportunities and decision-making, and comprises four main indicators:

1. The share of parliamentary seats occupied by women.
2. The proportion of legislators, senior officials and managers who are women.
3. The female share of professional and technical jobs.
4. The ratio of estimated female to male earned income (see Tables 2.5–2.7).

The UNDP gender indices reveal the increasing prominence given to gender in national and global accounting of development and poverty and are important complementary tools in the gender analysis in so far as they go some way to quantifying male–female disparities in opportunities, capabilities and access to resources (UNDP, 2001b: 5). Insofar as being in the public domain they are also claimed to be extremely important for policy since they draw (and expose) governments' attention (or inattention) to gender inequalities, as well as potentially galvanising them into action (Dijkstra and Hanmer, 2000; UNIFEM, 2002).

This said, and as will be discussed in more detail later, it is important to recognise that bases of the UNDP gender indices remain limited. For example, data on women's income relative to men's are restricted to formal sector remuneration (Kabeer, 2003: 87). Yet since women are disproportionately concentrated in informal economic activity (Table 2.8), this does not provide an accurate picture of male–female earning differentials, especially given that gender gaps in remuneration tend to be wider in the informal than formal sector (see Funkhouser, 1996: 1746; López de Mazier, 1997: 236).

On top of this, the indices neglect women's considerable inputs into household labour, and other unpaid activities such as subsistence farming, which play a crucial role in underpinning livelihoods. Indeed, while gender research has stressed the importance of incorporating the non-market work of women in GDP and poverty assessments, this tends to remain undervalued, if not invisible, despite increased use of terms such as such as 'care economy' and 'reproductive economy' intended to underline its significance (see Elson, 1999b; Folbre, 2006). As summarised by ECLAC (2004b: 19):

> The fact that monetary value is not placed on unpaid domestic work, and that methods for measuring household poverty do not incorporate an attribution of income in this category in households where one person is entirely dedicated to domestic work and care, limits the ability of traditional measures of poverty to capture gender inequalities.

Table 2.5 Gender Empowerment Measure (GEM): Latin American countries

	Gender Empowerment Measure (GEM) 2004		Seats in parliament held by women 2004 (as % of total)	Female legislators, senior officials and managers 2004 (as % of total)	Female professional and technical workers 2004 (as % of total)	Ratio of estimated female to male income 2001
	Rank[1]	Value				
Argentina	21	0.645	31.3	26	53	0.37
Bolivia	41	0.524	17.8	36	40	0.45
Brazil	–	–	9.1	–	62	0.42
Chile	58	0.460	10.1	21	52	0.38
Colombia	48	0.498	10.8	38	50	0.53
Costa Rica	19	0.664	35.1	53	28	0.39
Cuba	–	–	36.0	–	–	–
Dominican Republic	40	0.527	15.4	31	49	0.36
Ecuador	50	0.490	16.0	25	44	0.30
El Salvador	60	0.448	10.7	26	46	0.36
Guatemala	–	–	8.2	–	–	–
Honduras	70	0.355	5.5	22	36	0.37
Mexico	34	0.563	21.2	25	40	0.38
Nicaragua	–	–	20.7	–	–	–
Panama	52	0.486	9.9	38	49	0.50
Paraguay	63	0.417	8.8	23	54	0.33
Peru	42	0.524	18.3	27	44	0.27
Uruguay	46	0.511	11.5	37	52	0.52
Venezuela	61	0.444	9.7	27	61	0.41

Note:
1. Rank out of 78 countries.
– = No data.

Source: UNDP (2004: table 25).

Table 2.6 Gender Empowerment Measure (GEM): South-East Asian countries

	Gender Empowerment Measure (GEM) 2004		Seats in parliament held by women 2004 (as % of total)	Female legislators, senior officials and managers 2004 (as % of total)	Female professional and technical workers 2004 (as % of total)	Ratio of estimated female to male earned income 2001
	Rank[1]	Value				
Brunei Darussalam	–	–	–	–	–	–
Cambodia	69	0.364	10.9	14	33	0.77
China	–	–	20.2	–	–	–
Hong Kong, China (SAR)	–	–	–	26	40	–
Indonesia	–	–	8.0	–	–	–
Korea, Rep. of	68	0.377	5.9	5	34	0.46
Lao PDR	–	–	22.9	–	–	–
Malaysia	44	0.519	16.3	20	45	0.40
Mongolia	62	0.429	10.5	30	66	0.67
Papua New Guinea	–	–	0.9	–	–	–
Philippines	37	0.542	17.2	58	62	0.59
Singapore	20	0.648	16.0	26	43	0.50
Thailand	57	0.461	9.5	27	55	0.61
Vietnam	–	–	27.3	–	–	–

Note:
1. Rank out of 78 countries.
– = No data.

Source: UNDP (2004: table 25).

Table 2.7 Gender Empowerment Measure (GEM): sub-Saharan African countries

	Gender Empowerment Measure (GEM) 2004		Seats in parliament held by women 2004 (as % of total)	Female legislators, senior officials and managers 2004 (as % of total)	Female professional and technical workers 2004 (as % of total)	Ratio of estimated female to male earned income 2001
	Rank	Value				
Angola	–	–	15.5	–	–	–
Benin	–	–	7.2	–	–	–
Botswana	35	0.562	17.0	35	52	0.51
Burkina Faso	–	–	11.7	–	–	–
Burundi	–	–	18.5	–	–	–
Cameroon	–	–	8.9	–	–	–
Cape Verde	–	–	11.1	–	–	–
Central African Republic	–	–	–	–	–	–
Chad	–	–	5.8	–	–	–
Comoros	–	–	–	–	–	–
Congo, Dem. Rep. of the	–	–	7.4	–	–	–
Congo	–	–	10.6	–	–	–
Côte d'Ivoire	–	–	8.5	–	–	–
Equatorial Guinea	–	–	5.0	–	–	–
Eritrea	–	–	22.0	–	–	–
Ethiopia	–	–	7.8	–	–	–
Gabon	–	–	11.0	–	–	–
Gambia	–	–	13.2	–	–	–
Ghana	–	–	9.0	–	–	–
Guinea	–	–	19.3	–	–	–
Guinea-Bissau	–	–	7.8	–	–	–
Kenya	–	–	7.1	–	–	–

Table 2.7 (continued)

	Gender Empowerment Measure (GEM) 2004		Seats in parliament held by women 2004 (as % of total)	Female legislators, senior officials and managers 2004 (as % of total)	Female professional and technical workers 2004 (as % of total)	Ratio of estimated female to male earned income 2001
	Rank	Value				
Lesotho	–	–	17.0	–	–	–
Liberia	–	–	–	–	–	–
Madagascar	–	–	6.4	–	–	–
Malawi	–	–	9.3	–	–	–
Mali	–	–	10.2	–	–	–
Mauritius	–	–	5.7	–	–	–
Mozambique	–	–	30.0	–	–	–
Namibia	33	0.572	21.4	30	55	0.51
Niger	–	–	1.2	–	–	–
Nigeria	–	–	3.3	–	–	–
Rwanda	–	–	25.7	–	–	–
São Tomé and Principe	–	–	9.1	–	–	–
Senegal	–	–	19.2	–	–	–
Seychelles	–	–	29.4	–	–	–
Sierra Leone	–	–	14.5	–	–	–
Somalia	–	–	–	–	–	–
South Africa	–	–	30.0	–	–	–
Sudan	–	–	9.7	–	–	–
Swaziland	–	–	6.3	–	–	–
Tanzania, U. Rep. of	–	–	22.3	–	–	–
Togo	–	–	7.4	–	–	–
Uganda	–	–	24.7	–	–	–

Zambia	–	–	–	–	12.0	–	–
Zimbabwe	–	–	–	–	10.0	–	–

Notes:
1. Rank out of 78 countries.
– = No data.

Source: UNDP (2004: table 25).

Table 2.8   Gender and informal employment: selected developing countries

Region/country	Informal employment as % of non-agricultural employment	Women's informal employment as % of non-agricultural employment	Men's informal employment as % of non-agricultural employment
North Africa	*48*	*43*	*49*
Algeria	43	41	43
Morocco	45	47	44
Tunisia	50	39	53
Egypt	55	46	57
Sub-Saharan Africa	*72*	*84*	*63*
Benin	93	97	87
Chad	74	95	60
Guinea	72	87	66
Kenya	72	83	59
South Africa	51	58	44
Latin America	*51*	*58*	*48*
Bolivia	63	74	55
Brazil	60	67	55
Chile	36	44	31
Colombia	38	44	34
Dominican Republic	72	84	63
El Salvador	57	69	46
Guatemala	56	69	47
Honduras	58	65	74
Mexico	55	55	54
Venezuela	47	47	47
Asia	*65*	*65*	*65*
India	83	86	83
Indonesia	78	77	78
Philippines	72	73	71
Thailand	51	54	49

Source: UNIFEM (2002: table 5), based on ILO (2002) figures.

The statistical invisibility of 'the sexual division of labour', or the assignment of household chores to women also means that 'women are overloaded with work whose value is not socially or economically recognised' (ibid.: 2).[6]

Although some progress has been made towards improving the gender-sensitivity of enumeration in the last two decades, such as through greater recourse to time-use statistics and the provision of gender training for data collectors (see Corner, 2002; 2003), quantifying and assigning a value to women's work outside the realm of the formal paid economy represents one of the biggest methodological challenges of the twenty-first century (see Benería, 1999; UNDP, 1995; WEDO, 2005). A number of approaches have been devised, which range from attempting to match the particular type of unpaid labour performed by its corresponding market price, to assessing the opportunity cost of doing unpaid labour instead of participating in the paid sector (see Box 2.3). However, none is without problems. While focusing on persons, as in the opportunity cost approach, assigns different values to the unpaid work performed according to who does it, approaches which rely on average wages according to activity depress the general value of the work because paid housework or care of the young, elderly, infirm and so on, tend to be feminised occupations and, as such, to command lower remuneration. A further difficulty arises in respect of how to factor in the simultaneous performance of different unpaid (and paid) tasks, and issues around work intensity (see also Floro, 1995; Folbre, 2006).

The Importance of Participatory Methodologies

Aside from intra-household scrutiny, and consideration of factors beyond income, participatory tools have been regarded as crucial in assessing the gender dimensions of poverty (see Kabeer, 1996: 18 et seq.; Moser et al., 1996b: 2).

Evolving out of Participatory Rural Appraisal (PRA) methodologies, Participatory Poverty Assessments (PPAs) entail the deployment of 'outsiders', such as NGO personnel, as 'facilitators', with local people acting not so much as 'informants' but 'analysts' (May, 2001: 45). This nominally gives rise to broadened ownership of the term 'poverty' which is crucial given that in many contexts poverty is construed as being 'relational rather than absolute', and extends far beyond considerations of physical survival to incorporate notions of 'exclusion, powerlessness and stigma' (ibid.: 24; see also Clarke and Sison, 2003: 216). As underlined by Kabeer (2003: 80): 'The well-being of human beings, and what matters to them, does not only depend on their purchasing power, but on other less tangible aspects, such as dignity and self-respect' (see also Painter, 2004: 18; Rojas, 2003; van Vuuren, 2003: 51).

Even if the implementation, interpretation and use of PPAs leaves much to be desired, it is extremely significant, given traditional allegiance to quantitative approaches, that multilateral organisations have taken them on board, one of the most notable examples being the World Bank's 'Voices of the Poor' study for the millennial *World Development Report* (see World Bank, 2000). Since PPAs nominally offer scope for the inclusion of women's voices, this also represents a potentially important step towards enhancing the gender-responsiveness of poverty assessment.

BOX 2.3   APPROACHES TO ASSIGNING ECONOMIC VALUE TO UNPAID CARE WORK

1. The mean wage approach

Calculates the average hourly wage in the economy as a whole, usually on a sex-disaggregated basis, and assigns this to unpaid care work.

Can lower the overall estimated value of unpaid work (a) because women usually perform more unpaid care work than men, and (b) the mean female wage is generally lower than the mean male wage.

2. The opportunity cost approach

Calculates the value of unpaid care work by estimating what the person has forfeited by doing unpaid care work instead of working in a typical remunerated activity for someone with their particular educational and skill set.

Poses difficulties in that since the opportunity cost of a university graduate doing unpaid care work is estimated as higher than someone with less education, it confers different values to unpaid care work according not to the activity performed, but to the person performing it.

Another problem relates to the determination of what wage to use when people are normally unemployed and unwaged, or work in subsistence production.

3. The generalist approach

Calculates the mean wage of workers in the paid economy whose functions and circumstances best match those perfomed by persons in the unpaid sector. For example, childcare, the wages of crèche workers, for housework, paid domestic helpers and so on.

4. The specialist approach

Focuses on the activity as opposed to the person performing the activity at a more disaggregated level than the generalist approach. For example, values unpaid cooking time at the wage of a paid chef or cook, cleaning at the value of the wage of a paid cleaner and so on.

Source: Budlender (2004: 35–7).

OUTSTANDING CHALLENGES TO THE GENDER-SENSITIVITY OF POVERTY ANALYSIS

Having documented the influences of feminist research and advocacy on the conceptualisation and measurement of poverty, it is important to identify major barriers to further advances. Three which stand out in particular are, first, continued gender 'blindspots' in 'mainstream' approaches to poverty assessment; second, that inadequate data make it hard to expand the scope of gender-sensitive poverty indicators; and third, that advocacy for directing resources to women, usually through pronouncements about the 'feminisation of poverty', has often become wedded to unhelpful stereotypes which narrow the scope of analysis and policy.

Major 'Mainstream' Approaches to Poverty Analysis and Their Limitations Regarding Gender

The three dominant 'mainstream' approaches to poverty analysis are classified by Kabeer (2003: 79 et seq.) as follows:

1. The *'poverty line' approach*, which measures the economic 'means', notably income, through which households and individuals meet their basic needs.
2. The *'capabilities'* or *'human development''approach*, whereby 'means' other than earnings or transfer payments, such as endowments and entitlements are brought into the equation, along with 'ends' ('functioning achievements').
3. *'Participatory poverty assessments'* which explore the causes and outcomes of poverty in more context-specific ways, taking into account subjective views on poverty. This could also be described as a 'social inclusion' approach which, as noted by Chen et al. (2004: 6), focuses on 'political participation, social dialogue and "voice"'.

The poverty line approach and gender

Grounded in quantitative (or 'money metric') measures of income, consumption and/or expenditure, national (and international) 'poverty lines' are drawn at the point which divides poor from non-poor households on the basis of whether they are able to satisfy an officially determined minimum level of survival, comprising food with an allowance for non-food items (see Satterthwaite, 2005: 3). Poor households whose incomes cannot stretch to dietary sufficiency may be further categorised as 'food poor', 'extremely poor' or 'indigent'.

Regardless of the use of income or consumption, neither method is fool-proof. Where current income is the basis for official poverty, assessment data are often difficult to obtain, as well as subject to under-reporting (see World Bank, 1996). Yet where expenditure is used as a proxy for income this may not accurately reflect the 'real monetary cost for individuals or households of meeting their needs' (Satterthwaite, 2003: 29). More particularly, the allowance for non-food consumption is often small and may neglect or under-estimate what households spend on other necessities such as accommodation and transport (Satterthwaite, 2005: 3; see also ADB, 2005c: app. 1).[7]

Another problem with the poverty line approach is that it assumes that well-being can be equated with people's capacity to meet essential physical survival needs (usually food), and the 'ability – shown by income – to "choose" between different "bundles" of commodities' (Kabeer, 2003: 79; see also May, 2001: 24–5). While this is undoubtedly important, the poverty line approach discounts the impacts of public goods and services such as health and education (Satterthwaite, 2005; UNFPA, 2002). This tendency to focus on domestic as opposed to public resources can, in turn, lead to an 'implicit bias in policy choices in favour of the generation of private income as against public goods provision, and similarly, the identification of the poor for targeting purposes towards those lacking private income' (Ruggeri Laderchi et al., 2003: 9).

A related problem is that poverty lines ignore the non-monetary resources and non-market transactions through which people fulfil their survival needs, such as the 'social capital' generated among networks of kin, friends or neighbours. Work on Mexico, for example, indicates that the bearing on people's well-being of income and access to public services such as water and public transport may actually be less important than good relations with family and neighbours (Rojas, 2003). On the basis of this, Rojas (2003: 1) concludes that 'the abatement of poverty would be better served by a well-being concept based on the wholeness and complexity of human beings' (see also May, 2001). Because 'positive' social capital may mitigate people's poverty, so too is it also important to acknowledge that people may prioritise investment in these over material goods (see van Vuuren, 2003: 159 et seq.).

From a gender perspective, the focus on money-metric data clearly downplays women's contributions to survival because it disregards their vital unpaid work (Johnsson-Latham, 2004b: 41). Another major problem with poverty lines is their continued over-reliance on households as the unit of measurement which conceals gender-differentiated poverty burdens. As summarised by Baden (1999: 11): 'At the household level, income and consumption-based measures do not provide a good predictor of women's well-being because of intra-household inequalities in resource distribution and other institutional biases', it being quite possible for women to be deprived in rich households and for increases in household income to actually mean greater gender inequality in well-being (see also Jackson, 1996; Kabeer, 1996; 2003: 81; Mayoux, 2006; Srinivasan, 2004). Yet despite long-standing feminist concerns over resource-allocation inequities, it remains 'rare to find standard surveys, such as those carried out in the context of the PAs (poverty assessments), embarking on a quantitative exploration of intra-household poverty' (Razavi, 1999: 412).

Another, more general problem with money-metric methods is that they may underestimate poverty. On the basis of research in Peru, for example, Franco (2003) observes that despite some association between monetary poverty and capability poverty, around one-third of capability poor people are not actually monetarily poor, 'Hence monetary poverty which is a measure governments normally use, misses out very large numbers of people suffering important types of deprivation' (ibid.: 1; see also Staudt, 1998). Nonetheless, poverty lines often continue to be favoured by national as well as international bodies on grounds that: 'Income-based measures of poverty are objective, highly amenable to quantitative analysis, and accurately describe income poverty, provided household surveys are carefully administered' (UNFPA, 2002).

The capabilities approach and gender
Whereas the poverty line approach focuses mainly on 'means', the 'capabilities' approach to poverty deriving from Amartya Sen's work (see earlier) also focuses on 'ends', as well as blurring the distinction between 'means' and 'ends' (Kabeer, 2003: 84). Drawing on a broad range of factors beyond income such as drinking water, sanitation, shelter, health and clothing, which interact in manifold ways with people's 'functionings' (Kabeer, 2003: 83–4; also note 5): 'The capabilities approach represents a major contribution to poverty analysis because it provides a coherent framework for defining poverty in the context of the lives people live and the freedoms they enjoy' (Ruggeri Laderchi et al., 2003: 21: see also Sen, 1990). A major bonus as far as gender is concerned is that by concentrating on individuals as well as households, capabilities can be interpreted and measured in sex-disaggregated ways. In turn, among the most useful contributions to gender and poverty offered by the capabilities approach as identified by Kabeer (2003: 95) are, first, assistance in monitoring differences in basic achievements across space and time; second, drawing attention to regional differences in gender inequality; and third, revealing aspects of gender inequality that persist regardless of levels of economic growth.

Yet although the capabilities approach goes beyond poverty lines in respect of illuminating gender dimensions, much information relevant to gender inequality, such as time use and work intensity is not heeded. More generally, there are also difficulties in translating the capabilities approach into policies for poverty reduction. As argued by Greeley (2001: 55): 'The capabilities framework is very rich, but it is strongest as rights-based ethical theory and it does not translate neatly into a strategy for pro-poor policy formulation and implementation.' Greeley further notes that this problem is compounded by the lack of an agreed universal list of 'desirable capabilities' (ibid.; see also van Vuuren, 2003: 34).

Notwithstanding these caveats, some argue that the concepts of multidimensionality promoted by Sen and others have not only broadened poverty definitions, but, along with the major UN conferences of the 1990s, have helped to make for poverty reduction strategies which are more comprehensive, have a 'human face', and are potentially more effective (see Virola, 2002: 25). Generally speaking, gender is much likelier to feature in such initiatives than those which take a narrow, overly quantitative, 'top-down' view of poverty.

Participatory Poverty Assessments: constraints regarding gender
As identified earlier, PPAs have made an important contributions to 'engendering' poverty analysis, mainly by highlighting factors such as women's greater burden of 'time poverty', their vulnerability to domestic violence, and unequal decision-making (Kabeer, 2003: 99). Participatory Poverty Assessments have also revealed that *perceptions* of poverty at the household level are likely to differ by gender in so far as men usually define poverty as a lack of assets whereas women equate poverty with shortfalls in consumption, especially as they relate to inability to 'provide for the family' (May, 2001: 27). In the 'Voices of the Poor' study carried out by the World Bank, for example, men frequently defined poverty in terms of lack of respect and self-esteem, yet 'no women seem to have regarded themselves entitled to make demands for respect and self-esteem'. Instead, most poor women stated that 'the worst form of poverty was inability to feed their children' (Johnsson-Latham, 2004b: 23).[8]

Yet while potentially going some way to expose gendered perceptions and dimensions of poverty, as far as I am aware there has been no PPA to date which has been oriented to exploring grassroots views on the 'feminisation of poverty'. In turn, because PPA methodology is subject to the relative 'gender-blindness' or 'gender-awareness' of its facilitators, not all participatory assessments even make reference to gender issues (Kabeer, 2003: 101). Facilitator bias not only determines who is selected, encouraged, and/or available to participate at the grassroots, but can give rise to losses in gender-relevant information when it comes to aggregating and presenting the findings (ibid.: 102; see also Johnsson-Latham, 2004a).

Moreover, even if women as well as men are involved in consultations, where PPA data are left 'raw' rather than 'interpreted', the internalisation of gendered norms can conceal or minimise gender inequalities and their meanings (ibid.: 102; see also Baulch, 1996; Cornwall, 2003; McIlwaine, 2002; Razavi, 1999: 422; Whitehead and Lockwood, 1999). It has accordingly been argued that aggregate summaries from PPAs need to be much more explicit about gender-specific dimensions of poverty which appear in the 'raw' data (see Table 2.9).

More general problems with PPAs include the difficulty of verifying results and comparing them across places, the fact that the process of participation itself is so dialogic and power-laden that the knowledges produced may be more a function of the exercise itself than a window to people's opinions on, or responses to, privation, that informants' participation itself, and what they say, may be shaped by financial incentives, and that it is difficult (and costly) to recruit skilled communicators up to the task of genuine participatory assessment (see, for example, Cook, 2002; Gibson-Graham, 2005; also Tables 2.10 and 2.11). Another important limitation is that PPAs are often one-off exercises, despite the fact that 'getting underneath the political inflections of talk requires longer-term work that builds up relations with those we are seeking to understand' (Jackson, 2003: 455). Adding up these factors, it is no surprise that PPAs are often regarded as an adjunct rather than a substitute for more conventional methods (UNFPA, 2002), and are more symbolic than substantive. Although theoretically, for example, participatory input is required for PRSPs, as many as 39 organisations and regional networks in 15 African countries concurred at a meeting in Kampala in 2001 that the limited involvement by civil society organisations (CSOs) in policy discussions amounted to 'window-dressing' for a 'repackaged' version of structural adjustment programmes (Ruggeri Laderchi et al., 2003: 26; see also Chapter 1 in this volume).

To summarise this section, despite growing lip-service to the importance of 'social deprivation' (alongside 'physical deprivation'), in poverty evaluation, which, via more holistic, participatory methods nominally takes into account the 'voices of the poor' and considers (gendered) subjectivities, power relations and so on, mainstream development institutions and government departments seem to find it easier to fall back on traditional (quantitative) formulae, especially when it comes to assessing poverty levels and trends at a global scale. This is hardly surprising, first, because it is so difficult to collapse diverse and abstract data into a form amenable to international comparison, and second, because as Stryker (2001: 76) notes: 'The multidimensional conceptualisation of poverty reduction frequently becomes so broad that it is difficult to separate the poor from the non-poor' (see also Chambers, 1997: 5). As echoed by Lipton (2001: 47), 'new

Table 2.9 '*Engendering' PPA aggregate summaries: suggestions relating to the World Bank study 'Voices of the Poor'*

Current summary (gender-neutral)	Potential addition (to highlight gender dimensions)
Expression of poverty	*How women and men are affected*
Hunger	Women eat least and last in many regions
Disease (including HIV, alcoholism)	Women's reproductive health is neglected Men's care costs more Men's own actions increase risks
Lack of income	Few poor women have an income
No land/property	Few women own/control land or assets Property is taken from widows
Violence/insecurity	Most poor women are victims although many young men and/or men involved in crime also suffer male violence
Exclusion from decision-making	Women excluded because of their sex
Lack of water, electricity, roads	Increase in women's workloads
Current recommendations (gender-neutral)	Potential addition (to highlight gender dimensions)
From poverty to resources	*Women/men*
From isolation to resources	Eliminate discrimination with regard to land and so on
From sickness to health	Special attention to women's health, including reproductive health Action to combat root causes of men's alcoholism
From fear to security	Combat violence against women and ensure land rights for women
From corruption to rule of law	Legal education, support to women's groups, equal rights

Source: Johnsson-Latham (2004a: 12–13).

languages' of sustainable livelihoods, empowerment, entitlements and human rights: 'have great rhetorical (and some logical and ethical) force in mobilising support for anti-poverty programmes. But they are more diverse than the language of basic material needs. Also, progress is harder to monitor and less measurable in policy terms.' This said, in order to improve both the quality and gender-sensitivity of poverty assessment and alleviation, there is

Table 2.10 Seven types of public participation

Typology	Characteristics of each type
1. Manipulative participation	Participation is simply a pretence, with 'people's' representatives on official boards but who are unelected and have no power.
2. Passive participation	People participate by being told what has been decided or has already happened. It involves unilateral announcements by an administration or project management without listening to people's responses. The information being shared belongs only to external professionals.
3. Participation by consultation	People participate by being consulted or by answering questions. External agents define problems and information gathering processes, and so control analysis. Such a consultative process does not concede any share in decision-making, and professionals are under no obligation to take on board people's views.
4. Participation for material incentives	People participate by contributing resources, for example, labour, in return for food, cash or other material incentives. Farmers may provide the fields and labour, but are involved in neither experimentation nor the process of learning. It is very common to see this called participation, yet people have no stake in prolonging technologies or practices when the incentives end.
5. Functional participation	Participation seen by external agencies as a means to achieve project goals, especially reduced costs. People may participate by forming groups to meet predetermined objectives related to the project. Such involvement may be interactive and involve shared decision-making, but tends to arise only after major decisions have already been made by external agents. At worst, local people may still only be co-opted to serve external goals.

Table 2.10   (continued)

Typology	Characteristics of each type
6. Interactive participation	People participate in joint analysis, development of action plans and formation or strengthening of local institutions. Participation is seen as a right, not just the means to achieve project goals. The process involves interdisciplinary methodologies that seek multiple perspectives and make use of systemic and structured learning processes. As groups take control over local decisions and determine how available resources are used, so they have a stake in maintaining structures or practices.
7. Self-mobilisation	People participate by taking initiatives independently of external institutions to change systems. They develop contacts with external institutions for resources and technical advice they need, but retain control over how resources are used. Self-mobilisation can spread if governments and non-governmental organisations provide enabling framework of support. Such self-initiated mobilisation may or may not challenge existing distributions of wealth and power.

Source: FASE (2003: box 4.1).

perhaps nothing to preclude more dedicated efforts to 'triangulate' quantitative data on income or capabilities with the findings of PPAs and with qualitative gender analyses (such as case studies) which focus on gendered relations and processes as well as outcomes (see Razavi, 1999: 422; Whitehead and Lockwood, 1999: 539).

Deficiencies in Data on Gender and Poverty

Recognising that broader conceptualisations of poverty have not readily translated into the widespread development or application of tools which are able to capture the gendered complexities of poverty, another major outstanding obstacle to the gender-sensitivity of poverty analysis is constituted by data deficiencies.

Table 2.11 Modes of participation

Mode of participation	Associated with	Why invite/involve?	Participants viewed as
Functional	Beneficiary participation	To enlist people in projects or processes so as to secure compliance, minimise dissent, lend legitimacy	Objects
Instrumental	Community participation	To make projects or interventions run more efficiently, by enlisting contributions, delegating responsibilities	Instruments
Consultative	Stakeholder participation	To get in tune with public views and values, to garner good ideas, to defuse opposition, to enhance responsiveness	Actors
Transformative	Citizen participation	To build political capabilities, critical consciousness and confidence; to enable to demand rights; to enhance accountability	Agents

Source: Cornwall (2003: table 1).

One major problem is limited data coverage. Despite emphasis in CEDAW and the BPFA on the vital need for sex-disaggregated data in planning and evaluation, as of 2004 it had only been possible to compute the GDI for 144 out of 177 countries of the world for which the HDI is calculated, and a mere 78 for the GEM (see UNDP, 2004). Lack of relevant data is also a problem in relation to gender-sensitive MDG monitoring. While UNIFEM (2002: 55) claims that relevant statistics often exist, the only challenges being to 'liberate data from the files of national statistical offices', and to make information available in 'easy to use forms' (ibid.: 56), capacity often remains limited, despite the efforts of international entities such as the UNDP's Thematic Trust Fund on Gender to provide help in 'en-gendering indicators and methodologies'.[9] Indeed, even for very basic data on population, births and deaths, the United Nations Statistics Division (UNSD) (2005: 6) observes that there has been woefully little

Table 2.12   *Total number of countries or areas, and number of countries or*
areas which reported population by sex and age at least once in
the period 1995–2003

	Total		Reported population by sex and age at least once between 1995 and 2003	
	No. of countries	Population in 2000 (millions)	No. of countries or areas	Population (%)[1]
World	204	6069	151	90
Development Group				
More developed regions	47	1193	44	99
Less developed regions[2]	107	4208	90	95
Least developed countries	50	668	17	38
Continent				
Africa	55	796	23	59
North America	27	488	26	100
South America	13	347	11	98
Asia	50	3679	43	93
Europe	42	728	39	99
Oceania	17	31	9	79

Notes:
1.   As percentage of the total population shown.
2.   Excluding least developed countries.

Source: UNSD (2005: table 2.1).

progress towards sex-disaggregation in the past three decades, with 14
countries having failed to report to the UN at all. This is partly due to cost
and time considerations involved in conducting censuses at regular inter-
vals. Although 85 per cent of the world's population resides in a country in
which at least one census has been undertaken between the 1980s and
2000s, only three-quarters of the world's 204 countries were able to provide
sex-disaggregated vital statistics in the period 1995–2003 (see Table 2.12).

A second major data limitation relates to accuracy. Most indicator
systems rely on national censuses, which not only suffer from sporadic collection, but from unreliable information, suffering as they so often do from
poor enumeration, imprecise definitions, and gender bias (Beck, 1999). For
example, enumerators may not have had gender training appropriate to the
task of eliciting information that accurately records and/or represents

gender differences (Corner, 2003). While civil registration systems can offer an alternative, in many countries these are also incomplete (UNSD, 2005).

A third problem is the narrowness of data. As noted earlier, gender differences in earned income in the UNDP gender indicators (and in MDG 3) are based only on formal sector earnings, and do not take into account 'work' in general, land or other productive assets (Johnsson-Latham, 2004b). With formal sector earnings leading to a privileging of 'the most educated and economically advantaged' (Cueva Beteta, 2006: 221), this can clearly obliterate poor women (Chant, 2006). While there have been some attempts to devise more elaborate indicators of 'women's empowerment' on the part of organisations such as the World Economic Forum (WEF) (see Lopez-Claros and Zahidi, 2005), lack of baseline statistics has prevented scores being computed for more than 58 countries, most of which are outside the developing world.[10]

A fourth problem relates to standardisation. While to some degree this is necessary for international comparisons, the criteria selected, and the meanings ascribed to them, may not be easily transported across different cultural, social and economic contexts (Chant, 2006). Examining different variables in isolation can also be misleading. For example, Dijkstra and Hanmer (2000) point out that higher female income shares commonly equate with more gender-sensitive development (and, by implication, less likelihood of female poverty). Yet despite several positive impacts documented for women of increased earning, such as greater autonomy and financial security, in cases where women end up with heavy 'double' and/or 'triple burdens' then the implications for well-being are questionable. As indicated earlier, few women can count on much alleviation of their reproductive labour of housework and childcare (at least by male partners) to offset additional responsibilities in the paid economy. As such increased income may only come at the cost of depletion of other valued resources such as time and health. This is especially the case among low-income groups where women tend to work the longest hours and gender disparities in hours of labour are greatest (Pineda-Ofreneo and Acosta, 2001: 3). An additional factor is that women may be pressurised into surrendering their earnings to fathers, husbands, or other relatives, or be unable to determine how their money is spent. For example, the Zambian Demographic and Health Survey of 2002 indicated that as many as 60 per cent of married women could not decide on the use of their own earnings (Mboup and Amunyunzu-Nyamongo, 2005). In turn, the market value of women's work may be less important to women than whether their employment is 'decent', fulfilling, and/or compatible with the demands of motherhood. For example, Bradshaw and Linneker (2001: 206) point out in relation to women's low-skilled employment in '*maquilas*' (export processing plants), that becoming better off materially may be accompanied by 'frustrating' or 'demeaning' work conditions.

Leading on from this, a fifth data issue is that qualitative and subjective criteria are seldom incorporated in macro-level accounting. Most statistical measures of gender inequality which pertain to poverty continue to rely on readily quantifiable variables which are limited in their potential for illuminating male–female disparities. Gender differences in educational enrolment, for example, may give some notion of differential capabilities between women and men, but say nothing about quality of education, gender bias in educational choices, or vocational relevance. The prospects that existing indices might be extended to include more qualitative material of this nature, let alone that which is more abstract (power, independence, for example) and/or contentious (rape, sexuality, domestic violence), remain decidedly remote (see Johnsson-Latham, 2004b). In the Philippines, for instance, the Women's Environment and Development Organisation (WEDO) (2005: 95) notes that the under-reporting of domestic violence due to social and cultural stigmatisation leads to notoriously unreliable indicators. Violence is also subject to underestimation in Latin America, despite the fact that it possesses the most comprehensive sex-disaggregated data in the South, and that the costs of violence are extremely heavy at a number of levels (World Bank, 2003e: 7). As highlighted by ECLAC (2004b: 26):

> A thorough understanding of poverty must include an analysis of violence as a factor that erodes personal autonomy, the exercise of citizenship and social capital (social autonomy), the latter as a result of the isolation to which women are subjected. This is consistent with the definition of poverty as the lack of minimum survival conditions . . . On the one hand, poverty is a risk factor that makes the appearance of physical violence in the home more probable. In addition, violence produces more poverty, since it holds back economic development for a number of reasons: (i) dealing with the effects of both social and domestic violence requires spending on the part of the police, judicial and social services systems, and (ii) in the case of women, those who suffer domestic violence are less productive at work, which leads to a direct loss to national production.

Sixth, the manner in which indicators are selected is also contentious. Globally comparative measures tend to be determined by a handful of 'international experts' rather than through broad-based consultation with relevant stakeholders, such that the criteria chosen to measure women's 'progress' may not signify much at the grassroots in the Global South. This is arguably the case with both the GDI and the GEM, which, as Willis (2005: 135) describes, are based on ' "top-down" perspectives of "development" and the formal sphere of paid employment and politics'. Mounting female representation in parliament (as recorded by the GEM), for example, may well indicate a challenge to male bias in politics and governance, and/or growing capacity and will at a national level to address issues such as gender discrimination in employment, income, reproductive health or domestic violence (see ADB, 2002: 94; Baden, 1999: 6; UNMP/TFEGE, 2005: 14). Nonetheless, this measure leaves out the bulk of women whose daily lives in many societies may be relatively unaffected by formal politics, and whose own political interests are better advanced through other channels (see Cueva Beteta, 2006).

A final proviso concerning data deficiencies, is that gender indicators in general, whether poverty related or not, usually say little about differentiation among women (or men) on account of stage in the life course, household circumstances, marital and fertility status and so on. The fact is that particular groups of women – for example, elderly, adolescent, indigenous or ethnic minority women – may be more vulnerable to poverty than others. As with all aggregate measures, however, such differences are masked.

Blindness to, or insufficient appreciation of, differentiation among women is pertinent to the situation whereby gendered poverty analysis has produced a range of rather monolithic – and often contradictory – stereotypes which do not hold for all women, nor all contexts. The most obvious, and increasingly widely critiqued, of these relates first to the generic concept of the 'feminisation of poverty' ([all] women are poorer than men and getting poorer), and second, to its links with the progressive 'feminisation of household headship' (see Chant, 2003a). While these constructions have been shaped by the imperative of getting 'gender on the development agenda' and have had some degree of success in this regard, this has often come at the cost of extreme oversimplification if not misrepresentation of current complexities and trends, as discussed further in the next chapter.

CONCLUSION

While it has not been possible here to cover all the contributions made by feminist research to 'en-gendering' poverty analysis, it is clear that significant advances have been made since the 1970s, particularly in respect of expanding the concept of poverty in ways that expose and illuminate its gendered dimensions. As summed up by Razavi (1999: 417): 'From a gender perspective, broader concepts of poverty are more useful than a focus purely on household income levels because they allow a better grasp of the multidimensional aspects of gender disadvantage, such as lack of power to control important decisions that affect one's life.'

The idea that gender-sensitive frameworks for poverty analysis should become broader still is highly desirable, although this does not necessarily entail the rejection of existing frameworks. While poverty lines fall short of representing key dimensions of gendered poverty, for instance, it remains vital to know about income and consumption, and how these are changing among women and men over time. As summarised by Dietz (2001: 19):

> The debate on human deprivation, on poverty, has seen both a proliferation of complexity in concepts and a simplification to one basic concept: the number of people with less than PPP US$1.00 a day. Both complexity and simplicity are needed. Complexity arises in understanding the linkages between the many causes of human deprivation and in understanding the reasons for the success or failure of approaches to the reduction of poverty. Simplification is necessary to catch the eyes and ears of a world community of decision-makers and of public opinion leaders who have become the victims of a disease called aid fatigue.

This said, there is clearly scope to improve poverty line approaches in ways that increase their gender-responsiveness. One step in this direction would be to make greater use of per capita incomes and/or AEUs rather than relying solely on aggregate household data. Another fruitful revision would be to include a broader remit of quantifiable measures of privation in poverty lines, disaggregated, where possible, by sex. This could include a range of women's and men's capabilities, assets and entitlements (education, health status, land and property ownership, access to public goods and services and so on), along with resources such as *time* which is especially scarce among low-income women in the South (see Corner, 2002). Indeed, although the generation of quality time use data is a 'complex and necessarily expensive task', it is essential in challenging the persistent invisibility of much of women's contribution to developing country economies (ibid.: 2–3).[11] Highlighting the effort expended in unpaid tasks such as childcare, looking after the elderly and infirm, voluntary community and social work and so on, can, in turn, raise women's profile in policies and programmes (ibid.).

Aside from more comprehensive and better quality cross-sectional and panel data, attempts should also be made to break down sex-disaggregated statistics by age, if not by other factors such as marital and fertility status. Age disaggregation would be of particular importance in helping to determine whether there are major generational differences in the incidence of poverty among women relative to men over time, as well as pointing to the key underlying processes.

Another vital step will be to make data collection itself more gender-sensitive. Initiatives already taken in this direction include India's provision of comprehensive gender training for personnel involved in the 2001 census (see Corner, 2003: 7). Another strategy has been to set minimum targets for female enumerators and supervisors. Levels of 20 per cent and 10 per cent respectively were established for the 2001 Census of Nepal (representing a major rise on previous figures) following the widespread observation that use of female staff leads to significant increases in the enumeration of women's labour force participation. Another strategy has been to revise key terms and definitions which relate to gender such as 'work' (ibid.: 8).[12]

A further step forward would arguably be to encourage wider participation by different stakeholders in identifying key dimensions of gendered poverty which are significant to poor women (and men) themselves. While consensus across countries is unlikely to be easy, a gender-sensitive HPI – or Gendered Poverty Index (GPI) – which comprises measures culled from broad-based consultations is not out of the question (see Chant, 2006; Durbin, 1999; also Chapter 7 in this volume). Recognising that not all data are amenable to quantification, efforts to increase the space given to qualitative gender-sensitive poverty analysis and to approaches which assess subjective well-being (see Rojas, 2003) have an integral part to play here. Following Bradshaw's (2002: 12) point that women's poverty is not only multidimensional but is also 'multisectoral', namely 'women's poverty is experienced in different ways, at different times and in different "spaces"', it is also essential, particularly from the perspective of the 'feminisation of poverty', to look within as well as beyond household units, as discussed further in the next chapter.

NOTES

1. This has particular resonance for developing countries in so far as imposed, 'objective', universalising and preponderantly Eurocentric indicators of poverty have been regarded as 'disempowering' to people in the South. As asserted by Jackson (1997: 152): 'Poverty reduction appears in poststructuralist perspectives as an imperialist narrative, universalising, essentialising and politically sinister' which justifies 'hegemonic development interventions'.
2. The 'Lost Decade' (used mainly in relation to Latin America, but also sub-Saharan Africa) refers primarily to the 1980s when there was a reversal in many of the advances in wealth and social welfare which countries in these regions had achieved in the years prior to the debt crisis. Some would argue that two 'lost decades' had been experienced by the end of the twentieth century (see Arriagada, 2002: 148).
3. To some extent this is addressed by the use of Adult Equivalence Scales which refine per capita measures on the basis of the expected consumption needs of different household members at different stages of the life course. For example, a value of 1 is normally assigned to an adult equivalent unit (AEU), which is, by definition, an adult male aged 23–50 years. In turn, an adult woman of same age is assigned a value of 0.74, an infant of up to 6 months old, a value of 0.24 and so on. There are problems with AEU methodology, however, as identified in a recent poverty study of The Gambia. One major one is that the adult female AEU is based on a non-pregnant and non-lactating woman with medium and basal metabolic rate. Yet in The Gambia (as in many other sub-Saharan African countries) women grow around 80 per cent of food for household consumption,

and are often pregnant and lactating (see GOTG, 2000: 26–7). As such, their consumption needs are considerably higher than nominally projected by the standard female AEU.

4. The first UNDP index was the Human Development Index (HDI), which appeared in 1990. Based on the premise that 'people and their lives should be the ultimate criteria for assessing the development of a country, not economic growth', the HDI focuses on income, literacy and life expectancy (UNDP, 1990; 2002).

5. The UNDP (1997: 13) defines 'functionings' as referring to the 'valuable things that a person can do or be', such as being well-nourished, having long life expectancy, and being a fully integrated and active member of one's community. In turn, 'capability . . . stands for the different combinations of functionings the person can achieve', and their freedom to achieve various functionings (ibid.). Klasen (2004: 6) makes the point that in practice, most translations of Sen's ideas into indices such as the HDI, do not actually measure capabilities (or 'choice sets') so much as functionings (or outcomes), as the latter are easier to observe. Outcomes are then interpreted as a result of lack of capability, even in cases where people deny themselves exercise of a capability on a 'voluntary' basis. In respect of gender, this is particularly problematic. While on the one hand women's poor health or nutrition may potentially result from capability failure (that is, the inability to be adequately nourished), it may also be predicated on women's desire – albeit conditioned through social norms such as 'maternal altruism' – to sacrifice their own dietary intake for the sake of children.

6. Although the most recent revision of the System of National Accounts (SNA) in 1993 conceded to the inclusion of subsistence production in the calculation of GDP, unpaid care work continues to be omitted. The grounds for this are the prospective 'distortion' of accounts, rendering them less useful for market analysis and policy purposes, that unpaid care work is difficult to quantify, that the data required are not available, and that the sudden inclusion of unpaid care work would complicate GDP comparisons over time (see Budlender, 2004: 16).

Despite the difficulties involved in calculation, in 1995, the UNDP estimated that the combined value of the unpaid work of women and men, together with the underpayment of women's work in the market was in the order of US$16 trillion, or about 70 per cent of global output. Of the $16 trillion identified, approximately $11 trillion was deemed to be constituted by the 'non-monetised, invisible contribution of women' (UNDP, 1995: 6).

7. Theoretically, poverty lines are more suitable for urban areas where more goods and services are monetised. However they were first used in advanced economies where most people lived in dwellings with access to water, light and sanitation. Such assumptions cannot be made for developing countries, begging caution about an 'uncritical transfer' of standards (Satterthwaite, 2005: 3–6).

8. These preoccupations, which feature prominently among women in my case study countries, appear to be remarkably widespread (see Yeandle et al., 2003, on the UK).

9. The UNDP's Thematic Trust Fund on Gender was formed in 2001 with a view to supporting national capacity-building through four major lines of service. In addition to 'en-gendering indicators and methodologies', these were 'en-gendering policy', 'en-gendering legal frameworks' and 'en-gendering institutions' (see UNDP, 2001b; Zaoude, 2002).

10. Based on published national statistics and data from international organisations, together with qualitative survey data from the annual WEF Executive Opinion Survey, the WEF measure of 'women's empowerment' comprises economic participation, economic opportunity, political empowerment, educational attainment, and health and well-being. Each of these dimensions includes more than the conventional stock of criteria. For example, economic participation not only measures the gap between women and men in respect of levels of economic activity, but unemployment levels, and remuneration for equal work. Economic opportunity takes into account the quality of women's employment conditions, including maternity leave benefits, the impact of maternity laws on the hiring of women, the availability of state-provided childcare, and

equality between women and men in private sector employment (see Lopez-Claros and Zahidi, 2005).

11. Even use of the simple '24 hour day model' in which participants are asked to describe the use of time by women and men in their own or other households on a typical day, has been critical in underlining the fact that 'women are not "just sitting at home all day" waiting for a project or government programme to come along and "involve them in development" ' (Corner, 2002: 7). It has also helped to move analysis away from a WID to a GAD approach in so far as it permits systematic comparisons between women's and men's lives and activities. Some of the now widely accepted facts which the 24 hour day model has assisted in establishing are: (1) that women and men use time differently, (2) that women spend more time in work overall than men, but shorter hours in paid work, (3) that women have less 'discretionary' time, and (4) that women typically engage in multiple activities (childcare, housework, remunerative work, minding animals and so on), simultaneously (ibid.).

12. One innovation adopted in Nepal's 2001 Census, which was designed with the help of UNIFEM South Asia and other UN agencies, was the elimination of traditional labour force questions in order to take into account unpaid work (see Corner, 2003).

3. The 'feminisation of poverty' in the Global South: assertions, agendas and evidence

INTRODUCTION

As identified in Chapter 1, the 'feminisation of poverty' connotes the idea that women are a disproportionate percentage of the world's poor and that gender gaps in poverty incidence are widening. According to Wennerholm (2002: 10), the term has been responsible not only for drawing attention to the 'great number of women living in poverty', but in highlighting the impact of macroeconomic policies on women, and calling for women to be recognised in the development process. Additional corollaries have been to promote awareness of the existence of female-headed households and to illustrate their vulnerability (ibid.). That the 'feminisation of poverty' has, in turn, been a rallying point for gender advocacy and activism is in little doubt. As articulated by Williams and Lee-Smith (2000: 1): 'The feminisation of poverty is more than a slogan: it is a marching call that impels us to question our assumptions about poverty itself by examining how it is caused, manifested and reduced, and to do this from a gender perspective.'

Yet despite some value in these impacts, problems mentioned thus far include an overemphasis on income, the narrow and unsubstantiated bases of the term (especially in relation to trends), the often arbitrary depiction of women's poverty by data pertaining only to female-headed households, and generalisation of the latter as the 'poorest of the poor' (see Chapters 1 and 2). In order to set the scene for my detailed case studies of The Gambia, Philippines and Costa Rica, this chapter provides an overview of investigation and debate on the 'feminisation of poverty' in the context of the Global South. My principal objective is to disentangle the key assertions and agendas underpinning the construct from the evidence actually available to support its principal tenets – namely, that women bear a greater and rising share of poverty relative to men, and that female household headship is particularly implicated in this process.[1]

In order to examine the extent to which the 'feminisation of poverty', in crude terms, is as generalisable across the South as suggested by current orthodoxy, the first section of the chapter introduces the main reasons why poverty is thought to be more prevalent among women than men, and examines the extent to which this is borne out by an albeit relatively limited body of macro-level quantitative data. In the second section of the chapter I proceed to a more in-depth discussion of female-headed households which draws on a broader range of empirical material. This focuses on the reasons why they have been typecast as the 'poorest of the poor' and some of the challenges raised to the stereotype. I also analyse some of the political and policy consequences of the 'feminisation of poverty' along with the potential risks of rejecting the idea that women in general, or female household heads in particular, are poorer than their male counterparts.

FOUNDATIONS OF THE 'FEMINISATION OF POVERTY': WHY WOMEN ARE THOUGHT TO BE POORER THAN MEN

Gender gaps in income poverty have long been deemed a 'tragic conse-quence of women's unequal access to economic opportunities' (UNDP, 1995: 36). This is regarded as being shaped by a variety of factors, with Moghadam's (1997) uncharacteristically in-depth review of the 'femini-sation of poverty' identifying three main reasons which, prima facie, put women at greater risk of poverty than men. These are, first, women's dis-advantage in respect of poverty-inducing capabilities and entitlements (such as education, skills, access to land and property); second, their heavier work burdens and lower earnings, and third, constraints on socio-economic mobility due to cultural, legal, political and labour market barriers. As echoed by Kabeer (2003), there are probably as many non-economic as economic causes of women's poverty which not only play out in public arenas such as the law and labour markets, but also in the home. As a result of gender socialisation, intra-household power rela-tions and domestic divisions of labour, for example, some women are pre-vented from engaging in activities which may enhance their own and their households' resource base (see Lavinas and Nicoll, 2006). In turn, even where women earn reasonable incomes, they may not be able to glean much personal benefit because they have little control over the allocation of household resources, whether because their earnings are appropriated by men, or are diverted to expenditure on others. Indeed, Bradshaw and Linneker (2003: 9) draw attention to three fairly generalised patterns:

namely, that women have fewer possibilities to translate work into income; that when women do have income they find it more difficult to transform this into decision-making capacity, and that when women do make decisions these are less likely to enhance their own well-being as that of others.

Despite the complexity of reasons for, and manifestations of, women's poverty, and the fact that income, along with longevity, is argued to be one of the few indicators which seems less robust in confirming women's privation than access to land, agency in decision-making, legal rights within the family, vulnerability to violence and (self-)respect and dignity (Johnsson-Latham, 2004b: 26–7), 'feminisation of poverty' orthodoxy, especially in the arena of policy and planning, has tended to dwell mainly on money-metric poverty. While this is limited, it is still important to review what data there are for Africa, Asia and Latin America which support the notions that (a) the incidence of income poverty among women is higher than among men, and (b) that women's relatively greater poverty burden is intensifying.

What Evidence is There to Support a 'Feminisation of Poverty'?

As pointed out in Chapter 1, most of the data which do exist on gender differences in poverty in the Global South is actually extrapolated from comparisons between the aggregate incomes of male- and female-headed households, and not from women and men as individuals. Only Latin America possesses region-wide sex-disaggregated headcount figures on income poverty, and, interestingly, while on the surface these suggest that women are poorer than men, especially in rural areas, for the most part differences are fairly marginal (Table 3.1) Indeed, in urban areas in 10 out of 17 countries (Argentina, Bolivia, Brazil, Chile, Colombia, Guatemala, Honduras, Mexico, Paraguay and Uruguay), the proportion of men in poverty is actually on a par with or slightly higher than women, leading UNIFEM (2002: 61) to conclude that the 'feminisation of poverty' is only present in some countries in Latin America, and nowhere near the level of 70 per cent as popularly expounded. Moreover, if we are to take on board the notion of 'feminisation' as trend, then there is a strong indication that poverty gaps between women and men are not rising either. For example, Medeiros and Costa's (2006) detailed quantitative study of Argentina, Bolivia, Brazil, Chile, Colombia, Costa Rica, Mexico and Venezuela between the early 1990s and early twenty-first century found 'no solid evidence of a process of feminisation of poverty in the Latin American region' (ibid.: 13). This conclusion was drawn on the basis of an extremely comprehensive analysis which not only considered per capita income figures,

Table 3.1   Gender and poverty in Latin America

Country	Area	Proportion below poverty line (%)		Females per 100 males below poverty line
		Male	Female	
Argentina	Urban	23.8	23.6	99.3
Bolivia	Urban	48.6	48.2	101.4
	Rural	79.4	81.6	102.8
Brazil	Urban	33.0	32.6	99.5
	Rural	54.8	55.6	101.6
Chile	Urban	20.6	20.6	101.0
	Rural	26.4	28.8	109.1
Costa Rica	Urban	16.8	19.2	114.4
	Rural	20.8	23.8	114.5
Dominican Republic	Urban	33.9	36.9	110.2
	Rural	37.7	43.3	115.0
Ecuador	Urban	63.1	63.3	102.8
El Salvador	Urban	38.1	39.0	101.3
	Rural	64.9	65.4	100.8
Guatemala	Urban	45.7	45.4	101.0
	Rural	69.8	70.0	100.4
Honduras	Urban	66.6	65.4	99.3
	Rural	81.0	81.5	100.8
Mexico	Urban	38.7	38.7	101.0
	Rural	58.3	58.6	101.6
Nicaragua	Urban	63.4	64.5	101.7
	Rural	77.4	76.6	99.0
Panama	Urban	25.8	26.6	103.1
	Rural	40.4	43.6	107.9
Paraguay	Urban	49.7	47.4	97.1
	Rural	73.2	74.4	101.9
Uruguay	Urban	9.7	9.4	97.3
Venezuela	Total	48.6	50.0	104.4

Sources: CEPAL (2002: cuadros 6a and 6b); UNIFEM (2002: table 15).

but examined women and men in general and according to household headship, as well as exploring the incidence, severity and intensity of poverty (see also Lavinas and Nicoll, 2006, on Brazil).

For most of the rest of the Global South, there are not only insufficient data to establish trends, but even to determine the actual share of 'feminised' poverty at any moment in time. As summarised by Rodenberg

(2004: 1): 'a large proportion of the 1.3 billion people living in absolute poverty are women, though there is too little gender-specific data to substantiate the oft-quoted figure of 70 per cent (see also Chen et al., 2004: 37; Elder and Schmidt, 2004: 3n; Lampietti and Stalker, 2000; Marcoux, 1998a; 1998b). Yet accepting the challenge that, 'Although it is difficult to estimate gender differences in the incidence of poverty . . . it is reasonable to assume that women constitute a disproportionate share of the world's poor given their constrained access to capital and land, their lower labour market status, and their disproportionate responsibility for the provision of unpaid domestic and care work' (UNRISD, 2005: 6) it is important to interrogate other kinds of data which potentially afford a handle on how gender gaps in poverty may be changing over time.

The GDI and the GEM provide useful starting points here, assessing as they do literacy and education, gender in parliamentary processes, some gender dimensions of occupational status, and male–female differences in earned income (see UN/UNIFEM, 2003: 20; also Chapter 2 in this volume). Notwithstanding difficulties in assessing trends in the GDI given methodological changes over time, values for selected countries, including The Gambia, Philippines and Costa Rica, indicate that some advances towards gender equality have been made during the last decade, even if disaggregating the index reveals a rather different story (see Table 3.2). In Latin America, for example, the main gains between 1997 and 2002 were in respect of education and life expectancy rather than earned income (Table 3.3). Gains in women's share of earned income were also negligible in South-East Asia, and in some countries (for example, China, Indonesia and Malaysia), there was a downward shift (Table 3.4). As for sub-Saharan Africa, most of the increase in GDI values seems to have been accounted for by increases in female literacy and education, albeit from low levels and without substantial shrinkage in male–female gaps (Table 3.5).

As for trends in GEM components, in Latin America there has been quite a lot of upward movement in respect of women's share of parliamentary seats, and their representation among administrative and managerial personnel. Yet these advances are, again, checked by relative stasis in women's share of earned income (Table 3.6). Similar patterns are observable in South-East Asia (Table 3.7), and may also be the case for sub-Saharan Africa, although the patchiness of longitudinal information only allows for confirmation of increased political representation (Table 3.8).

Notwithstanding that the GDI and the GEM cover only a few factors pertinent to gendered poverty, and that earned income, in relating to formal sector employment only, is restricted to better-off segments of the population, there is some indication here that women's economic disadvantage is persistent, if not deepening relative to men.

The significance of women having lower shares of income is brought into further relief by quantitative data on time-use for a range of countries which point to their overall hours in work exceeding those of men (see Table 3.9). That women spend more time in non-market than market activities is also important in so far as a large amount of their labour efforts remain unremunerated, and undoubtedly impinge on their scope to earn more income.

Athough intra-household and extra-domestic resource transfers are clearly also vital in establishing people's levels of income poverty, the statistical evidence discussed above does point to a likelihood of women being poorer than men despite advances in education, employment and politics. However, when it comes to female-headed households being the 'poorest of the poor', existing evidence seems to be more contentious.

ASSERTIONS ABOUT THE LINKS BETWEEN THE FEMINISATION OF POVERTY AND THE FEMINISATION OF HOUSEHOLD HEADSHIP

The general assumption that women-headed households are likely to face an above-average risk of income poverty is by no means implausible. Indeed, there are several persuasive reasons why we might expect a group disadvantaged by their gender to be further disadvantaged by allegedly 'incomplete', or 'under-resourced', household arrangements (see Box 3.1). This is especially so given the notion that female headship is prone to arise in situations of economic stress, privation and insecurity, whether through labour migration, conjugal instability, and/or the inability of impoverished kin groups to assume responsibility for abandoned women and children (see Benería, 1991; Chant, 1997b; Chen and Drèze, 1992: 22; Fonseca, 1991: 138).

Extrapolating Women's Disadvantage to Women-Headed Households

One of the main reasons why female-headed households, especially lone mother units, are regarded as the 'poorest of the poor' is because women's general disadvantage is deemed to be aggravated when they raise children alone. As articulated by Elson (1992: 41):

> The growth of female-headed households is no sign of emancipation from male power; in a society in which women as a gender are subordinate the absence of

Table 3.2 Gender-Related Development Index (GDI) summary, by regional examples, 1994–2002

| Country | Gender-related Development Index (GDI) | | | | Post-1999 HDR HDI/GDI methodology/data changes[1] | | | | | | | | |
| | 1994 HDR[2] | 1995 HDR[3] n=130 | | | 1999 HDR n=143 | | | 2002 HDR[4] n=146 | | | 2004 HDR n=144 | | |
	1991 GDA HDI	1992/93 GDI	1992/93 GDI rank	1992/93 HDI-GDI rank	1997 GDI[5]	1997 GDI rank	1997 HDI-GDI rank	2000 GDI	2000 GDI rank	2000 HDI-GDI rank	2002 GDI[6]	2002 GDI rank	2002 HDI-GDI rank
Sub-Saharan Africa													
Côte d'Ivoire	–	0.341	107	–1	0.404	154	–2	0.411	132	0	0.379	132	0
The Gambia	–	0.277	119	–1	0.384	163	2	0.397	136	–1	0.446	125	1
Mauritania	–	0.309	116	–5	0.438	122	1	0.429	127	1	0.456	124	0
Senegal	–	0.316	111	2	0.417	127	0	0.421	130	0	0.429	128	0
Sierra Leone	–	0.195	129	0	na	na	na	na	na	na	na	na	na
South-east Asia													
China	0.471	0.578	71	7	0.699	79	2	0.724	77	3	0.741	71	5
Indonesia	–	0.591	68	4	0.675	88	0	0.678	91	1	0.685	90	–1
Korea, Rep. of	–	0.78	37	–11	0.845	30	–1	0.875	29	–2	0.882	29	–1
Philippines	0.476	0.625	64	6	0.736	65	–2	0.751	63	4	0.751	66	3
Thailand	0.666	0.798	33	15	0.751	58	2	0.76	60	1	0.766	61	1
Latin America													
Colombia	–	0.72	50	–3	0.765	51	1	0.767	56	3	0.77	59	1
Costa Rica	0.654	0.763	42	–18	0.795	42	1	0.814	41	0	0.823	44	–2
Guatemala	–	0.481	87	–7	0.608	101	–2	0.617	100	0	0.635	98	1
Nicaragua	–	0.56	73	3	0.609	100	2	0.629	97	2	0.66	97	–1
Venezuela	–	0.765	40	–1	0.786	46	0	0.764	57	3	0.775	58	–2

Notes:

1. Various methodological changes in the calculation of the HDI were made in the 1999 Human Development Report. These included the use of improved life expectancy statistics, revised data from UNESCO on adult literacy and primary, secondary and tertiary enrolment, more gradual discounting of income above the world per capita average, and revised PPP data from the World Bank (see Anand and Sen, 2000). This means that there is no direct comparability between pre- and post-1999 HDI scores, which, in turn, has implications for the GDI. In addition, in the 1999 report, real GDP by gender was used instead of women's and men's share of earned income, although this was reversed in the 2001 report.

2. The 1994 Human Development Report used a 'Gender-Disparity-Adjusted HDI' (GDA), which amended the HDI by taking the average female–male ratio for the three HDI components as a percentage, by which the HDI was multiplied.

3. The GDI and GEM were introduced in the 1995 Human Development Report.

4. Because of a lack of gender-disaggregated income data, female and male earned income are crudely estimated on the basis of the ratio of the female non-agricultural wage to the male non-agricultural wage, the female and male shares of the economically active population, the total female and male population, and per capita GDP (in US$ PPP). Estimates for 2000 are based on the latest available year between 1991 and 2000.

5. HDI ranks have been re-calculated for the countries with a GDI value in 1997, namely 143.

6. HDI rank re-calculated for 144 countries with a GDI in 2002.

– = No data.

Sources: UNDP (1994; 1995; 1999; 2002; 2004).

85

Table 3.3   Components of the GDI, 1997–2002: selected Latin American countries

	Share of earned income (%)		Life expectancy (years)		Adult literacy rate (%)		Combined primary, secondary and tertiary gross enrolment ratio (%)		Estimated earned income (US$ PPP)		GDI
	Female	Male	Female	Male	Female	Male	Female	Male	Female	Male	
1997											
Brazil	29	71	71.0	63.1	83.9	84.1	77	82	3813[1]	9205	0.733
Colombia	35	65	74.3	67.3	90.8	91.0	71	70	4725	8945	0.765
Costa Rica	26	67	78.9	74.3	95.1	95.0	65	68	2220	4414	0.795
Guatemala	23	77	67.2	61.4	58.9	74.2	43	51	1861	6298	0.608
Mexico	27	73	75.5	69.5	87.9	92.3	69	66	4594	12216	0.778
Nicaragua	29	71	70.6	65.8	63.4	63.3	65	61	1169	2835	0.609
Venezuela	28	72	75.7	70.0	91.6	92.5	68	66	5006	12661	0.786
1999											
Brazil	29	71	71.8	63.9	84.9	84.8	80	79	4067	10077	0.743
Colombia	31	69	74.6	67.8	91.5	91.5	73	73	3582	7965	0.760
Costa Rica	26	74	79.2	74.5	95.5	95.4	66	67	4518	13080	0.813
Guatemala	23	77	67.7	61.9	60.5	75.6	45	53	1691	5622	0.610
Mexico	27	73	75.8	69.8	89.1	93.1	70	71	4486	12184	0.782
Nicaragua	29	71	70.8	66.1	69.8	66.6	65	61	1338	3231	0.628
Venezuela	28	72	76.0	70.2	91.8	92.9	66	64	3104	7855	0.759

2002

Brazil	29.7	70.3	72.5	63.9	86.5	86.2	94	90	4 594	10 879	0.768
Colombia	34.5	65.5	75.2	69.0	92.2	92.1	70	67	4 429	8 420	0.770
Costa Rica	27.8	72.2	80.5	75.7	95.9	95.7	70	69	4 698	12 197	0.823
Guatemala	24.8	75.2	68.7	62.8	62.5	77.3	52	59	2 007	6 092	0.635
Mexico	27.5	72.5	76.3	70.3	88.7	92.6	74	73	4 915	12 967	0.792
Nicaragua	30.7	69.3	71.8	67.1	76.6	76.8	66	63	1 520	3 436	0.660
Venezuela	29.3	70.7	76.6	70.8	92.7	93.5	74	69	3 125	7 550	0.770

Note: 1. In the 1999 Human Development Report, the figures for women's and men's earned income were calculated on the basis of real GDP rather than estimated earned income.

Sources: UNDP (1999: table 2; 2001a: table 21; 2004: table 24).

Table 3.4 Components of the GDI, 1997–2002: selected South-East Asian countries

	Share of earned income (%)		Life expectancy (years)		Adult literacy rate (%)		Combined primary, secondary and tertiary gross enrolment ratio (%)		Estimated earned income (US$ PPP)		GDI
	Female	Male	Female	Male	Female	Male	Female	Male	Female	Male	
1997											
China	40	60	72.0	67.9	74.5	90.9	67	71	2485[1]	3737	0.699
Indonesia	34	66	67.0	63.3	70.5	90.6	61	68	2395	4626	0.675
Korea, Rep. of	31	69	76.0	78.0	95.5	98.9	84	94	8388	18708	0.845
Malaysia	32	68	74.3	69.9	81.0	90.2	66	64	5115	11081	0.763
Philippines	36	64	70.2	66.5	94.3	94.8	85	80	2510	4513	0.736
Singapore	33	67	79.3	74.9	87.0	95.9	71	74	18947	37883	0.883
Thailand	37	63	72.0	65.8	92.8	96.7	59	58	3221	5435	0.751
1999											
China	40	60	72.5	68.3	75.5	91.2	73	73	2841	4350	0.715
Indonesia	34	66	67.7	63.9	81.3	91.5	61	68	1929	3780	0.671
Korea, Rep. of	31	69	78.4	70.9	96.2	99.1	85	95	9667	21676	0.868
Malaysia	32	68	74.8	69.9	82.8	91.1	67	64	5153	11183	0.768
Philippines	35	65	71.1	67.0	94.9	95.3	84	80	2684	4910	0.746
Singapore	33	67	79.5	75.2	88.0	96.2	75	76	13693	27739	0.871
Thailand	38	62	72.9	67.0	93.5	97.0	61	60	4634	7660	0.755

2002											
China	39.7	60.3	73.2	68.8	86.5	95.1	64	69	3 571	5 435	0.741
Indonesia	33.9	66.1	68.6	64.6	83.4	92.5	64	66	2 138	4 161	0.685
Korea, Rep. of	31.6	68.4	79.2	71.7	96.6	99.2	85	98	10 747	23 226	0.882
Malaysia	28.4	71.6	75.6	70.7	85.4	92.0	72	69	5 219	13 157	0.786
Philippines	37.1	62.9	71.9	67.9	92.7	92.5	82	81	3 144	5 326	0.751
Singapore	33.1	66.9	80.2	75.8	88.6	96.6	75	76	15 822	31 927	0.884
Thailand	37.9	62.1	73.4	65.2	90.5	94.9	72	74	5 284	8 664	0.766

Note: 1. In the 1999 Human Development Report, the figures for women's and men's earned income were calculated on the basis of real GDP rather than estimated earned income.

Sources: UNDP (1999: table 2; 2001a: table 21; 2004: table 24).

Table 3.5 Components of the GDI, 1997–2002: selected sub-Saharan African countries

	Share of earned income (%)		Life expectancy (years)		Adult literacy rate (%)		Combined primary, secondary and tertiary gross enrolment ratio (%)		Estimated earned income (US$ PPP)		GDI
	Female	Male	Female	Male	Female	Male	Female	Male	Female	Male	
1997											
Côte d'Ivoire	27	73	47.3	46.2	33.7	51.0	32	48	991[1]	2656	0.404
Gambia, The	38	62	48.6	45.4	26.4	40.1	35	48	1115	1834	0.384
Mali	39	61	54.6	52.0	28.3	43.1	20	31	583	902	0.367
Mauritania	37	63	55.1	51.9	27.8	49.4	36	45	1283	2185	0.438
Nigeria	30	70	51.5	48.7	50.8	68.5	48	61	553	1293	0.442
Senegal	36	64	54.2	50.5	24.8	44.5	31	40	1253	2209	0.417
Sierra Leone	30	70	38.7	35.8	20.0	47.5	–	–	246	581	–
1999											
Côte d'Ivoire	27	73	48.1	47.5	37.2	53.8	30	46	892	2379	0.409
The Gambia	37	63	47.3	44.5	28.5	43.1	37	53	1181	1987	0.390
Mali	39	61	52.2	50.2	32.7	47.3	22	34	582	928	0.370
Mauritania	36	64	52.7	49.5	31.4	52.2	37	44	1163	2062	0.428
Nigeria	31	69	51.7	51.3	54.2	71.3	41	49	520	1182	0.443
Senegal	35	65	54.8	51.1	26.7	46.4	31	40	996	1844	0.413
Sierra Leone	–	–	39.6	37.0	–	–	21	32	–	–	0.19

2002

Côte d'Ivoire	26.9	73.1	41.5	40.9	38.4	60.3	34	50	818	2222	0.379
The Gambia	37.3	62.7	55.4	52.5	30.9	45.0	41	49	1263	2127	0.446
Mali	37.8	62.2	49.0	47.9	11.9	26.7	21	31	635	1044	0.309
Mauritania	35.8	64.2	53.9	50.7	31.3	51.5	42	46	1581	2840	0.456
Nigeria	29.8	70.2	52.0	51.2	59.4	74.4	41	49	562	1322	0.458
Senegal	35.5	64.5	54.9	50.6	29.7	49.0	35	41	1140	2074	0.429
Sierra Leone	29.3	70.7	35.6	33.1	–	–	38	52	337	815	–

Notes:
1. In the 1999 Human Development Report, the figures for women's and men's earned income were calculated on the basis of real GDP rather than estimated earned income.
–   = No data.

Sources: UNDP (1999: table 2; 2001a: table 21; 2004: table 24).

Table 3.6   Components of the GEM, 1994–2004: selected Latin American countries

	GEM		Seats in parliament held by women (% of total)	Female legislators, senior officials and managers (% of total)	Female professional and technical workers (% of total)	Ratio of female to male earned income
	Rank	Value				
1994 (n = 116)						
Brazil	58	0.358	5.5	17.3[1,2]	57.2[3]	22.9[4]
Colombia	29	0.435	9.4	27.2	41.8	20.1
Costa Rica	22	0.474	14.0	23.1	44.9	19.0
Guatemala	46	0.390	5.2	32.4	45.2	13.8
Mexico	42	0.399	16.3	19.4	43.2	22.3
Nicaragua	34	0.427	16.3	12.4	42.9	24.2
Venezuela	45	0.391	6.0	18.6	55.2	22.8
1999 (n = 102)	70	0.367	5.9	17	63	29[5]
Brazil						
Colombia	31	0.515	12.2	39	46	31
Costa Rica	23	0.550	19.3	27	48	26
Guatemala	44	0.482	12.5	32	45	23
Mexico	33	0.511	16.9	20	45	27
Nicaragua	–	–	10.8	–	–	29
Venezuela	43	0.484	12.1	23	57	28
2004 (n = 78)						
Brazil	–	–	9.1	–	62	0.42
Colombia	48	0.498	10.8	38	50	0.53
Costa Rica	19	0.664	35.1	53	28	0.39
Guatemala	–	–	8.2	–	–	0.33
Mexico	34	0.563	21.2	25	40	0.38

Nicaragua	–	61	20.7	–	27	–
Venezuela	–	0.444	9.7	–	61	0.41

Notes:

1. In the 1995 Human Development Report, and in each report until 2001, the nomenclature for this category was 'female administrators and managers'. Thereafter the classification was changed to 'female legislators, senior officials and managers'.
2. Data here pertain to 1992.
3. Data here pertain to 1992.
4. In the 1995 report, figures are expressed in respect of women's percentage share of earned income, rather than as the ratio of female to male earned income (as in 2004).
5. In the 1999 Human Development Report, the GEM listed the average real GDP of women, but in the interests of comparability, the estimated female share of earned income is substituted here.
– = No data.

Sources: UNDP (1995: table 3.5; 1999: table 3; 2004: table 25).

Table 3.7 Components of the GEM, 1994–2004: selected South-East Asian countries

	GEM Rank	GEM Value	Seats in parliament held by women (% of total)	Female legislators, senior officials and managers (% of total)	Female professional and technical workers (% of total)	Ratio of female to male earned income
1994 (n = 116)						
China	23	0.474	21.0	11.6[1,2]	45.1[3]	31.2[4]
Indonesia	56	0.362	12.2	6.6	40.8	25.3
Korea, Rep. of	90	0.255	1.0	4.1	42.5	22.0
Malaysia	49	0.384	10.0	8.3	38.2	29.3
Philippines	28	0.435	11.2	27.7	63.2	21.1
Singapore	35	0.424	3.7	15.7	40.3	28.9
Thailand	54	0.373	3.7	22.2	52.7	34.6
1999 (n = 102)						
China	40	0.491	21.8	11.6	45.1	40[5]
Indonesia	–	–	–	–	–	34
Korea, Rep. of	78	0.336	3.7	4.2	45.0	31
Malaysia	52	0.451	10.3	19.2	43.2	32
Philippines	45	0.480	12.9	34.8	65.1	35
Singapore	32	0.512	4.8	34.3	16.1	33
Thailand	–	–	–	22	55	38
2004 (n = 78)						
China	–	–	20.2	–	–	–
Indonesia	–	–	8.0	–	–	–
Korea, Rep. of	68	0.377	5.9	5	34	0.46
Malaysia	44	0.519	16.3	20	45	0.40

Philippines	37	0.542	17.2	58	62	0.59
Singapore	20	0.648	16.0	26	43	0.50
Thailand	57	0.461	9.6	27	55	0.61

Notes:
1. In the 1995 Human Development Report, and in each report until 2001, the nomenclature for this category was 'female administrators and managers'. Thereafter the classification was changed to 'female legislators, senior officials and managers'.
2. Data here pertain to 1992.
3. Data here pertain to 1992.
4. In the 1995 report, figures are expressed in respect of women's percentage share of earned income, rather than as the ratio of female to male earned income (as in 2004).
5. In the 1999 Human Development Report, the GEM listed the average real GDP of women, but in the interests of comparability, the estimated female share of earned income is substituted here.
– = No data.

Sources: UNDP (1995: table 3.5; 1999: table 3; 2004: table 25).

Table 3.8 Components of the GEM, 1994–2004: selected sub-Saharan African countries

	GEM		Seats in parliament held by women (% of total)	Female legislators, senior officials and managers (% of total)	Female professional and technical workers (% of total)	Earned income share of women (% of total)
	Rank	Value				
1994 (n = 116)						
Côte d'Ivoire	112	0.157	4.6	0[1,2]	15.2[3]	27.8[4]
Gambia, The	74	0.315	7.8	14.5	26.5	32.6
Mali	97	0.237	2.3	19.7	19.0	11.8
Mauritania	111	0.613	0	7.7	20.7	18.5
Nigeria	108	0.198	2.1	5.5	26.0	28.5
Senegal	88	0.265	11.7	3.7	16.5	31.3
Sierra Leone	–	–	–	–	–	–
1999 (n = 102)						
Côte d'Ivoire	–	–	8.0	–	–	27[5]
Gambia, The	93	0.243	2.0	16	24	37
Mali	74	0.353	12.2	20	19	39
Mauritania	99	0.197	2.2	8	21	36
Nigeria	–	–	–	–	–	31
Senegal	–	–	–	–	–	35
Sierra Leone	–	–	–	–	–	–
2004 (n = 78)						
Côte d'Ivoire	–	–	8.5	–	–	–
Gambia, The	–	–	13.2	–	–	–
Mali	–	–	10.2	–	–	–

Mauritania	—	—	4.4	—	—
Nigeria	—	—	5.8	—	—
Senegal	—	—	19.2	—	—
Sierra Leone	—	—	14.5	—	—

Notes:

1. In the 1995 Human Development Report, and in each report until 2001, the nomenclature for this category was 'female administrators and managers'. Thereafter the classification was changed to 'female legislators, senior officials and managers'.
2. Data here pertain to 1992.
3. Data here pertain to 1992.
4. In the 1995 report, figures are expressed in respect of women's share of earned income, rather than as the ratio of female to male earned income (as in 2004).
5. In the 1999 Human Development Report, the GEM listed the average real GDP of women. In the interests of comparability, the estimated female share of earned income is substituted here.

— = No data

Sources: UNDP (1995: table 3.5; 1999: table 3; 2004: table 25).

Table 3.9 Gender, work burden and time allocation: selected developing countries

	Year	Burden of work			Total work time		Time allocation (%)			
		Total work time (minutes per day)		Female work time (% of male)	Market activities	Non-market activities	Time spent by women		Time spent by men	
		Women	Men				Mkt	Non-mkt	Mkt	Non-mkt
Country										
Urban areas										
Colombia	1983	399	356	112	49	51	24	76	77	23
Venezuela	1983	440	416	106	59	41	30	70	87	13
Kenya 1986	590	572	103	46	54	41	59	79	21	
Nepal 1978	579	554	105	58	42	25	75	67	33	
Indonesia	1992	398	366	109	60	40	35	65	86	14
Average[2]		481	453	107	54	46	31	69	79	21
Rural areas										
Guatemala	1977	678	545	117	59	41	37	63	84	16
Kenya 1988	676	500	135	56	44	42	58	76	24	
Bangladesh	1992	545	496	110	52	48	35	65	70	30
Nepal 1978	641	547	117	56	44	46	54	67	33	
Philippines	1975–7	546	452	121	73	27	29	71	84	16
Average		617	515	120	59	41	38	62	76	24

Notes:

1. Mkt = market activities; non-mkt = non-market activities. Market activities refer to market-oriented production activities as defined by the 1993 revised UN System of National Accounts (SNA).

2. Averages for urban and rural areas refer to unweighted averages for countries listed in relevant sections.

Source: UNDP (2004: table 28).

BOX 3.1   FACTORS INFLUENCING THE
CONSTRUCTION OF FEMALE-HEADED
HOUSEHOLDS AS THE 'POOREST OF
THE POOR'

- Assumption that female-headed households are most likely to form in situations of poverty.
- Equation of female-headed households with 'lone mother and children' households.
- Assumption that female heads themselves are primary or sole 'breadwinners'.
- Assumption that female household heads will have limited time for reproductive labour.
- Extrapolation of women's labour market disadvantage as individuals (for example, in occupational status, earnings, and so on) to female-headed households.
- Overemphasis (or exclusive emphasis) on economic status of household head as signifier of well-being for all household members.
- Perceived impacts of gender inequalities in respect of land, property and other material assets on female-headed households.
- Assumption that women-headed households have greater proportions of female members than male-headed units.
- Limited state/institutional transfers to female-headed households.
- Limited financial support to children in female-headed households from absent fathers.
- Conjectured limitations in access to and/or use of social capital of female-headed households in respect of networks of kin, neighbours, friends.
- Historical association of 'feminisation of poverty' concept with poor lone mothers and their children.
- Repeated 'statements of fact' in academic and policy literature.
- Endorsement of greater incidence and degrees of poverty among female-headed households by mainstream development institutions.
- Reliance on aggregated household (rather than per capita) figures for income, consumption and expenditure.

- Priority attached to quantitative/'physiological deprivation' indicators of poverty.
- 'Visibility' of female-headed households in conventional poverty statistics.
- Justification for selective/targeted poverty-alleviation programmes.
- Social pathology discourses of lone mother households as 'incomplete families', 'problematic families' and/or as symptomatic of 'family breakdown', and dominance of normative assumptions about the advantages of the 'natural' and/or 'traditional' (patriarchal/male-headed) family unit for material well-being.
- Concern for children's rights and well-being.
- Instrumental value of 'poorest of the poor' orthodoxy in securing resources for women in development/social programmes.

Source: Chant (2003a: 57).

a husband leaves most women worse-off. The core of gender subordination lies in the fact that most women are unable to mobilise adequate resources (both material and in terms of social identity), except through dependence on a man.

In lacking an adult male 'breadwinner' lone mother units are not only deprived of men's earnings and assets but relatively speaking have more dependants to support (see Fuwa, 2000: 1535; IFAD, 1999; ILO, 1996; McLanahan and Kelly, n.d.: 6; Safa and Antrobus, 1992: 54; UNDAW, 1991: 38). Women's purported single-handed management of income-generation, housework and childcare further compromises economic efficiency and well-being (see ECLAC, 2004b: 18). On one hand, female heads are conjectured to have less time and energy to perform the full range of non-market work so essential to income conservation in poor neighbourhoods, such as shopping around for the cheapest foodstuffs, or cutting costs by self-provisioning rather than relying on market goods and services (see World Bank, 2003a: 8). In turn the burden of women's 'reproduction tax' (Palmer, 1992) means that lone mothers are often confined to poorly paid part-time, informal and/or home-based occupations. This is compounded by women's lower education and training, gender discrimination in the workplace, and minimal state support to mothers and carers (see Dia, 2001; Elson, 1999a; Finne, 2001; Kabeer, 2003; also Christopher et al., 2001; England and Folbre, 2002; Folbre, 1994; Rogers, 1995). Since female heads are much more commonly engaged in informal activity than their male counterparts, and in the lower tiers too (see Bolles, 1986; Brown, 2000; Chant, 1991a; Chen et al., 2004; Merrick and Schmink, 1983; Sethuraman, 1998), it is no surprise that they are thought to be at an above-average risk of poverty, especially in house-holds where they are the sole 'breadwinning' adult.

Given the common disadvantages of informal employment not only in respect of earnings (see Chapter 2) , but regularity, social security and pen-sions, the short- and long-term implications for female heads of household are potentially serious. It is also important to remember that women's con-ventionally limited access to 'physical capital assets' (Rakodi, 1999) or 'non-labour resources' (Kabeer, 2003: 198), such as land and property, may exacerbate financial difficulty (ECLAC, 2004b: 51; also Mboup and Amunyunzu-Nyamongo, 2005). Since informal sector businesses are often based in or from the home, female heads who have no option but to rent or share accommodation may find their choice and scale of entrepreneurial activities constrained by landlords (see Chant, 1996: ch. 3). Indeed, even rental accommodation might be hard to obtain or hold onto in the face of aspersions about the sexual propriety of women without male 'guardians' (see Vera-Sanso, 2006, on southern India).

Disadvantage in labour supply, opportunities and assets is also thought to be exacerbated in women-headed households on account of their higher proportions of female vis-à-vis male members (Marcoux, 1997; also Box 3.1). While there is scant data on this for most parts of the South, evidence from Vietnam, Bangladesh and South Africa suggests that women's lower average earnings translate into a virtually 'unequivocal' risk of poverty in households which have only female members (Kabeer, 2003: 141), even if the matter of how the 'femaleness' of the household is constituted, for example, in terms of age and economic activity rates of members, may well mediate gender-poverty linkages (see Kusakabe, 2002: 8, on Cambodia).

Limited Support from External Parties

Another important set of factors in the construction of women-headed households as 'poorest of the poor' is that in most developing countries they receive scant 'transfer payments' from external parties such as the state, or 'absent fathers'. While some countries, as discussed in greater detail later, have launched targeted initiatives to alleviate the poverty of female-headed households, where these do exist, they have rarely made an appreciable difference to household incomes or assets.[2] The same applies where female heads, along with other 'vulnerable' groups such as the elderly, disabled or orphaned, receive benefits from residual social programmes designed to cater to those excluded from mainstream contributory aid and welfare schemes.

The latter is noted by Bibars (2001: 83 et seq.) in relation to Egypt, where non-contributory programmes of poverty alleviation have not 'provided women with an institutional alternative to the male provider'. This is significant more generally since in most parts of the South there is limited enforcement of legal stipulations pertaining to absent fathers. While legislation governing maintenance payments in many contexts seems to be extending to cover children born in consensual unions as well as formal marriage, in practice levels of 'paternal responsibility' are notoriously low, especially among the poor, and men are seldom penalised for non-compliance (see Chant, 1997a; 2003a; van Vuuren, 2003: 73). Recognising that men's incapacity to pay because they are unemployed or underemployed or have low earnings may be an important factor, unwillingness to pay seems to be an equally important issue (see Chant, 1997b).

Another factor offered to explain poverty among female-headed households is that their social networks (and hence access to social capital) may be smaller (see Box 3.1). This is sometimes attributed to the fact that female heads lack ties with ex-partners' relatives, or because they 'keep themselves to themselves' in the face of hostility or mistrust on the part of their own family networks or others in their communities (see Chant, 1997a; Lewis, 1993; Willis, 1994). Indeed, lone mothers may deliberately distance themselves from kin as a means of deflecting the 'shame' or 'dishonour' attached to out-of-wedlock birth and/or marriage failure, not to mention, in some instances, stigmatised types of employment such as sex work (see Chant and McIlwaine, 1995: 302; also Bibars, 2001: 60–61). Added to this, some female heads are unable to spare the time to actively cultivate social links and/or may eschew seeking help from others in order to reduce demands for assistance in return – deficits in material and other resources preventing ready reciprocation of favours (Chant, 1997a: 206; González de la Rocha, 1994a: 211; 2003a: 23; van Vuuren, 2003: 101; see also Chen and Drèze, 1992: 23).[3]

However, we cannot necessarily assume that women heads lack transfers from external parties (especially non-resident children). Nor can we assume that women's general disadvantage as individuals translates into greater disadvantage for female-headed households, or, indeed, that living with men automatically mitigates women's risks of poverty. Nonetheless, there are probably three main factors over and above those already discussed which help to explain the frequently unproblematised construction of women-headed households as the 'poorest of the poor'.

Historical Legacies

A first, and fairly plausible, reason for the conjectured links between poverty and female household headship owes to historical legacy. The coining of the term 'feminisation of poverty' is usually attributed to Diana Pearce (1978) who observed a rising incidence of poverty among women relative to men in the USA, and linked this in large measure with the mounting presence of households headed by women, particularly of Afro-Caribbean descent (Goldberg, 1998: 178n; see also McLanahan and Kelly, n.d.; Medeiros and Costa, 2006; Moghadam, 1997: 6; Staudt, 1998: 217). While higher poverty rates among women relative to men had also been noted in previous historical periods such that it may have been more appropriate to talk about a *'re-feminisation* of poverty' (Goldberg 1998: 162; emphasis added), and the trend for this to concentrate among female-headed households was more marked in the USA than in many other industrialised countries (Goldberg and Kremen, 1987), Pearce's work seems to have been a starting point for the association between female headship and poverty, which has been nailed to the mast by ongoing, if unwarrantedly generalised, repetition (see Chant, 2003a; Jackson, 1998; also Box 3.1).

Continued Reliance on Quantitative Poverty Indicators

A second important factor in the 'poorest of the poor' epithet derives from the continued precedence of quantitative measures in poverty assessments, be these in relation to incomes, expenditure or consumption. As noted in Chapter 2, poverty analyses continue to be grounded in the predominantly 'physical aspects of deprivation, rather than the more intangible ones' (Kabeer, 1994: 161). Notwithstanding Johnsson-Latham's (2004b: 26–7) argument that income data can often underestimate women's poverty, when considering that aggregate household (rather than per capita) incomes, usually based on earnings, are often taken as the benchmark for measuring income poverty (see Kabeer, 2003: 79–81), it is no surprise that female-headed households show up as a particularly vulnerable constituency because of their smaller average size (see Chant, 1997b; also Bongaarts, 2001; Box 3.1).

Political Agendas

Third, and related to this, the fact that female-headed households are a 'visible and readily identifiable group in income poverty statistics' (Kabeer, 1996: 14), has provided rich justification for GAD lobbyists, serving as a tactical peg on which to allocate resources to women (see Baden and Goetz, 1998: 23; Chant, 2003a; Jackson, 1998). Even if there are many less auspicious consequences of the orthodoxy that female-headed households are the 'poorest of the poor', including fuel for neoliberal targeting, and neglect of the needs of the majority of women (who are in male-headed households), that it has been able to secure funds for women is undoubtedly a major reason why many stakeholders, including those within the GAD arena, have clung to the construction.

CHALLENGES TO THE CONSTRUCTION OF WOMEN-HEADED HOUSEHOLDS AS THE 'POOREST OF THE POOR'

Despite pervasive emphasis on female household headship in exacerbating women's poverty, and the idea that the mounting 'feminisation of poverty' can be attributed partially, if not primarily, to rising female household headship, challenges to the blanket stereotyping of women as 'poorest of the poor' have emerged from a number of quarters.

Lack of Supporting Data

One of the most important challenges is that data are inconclusive, and at a variety of levels. Bearing in mind that comparisons of poverty among female- and male-headed households often rely on aggregate household incomes which do not take size into consideration let alone intra-household resource distribution (see Klasen, 2004), several inter-regional and/or international assessments based on data compiled by the World Bank and other multilateral organisations such as the International Fund for Agricultural Development (IFAD), and the International Food Policy Research Institute (IFPRI), confirm that female household headship does not predict an above-average probability of income poverty in any consistent manner (for details see Chant, 1997b; Chen et al., 2004: 37; IFAD, 1999; Kennedy, 1994: 35–6; Lampietti and Stalker, 2000; Moghadam, 1997: 8; 1998; Quisumbing et al., 1995). On top of this, there is no apparently systematic linkage between general levels of poverty and female household headship in particular countries or regions, with the latter often increasing as levels of poverty decline.[4] Despite a rise in the share of households in poverty and extreme poverty headed by women in parts of Latin America in recent years, for example (see Arriagada, 2002; ECLAC, 2004b: 58; also Table 3.10), in some countries – notably Mexico, Brazil and Guatemala – women-headed households appear to be more prevalent among the *non-poor*, albeit by a small margin. Moreover, in countries not included in Table 3.10, such as Colombia, female headship has shown a tendency to concentrate more in upper than lower income deciles over time. In 1995, for example, when 22.5 per cent of Colombia's households were female headed, only 20.9 per cent of households in extreme poverty (equating to

Table 3.10 *Female-headed households by poverty status over time in urban Latin America*

Country and year	Total % of households headed by women	Extremely poor (%)	Poor (%)	Non-poor (%)
Argentina (Gran Buenos Aires)				
1990	21.1	26.2	11.6	22.3
1994	24.0	22.0	20.0	24.0
1997	26.1	31.7	24.1	26.5
1999	26.9	36.9	28.0	26.5
Bolivia				
1989	16.7	22.0	24.1	26.1
1994	18.0	20.0	17.0	18.0
1997	20.7	24.0	22.4	18.6
1999	20.9	24.4	18.9	20.7
Brazil				
1990	20.1	24.2	22.6	18.4
1993	21.7	22.9	21.0	21.7
1996	23.7	24.1	22.1	24.0
1999	25.4	24.2	24.2	25.9
Chile				
1990	21.4	24.5	19.8	21.5
1994	22.0	27.0	21.0	22.0
1996	23.0	29.0	22.0	23.0
1998	24.0	28.0	23.0	24.0
Costa Rica				
1991	24.1	27.7	22.3	24.0
1994	24.0	24.0	24.0	24.0
1997	26.8	51.0	35.5	24.0
1999	27.9	55.8	38.5	24.9
Ecuador				
1990	16.9	21.6	15.9	15.3
1994	18.7	22.7	17.5	15.3
1997	18.6	23.8	18.6	16.7
1999	20.1	22.9	20.5	18.0
El Salvador				
1995	30.8	38.2	31.3	29.0
1997	30.2	35.8	33.2	27.8
1999	31.4	35.5	35.5	29.2

Table 3.10   (continued)

Country and year	Total % of households headed by women	Extremely poor (%)	Poor (%)	Non-poor (%)
Guatemala				
1989	21.9	23.1	21.0	21.7
1998	24.3	24.2	21.9	25.3
Honduras				
1990	26.6	35.4	21.2	21.4
1994	25.0	28.0	25.0	21.0
1997	29.2	31.9	27.7	27.5
1999	30.3	32.2	30.4	28.1
Mexico				
1989	15.7	13.9	14.0	16.7
1994	17.0	11.0	16.0	18.0
1996	17.5	17.1	14.7	18.9
1998	19.0	18.0	16.0	20.0
Nicaragua				
1993	34.9	39.9	33.8	31.7
1998	34.5	39.2	36.4	29.6
Panama				
1991	26.0	33.7	29.0	23.5
1994	25.0	35.0	25.0	24.0
1997	27.5	36.5	28.8	26.2
1999	27.4	44.6	28.0	25.8

Source: CEPAL (2002: cuadro 6E).

the bottom two income deciles) were headed by women, and 19.3 per cent among the poor (deciles 3–5), whereas female-headed households made up 25.1 per cent and 26.2 per cent respectively of the top two deciles (9 and 10) (see Wartenburg, 1999: 80–81). That female headship plays little role in determining poverty has also been found and/or confirmed in Peru, where the incidence of monetary poverty may be the same if not higher in male-headed households (Franco, 2003: 7), in Guyana (see Gafar, 1998), Panama (Fuwa, 2000), and Argentina (Geldstein, 1994; 1997) (see also Medeiros and Costa, 2006, for a more general overview of eight Latin American countries).

Across a wider geographical remit, detailed micro-level research based on varying combinations of primary and secondary data also provides limited grounds for generalisation. On the one hand, there are countries where female headship and poverty seem to be linked, including Botswana (van Driel, 1994: 216), Egypt (Bibars, 2001: 68), Iran (ILO, 2004b), Zambia (Nauckhoff, 2004: 54), Kenya (Rodenberg, 2004: 46), Lesotho (Tuoane et al., 2001), South Africa (Todes and Walker, 1993: 48), and Venezuela (Paolisso and Gammage, 1996: 18–21). Moreover, one of the biggest comparative reviews to date, based on over 60 micro-level studies from Latin America, Africa and Asia, concluded that in two-thirds of cases women-headed households were poorer than male-headed households (see Buvinic and Gupta, 1993; 1997).[5] On the other hand, numerous other studies indicate either that there is no relationship between the sex of household heads and income and/or that women-headed households are just as likely to be present among middle- and/or upper-income groups as among the poor (see Appleton, 1996, on Uganda; Kukusabe, 2002, on Cambodia; Kumari, 1989: 31, on India; Lewis, 1993: 23, on Bangladesh; van Vuuren, 2003, on Tanzania; Weekes-Vagliani, 1992: 142, on the Côte d'Ivoire).

In turn, even where women-headed households in some countries do fall disproportionately into the category of poor or extremely poor, it is by no means clear that they are responsible for an 'inter-generational transmission of disadvantage'. Low incomes may well predispose dependants in female-headed units to greater risk, but this does not necessarily materialise in practice. Indeed, due to the intervening effects of intra-household resource allocation, which are often prone to greater inequality and male bias in male-headed units, girls in female-headed households may fare better in respect of well-being and accumulation of capabilities (see Chant, 1997a; 1997b; Hoddinott and Haddad, 1991; Moghadam, 2005; also Chapter 1 in this volume). In addition, notwithstanding the common assumption that female heads of household send young children out to work, levels of child labour are not noticeably higher in female-headed units (see Chant, 1997a: 230 et seq.; Chant and Jones, 2005). As concluded by Delamonica et al. (2004: 1) on the basis of UNICEF data from 17 countries in which at least 15 per cent of children were living only with their mother: 'despite the many challenges that single mothers face, they still manage to raise their children with outcomes similar to those of two-parent families'. The same study also showed that children living with single fathers (as well as with neither biological parent), actually had the poorest outcomes (ibid.: 25).

In light of the above, it is clearly wise to refrain from overemphasising the 'plight of female-headed households' (Scott, 1994: 86). Indeed, given that so much evidence goes against the grain of prevailing orthodoxy, it is arguably more important to establish how female heads do not necessarily end up poorer than their male counterparts.

Heterogeneity of Female-Headed Households: Configuration and Context

The diversity of female-headed households presents a major qualification to generalised statements about their poverty (Box 3.2). Differentiation occurs, *inter alia*, through routes into the status (whether by 'choice' or involuntarily, and/or through non-marriage, separation, divorce, widowhood, migration and so on), by rural or urban residence, by 'race', by composition, by stage in the life course (including age and relative dependency of offspring), and by access to resources from beyond the household unit (from absent fathers, kinship networks, state assistance and the like) (see Baylies, 1996; Chant, 1997a; Feijoó, 1999; Safa, 2002; Varley, 2002; van Vuuren, 2003; Whitehead and Lockwood, 1999). The significance of these variables – which can intersect in myriad ways – is, in turn, mediated by the particular social, cultural, demographic, political and economic contexts in which female heads are situated.

BOX 3.2   FACTORS CHALLENGING THE CONSTRUCTION OF FEMALE-HEADED HOUSEHOLDS AS THE 'POOREST OF THE POOR'

- 'Poorest of the poor' not borne out consistently by quantitative data pertaining to incomes, consumption, indicators of well-being among children and so on.
- Heterogeneity of female-headed households (in respect of routes into status, composition, stage in the life course and so on).
- Recognition that households are permeable units with flows from beyond household boundaries affecting internal well-being.
- Likelihood in many cases that female heads of household will be at later stage in life course and have fewer dependent children.
- Above-average receipt of financial support from working children within and beyond the home.
- Recognition that female-headed households are not necessarily 'male absent' households.
- Recognition that household well-being cannot be automatically equated with economic status of heads.
- Strategies adopted by female-headed households to compensate for gender bias and/or household vulnerability (for

---

example, household extension, increases in occupational density, optimal utilisation of labour supply [especially that of women]).

- Multidimensional/'social deprivation' conceptualisations of poverty which extend beyond incomes and consumption, emphasising, *inter alia*, assets, subjective experiences of privation, 'vulnerability' and poverty-generating processes.
- Gender disparities in resource distribution and poverty relations as power relations, namely, that *command and control over resources* may be equally, if not more, important as *level of resources* in determining individuals' experiences of poverty.
- Acknowledgement of agency among female heads of household who may make 'trade-offs' between different dimensions of poverty (for example, 'income poor' but 'power-rich').
- Rejection of unitary household models in favour of models emphasising household as a sites of bargaining, 'cooperative-conflict', and intra-household inequalities along lines of gender in respect of resource generation and distribution.
- Recognition that some women may actively choose female household headship on grounds of improved material and/or other aspects of well-being, and/or resist becoming part of new male-headed arrangements following conjugal breakdown or widowhood.

Source: Chant (2003a: 58).

In terms of routes into the status, for example, when female headship occurs through bereavement, it may well be that this brings a downturn in economic well-being, especially where women have low rates of labour force participation and/or few employment opportunities. One case in point is Iran, where the majority of households headed by women enter the state through widowhood, and 17.5 per cent are poor compared with 15.3 per cent of households as a whole (see ILO, 2004b: 22). Yet in situations where women have greater access to employment, or are more accustomed to working, they may find their economic circumstances improving following widowhood (or divorce or separation), especially if they were previously unable to count on spousal support.

Similar contingencies apply when female headship comes about through male labour migration. Although de facto female-headed households may be better off than their *de jure* counterparts, as observed in the case of India (see Gangopadhyay and Wadhwa, 2003), when male labour migrants fail to remit money, women and their dependants can end up more impoverished. As pointed up by Elson (1992: 41): 'Male migration reduces the expenses of the household – but all too frequently reduces household resources to an even greater extent . . . Migration in a growing number of cases appears to be a polite word for desertion. It is a male survival strategy rather than a female survival strategy.'

Age also plays a role in affecting disadvantage, recognising, again, that the way it does so may vary substantially from one context to another, and for different reasons. In Egypt, for example, Bibars (2001: 67) points out that female heads tend to be poor because the majority are 'old and illiterate and unable to work', and in Iran, older women are identified as being particularly prone to poverty where children have left home and set up their own households (ILO, 2004b: 28). In Chile, by contrast, the mean age of 'non-poor' female heads is higher (at 56.9 years) than for those classified as 'poor' (51.9 years), or 'destitute' (46 years) (Thomas, 1995: 82; Table 3.3). One reason for less poverty among older female heads is that they have fewer dependent children, and more of working age (whether co-resident or who have left home) who provide financial assistance, as observed in Mexico and Costa Rica for example (Chant, 1997a). Indeed, here and in other parts of the South it is widely noted that female heads tend to receive larger and more regular remittances than male heads from non-resident offspring (see Appleton, 1996, on Uganda; Brydon and Legge, 1996: 49 and 69 and Lloyd and Gage-Brandon, 1993: 121 and 123, on Ghana; Chant and McIlwaine, 1995, on the Philippines; Kusakabe, 2002: 6, on Cambodia). As summarised by Safa (2002: 13) in the context of the Dominican Republic, 'female-headed households can function quite adequately as long as the consanguineous ties that provide crucial financial, domestic, and emotional support are maintained'. In fact, in some parts of the world, such as the Netherlands Antilles, it has been argued that 'family networks provide women with more security than an individual male partner' (Ypeij and Steenbeek, 2001: 73).

Leading on from this, another fairly general finding is that female-headed units have a greater tendency to comprise extended kin members which can bolster security and well-being, whether because this adds wage earners to the household unit, or because it facilitates engagement in wage-earning among other individuals in the household. In Latin America, for example, over one-third of extended families are headed by women, as compared to one-fifth of non-extended parent-child units (ECLAC, 2004a: 35). Among the poor, levels are often higher still. Research on low-income households in urban Mexico, for example, has revealed that more than one-half of female-headed households are extended, compared with just over one-quarter of male-headed units (Chant, 1997a), and in rural and urban Nicaragua, the differentials are even more marked, at 54 per cent versus 21 per cent (Bradshaw, 2002: 16).

There are often important interactions between stage in the life course and composition in so far as older heads are more likely to extend their membership through the marriage of sons and daughters. Accordingly female-headed households may well contain male adults, which underlines Fonseca's (1991) point that female-headed households do not necessarily equate with 'male-absent' households (see also Box 3.2). Notwithstanding that in some cases, especially where there are few opportunities for productive work, household extension 'may actually serve to increase rather than decrease vulnerability' (Bradshaw, 2002: 21), in other instances it can reflect a proactive measure to improve well-being.

Although it is impossible to generalise about different features of female-headed households and their links with poverty across different contexts, at the bottom line, diversity in respect of socio-economic status, age, composition, dependency levels, access to resources from beyond the household and so on, precludes categorical labelling. Rather than basing analysis solely on the characteristics of one individual, therefore, evaluations need also to take into account composition and extra-domestic relations (see Chant, 1997a; 1997b; Feijoó, 1999; Kusakabe, 2002; Oliver, 2002; Varley, 2002; Whitehead and Lockwood, 1999). Indeed, focusing on livelihood strategies and the activities of other household members reveals that potential shortfalls in the income and assets of female-headed households are often compensated in other ways.

Variations in Household Employment and Earning Strategies

Even if female heads of household may be disadvantaged by gender inequalities in earnings, it is mistaken to assume that they are necessarily the sole or even main breadwinners in households (Mookodi, 2000; Rosenhouse, 1989; Varley, 1996; also Box 3.2). Indeed, in many parts of the South, especially those which have experienced major debt crises and/or undergone neoliberal restructuring, multiple earning has been one of the most common strategies adopted by low-income households to keep afloat.[6] In turn, mounting contributions from other household members have diminished the share of total income apportioned by heads (González de la Rocha, 2002: 64). Furthermore, much research, especially on Latin America, suggests that relative to household size, female-headed households may have more earners (and earnings) than their male-headed counterparts because of failure on the part of the latter to make full use of their labour supply. Whether motivated by pride, honour, or sexual jealousy, for example, studies of Mexico and Honduras, indicate that men may forbid their wives (and even daughters) to work, especially in jobs outside the home or neighbourhood (see Benería and Roldan, 1987: 146; Bradshaw and Linneker, 2001: 199, on Honduras; Chant, 1997b; Fernández-Kelly, 1983; Proctor, 2003: 303; Townsend et al., 1999: 38; Willis, 1993: 71). When this leaves households reliant on a single wage, there are greater risks of destitution. Moreover, although female-headed households may clearly *need* more workers (that is, to supplement their own remuneration), more efficient use of female labour can add to the effects of household extension and/or multiple earning strategies in reducing dependency ratios and enhancing per capita incomes (see Chant, 1991a: 204, table 7.1; Selby et al., 1990: 95; Varley, 1996: table 5, on Mexico; also Chant, 1997a: 210; Kennedy, 1994; Oliver, 2002: 47; Paolisso and Gammage, 1996: 21; Quisumbing et al., 1995; Shanthi, 1994: 23, on other contexts). As summed-up by Wartenburg (1999: 95) in relation to Colombia, the manner in which female-headed households organise themselves can optimise the positive elements of such arrangements and thereby contribute to neutralising the negative effects of gender bias. Aside from the fact that the diverse livelihood strategies entered into by female-headed households can raise earning capacity and reduce vulnerability, earnings seem to have a greater chance of being translated into disposable income for household use because female heads are better able to exert power and exercise their preferences.

Intra-Household Resource Distribution

Leading on from the above, that earning differentials between households may be tempered by *intra*-household distributional factors (Folbre, 1991: 110), is extremely pertinent given evidence from a range of contexts that more money, in relative terms, may be available for common expenditure within households headed by women, with positive effects on members' nutritional intake, health care and education (Chant, 1997a: 227–8; Engle, 1995; Kabeer, 1996: 13; 2003: 165 et seq.). This not only means greater well-being in the short-term, but, given investments in human capital, also encompasses potential for greater socio-economic security (or indeed mobility) over a longer time frame.

As flagged up in Chapter 2, this situation is in part explained by gender disparities in the use and allocation of earnings, with men's tendency to income retention for discretionary spending often exposing women and children to 'secondary poverty' (see Dwyer and Bruce, 1988; also Bradshaw, 1996b; 2002; Chant, 1997b; González de la Rocha, 1994b: 10). Over and above the resultant observation that 'The presence of two parents in the same residence gives no guarantee of either financial or emotional support' (Baylies, 1996: 77; also van Driel, 1994: 208 et seq.), it should also be noted that where women are earning, men may not only let women's incomes substitute theirs (see Bradshaw and Linneker, 2003; Mayoux, 2006), but make additional claims for 'top-up' money. In Thailand, for instance, Blanc-Szanton (1990: 93) observes that it is culturally acceptable for husbands to gamble and go drinking with friends after work and to demand money from their spouses to do so. Such findings underline Folbre's (1991: 108) argument that male heads may command a larger share of resources (due to their privileged bargaining position) than they actually bring to the household (see also Baylies, 1996: 77). Added to this, financial contributions from men may be so irregular that this makes for excessive vulnerability on the part of women, who may be forced into borrowing and indebtedness in order to get by (Chant, 1997a: 210).

Female Household Headship as a 'Trade-Off'

Following on from the discussion in Chapter 2 which identified how actual levels of income may mean little in respect of women's subjective evaluations of their situations, it is important to recognise that 'A lower income may even be preferred over a position of dependence and domination' (Davids and van Driel, 2001: 164; see also González de la Rocha, 1994a: 210; also Box 3.2). This is central to the notion of 'trade-offs' and helps to explain why some low-income women make choices which, at face value, appear prejudicial to their well-being. Although women are less likely to leave men as be deserted, empirical evidence suggests that in some cases their need or desire to do so is such that they make considerable financial sacrifices. Leaving spouses not only means doing without male earnings, but potentially forfeiting the conjugal home and other assets such as neighbourhood networks in which considerable time, effort and/or resources may have been invested (Chant, 1997a; 2003a). In the interests of preserving their autonomy, separated women may also resist men's offers of child support (see Chant, 1997b: 35). In short, some women prefer to cope with financial hardship than pay the price that maintenance can bring with it. Although leaving men or eschewing assistance may at one level lead to an exacerbation of material poverty, and, accordingly, attach a high price to women's independence (see Jackson, 1996; Molyneux, 2001: ch. 4), benefits in other dimensions of women's lives may be adjudged to outweigh the costs. While women's lower average wages clearly inflate these costs, as Graham (1987: 59) argues: 'single parenthood can represent not only a different but a preferable kind of poverty for lone mothers' (see also UNDAW, 1991: 41). Indeed, although financial pressures force some women to marry, or to search for new partners following conjugal breakdown, others choose to remain alone (see Chant, 1997a: ch. 7; also Bradshaw, 1996a; van Vuuren, 2003: 231; Ypeij and Steenbeek, 2001). As noted by Fonseca (1991) in relation to research in Porto Alegre, Brazil, women who live without partners often do so not through lack of opportunity, but by choice (ibid.: 156). In many cases these are older (post-menopausal) women, who, 'having gained a moment of respite in the battlefield of the sexes', prefer to rely upon sons than spouses (ibid.: 157; see also Box 3.2).

Notwithstanding that the 'trade-offs' available to most low-income women are usually 'bleak', not to mention 'painful' (see Kabeer, 1997; 1999; also van Driel, 1994), men's incomes can carry too many conditions to make them worthwhile (Chant, 2003a). As summarised by Rodenberg (2004: 13):

> Women are . . . more often affected, and jeopardised by poverty. Lacking powers of self-control and decision-making powers, women – once having fallen into poverty – have far fewer chances to remedy their situation. This fact, however, should not be understood to imply globally that e.g. a rising number of women-headed households is invariably linked with a rising poverty rate. It is instead advisable to bear in mind that a woman's decision to maintain a household of her own may very well be a voluntary decision – one that may, for instance, serve as an avenue out of a relationship marred by violence. If poverty is understood not only as income poverty but as a massive restriction of choices and options, a step of this kind, not taken in isolation, may also mean an improvement of women's life circumstances.

Although the above suggests that sweeping stereotypes about the poverty of women-headed households are misplaced, a counter-stereotypical proposition would be equally ill-advised. Female headship is far from being a 'panacea for poverty' (see Feijoó, 1999: 162). It is clear that some women's individual endowments and household characteristics make them more vulnerable than others. Lone-parent households (especially those with young children), rarely 'compete on an equal playing field' with their two-parent counterparts (Hewitt and Leach, 1993: v), whether in terms of labour resources, access to jobs or other productive assets. This puts some female heads in the position of having to become 'time poor' and/or to self exploit in the interests of overcoming income deficiency and enabling them to cope with multiple responsibilities for economic provisioning and reproductive work (see also Delamonica et al., 2004: 2; Fuwa, 2000: 1517; 2001: 18; Panda, 1997). This may clearly constrain their possibilities for rest and leisure, with major implications for personal well-being, health, income-generating activities, and time available to spend with children. As such, recognising that poverty is multi-causal and multifaceted, and that, in some ways and in some cases, female household headship can be positive and empowering, is no justification for lack of assistance from state agencies and other institutional providers (Bibars, 2001: 67; Chant, 2003a).

IMPLICATIONS OF STEREOTYPING FEMALE-HEADED HOUSEHOLDS AS THE 'POOREST OF THE POOR'

While recognising the need to avoid undermining the case for policy attention, a number of undesirable (if unintended) consequences result from persistent emphasis on an association between female household headship and the 'feminisation of poverty' (see Box 3.3). One of the most important is that the typecasting of female-headed households as the 'poorest of the poor' conveys an impression that poverty owes more to women's personal and/or household characteristics than to the wider socio-economic contexts in which they are situated. The centrality of lone motherhood in debates about the UK's growing 'underclass', for example, are levelled by Phoenix (1996: 174) as having contributed to 'a construction of lone mothers as "feckless", wilfully responsible for the poverty that has been well-documented to be a feature of lone parenting', or as Laws (1996: 68–9) puts it: 'It is argued that lone parenthood itself is the problem, not the conditions in which it occurs' (see also Lewis, 1989; Moore, 1996; Roseneil and Mann, 1996: 205; Stacey, 1997; Waldfogel, 1996).

BOX 3.3 IMPLICATIONS OF STEREOTYPING FEMALE-HEADED HOUSEHOLDS AS THE 'POOREST OF THE POOR'

- Can potentially secure resources for women in development/social programmes.
- Homogenises negative economic circumstances of female-headed households.
- Neglects and/or deflects attention from situation of women in male-headed households.
- Ignores 'secondary poverty' and suggests that women in male-headed households do not experience poverty.
- Places undue emphasis on household configuration in exacerbating the poverty of women, rather than (a) intra-household dynamics, and/or (b) wider gender inequalities.
- Devalues the efforts made by female-headed households to overcome gender bias and/or household vulnerability.

- Ignores subjective meanings of household headship for women such as power, autonomy, self-esteem.
- Ignores non-economic aspects of disadvantage in women's lives, such as unequal gender roles and relations, domestic violence, and so on.
- Objectification of female heads as a group in need (rather than as a group with rights).
- Bolsters neoconservative agendas for strengthening marriage and the 'traditional family'.
- Pathologisation of female headship can contribute to narrowing their livelihood possibilities.
- Contributes to negative image of female-headed households.
- Gender inequality becomes conflated with poverty.
- Gives rise to programmes which focus on women only rather than on women and men, and/or gender relations (WID v. GAD).
- Leads to targeted programmes for female heads of household which, to date, do not seem to have appreciable benefits in respect of raising women's status, social legitimacy and well-being, and/or diminishing inequalities in gender or between household structures.
- Serves neoliberal agendas for efficiency and the substitution of universal social programmes by targeted programmes.
- Ignores lone-father households.

Source: Chant (2003b: 60).

This, in turn, does little to arrest the idea that motherhood is only viable and/or acceptable in the context of marriage (see Chant, 1997b; Collins, 1991: 159; Hewitt and Leach, 1993), or that female-headed households are deviant and/or 'inferior' to their male-headed counterparts (Feijoó, 1999: 156). As stated by Johnsson-Latham (2004b: 30):

> the tendency to disregard female poverty in male-headed households and to stigmatise FHHs [female-headed households] as poor can be seen as a political choice, and as part of a neo-conservative agenda which seeks to portray male-headed households as superior to FHHs. This approach runs contrary to the politically agreed texts from Beijing in 1995 where, in the end, an agreement was reached to refer to various forms of families, and not (as suggested by the Vatican and many Muslim countries) to indicate the family – supposedly male headed – to be the norm.

At one level, constructions of female-headed households as 'problematic' may lead to palliative interventions such as the provision of assistance to affected parties with child-feeding, day care, access to credit, skills-training, or shelter (see for example, Bibars, 2001: 81 et seq.; Chant, 1997a; Grosh, 1994; Lewis, 1993; Safa, 1995: 84). However, at another extreme: 'Eurocentric emphasis on the nuclear family as the norm and the embodiment of modernity and progress, leads to pathological views of female-headed households' (Safa, 1998: 203), and to the equation of female household headship with 'family breakdown' (Chant, 2002b).[7] Both of these, in turn, provide grounds to strengthen the 'traditional' (male-headed) family despite its often injurious effects on women's well-being.

Indeed, another adverse outcome of persistent portrayals of the economic disadvantage of female-headed units is that this misrepresents and devalues the enormous efforts made by female heads to overcome the problems they face on account of their gender, as well as missing the meanings of female headship for women. As asserted by Davids and van Driel (2001: 166): 'Female-headed households appear as an objective category of households in which the subject position of the female head vanishes completely as does the socio-cultural and psychological meaning that their status has for them personally.' Uncompromisingly negative images of female heads can also condemn them to greater privation, for example, by limiting their social networks which, in many parts of the world, act as sources of job information, as arenas for the exchange of labour and finance, and as contexts for securing the prospective marriages of offspring (see for example, Bruce and Lloyd, 1992; Davids and van Driel, 2001: 164; Lewis, 1993: 34–5; Monk, 1993: 10; Winchester, 1990: 82; see also Box 3.43.

In turn, emphasis on female-headed households as the 'poorest of the poor' suggests that gendered poverty is confined to this 'minority' group alone, regardless of resounding evidence of disadvantage among women in general, and that male household headship can render them vulnerable to 'secondary poverty' (Bradshaw, 1996a; Chant, 1997a; Feijoó, 1999: 156; Fuwa, 2001; Jackson, 1996; 1997: 152; Kabeer, 1996; May, 2001: 50; Varley, 1996). As summarised by Davids and van Driel (2001: 162):

> What is implied is that female-headed households are poorer than male-headed households. The question that is not asked, however, is whether women are better-off in male-headed households. By making male-headed households the norm, important contradictions vanish within these households, and so too does the possibly unbalanced economical (*sic*) and social position of women compared to men.

Last but not least, the aforementioned tendency for the 'feminisation of poverty' to produce policy interventions which either target women in isolation or focus mainly on those who head their own households can neglect vital relational aspects of gender which are likely to play a large part in accounting for women's disadvantage within and beyond the home (see Buvinic and Gupta, 1997; Jackson, 1997; May, 2001; Moore, 1996). This seems to compound a palpable reluctance on the part of policy-makers to engage with gender (rather than women) in anti-poverty initiatives on grounds of ignorance, fear and/or concern to conserve resources. One appeal of directing resources to female-headed households, for instance, is that they are 'a "target group" which is less politicised, for development interventions, than intrahousehold "interference"' (Jackson, 1997: 152). Targeted strategies, in turn, are also cheaper than universal social programmes (see Budowski and Guzmán, 1998; Chant, 2002a). Yet part of the reason for the relatively limited success of targeted schemes is precisely because they have focused on the supposed 'victims' rather than attempting to unseat the structures of gender inequality which make many women vulnerable in the first place.

Experiences with Targeted Programmes

The targeting of anti-poverty programmes to female-headed households was identified as one strategy to combat women's poverty by the BPFA (Moghadam, 1998: 227), and has been implemented in various guises in a number of countries in the Global South, including the Philippines, Singapore, Cambodia, Iran, Bangladesh, India, Honduras, Puerto Rico, Chile, Colombia and Costa Rica. Among the potential benefits of dedicated initiatives for female heads of household, Buvinic and Gupta (1997), pinpoint three in particular. The first is that in situations where data on poverty are unreliable, isolating households headed by women is likely to capture a significant share of the population 'in need', especially where there are substantial gaps in male and female earnings, and limited subsidised childcare facilities. Second, targeting assistance to lone mothers may be an effective means of improving child welfare given widespread empirical evidence that children fare better where women have resources at their own disposal. A third potential benefit is greater gender equitability in development resource allocation.

Arguments against targeting highlighted by Buvinic and Gupta (1997) include the fact that female-headed households may become male headed over time through remarriage or cohabitation, thereby resulting in a leakage of benefits to male-headed households. Another potential slippage of benefits is to non-poor households given that not all female-headed households suffer low incomes, and some may receive support, albeit periodically, from men. Further problems arise from difficulties inherent in screening processes whereby some female heads may not be classified as such due to cultural bias towards naming men for this role, even if they are largely or permanently absent, or make little contribution to family life and welfare. Tactics for determining female heads most in need may also be problematic. In Honduras, for example, a food coupon programme targeted at primary school children from female-headed households attempted to ascertain the financial status of mothers through questioning children and neighbours in the community. This was not only construed as intrusive, but did not always lead to appropriate decisions (Grosh, 1994).

On top of this, many women may not want to be identified as lone mothers given the stigma attached to the status. They may also feel that taking public money will increase antagonism against them.[8] In Egypt, for example, Bibars (2001: 83) notes the build-up of a 'distrustful, punitive and contemptuous attitude towards female-headed households and the poor in general' in recent years. More generally Buvinic and Gupta (1997: 271) draw attention to the fact that targeting can alienate and/or provoke conflict with male-headed households when female heads are granted assistance which is not perceived as 'female-specific' such as housing subsidies and food coupons.

Other problems of targeting include the construction of female-headed households as a vulnerable and residualised group. As Bibars (2001: 83 et seq.) notes of Egypt, while the beneficiaries of mainstream contributory aid and welfare schemes (who are primarily men) are perceived as having 'rights', the recipients of non-contributory programmes (who are predominantly female) are treated in a disparaging light as 'charity cases' (see also Johnsson-Latham, 2004b: 38).

Another argument against targeting, particularly common among government bodies, is that it may produce so-called 'perverse incentives'. In Egypt, Bibars (2001: 67) comments that free and unconditional assistance is thought not only to increase the numbers of female household heads, but to encourage them 'to relax and not work'. In Costa Rica, fear that more women might be encouraged to opt for female headship has been so pronounced that when the government established its first programme for female household heads in 1995 specific declaration was made in the supporting documentation that there was no intention to promote rises in lone motherhood (Chant, 1999; see also Chapter 6 in this volume).

Another set of reasons for the limited impact of targeted schemes owes to their palliative nature and small resource allocations. As argued by ECLAC (2004b: 62): ' "targetted" programmes to alleviate poverty and provide emergency aid cannot substitute for universal social policies that should be designed to overcome the chronic, structural problem of poverty by promoting enforcement of individuals' economic and social rights'.

Last, but not least, continuing gender inequalities in society at large have also acted as a brake on success. In Chile, for example, which piloted a Programme for Female Heads of Household in 1992–93, that was later extended nationally, efforts to increase women's access to employment through vocational labour training, access to childcare and so on, were tempered by the government's failure to address the social and cultural structures underlying gender segmentation in the labour market and the perpetuation of poverty among women (Arriagada, 1998: 97; Badia, 1999; see also Budowski, 2002, 2003; Marenco et al., 1998, on Costa Rica; Rico de Alonso and López Téllez, 1998: 197, on Colombia; Mayoux, 2006, and Pankurst, 2002, on savings and credit schemes for women more generally). Indeed, it is instructive that in Cuba, where there has been resistance to special welfare benefits to female heads, policies favouring greater gender equality in general, high levels of female labour force participation and the availability of support services such as day care, have all made it easier for women to raise children alone (see Safa, 1995). This endorses Moghadam's (1997) more general point that the varying economic circumstances of female-headed households depend not only on women's access to employment and property, but on social policies and their interplay with economic and political regimes in different countries (see also Neumayer and de Soysa, 2005).

CONSEQUENCES OF PERSISTING WITH THE NOTION OF A 'FEMINISATION OF POVERTY' MORE GENERALLY

Beyond the problems associated with targeting female-headed households, it is important to consider other consequences of persisting with an unqualified notion of a 'feminisation of poverty' more broadly (that is, which upholds the idea that the incidence of poverty among women is becoming greater over time). Aside from the fact that unsubstantiated assertions may provoke backlash and ridicule among those hostile to a GAD agenda, as well as provide little guidance as to how to shape appropriate policies, one unfortunate, if unintended, consequence of an overly categoric association between women and poverty is that it tends to place gender in the 'poverty trap' (Jackson, 1996).

Leading out of this, repeated emphasis on the links between women and poverty, and the idea that investing in women is one of the most efficient routes to ensuring all-round development gains, seems to have translated into a generalised bid to alleviate poverty primarily, or even exclusively, *through* women (see Jackson, 1996: 490; Kabeer, 1997: 2; Molyneux, 2001:

184; Pankhurst, 2002; Razavi, 1999: 419). As discussed earlier in the book, although so-called 'gender-responsive' poverty alleviation initiatives are often couched in the language of 'women's empowerment' efficiency often prevails over equity, with the underlying impetus being that investing in women makes 'good economic sense'. As reflected in an indicative statement by Finne (2001: 9):

> Economic progression and improvements in the quality of life for all people is more rapidly achieved where women's status is higher. This is not simply a focus on a single individual, but because of women's communal role, positive effects will be seen in the family, home, environment, children, elderly and whole communities and nations.

Such thinking is common in major institutions such as the World Bank, which talks at one level about 'empowering' women while at the same time emphasising the 'pay-offs' or 'returns' from investing in them. One particularly pertinent example is the World Bank's line that education for girls is the single most effective strategy for tackling poverty since it not only enhances their earning capacity, but has positive spin-offs for child morbidity and mortality, nutrition, and the schooling of subsequent generations (World Bank, 1994; see also UNRISD, 2005: 11; World Bank, 2000; 2002a). While not disputing these claims, nor the strategic value of arguments which urge the reduction of gender inequalities to fulfil broader societal objectives, it is important to maintain boundaries between empowerment as a route to poverty alleviation, and empowerment as a goal for women per se. Otherwise, women may simply be being used as a means to other ends, as exemplified by the more general syndrome of women working *for* development rather than vice versa (see Blumberg, 1995: 10; Elson, 1989; 1991; Jackson, 1996: 490; Kabeer, 1994: 8; Molyneux, 2001: 184; Razavi, 1999: 419; de Vylder, 2004). As summed-up by Bradshaw and Linneker (2001: 207): 'in general gender has been included as a variant on the poverty problem. That is, women have been added in to existing policies most usually for their capacity as efficient service providers rather than as people with rights, agendas and needs'.

Other consequences of an over-reliance on the unpaid or underpaid labour of women in anti-poverty initiatives include the reinforcement of gender divisions and discrimination, the burdening of women with the costs of cutbacks in public spending, and few tangible benefits for women as 'autonomous individuals entitled to rights and benefits related to activities designed to improve their quality of life' (ECLAC, 2004b: 54; also Rodenberg, 2004: 25; UNRISD, 2005: 139). Such observations find fertile ground in the Mexican programme, *Progresa/Oportunidades*, which ties cash transfers and food handouts to 'co-responsibility' on the part of parents to ensure children's school attendance and health-care usage. In relying mainly on the unpaid volunteer work of mothers, Molyneux (2006a) claims that the programme has 'built upon, endorsed and entrenched a highly non-egalitarian model of the family', in which women's position as a 'conduit of policy' is motivated primarily by the calculated improvements of well-being of others (see also González de la Rocha, 2003a: 25).

While not denying that increasing women's income-generating capacity can go some way to addressing material poverty, as well as giving women greater confidence (see Mukhopadhyay, 2000), this can also come at the cost of draining other resources such as time and energy, or curtailing opportunities to save money through reproductive labour, or even changing intra-household gender dynamics in adverse ways. For example, evidence suggests that growing pockets of social, educational and economic vulnerability among men, coupled with unease about wives working, can manifest itself in violence in the home and in the community, in drug or alcohol abuse and other forms of disaffected behaviour (see Chant and Gutmann, 2000; Moser and McIlwaine, 2000a; 2000b; UNESCO, 1997: 6).

Indeed, aside from the costs attached to making women responsible not only for curing their own poverty, but reducing poverty more generally, that little room has yet been made in feminisation of poverty discussions for men and gender relations means that we know little about which other groups face growing threats of poverty or what the repercussions might be in terms of inter-group dynamics. Patriarchal structures both within and outside the home assist in explaining, for example, how micro-credit programmes for women often lead to their accumulating greater debt where husbands commandeer the loans (see Mayoux, 2006), or why the relationship between women's employment and empowerment remains a 'vexed one' (Moore, 1988: 111; see also McClenaghan, 1997; Tiano, 2001). In short, the preoccupation with women and income in the 'feminisation of poverty' is dangerous for two main reasons: first, because, analytically, it occludes the social dimensions of gender and of poverty, and second, because in policy terms, it translates into single-issue, single group interventions which have little power to destabilise deeply embedded structures of gender inequality in the home, the labour market, and other institutions (Chant, 2006; Gangopadhyay and Wadhwa, 2003; Mayoux, 2006; Rodenberg, 2004). As Baden (1999: 7) has argued: 'The "feminisation of poverty" argument is not helpful if it is used to justify poverty reduction efforts which uncritically target women-headed households or even "women" in general, but which do not challenge the underlying "rules of the game".'

CONCLUSION

In summarising this chapter, three factors are in need of emphasis. The first is that there is little evidence to support the principal tenets of 'feminisation of poverty' orthodoxy, namely, that the incidence of income poverty is greater among women than men, that this gender-differentiated incidence is rising, and that women-headed households are systematically the 'poorest of the poor'.

A second, and related, point is that the 'feminisation of poverty' conveys little of the complexity of gendered experiences of poverty or diversity among women. In line with Lampietti and Stalker's (2000: 2) argument that: 'Headship analysis cannot and should not be considered an acceptable substitute for gender and poverty analysis', one of main tasks is surely to interrogate the often reactive monolithic stereotypes which have come to be associated with – if not created by – 'feminisation of poverty'. This means going beyond headship, and exploring in much greater detail which particular women are at greatest risk of privation in relation to other women as well as to men, and how this varies, and is changing, across space and time.

The third point is that the ways in which the 'feminisation of poverty' has translated into practice – primarily in the form of targeted interventions for women and female-headed households – seem unlikely to make major inroads into changing the gender status quo, or women's poverty burdens. While some alternatives are suggested in Chapter 7, the next three chapters attempt to assess whether in The Gambia, the Philippines and Costa Rica anything akin to a 'feminisation of poverty' is occurring, and if so, on what grounds.

NOTES

1. I have chosen to concentrate on female headship in this chapter because this has been such an important element in the 'feminisation of poverty' thesis, besides which I am more interested in looking at women (and men) as individuals and taking into consideration such factors as age and position in the household in the case study discussions (Chapters 4–6).
2. For many countries in the North, low levels of public assistance are held to account for the poverty of lone mother households (see, for example, Edwards and Duncan, 1996; Hardey and Glover, 1991: 94; Hobson, 1994: 180; Mädge and Neusüss, 1994: 1420; Millar, 1992: 150), although some assert that state support for women of various forms (for example, full employment) can greatly increase the viability of lone motherhood (see Goldberg, 1998; Moghadam, 1998: 243; Ypeij and Steenbeek, 2001).
3. In the context of research on informal mutual insurance networks in Southern Ghana, Goldstein et al. (2001: 7) note that these do not always work because people fail to ask others for assistance. This tends to apply more to women than men, the main reason being

that: 'not asking largely reflects internalising rejection, or not wanting to incur the transaction costs associated with asking'. González de la Rocha (2003b: 23) echoes that it is necessary to take into account that greater embeddedness in a network of relations generally implies more obligations, while Yeandle et al. (2003) refer to 'problem debt' where inability to pay back loans from friends and family can undermine relationships and have negative social and economic consequences.

Another factor, pointed up in relation to Afro-Caribbean women in the Netherlands, is that declining favours from kin can be a means of reducing interference in their lives (Ypeij and Steenbeek, 2001: 78).

4. It is important to note that the overall average incidence of female headship remains higher in the richer than poorer nations of the world (see Varley, 1996: table 2).

5. Thirty-two of the studies had been conducted in Latin America, 20 in Africa and 14 in Asia, between 1979 and 1989 (see Buvinic and Gupta, 1993, 1997). The indicators of poverty comprised total and/or per capita household income and consumption, AEUs, expenditure, access to services, and ownership of land or assets.

6. Context is highly important here however. For example, a study of four rural and urban communities in Nicaragua in the aftermath of Hurricane Mitch indicated that as many as 16 per cent of households reported no one working at the time of interview, and those households with only one earner (42 per cent) were the single biggest category (Bradshaw, 2002: 18).

7. Although 'family breakdown' is often associated with higher rates of delinquency among young people, it is interesting that an in-depth longitudinal study of youth gangs in Managua, Nicaragua, found that membership was not consistently influenced by family background or any other factors (see Rodgers, 2006).

8. This does not appear to be the case in Nicaragua where female heads expressed preference to receive help from institutional providers rather than kin or neighbours (Linneker, 2003). Many women in Costa Rica also seem to have welcomed the support granted through targeted state initiatives (see Budowksi, 2003; also Chapter 6 in this volume).

4. Gender, generation and poverty in The Gambia

INTRODUCTION

Having traced some general parameters of gendered poverty in the Global South, in this chapter on The Gambia, and in the following two on the Philippines and Costa Rica, my aim is to ascertain if poverty is becoming progressively 'feminised' and, if so, on what grounds. Acknowledging the importance of both 'objective' and 'subjective' interpretations of poverty, each of the three chapters draws on a combination of primary and secondary source material. The latter comprises statistical, bibliographic and policy documentation, whereas the former consists of findings from interviews conducted with personnel from key state organisations, NGOs and international agencies, and with poor women and men at the grassroots. As identified in Chapter 1, low-income respondents were drawn from different age groups and their views are vital not only in highlighting subjective experiences of poverty, but in revealing the extent to which poverty affects (or at least is perceived to affect) women and men at different stages of the life course and how this is changing (or not) over time.

The first section of each chapter provides a general synopsis of key characteristics of development, poverty and gender in the country concerned, including discussion of pertinent factors such as education, employment, wages and incomes, and demographic and household transitions. Attention is also given to state, international and NGO initiatives to reduce poverty and gender inequality. In the second part of each chapter I draw on my primary fieldwork with women and men at the grassroots, and with key institutional personnel, to explore the personal opinions of different stakeholders on gender and generational dimensions of poverty. While most of the comparative analysis between countries is left to Chapter 7, some reference is made to data on the Philippines and Costa Rica, especially in tables.

DEVELOPMENT AND POVERTY IN THE GAMBIA

Gambian Society and Economy in Brief

The Gambia was a British colony for three centuries prior to gaining its independence in 1965. Although for the first five years The Gambia was a constitutional monarchy within the Commonwealth, following a 1970 referendum it became a republic (UNSD, 2005). Currently The Gambia is nominally a democracy with six parties, although the Alliance for Patriotic Reorientation and Construction (APRC, formerly the Armed Forces Provisional Ruling Council), under the leadership of President Yahya Jammeh, has been in power since his 1994 military coup. Although the People's Progressive Party (PPP) of the displaced former President, Sir Dawda Jawara, was not allowed back into politics until 2001, the supposed restoration of democracy with the 'Second Republic' came in 1997. Even then, another party – the National Convention Party (NCP) – is in coalition with the APRC which holds 46 out of a total of 53 seats in the National Assembly (48 of which are elected by universal suffrage) (EIU, 2006a: 23). The only major opposition party to have made a mark to date is the United Democratic Party (UDP) which has a staunchly civilian following. This is headed by the lawyer, Ousainou Darboe, who managed to garner 32.7 per cent of the votes against Jammeh's 52.9 per cent in the 2001 election. Yet although the UDP was also a major player in an attempt to consolidate a multi-party opposition coalition – the National Alliance for Democracy and Development (NADD) – this fragmented in the run-up to the 2006 presidential election, leading to a 'landslide' victory and third term for Jammeh.

Administratively The Gambia is divided into the seat of government and capital territory – Banjul City Council-Kanifing Municipal Council (BCC-KMC), where my grassroots interviews were carried out – plus five divisions (see Figures 4.1 and 4.2). Each of these is headed by a Governor who is presidentially appointed, as are the Chiefs who head the 35 district sub-divisions. At village level power is in the hands of elected *alkolulu*, who number 1800. Controversially, and somewhat paradoxically, current plans for decentralisation of governance in The Gambia include the proposal that *alkolulu* might also be appointed by the president.

The Gambia is one of the smallest countries in West Africa, occupying a land area of only 11 300 km², and except for its coastal perimeter, being completely encircled by its much larger neighbour, Senegal. Lying between 13 and 14 degrees north of the equator, The Gambia has a sub-tropical Sahelian climate with a three-month rainy season between July and October.

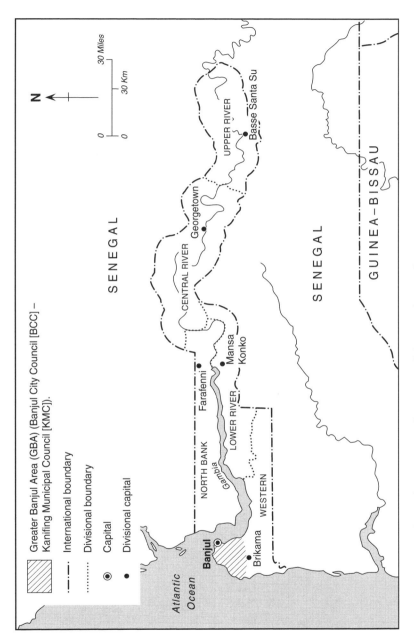

Figure 4.1 The Gambia: administrative divisions and divisional capitals

127

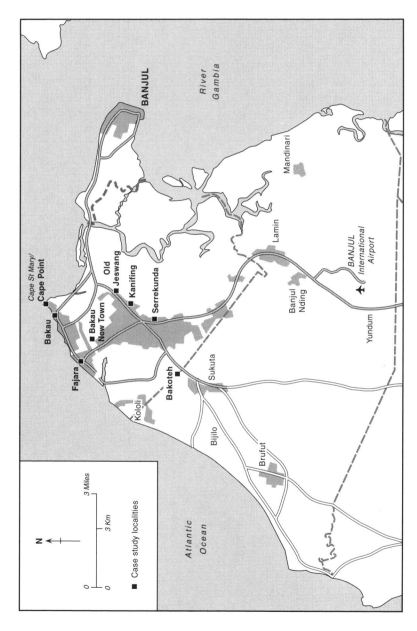

Figure 4.2 Greater Banjul Area: case study localities

As pointed out in Chapter 1, The Gambia is also the poorest of the three case study countries. This is partly due to its weak and non-diversified economy deriving, *inter alia*, from its small size and limited internal market, the population as of 2005 being only 1.5 millions (EIU, 2006a). This, in turn, is widely held responsible for the fact that as of 2003 The Gambia was more aid dependent than it was in the 1970s, with the ratio of aid to Gross National Product (GNP) being greater than 20 per cent (SPACO, 2003d: 25). While more than 50 per cent of foreign aid goes to economic management and development planning (ibid.: 26), the country continues to carry a heavy debt burden. In 2003 external debt amounted to US$576 millions, leading to a ratio of debt service to GDP of 18 per cent, and consuming more than 40 per cent of The Gambia's annual domestic revenue (DOSFEA, 2004: 17; SG, 2005).

One of the Gambia's few sources of export earnings is groundnuts, which renders the country vulnerable both to vagaries of the weather, as well as to fluctuations in prices of primary commodities on the world market. Even if better rainfall in the last three years has led to a pick-up in production (EIU, 2006a: 29), as recently as 2002 drought resulted in the halving of the groundnut harvest, which, together with a 30 per cent reduction in other agricultural commodities, provoked a 3 per cent drop in real GDP, and the declaration of a National Emergency on Crop Failure and Food Shortage (RTG, 2003a: 6 and 18).

The only other major foreign exchange earners are the trade in re-export and international tourism. The former has long been one of The Gambia's most secure sectors on account of reliance of landlocked countries such as Mali and Burkina Faso for channelling to Europe goods such as rice, sugar and textiles (SPACO, 2003d: 11). Located in one of the busiest import and export points in West Africa, the sector is also highly remunerative, with the value of the Gambian re-export trade in 2003 outstripping that of groundnut exports seven times over (EIU, 2005a: 25).

The international tourist industry, which has a 35-year history, is also fairly buoyant, employing around 12 000 people, and, as of the late 1990s, generating over US$30 billions in foreign exchange and 13.3 per cent of GDP (ITC, 2001: table 1; PPTP, 2004: table 2). Air charter tourists (mainly from the UK and Germany) rose from 58 000 a year to 91 500 between the early and late 1990s, with hopes that this will reach 100 000 in the near future (EIU, 2005a: 29). This said, while tourism has been responsible for major FDI increases, much of the infrastructure is managed by expatriates and serviced by foreign tour companies and airlines, which, as for developing countries more generally, can result in significant leakage of profits. A second issue is that the sector has proved vulnerable to national and international political events. For example, Jammeh's coup of 1994 not only provoked a reduction in aid flows and private investment in the mid-1990s, but a fall-off in tourist arrivals (IMF/IDA, 2002: 1). On top of these difficulties, The Gambia's 'mass market, winter sun' tourism is seasonal (Roe et al., 2002: 1). With the drop in tourism coinciding with the cropping period, the rainy summer months are a particularly lean time (SPACO et al., 2002b: 22). Following the establishment of The Gambia Tourism Authority, current plans for the sector are greater involvement by Gambian nationals in tourism investment and infrastructure, the expansion of eco-tourism, cultural and conference tourism, diversification of countries of origin, and the upgrading of tourism products such as luxury hotels (see DOSFEA, 2006: 77–81; GOTG, 2000: 13).

With the latter expected to attract higher-spending visitors and to improve tourism receipts, there is some cause for optimism, especially given the healthy performance of the re-export trade, increased groundnut production, and some diversification into non-traditional agricultural produce such as cotton, sesame, fresh fruit and vegetables.[1] Real GDP growth in the last three years has sustained an average of 5 per cent or more, the national currency (dalasi) has shown greater stability, and in 2005, inflation was lower than previous years at only 5.9 per cent (EIU, 2006a: 24).

Population and demographic dynamics

The Gambia is a predominantly Muslim country, with only 5 per cent declaring themselves Christian, and a further 5 per cent estimated to practice animism (Bjinsdorp and Montgomery, 2003: 5). While there are more conversions to Islam than to Christianity, the country is noted for its religious tolerance, and respect for others' beliefs and practices.

The major ethnic groups in The Gambian are the Mandinka (39.5 per cent), Fula (18.8 per cent), and Wolof (14.6 per cent). However, smaller groups include the Jola and Karoninka (10.6 per cent), Serahuli (9.9 per cent), Serere (2.8 per cent), Creole and Aku Marabout (1.8 per cent), Manjago (0.8 per cent), Bambara (0.8 per cent), and 'other Gambians' (mainly of Lebanese origin) (1.5 per cent) (FASE, 2003). Intermarriage is also common (Wadda, 2000).

Although the official language of the country is English, and, being the medium of instruction in schools is most widely spoken among youth, most people speak at least two indigenous languages, with Wolof being the most common. Ethnic and linguistic diversity is arguably on the increase given the influx of migrants and refugees from other parts of West Africa who now constitute around 10 per cent of the population. Just as much as many Gambians seek work overseas, being more peaceful and politically stable than many of its neighbours, The Gambia has also proved to be an important migrant destination itself, especially from the Economic Organisation of West African States (ECOWAS) countries which have been afflicted by war, such as Sierra Leone, Liberia and Senegal. While in 2004 one-fifth of overseas migrants were constituted by women who were mainly refugees from Sierra Leone and Liberia,[2] the source countries of male migrants were more diverse, including Guinea, Guinea Bissau, Mali and Nigeria (see Toulmin and Guèye, 2003).

Migrants from most of the above-mentioned countries work in agriculture, the restaurant trade or security services. However, Nigerians tend to fill skilled positions in such areas as finance, law, accountancy and medicine, often left vacant by the external migration of skilled Gambians, especially men (see Badjie, 2003: 3; Wadda, 2000). Non-indigenous Gambians are also estimated to own around 60 per cent of informal sector businesses (Badjie, 2003: 18–19; Sanneh, 2003: 8). The extent to which international migration to The Gambia has sustained the country's high rates of population growth is not clear, although estimates point to the fact that out of the 4.2 per cent annual growth rate in the inter-censal period 1983–93, only two-thirds could be attributed to natural increase (Taal, 2003: 14). Whatever the case, growth has caused population density to double from from 64 to 128 persons per km^2 between 1983 and 2003 (DOSFEA, 2006: 21).

Although annual population growth declined to 2.8 per cent per annum between 1993 and 2003, population size increased by 31 per cent (DOSFEA, 2006: 21). While migrants are often scapegoated for flooding the labour market, straining the country's skeletal public services and exacerbating poverty, this should not detract from the fact that The Gambia has one of the highest total fertility rates (TFRs) in the world, with each woman still giving birth to an average of nearly five children (Table 1.2). While there is some evidence that couples are beginning to limit family size, teenage pregnancy, early marriage and high infant and child mortality (at 130 per 1000 births for boys, and 116 for girls – WHO, 2005b), conspire against this. Additional factors are that nearly 45 per cent of the population is under 16 (Wadda, 2000), and contraceptive prevalence low, at only 24 per cent in the capital Banjul and 9 per cent nationally, with women with no education having a much lower level of contraceptive use (8 per cent) than those with secondary or higher education (18 per cent) (RTG, 2003b: 231). Socially, the use of condoms within marriage (even polygamous marriages) is frowned upon because it implies that one partner is being unfaithful to the other (Shaw and Jawo, 2000: 73). Abortion is illegal in The Gambia and punishable by life imprisonment under Section 198 of the Criminal Code (GOTG, 1998: 18). This is a major reason why the maternal mortality rate (1050 per 100 000 live births) is one of the highest in sub-Saharan Africa (GOTG/UNICEF, 2000: 17).

Although The Gambia's Family Planning Association, which is a member of the International Planned Parenthood Federation (IPPF), was established in the 1970s, and educational literature stresses the strategic importance of lower fertility for poverty reduction (see METG, 1997), one major barrier is religion. While the United Nations Fund for Population Activities (UNFPA) is working with Islamic NGOs to promote, *inter alia*, reproductive health and the rights of the girl child (UNFPA The Gambia, 2003), Islamic leaders regularly resort to 'virulent campaigns' against the use of contraceptives on radio, television and during Friday prayers (GOTG/UNICEF, 2000: 36). Aside from the fact that many Muslims claim that contraception is 'against the Koran', some men have a vested interest in high fertility for economic reasons, especially in farming communities, where the male TFR is 12, as opposed to 6.8 among women (see Shaw and Jawo, 2000: 73; also Sear et al., 2007).

Although potentially exerting more pressure on agricultural land, the prospects are that youth, who have more education than their elders and who generally aspire to 'modern' careers, will move instead to urban settlements on the coast. Indeed, as of 1993, just over one-quarter (26.1 per cent) of the national population was concentrated in the Greater Banjul Area (GBA), which covers just 16 per cent of national territory, and consists of Banjul together with KMC which comprises Serrekunda and smaller urban settlements such as Bakau and Fajara (Figure 4.2). By 2003 the concentration of population in this area had risen to 47 per cent (SPACO, 2003a: 29), constituting the bulk of the national urban population which currently stands at 50.4 per cent (DOSFEA, 2006: 21). Urban migration is not only driven by the lure of higher earnings, but the alleged irrelevance of the school curriculum to people in rural areas. This has depleted the rural resource base and is widely alleged to have contributed to urban unemployment, drug abuse, and 'bumstering' (loitering and petty crime) (see TANGO, 2001: iii).

Employment

Leading on from the above, employment opportunities in The Gambia are limited in rural and urban areas alike. The majority of the workforce (67.9 per cent) relies on agricultural production which commands such low profits that many have to supplement their incomes with non-farm activities such as tailoring, carpentry, soap-making, pottery and transportation, often in conjunction with seasonal migration (see Tables 4.1 and 4.2). In urban areas there is only a small formal sector, employing a mere 10 per cent of the labour force, and industry is minimal, accounting for less than 8 per cent of GDP and engaging only 4.3 per cent of the workforce (GOTG,

Table 4.1   Employment in The Gambia

Branch of employment	% of workforce
Agriculture	67.9
Fishing	1.0
Mining	0.3
Manufacturing	4.3
Utilities	0.5
Construction	1.5
Transport, storage and communications	2.4
Wholesale and retail commerce	9.7
Hotels and restaurants	1.2
Finance and real estate	0.5
Public administration	1.4
Social and recreational services	5.1
Personal services	3.6
International	0.6
Total	100.0

Source: SPACO (2003a: table 11).

Table 4.2   The Gambia: branch of employment of household members by poverty status

Branch of employment	Extremely poor (%)	Poor (%)	Non-poor (%)	All (%)
Agriculture	47.4	16.6	35.9	100.0
Fishing	20.8	13.2	66.0	100.0
Manufacturing	11.9	13.6	74.6	100.0
Construction	13.4	11.0	75.6	100.0
Transport, storage and communications	3.9	18.6	77.5	100.0
Wholesale and retail commerce	9.6	12.8	77.7	100.0
Hotels and restaurants	6.0	6.0	88.1	100.0
Public administration	8.9	6.3	84.8	100.0
Social and recreational services	8.2	13.3	78.5	100.0
Personal services	11.6	19.2	69.2	100.0

Source: SPACO (2003a: table 10).

Table 4.3   The Gambia: employment status of household members by poverty status

Employment status	Extremely poor (%)	Poor (%)	Non-poor (%)	All (%)
Employer	0.4	0.6	1.0	0.7
Private sector salaried employee	2.1	8.6	14.6	9.2
Public sector salaried employee	0.8	3.7	9.0	5.3
Own account worker	59.1	58.6	59.4	59.2
Family helper	37.7	28.6	16.0	25.6
All	100.0	100.0	100.0	100.0

Source: SPACO (2003a: table 9).

2000: 13). Even in the GBA only 34 per cent of households have a salaried worker (SPACO, 2004: 28), with the bulk of the economically active engaged in petty commerce or other own-account activities such as plumbing, metalwork and hair-plaiting (see SPACO et al., 2002a: 20). Own-account workers tend to be poorer than their salaried counterparts (GOTG, 2000: 60; see also Table 4.3), with low levels of literacy and vocational training viewed as constraints on small-scale entrepreneurialism (see FASE, 2003: 7; Sanneh, 2003: 8).

Unemployment is extremely high – at 26 per cent – with particular concerns expressed about youth unemployment, especially in the 16–25-year age cohort (DOSFEA, 2006: 118; GOTG, 2000: 147). This is in part due to a mismatch between content and quality of educational provision and labour market needs (see Chant and Jones, 2005). A commonly voiced opinion is that boys in particular are becoming 'over-educated' and either encounter few openings in the labour market deemed to be sufficiently highly paid, or lack the necessary skills or capital to set up in self-employment (Sanneh, 2003: 8; TANGO, 2000b: 4).

As it is, even where people do have an education, access to employment is constrained by personalism, with 'who you know' often being more important than 'what you know' or formal levels of education or training (see Chant and Jones, 2005). Some constraints on labour market mobility are also posed by the 'caste system' whereby certain manual trades are deemed unsuitable for people of 'noble' ancestry (see Box 4.2).

Education

Literacy levels in The Gambia are very low, with only 37.8 per cent of persons 15 years or more being able to read and write (see Table 4.4), even

Table 4.4   The Gambia, Philippines and Costa Rica: selected features of literacy and education

	The Gambia	Philippines	Costa Rica
Adult literacy rate (% age 15 and above) 2001	37.8	95.1	95.7
Youth literacy rate (% age 15–24 years) 2001	58.6	98.8	98.3
Combined primary, secondary and tertiary gross enrolment ratio (%) 2001	47	80	66
Net primary enrolment ratio (%) 2000–2001	69	98	91
Net secondary enrolment ratio (%) 2000–2001	35	53	49
Children reaching grade 5 (%) 1999–2000	69	–	80
Public expenditure on education as % of GDP			
1990	3.8	2.9	4.4
1998–2000	2.7	4.2	4.4
Public expenditure on education as % of total government expenditure			
1990	14.6	10.1	20.8
1998–2000	14.2	20.6	–

Note: – = No data.

Source: UNDP (2003a: tables 1, 9 and 10).

if major strides have been taken to increase enrolment in primary and secondary education in the last decade. For example, rising government expenditure on education (equating to 60 per cent of all expenditure on social services in the latter part of the 1990s – GOTG, 2000: 52), helped to underpin an annual growth rate of 8 per cent in enrolment in lower basic schools[3] between 1990–91 and 1997–98 (SPACO, 2003a: 27). Even if the growth rate was only 4 per cent per annum between 1995 and 2001, by 2000, net enrolment in primary education was 60 per cent, compared with 44 per cent in 1990 (RTG, 2003b: 18). This has helped to boost the literacy rate of 15–24-year-olds to 60 per cent, from a level of 29 per cent in 1980. Moreover, attempts have been made to bring English into the curriculum in *madrassah* (Islamic) schools, where many poorer families send their children, especially girls, for 'moral and religious reasons' (GOTG, 2000: 122).

With The Gambia having become (in 2003) one of 18 countries selected for the Education For All – Fast Track Initiative (EFA-FTI), there is likely to be further progress towards universal primary schooling. In line with the MDGs (see Chapter 1), the major goal of The Gambia's 2004–15 Education Policy is to provide 'quality basic education for all', alongside expansion of non-formal education, skills training and appropriate technology (DOSFEA, 2004: 35). This said, donor pressures to increase the proportion of the education budget to primary schooling have de facto reduced funding for secondary schools and there are concerns that the quality of primary education could be compromised by emphasis on numbers (see Martin, 2003: 14).[4] It should also be taken into consideration that there are persistent rural–urban disparities, with the enrolment rate being only 45 per cent in the former, compared with 64 per cent in the latter (RTG, 2003b: 11).

An additional factor which could continue to militate against significant increases in education is poverty, it being estimated that over 90 per cent of children not in school (the majority of whom are female) are from households in the two lowest income quintiles (RTG, 2002: 102).

Although fees for state primary ('lower basic') education have been waived, and for girls, fees for 'upper basic' (junior secondary) as well, there are many other costs – for example, for uniforms, exercise books, pens and so on (GOTG, 2000: 110; see also Ansell, 2003; Brydon and Legge, 1996; ILO, 2003a). Moreover, while most primary schools are in the state sector, the majority of senior secondary schools (21 out of 26) are private, usually run by Christian or Muslim missions, do not receive subsidies from the government and have limited enrolment (see Taal, 2003: 20). Similar provisos obtain to the tertiary sector which comprises University of The Gambia, founded in 1999, and three major higher education establishments: the Gambia Technical Training Institute (GTTI), the Gambia College, and the Management Development Institute (MDI) (GOTG, 2000: 52).

In a situation where schooling puts pressure on exiguous resources, non-attendance and drop-out are common (Martin, 2003: ch. 6), and many children are forced to engage in remunerated activities if they wish to further their education (Chant and Jones, 2005). Notwithstanding the frequent under-enumeration of child labour in national statistics (Robson, 1996), official data point to 16.4 per cent of 10–14-year-olds being in work, with higher levels of economic activity among girls than boys in both the 10–14 and 15–19 year cohorts (the respective female economic activity rates being 7.8 per cent and 13.1 per cent, and males' 4.5 per cent and 7.9 per cent) (GOTG, 2000: 66).[5] That this particularly affects poor households is borne out by previous research on 30 young people in the GBA, where around half had engaged in a remunerative activity by the time they were 11 or 12 years old, and in unpaid household tasks by the age of 7 or 8 (Chant and Jones, 2005).

Recognising that child labour and education are not necessarily 'polarised choices for poor households' (Subrahmanian, 2002: 403; also Punch, 2002; 2003), few young people seem to see part-time work as detrimental to their academic progress. Instead, they are often proud of their contributions to household income and their ability to resist what they deem to be an unappealing situation of having to rely on others. Nonetheless, as noted by Bjinsdorp and Montgomery (2003: 32): 'In African culture, the family rather than the individual is the most important unit and this clashes, at times, with the best interests of the child.' The fact that many young people spend up to four hours a day in a combination of paid and unpaid work, clearly robs them of time for homework, after-school private study, rest and play. When considering the more general evidence that child labour is a major factor in perpetuating poverty cycles, and the positive correlation between years of schooling and increased lifelong income (see Harper, 2004), the situation does not bode well for poverty, especially among women.

Health and Other Social Services

Education is not the only service to which Gambians have limited access. Although 84 per cent of the population purportedly have a water source at their disposal, piped supplies are often closed off for several hours at a time, and uncovered wells are vulnerable to contamination (SPACO, 2003a: 15). Only 37 per cent of the population has access to sanitary facilities and electricity. The latter is not only mainly confined to urban areas, but is also erratic with frequent and lengthy power cuts (TANGO, 2001: 8). The poor state of rubbish collection and use of idle public land for dumping are such that in April 2004 President Jammeh launched the controversial and unpopular measure of 'Operation Clean The Nation'. This bans traffic between 9 a.m. and 1 p.m. on the first Saturday of each month during which time people are expected to clean the streets and their own compounds. Somewhat ironically, the lack of garbage trucks to cope with disposal forces people to light polluting fires in open spaces.

Adding to the problem of service deficiencies is the poor condition of housing. Demand has risen with population growth and urbanisation leading to overcrowding, high rents relative to income, and, more recently, homelessness (see GOTG, 2000). Public support for housing is extremely limited despite the existence of three agencies to address provision, and that some schemes are alleged to have contributed to rural–urban migration (TANGO, 2001: ii–iii).

Notwithstanding some expansion in the health service in the last 30 years, and the fact that the government's stated aims are to ensure delivery by qualified and motivated staff, economic accessibility, and availability of quality essential drugs, vaccines and other medical supplies (SPACO, 2004: 3), per capita annual expenditure on health in 2002 was only US$18 (WHO, 2005b). There are only three state hospitals in the whole country, shortages of personnel and beds are commonplace, and given the dearth of ambulances, emergencies force people to use private vehicles, taxis or 'horse carts' (GOTG/UNICEF, 2000: 17). The frequent absence of drugs in government facilities exposes people to exploitation by commercial pharmacies (SPACO, 2004: 24), with the introduction of user fees for many services such as operations, X-rays and laboratory tests hitting the poor particularly hard. Indeed, recent calculations on the affordability of health care indicated that the majority of Gambians cannot meet their health needs (SPACO, 2004: 23). Although the non-poor spend more on private health, and some of the poor resort to the cheaper option of traditional healers and marabouts (GOTG, 2000: 98), health expenditure constitutes the second biggest item in household budgets (18.7 per cent), after food (39.1 per cent) (SPACO, 2004: 38).

The Gambia has only recently (2002) started training its own doctors, and although the number of doctors and dentists working in government-run health services increased by over 150 per cent between 1987 and 1997 (GOTG/UNICEF, 2000: 16), The Gambia still has only 0.2 physicians per 1000 persons (RTG, 2002: 38). Moreover, more than four-fifths of doctors in the public sector are expatriates, mainly from Cuba, which poses problems of language and different medical regimes (GOTG/UNICEF, 2000: 16; RTG, 2002: 39). Another source of vulnerability is that as much as 44.6 per cent of the funding for The Gambia's health service comes from external sources compared with only 2.8 per cent in the Philippines, and 1.3 per cent in Costa Rica (WHO, 2005b).

Despite the fact that The Gambia adopted the Primary Health Care (PHC) approach as far back as 1979, and has aimed to provide rural settlements with 400 or more inhabitants with both a Village Health Worker (VHW) and Traditional Birth Attendant (TBA), coverage is less than 60 per cent. This undoubtedly helps to explain why preventable communicable diseases such as malaria, acute respiratory infections, and diarrhoea still account for 60 per cent of child deaths (GOTG, 1998: 28). It is also disturbing that even in Banjul, where the last few decades have seen some signs of a 'health transition' marked by the progressive emergence of degenerative conditions such as cancer, deaths by 'diseases of poverty' continue to prevail (van der Sande et al., 2000).

The rising prevalence of sexually transmitted infections (STIs) is also a cause for concern. While low compared with many other sub-Saharan African countries, The Gambia's HIV/AIDS adult prevalence rate doubled between 1993–95 and 2000 to 1.6 per cent (RTG, 2003b: 21). By 2004 the number of people living with HIV/AIDS (PLWHA) had grown to an estimated 8000–13 000, and in one of the two support groups in the country – the Santa Yalla Support Society – women comprised 65.5 per cent of its 421 members.

Some of the factors held responsible for the mounting incidence of HIV/AIDS include lack of knowledge, unprotected sex, wife inheritance, the sharing of cutting instruments at circumcision ceremonies, and mother-to-child transmission (RTG, 2003b: 21; SPACO, 2003a: 14). In light of this the National Aids Control Programme of the Department of State for Health (DOSH), has not only played a major role in attempting to create awareness (see Figure 4.3), but also expanded provision of testing kits, training for health workers, and schemes to increase income among HIV/AIDS-affected persons. Nonetheless, it looks unlikely at present that The Gambia will meet MDG 6's target of halving or reversing the spread of HIV/AIDS (RTG, 2003b: 36; see also Box 1.3).

As for elderly and disabled citizens, support is extremely meagre, with a substantial number being forced to beg outside shops or at traffic junctions. Given low average life expectancy (Table 1.2), the proportion of people aged 60 or more is relatively small – at only 5.8 per cent. However, those who lack children or relatives able to help them out are at a severe disadvantage, with a micro-level survey conducted in Kanifing by The Gambian Association of Non-Governmental Organisations (TANGO)[6] concluding that the isolated elderly are at a disproportionate risk of poverty (TANGO, 2001: 11).

Individuals in such circumstances are relatively rare, but apply where men have split with their wives and no longer have contact with children, or where people suffer from a disability. Another group are people who have migrated whether from overseas or intra-nationally, who have reached the end of their working lives and lost ties with kin. The needs of this population have at least been acknowledged in the opening of The Gambia's first residential care home for the elderly, opened in Bakoteh in 2003, with 90 per cent funding from the World Bank, and 10 per cent from the Department of State for Social Welfare (DOSSW).

Poverty Levels and Trends

Mapping poverty in the Gambia is fraught with difficulty, not only on account of long lapses between poverty assessments (and their publication) but changes in the construction of poverty lines over time (see DOSFEA, 2006: 19).[7] Bearing in mind these caveats, it would appear that income poverty in The Gambia has been on the increase since the early 1990s, from

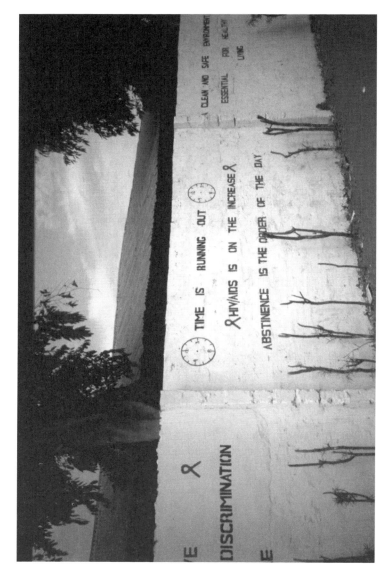

Note: Photograph by Sylvia Chant.

Figure 4.3 The Gambia: HIV/AIDS prevention campaign

Table 4.5   Poverty in The Gambia, 1992–2003

	Total population (%)	Greater Banjul (%)	Other urban population (%)	Rural population (%)
1992				
Extremely poor	18	5	9	23
Poor[a]	34	22	49	64
Non-poor	66	78	51	36
1998[b]				
Extremely poor	29.7	7	22	45
Poor	46.9	21	48	61
Non-poor	53.1	79	52	39
2003[c]				
Extremely poor	–	–	–	–
Poor	61	10.6[d]	57	63
Non-poor	39	89.4	43	37

Notes:
–   = No data.
a.   Percentages for the poor in this table include the extremely poor.
b.   1998 figures adjusted for comparative purposes using a Consumer Price Index based inflation of the 1992 poverty lines. When not adjusted, the figure for the total population in poverty in 1998 comes to 69 per cent, and to 37 per cent for extreme poverty (see RTG, 2003b: 1).
c.   No published data from the 2003 Integrated Household Poverty Survey were available on extreme poverty at the time of compiling this table.
d.   In the breakdown of the 2003 survey provided by DOSFEA (2006) Banjul was used rather than Greater Banjul.

Sources: DOSFEA (2006: 19); RTG (2002: 23); SPACO (2003a: table 1); TANGO (2001: 7).

38 per cent of the population in 1992, to 47 per cent by 1998, and 61 per cent in 2003 (see Table 4.5). Moreover, there are indications that inequality has grown, with the Gini coefficient rising from 0.47 to 0.50 between 1992 and 2000.[8] Although 'human development' definitions of poverty appear liberally in almost every Gambian policy document on the subject (see RTG, 2002: 4), and a major self-rated poverty (SRP) exercise conducted in 2000 revealed that 79 per cent of the population deemed themselves to be poor (GOTG, 2000: 42), trends in poverty are officially determined through money-metric methods. Given the difficulties of getting data on incomes, expenditure, together with the value of subsistence production, is used as a proxy (ibid.: 23; also DOSFEA, 2006: 19).

Beyond a higher incidence of poverty in rural than urban areas (63.3 per cent versus 57.2 per cent), there is a long-standing pattern for large

Table 4.6   Poverty by age cohort in The Gambia

Age group (years)	Extremely poor (%)	Poor (%)	Non-poor (%)	All (%)
0–4	15.0	14.9	14.0	14.4
5–9	18.0	17.2	14.8	16.1
10–19	25.9	24.8	21.6	23.4
20–39	24.2	26.3	31.5	28.5
40–59	11.0	12.7	12.7	11.9
60+	5.9	5.9	5.4	5.7
Total	100.0	100.0	100.0	100.0

Note: Figures taken directly from source, but do not add up exactly to 100 in poor column possibly due to rounding.

Source: RTG (2002: 25).

households to be disproportionately at risk. In 2003, for example, the incidence of poverty among households with one to three persons was only 18.9 per cent compared with 53.9 per cent among households with seven to nine members, and 73.4 per cent among households of ten persons or more (DOSFEA, 2006: 22). This is significant since average household size in The Gambia only fell slightly – from 8.95 to 8.61 – between 1993 and 2003 (ibid.: 21).

Official data also reveal a greater likelihood of poverty at both ends of the age spectrum (see Table 4.6). Among youth, the main factors seem to be poor educational and vocational provision and lack of employment opportunities (see Badjie, 2003; FASE, 2003: 7), whereas the elderly are most likely to be poor where they have no work or retirement benefits (RTG, 2002: 27; TANGO, 2001: 12). Even if only 0.5 per cent of senior citizens live alone, and as many as one-quarter of household heads are aged 60 or more, calculations by Kakwani and Subbarao (2005: 13) suggest that 68.2 per cent of the elderly are poor, compared with 62.2 per cent of the population as a whole. In turn, while 72 per cent of households headed by elderly persons in 1998 were living in poverty, this applies to only 53.9 per cent of households with no elderly persons was 53.9 per cent (ibid.: 38).

Over and above the disabled, who generally lack education, skills and employment (TANGO, 2000a: 9), women are also widely identified as a group at risk. Even if there are no official sex-disaggregated headcount data to support this, the Gambian government maintains that 'women fare worse than their male counterparts in all spheres of human development' (GOTG, 2000: 3), and that the 'higher incidence and severity of poverty among women as compared to men leads to the relationships between gender and poverty referred to as the feminisation of poverty' (RTG, 2002: 28; see also SG, 2002). Among reasons identified as giving rise to greater poverty among women elicited through PRSP consultative workshops are women's lack of information on reproductive health and lack of control over their own bodies, coupled with limited education and productive resources. In turn, women's hardship appears to be particularly marked in the realm of income and property (RTG, 2002: 4).

If there is widespread consensus that women are poorer than men, there appears to be rather more 'cloudiness' around the issue of female household headship and poverty. One potentially significant finding of the National Household Poverty Survey (NHPS) of 1998, for example, was that women-headed households (who at the time were around 16.7 per cent of households nationally, and as many as 19.7 per cent in Banjul), did not seem to be the 'poorest of the poor'. In this year only 45.1 per cent of female-headed households were classified as poor compared with 57 per cent of male-headed households, with the respective figures for extreme poverty being only 23.3 per cent versus 39.7 per cent (GOTG, 2000: 176). One reason for this situation may have been that polygamous households, which are designated as male-headed where co-wives share the same residential compound, are often poorer than others (SPACO et al., 2002a: 14). Another reason is lack of disaggregation between *de jure* and *de facto* female heads: given that the latter are more likely to be in receipt of remittances from partners who have migrated overseas, this may well have raised the economic status of the group as a whole.[9] Indeed, according to one analysis of 1998 data, the most important source of expenditure financing (51 per cent) in female-headed households was inter-household transfers, compared with 24 per cent in male-headed households (GOTG, 2000: 40). Although it is unlikely that these patterns have changed much, and no shifts in the classification of female household headship seem to have occurred either, 2003 data record a rather dramatic about-turn, with poverty purportedly affecting 63 per cent of households headed by women yet only 48 per cent of those headed by men (DOSFEA, 2006). Although one contributory factor might be the fairly steep rises in levels of female household headship between 1998 and 2003 – to 19.9 per cent nationally, and 25 per cent in Banjul – this remains as yet an unexplained conundrum among Gambian officialdom.[10]

Poverty Reduction Initiatives

The Gambia started devising its first Strategy for Poverty Alleviation (SPA I) in 1992. Launched two years later, this comprised four main objectives:

enhancing productive capacity, increasing access to and performance of basic social services, building capacity at the local level, and promoting participatory communication processes (GOTG, 2000: 49). In order to improve coordination, the Strategy for Poverty Alleviation Coordinating Office (SPACO) was formed in 1997 with funding for its first three years being provided by the UNDP. During this time some advances included investments in education aimed at increasing accessibility, enhancing opportunities for vocational and skills-based training, and stimulating entrepreneurship (GOTG, 2000: 51).

Given the ongoing increase in poverty in the 1990s, however, it was clear that revisions were necessary, and a first step was a participatory assessment of SPA I in 2000. This has since evolved into a 'homegrown' PRSP known as 'SPA II' supported by concessional lending from the IFIs through the Poverty Reduction and Growth Facility (PRGF).[11] In November 2000, the Executive Boards of the World Bank and IMF decided that The Gambia was eligible for debt relief under the Enhanced HIPC Initiative due to its unsustainable debt burden, its satisfactory track record in macroeconomic management and structural reform, and the unlikelihood that per capita GDP would exceed US$500 by 2019 (RTG, 2003a: 7). Proclaiming poverty as a 'human condition characterised by sustained or chronic deprivation of the resources, capabilities, choices, security and power necessary for the enjoyment of an adequate standard of living and other civil, cultural, economic, political and social rights' (ibid.: 5), SPA II was submitted to the IMF and World Bank in April 2002, and is conceived of as a 'rolling and dynamic medium-term inter-sectoral planning instrument' (DOSFEA, 2004: 8).

The overall goal of SPA II is to create an enabling environment for economic growth and poverty reduction (RTG, 2002: 5), with more specfic objectives being to enhance productive capacity and social protection among the poor, to increase coverage of basic social services, to build capacity among CSOs, and to mainstream 'cross-cutting' issues – gender, environment, nutrition, governance and HIV/AIDS – into development management (ibid.: 7). The PRSP is billed as the government's 'Strategic Blueprint of Development' (SG, 2005), and is also the 'first operational block' of The Gambia's medium-term development plan 'Vision 2020' (RTG, 2003a: 19). Adopting the 'centrality of private development to poverty reduction' (DOSFEA, 2004: 29), this aims to turn The Gambia into a middle-income country by the end of the second decade of the twenty-first century (GOTG, 2000: 49).

While SPACO's role since 1997 had been one of overall coordination, monitoring and feedback on poverty (see DOSFEA, 2004), 2003 saw the foundation of the NGO 'Pro-Poor Advocacy Group' (PROPAG), a network of CSOs, whose aims are to enhance dialogue on poverty issues between the state and civil society, to institutionalise civil society participation in budgetary processes, and to link pro-poor policies to budget allocations. As articulated in PROPAG's first Strategy Plan (2003–05), PROPAG's intention is to:

> work constructively and critically with Government, NGOs and all other stakeholders to encourage public servants to be responsible and accountable to the poor. This is intended to be achieved by monitoring and tracking government policy against planned and actual budgetary expenditure and by forming alliances and linkages with the Government, other stakeholders and local communities to influence the budget formulation process and national and international policies that militate against the poor's economic livelihood. (PROPAG, 2003: 1–2)

This initiative is essential given that efforts made thus far to incorporate the poor's priorities into macro-level economic policy have been ambitious in principle but rather limited in practice. For example, open budget-making theoretically started with the 2002 budget which involved civil society, local governments and communities in budget-making and delivery, guided by SPA II's call for a minimum of 30 per cent of the budget to be directed to poverty reducing activities (DOSFEA, 2004: 18). Despite this, the overall allocation to the three priority sectors – agriculture, health and education – fell from 27.3 per cent of total recurrent expenditures in 2002, to 25.9 per cent in 2003. Although in part this was due to increased debt service, the failure of government to take on board the 'voices of the poor' cannot be disregarded (ibid.). Yet from 2003 onwards, when a link was established between the Budget and SPA II, there has been some increase in poverty coding of the Budget and spending on the social sectors (RTG, 2003b: 3; SG, 2005). However, given macroeconomic instability – with a sustained annual GDP growth of 6 per cent being deemed necessary to reduce poverty, and failure of donor funding to match pledges – it seems highly unlikely at present that The Gambia will achieve its aim of halving the population living in extreme poverty by 2015, and bringing down poverty overall to 27 per cent (RTG, 2003b: 36; SG, 2005). Whether it will succeed in improving the situation of women, and more specifically achieve the country's MDG target of reducing the number of women living in poverty by 2015 by 66 per cent (RTG, 2002: 10), is another matter.

Although gender appears in the rhetoric of successive drafts of the PRSP, and the government claims to have 'realised that in women lay a potent force against poverty, hence our efforts at mainstreaming women's issues into all development programmes and projects' (SG, 2002), NGOs and international agencies have been highly critical of the failure to spell out what kinds of gender initiatives are required from specific institutions. Moreover, despite a dedicated consultation by SPACO in 2003 with the National Women's Bureau (NWB) (see SPACO, 2003c: 31 et seq.; also later), together with little change 'on the ground', the latest update of the SPA II in June 2006 gives grounds for concern. Although the latter states that since 'Gender participation and voice is (*sic*) a critical component of social justice as well as good economies (*sic*) to ensure development effectiveness', and there is mention, *inter alia*, of 'ensuring their legal and property rights' (DOSFEA, 2006: 25), nothing on these issues appears in the 'specific recommendations', which also fail to spell out how ambitious goals such as 'the removal of all cultural, policy and legal obstacles to the (*sic*) gender equity and equality' (ibid.: 112) might be realised. Indeed, the fact that in the same document it is asserted that 'there is no empirical evidence in The Gambia to show that a man earns more than a woman' (DOSFEA, 2006: 25), which contradicts other government figures (see later), casts major aspersions on how seriously gender considerations are actually taken.

Indeed, relatively speaking the Gambian government seems to have left most 'gender work' to NGOs and international agencies, concentrating the bulk of its own efforts in poverty alleviation on non-gender-specific initiatives such as introducing vocational training into the academic curriculum, providing occupational advisory bodies within the school environment, and creating the Gambia National Youth Service Scheme (GNYSS) to train 'early school leavers' (see GNYSS, 2001).

International agencies play a major role in poverty reduction initiatives in The Gambia through providing support to state departments or agencies, or to local NGOs and alliances. They also run 'stand-alone' programmes which complement existing national interventions, one notable example being that of the Fight Against Social Exclusion (FASE) programme which is funded by the UNDP, executed by the International Labour Organisation (ILO), and works with DOSFEA as a national counterpart. Launched in 2000, the main mission in the first three years was to strengthen community responses to poverty, to promote the full participation of the poor in national life, and to develop national policies favourable to the poor through training in entrepreneurial skills and management, with a major focus being women and youth. Additionally, FASE helps to establish community organisations and in the period 2000–2002 assisted in the formation of a total of 135 with an overall membership of nearly 13 000 among whom 94 per cent were women (FASE, 2003: 21).

Another important actor on the scene has been the Social Development Fund (SDF), which is co-funded by the Gambian Government and the African Development Bank (AfDB), and was set-up to 'counter the menace of poverty through a grassroots demand-driven approach with the extension of micro-credit, social service infrastructure and the provision of technical support towards poverty alleviation for CBOs (community-based organisations), NGOs and CSOs' (SG, 2002). In the interests of reducing poverty, the SDF gives small loans to organised local groups (usually referred to as '*kafos*')[12] many being all-female given SDF's mandate to 'empower women through skills development'. One such group, comprised entirely of women whose members participated in my grassroots survey, is the Sunwing Fruitsellers Association. The members had previously sold fruit and crafts on the roadside or in dilapidated shacks at Cape Point market, but with the assistance of an SDF grant were able to build a modern market comprising 36 new stalls complete with electricity, a shower room and a communal toilet. The grant also provided for training in batik and tie-and-dye, and in various aspects of enterprise development such as marketing concepts and pricing. Among the women I interviewed, who were, incidentally, among the most vocal of my women's groups, the consensus was that this had greatly enhanced their livelihoods. As mentioned by Hadi (30 years old): 'My education is not far, but due to the Association I can now do batik. I can now make jam. Before the fruit spoiled, but now I make jam. You make it for yourself. You are proud of yourself.'

Women and out-of-school youth are also the principal beneficiaries of a six-year nationwide Community Skills Improvement Programme (CSIP), funded by the AfDB. Among CSIP's specific objectives are to provide functional literacy and numeracy, income-generating skills and micro-credit facilities. Some of the programme's outputs in 2003 included the training of 87 literacy supervisors, the establishment of 182 fully operational literacy classes and the printing and distribution of 43 800 literacy primers. As summarised by DOSFEA (2004: 34):

> CSIP is a crucial intervention for poverty reduction as it targets women primarily providing marketable skills to enhance their productive capacities . . . where implementation has started, skills imparted on women (*sic*) are already beginning to have impact as trainees are engaging in small scale business activities thus earning additional income for the family.

GENDER IN THE GAMBIA

Despite the foregoing, and partly on account of its general level of poverty and low HDI score, The Gambia performs worse on the GDI than the Philippines and Costa Rica by a substantial margin (see Table 4.7).[13] The Gambia is also deemed to making only slow progress to the fulfilment of MDG 3 (see RTG, 2003b).

*Table 4.7   The Gambia, Philippines and Costa Rica: Gender-Related
Development Index and inequalities in political and economic
activity*

	The Gambia	Philippines	Costa Rica
Gender-Related Development Index (GDI) Value[a]	0.457	0.748	0.824
Gender-Related Development Index (GDI) Rank[b]	123	66	41
Female economic activity rate (age 15 and above) (%)	69.7	49.7	37.4
Female economic activity rate as % of male rate	78	61	46
Estimated earned income (PPP US$) 2001			
Female	1 530	2 838	5 189
Male	2 581	4 829	13 589
Ratio of estimated female to male earned income	0.59	0.59	0.38
Seats in parliament held by women (as % of total)	13.2	17.2	35.1

Notes:
a.   The GDI comprises four gender-differentiated indicators: life expectancy at birth; adult literacy; combined primary, secondary and tertiary gross enrolment ratio, and estimated earned income. The highest value of the GDI in 2001 was 0.941 (Norway), and the lowest Niger (0.279).
b.   Rank out of 144 countries.

Source: UNDP (2003a: tables 22, 23 and 25).

Although Gambian women have much higher economic activity rates than their Filipino and Costa Rican counterparts, and gender earning differentials in The Gambia are actually less than in Costa Rica, women have traditionally been excluded from many aspects of public life and leadership. Despite being granted the vote in 1960, it was not until 1982 that the first woman was elected to parliament. While as of 2004 there were five elected female MPs out of a cabinet of 14 (including a female Vice President and three Secretaries of State – for Education, Tourism and Culture and Women's Affairs) (see also Table 3.8), at a sub-national level women remain extremely under-represented among the ranks of governor, chief and *alkolulu* (see GOTG, 1998: 6).

Despite the fact that The Gambia is a signatory to the African Charter for Human and People's Rights, and to CEDAW, 'male dominance and hostile societal attitudes prevent women from exercising many of their rights' (NWB, 2002: 7), and in all ethnic groups women are regarded as having 'relatively low status' (Wadda, 2000). As summarised by UNICEF The Gambia (1999): 'Women and girls are key beneficiaries in many development programmes, but the gender gap remains wide in terms of participation in decision-making and control of resources.' This is attributed to the fact that male dominance prevails, that women's main role is regarded as that of procreation, and that 'It is still generally accepted by the majority of people that the status of women is inferior' (FASE, 2003: 5). As echoed by GOTG (2000: 53) 'women continue to be one of the most marginalised groups in our society. This is mainly due to deep-seated cultural beliefs that stereotype women as primary producers, reproducers and home managers.'

Cultural notions of femininity are very much bound up with marriage, motherhood and the significance of the extended family in Gambian culture which for women in particular implies obligations to others at different stages of their life course which are rarely perceived as negotiable, let alone actually negotiated.

Marriage, Family and Sexuality

Marriage is deemed extremely important by Gambian women and men alike, although its particular importance for women is underlined by the expectation that they will marry young. Indeed, census data reveal that 5 per cent of girls aged 10–14 are married, and as many as 53 per cent by the age of 20 (Taal, 2003: 27), with early marriage (between 12 and 17 years) being particularly common among the Mandinka, Fula and Serahuli (GOTG, 1998: 16). This, along with early pregnancy, tends to curtail women's personal and professional development. As summarised by FASE (2003: 5):

> Early marriage is widely practiced [*sic*] and it is one of the contributing factors to low female literacy, especially in rural areas. Other cultural practices such as female genital mutilation and various post-natal rituals aggravate the risk of maternal and child mortality and morbidity. Reproductive roles, coupled with other traditional practices make females less available for schooling and self-improvement possibilities as well as undermining their wealth.

Most men, on the other hand, do not marry until their late twenties or thirties, and in the context of polygamous marriage, embark on second or third marriages even later. As noted by Bjinsdorp and Montgomery (2003: 20) 'Traditionally a man might get married in his twenties, and take a new wife in each of his next three decades.' In one group of ten Serere women I interviewed in Old Jeswang, most of the younger women had husbands who were 25 to 30 years older and already had two or more wives.

Large spousal age gaps add an extra dimension to the power dynamics of conjugal relations in so far as men's seniority requires even greater deference and respect on the part of wives. Yet whatever the difference in age, once married, women are usually expected to serve and 'obey' their husbands, and to see this state as a 'blessing'. To reinforce this, newspaper articles appear every so often reminding wives that they should be obedient and submissive.[14] As part and parcel of their subjugation, women often work harder than men both inside and outside the home. One group of predominantly elderly women vegetable sellers interviewed in Bakau concurred that women are 'slaves' to men and 'very backward', adding that 'this is our culture, we have to accept'.

Leading on from this, motherhood is regarded as integral to marriage, with the Gambia Committee on Traditional Practices Affecting the Health of Women and Children (GAMCOTRAP) (1999: 22) asserting that: 'In the Gambian situation, the sexual life of women is not complete without a child, and preferentially, a boy child.' In turn, the pressure upon women to procreate is such that 'Women . . . do not have any reproductive rights or control over their bodies including the right to determine the size of their families through modern methods of family planning.' This is exacerbated by lack of access to information on sexual and reproductive health, and the consequent inability to make informed choices (TANGO, 2001: ii). Although the fertility rate among 15–19-year-olds dropped by 20 per cent between 1985 and 2005, the level is still extremely high at 157 per 1000, being more than three times that of Costa Rica.

Children are seen primarily as women's responsibility, and as articulated in one newspaper article: 'Most male parents in our lower-class families play a hands-off attitude in the socialisation of the children in the home. They leave the whole education to the child entirely in the hands of the female parents who are overloaded with home economics (*sic*) management' (see also Sear et al., 2000; 2007).[15] In turn, where children offend paternal expectations or desires then the blame is laid squarely at women's feet, who may even risk divorce if they are unable to change their offspring's ways (Box 4.1). To add insult to injury, women stand to lose their children in the event of divorce, which Muslim men can continue to execute though repudiation.[16] Although women are entitled to seek divorce in their own right, and may even attempt to keep their children through the courts, under Islamic law custody only goes to the mother where male children are under 7 and female children under 9. Thereafter the father is able to reclaim them (GOTG, 1998: 78). As noted by NWB (2002: 20): 'While the Gambian Constitution states that women shall have equal rights and treatment to men, women cannot seek protection with respect to those areas that are subject to customary or personal law, such as marriage and other domestic disputes' (see also Njie-Saidy, 2000).

BOX 4.1   THE GAMBIA: CHILDREN AS WOMEN'S RESPONSIBILITY

The following is an excerpt from the *Micro-Enterprise Development Training Manual* prepared by the FASE Programme in The Gambia. With a view to sensitising participants to the obstacles to entrepreneurship posed by the caste system, a 'Discussion between parents and son on the practice of a chosen trade' is presented, which also reveals some interesting gender dimensions of parenting and marriage.

Bakary, aged 65, the head of a village kabilo (committee) is a well-known trader in the village and a district tribunal member. His son Karamo has at an early age been always interested in leatherwork. In spite of discouragement from the parents, he continued to learn and developed skills for the trade. To practice [*sic*] his skills, he left his village and started a leatherwork service in a nearby town. His impressive skill, talent and the quality of his work soon earned him many customers and he became very popular and successful. One day his father visited him and the following conversation took place:

Bakary: 'You are a disgrace to the family. You come from a noble, royal ancestry, as a freeborn, now you have degraded yourself to the rank of an "oudeh" a lower class in our society.'

Karamo: 'Father, social class considerations should not be brought into the business field. I have always been interested in leatherwork and have worked hard and studied to develop skills and talents for it. Why should you prevent me from practising a trade I like and earn me (*sic*) honest living?'

Bakary: 'If you continue to practice this trade, no woman from the other superior classes will marry you and the children you get will inherit ill-luck, lack of blessing and the social stigma. Society will look down upon them and they will face many problems in life.'

Karamo: 'Father with all due respect, there is no basis for this. The best person in the sight of Allah as explained in the Holy Quran is the righteous, not a member of a social class.'

Bakary goes away in a rage and on arrival at the house, calls the mother and shouts: 'Your child has gone astray. He has no blessing. This is the reward you get for not caring for me and treating me properly. God is showing you in your children the effects of your marriage and your behaviour towards me.'

A day later the mother went to Karamo in tears and said:

'Karamo, please save my marriage and my good name and status in society. Your father curses me everyday [*sic*] and threatens to divorce me and my friends are keeping away, because the leather-work is cursed and brings bad luck to families. For the sake of pre-serving my marriage and the good name of my children, please stop your business.'

Upon abandoning his trade Karamo returned to the village where he remained unemployed and became very poor.

Source: FASE (2001: 40–42).

In cases of separation and divorce, obtaining maintenance for children from husbands is technically possible through the judicial system, with the Family Welfare Unit of the DOSSW nominally providing assistance towards peaceful resolution of disputes, or in cases where maintenance is refused, subjecting offending parents to attachment of earnings orders (GOTG, 1998: 25). Nonetheless many women do not proceed down this route for fear of spousal backlash. Indeed, a substantial number do not exit unhappy marriages in the first place given the likelihood that they will be cast out of the compound with no material possessions, and have no home or economic wherewithal to support their children.

Only children born out of wedlock are considered to be the sole respon-sibility of the mother (see GOTG, 1998: 25). Despite nominal protection under the Maintenance of Children Act, illegitimate children are often denied inheritance from their fathers' estates with the full sanction of Islamic and Customary Law (ibid.: 16), and are also targets of stigma and discrimination. Indeed, recent rises in divorce and non-marriage are often held responsible for weakening family life, creating 'more child poverty, adolescent pregnancy, juvenile crime, substance abuse, and other serious social problems' (Taal, 2003: 15).

One of the most serious contemporary social 'problems' in The Gambia, if discussions in the media and among officialdom, as well as at the grassroots, are anything to go by, is sexuality. Over and above continued denial of, and antipathy towards, same-sex love, discourses around hetero-sexual relationships are often heated and bi-polar. On the one hand, high rates of teenage and extramarital pregnancy suggest that a substantial segment of the population indulge in 'playing love' before (and outside) marriage. Indeed, a Youth Health Survey conducted in 1999–2000 found not only that the mean age at first birth was 16.9 years, but that some girls had their first intercourse at the age of 11 or 12 (Taal, 2003: 19). Normatively, however, 'Sex outside marriage is socially frowned upon and seen as contrary to religious and moral beliefs' (Bjinsdorp and Montgomery, 2003: 20). For example, in a standard 'Population and Family Life Education' book for children in junior secondary ('upper basic') school, it is stated that 'Sex before marriage is a social taboo and a religious sin in The Gambia. It is unacceptable for people to have children unless they are married' (METG, 1997: 50). It is also not uncommon to see letters to the press (often from young men) complaining about their female peers ('our Muslim sisters') wearing 'revealing dress', or deploring information campaigns on condoms which they feel encourage young unmarried people to believe that sex is acceptable,[17] even if abstinence is the more common message in HIV/AIDS awareness programmes (Figure 4.3).

The weight placed on women's propriety is reinforced through practices such as female genital mutilation (FGM) which is estimated to affect between 60 and 80 per cent of the female population, can entail infibulation as well as clitoridectomy, and is primarily to 'ensure a woman's virginity before marriage and chastity thereafter' (GAMCOTRAP, 1999: 8; also SCS, 2005). In contrast to other West African countries which have outlawed FGM since the late 1990s, including Benin, Burkina Faso, Senegal, Togo, Ivory Coast, Ghana and Kenya (see Adjamagbo-Johnson, 2004: 9; WEDO, 2005: 48), only two organisations in The Gambia are openly challenging the practice, notably GAMCOTRAP and the Foundation for Research on Women's Health, Productivity and Development (BAFROW). The political costs of this have been high, and, as articulated by Sosseh-Gaye (2001: 7) the anti-FGM lobby is regarded as a 'remote control cultural invasion from outside which is threatening the status quo. The advocates are labelled as unpatriotic and un-Islamic with more pressing issues to address such as baby dumping, teenage pregnancy and a general decline in the moral standards of women'. Even if support for a ban on FGM may grow in response to increased promotion of child rights on the part of the recently formed Child Protection Alliance (CPA), one unfortunate reaction to date has been increased secrecy around the ritual, and an alleged dropping of the age at which girls are circumcised from 11–12 years old, to only 2–3 (GAMCOTRAP, 1999: 8).

While seeds of challenges to other expressions of sexual double standards – such as polygamy – are also in place,[18] many men continue to marry more than one wife, not to mention have extramarital liaisons. Since the pressures on men to sire children are also high, there are possibly serious consequences given a context in which HIV/AIDS is increasing (TANGO, 2001: iii).

As for other changes in the family, there is some talk about the break-up of family networks through poverty and migration, even if fewer than 30 per cent of Gambian households are nuclear, and among female-headed households (see earlier), proclivities to extension appear to be fairly generalised, owing, *inter alia*, to housing shortages, the necessity for people to pool resources, and the sociocultural importance attached to assisting kin. An additional factor is the continuity of the '*kabilo* system' whereby clusters of households with biological and social links are presided over by elderly males (GOTG, 1998: 9).

Extra-domestic resource flows between kin members are also considerable. As in many other parts of sub-Saharan Africa, for example, children from rural homes are often fostered out to relatives in urban areas for schooling (see GOTG, 1998: 26; also Porter and Blaufuss, 2002; van Vuuren, 2003: 64). Indeed, a UNICEF survey conducted in the late 1990s revealed that a total of 10.2 per cent of children in The Gambia were not living with either of their parents, as against an overall average of 5.5 per cent for 41 countries in Asia, Africa and Latin America and the Caribbean (see Delamonica et al., 2004: 9, table 1). As with families in general, the burden of daily care for fostered children falls mainly on women, who usually become referred to as 'mother' by the child in question, as distinct from the woman who gave them birth ('born mother').[19]

Gender Dimensions of Education

Women represent around two-thirds of the illiterate population in The Gambia (GOTG, 2000: 4), although there is some evidence of declining gender gaps in literacy and schooling over time, with 30.9 per cent of Gambian women being literate in 2001, compared with only 21.3 per cent ten years earlier (see Table 4.8). Among young women in the same year, literacy as a proportion of the male was 76 per cent as against 69 per cent among women in general (Table 4.8). This positive trend undoubtedly reflects the fact that girls' enrolment in lower basic education in The Gambia grew at an annual average of 6 per cent during the 1990s compared with 2 per cent among boys. Although the male Gross Enrolment Ratio (GER) stood at 77 per cent in 2000, for girls it had climbed to 71 per cent. In the academic year 2002–03, by which time scholarships for girls had begun to bear fruit, the overall rate of enrolment in schools, including *madrasah* establishments, had reached 90 per cent (DOSE, 2003, cited in Martin, 2003: 14), with the gap between male and female enrolment minimal at the primary level, Table 4.8). However, further up the education hierarchy, gender gaps continue to be notable. Data pertaining to 1996 reveal that the GER for girls in senior secondary education was 14 per cent compared with 22 per cent among boys (RTG, 2002: 50–51), and, in extremely poor households, just under 14 per cent of girls aged 16–18 years

Table 4.8   The Gambia, Philippines and Costa Rica: gender inequalities in literacy and education

	The Gambia	Philippines	Costa Rica
Adult literacy rate (% aged 15 and above) 2001			
Female	30.9	95.0	95.8
Male	45.0	95.3	95.6
Adult female literacy rate as % of male rate, 2001	69	100	100
Youth female literacy rate as % of male rate, 2001	76	100	101
Net primary enrolment – ratio of females to males, 2000–2001	0.93	1.01	1.01
Net secondary enrolment – ratio of females to males, 2000–2001	0.70	1.18	1.11
Gross tertiary enrolment – ratio of females to males, 2000–2001	–	1.10	1.21
Combined primary, secondary and tertiary enrolment ratio (%) 2000–2001			
Female	43	81	66
Male	51	79	65

Note: – = No data.

Source: UNDP (2003a: tables 22 and 24).

are in school, versus 39 per cent of their male counterparts (ibid.; see also Martin, 2003: ch. 6).

One critical factor explaining gender differentials in education is that parents place more emphasis on educating sons. The Gambian government, for example, reports that in addition to girls being disadvantaged by domestic chores, their education is often sacrificed in households with limited financial resources (GOTG, 1998: 34). This is echoed by UNICEF The Gambia (1999) who note that 'Cultural practices of gender discrimination and the high cost to families of formal basic education limit school enrolment and retention, especially of girls'. Important contributory factors here are fourfold. First, there is a pervasive normative ideal that men should be the principal breadwinners and providers of accommodation – the latter being more prevalent than the former due to male-biased inheritance (see also below). Second, unemployment is higher among women than men (19 per cent versus 14 per cent in The Gambia – VPSSWA, 1999: 7). Third, women are much less likely to ascend to the upper tiers of the employment hierarchy (only 4.9 per cent of the skilled workforce in The Gambia is female for example – GOTG, 2000: 138). Fourth, the average earnings of men are consistently higher than those of women, regardless of poverty status and type of occupation (CSD, 1998; GOTG, 2001; see also later). Additional factors pointed up in the first national report on the MDGs is that early marriage depresses girls' access to education, along with the 'belief that schoolgirls tend to become sexually active whilst in school and remain unmarried thereafter' (RTG, 2003b: 14). As summarised by TANGO (2001: 8), although more than half of Gambian children live in poverty, in terms of nutritional status, access to resources and services and use of child labour, the girl child undoubtedly fares worse.

Gendered Divisions of Labour and Employment

Leading on from the above, gender inequalities in divisions of labour start young. The workload of girls within the home is often far heavier than boys, as they perform a wider range of chores and dedicate more time to these overall. Whereas boys may only be expected (or asked) to run the occasional errand, for example, girls are regularly involved in cooking, cleaning, sweeping, washing, sewing, and minding younger siblings. Indeed, sisters often have to service their brothers such as cleaning their rooms, turning down their beds at night, laundering their clothes, making small purchases on their behalf, hand-delivering messages to friends or girl-friends, and providing credit for mobile phones.[20] This gender disparity stems mainly from the fact that domestic labour and care of others is deemed fundamentally to be 'women's work' in accordance with the normative ideal that in adulthood women should be the chief 'homemakers' (see VPSSWA, 1999: 8).

Yet despite the fact that household labour is assigned primarily to women, most women have some form of income-generating activity as well, with two discernible impacts upon their younger counterparts. First, mothers have less capacity to assume full responsibility for reproductive labour and so pass on the 'excess' burden to daughters (or foster daughters). Second, it establishes the notion that young women should also contribute economically (Chant and Jones, 2005).

Although normatively men are supposed to be, and frequently claim to be, the primary breadwinners in The Gambia, in practice, as elsewhere in sub-Saharan Africa, women have growing economic responsibilities as daughters, wives, and as heads of their own households (see Barrett and Browne, 1996; also Adepoju and Mbugua, 1997; Tacoli, 2002). A total of 69.7 per cent of Gambian women aged 15 or over are economically active, which is as much as 78 per cent of the male rate (see Table 4.7).

Table 4.9   The Gambia: gender distribution of employment

Branch of employment	% of male workforce	% of female workforce
Agriculture	56.7	78.3
Fishing	1.4	0.5
Mining	0.4	0.3
Manufacturing	6.3	2.2
Utilities	0.9	0.0
Construction	2.8	0.2
Transport, storage and communications	3.9	0.8
Wholesale and retail commerce	9.6	10.0
Hotels and restaurants	2.1	0.3
Finance and real estate	0.5	0.6
Public administration	2.4	0.6
Social and recreational services	7.9	2.5
Personal services	4.4	3.2
International	0.7	0.4
All	100.0	100.0

Source: SPACO (2003a: table 14).

In agriculture, for example, which occupies 78 per cent of women workers, and in which women are around 50 per cent of the labour force, activities are mainly restricted to sowing, weeding and harvesting between late April and October (SPACO et al., 2002c: 16). Moreover, women represent more than 70 per cent of unskilled labour in agriculture (GOTG, 2000: 138), have limited land entitlement (usually gaining access only through male kin), and seldom own substantial livestock (TANGO, 2000a: 20).

Although women have a growing presence in formal urban employment (see Table 3.8), a 2000 study by the MDI Gender Unit revealed that there were four times as many men as women in top management positions, even where the former did not possess the appropriate qualifications.[21] This underlines the argument that: 'women's access to employment is limited in terms of getting employed in the first place, staying in employment and making it to the top' (VPSSWA, 1999: 3). Women are also subject to having their choice of work constrained by husbands (see Box 4.2), which is why so many restrict themselves to small-scale commerce and services. Indeed, while women are also widely noted to be becoming more visible and successful in small enterprises, they have yet to make their mark in big business.

BOX 4.2   THE GAMBIA: CONSTRAINTS ON FEMALE LABOUR FORCE PARTICIPATION

The following is an excerpt from Section 2 'Gender and Social Exclusion Considerations' in the *Micro-Enterprise Development Training Manual* prepared by FASE:

Gender Bias Ruins the Successful Business of Ramatoulie

Ramatoulie, a London-trained seamstress decides to start tailoring service in her small town, using funds saved and borrowed from the Bank. She gives the businesses full attention and because of her skills and efficiency, attracts many customers including schools and organisations in the town. Ramatoulie specialised in sewing dresses such as 'Asobi' for social functions and school uniforms. The business grew and the profit increased. Ramatoulie has little time for family and domestic chores but helps her husband, Mustapha, to run the house, to pay children's school fees and other domestic bills. She loves Mustapha, her marriage and family but she also loves her business, which she likes to expand. Unlike her in-laws and many people in the town she does not believe that a woman's place is in the home.

She avoids expensive social functions and ceremonies organised by the local community and is called: 'A Gambian in appearance but a Tubab at heart'. Ramatoulie's answer is 'I have no money to waste. Local custom will not ruin my business. He who walks slowly to catch a thief should not cough'.

As the business expands and customers increase, Ramatoulie's time for the family and society decreased. She travelled to buy materials, to give supplies, to organise fashion shows in hotels at night. These activities (including visits to hotels, late at night) made the family and community elders extremely angry and Mustapha's respect in society decreased. The elders and family members condemn the practice of visiting hotels at night, and frequenting the company of men and tourists.

Family members and community elders put pressure on Mustapha to act as a man and to protect his wife from evil. As the pressure increased, Mustapha called Ramatoulie and gave her an ultimatum: 'Enough is enough, you have to choose one husband (*sic*), either your business or your family!' Ramatoulie chose (*sic*) the husband and the family, reduced her business activities, lost her customers and faced many problems in the business, She applied for credit but needed the help of Mustapha to offer collateral. In the end, she failed to respect the business cycle and the business collapsed.

Source: FASE (2001: 43–5).

These gender divisions in work translate into disparities in earnings, with women's incomes being only 59 per cent of men's in the formal sector (Table 4.7), and dropping to 34 per cent when taking into account informal earnings (TANGO, 2001: 8). Aside from earning less than men, women also work longer days, especially as housemaids where ten-hour shifts for less than the minimum wage are not uncommon (GOTG, 1998: 22; TANGO, 2000a: 9). As informal workers, domestic workers are excluded from the Labour Act of 1990, which reinforces 'society's perception of domestic activity as a female domain and not worthy of legalisation or monetisation' (VPSSWA, 1999: 3). It should also be noted that only salaried female employees are entitled to three months' maternity leave, and there is no paternity leave for men.

Policy Responses to Gender Inequality

In light of persistent gender inequalities in The Gambia, and in response to international calls for the integration of women in development, an Act of Parliament in 1980 established a National Women's Council (NWC) comprising 31 women. The Council now has 51 members, 45 being elected on the basis of active participation in community and development activities, and six who are nominated on the basis of relevant skills and qualifications (NWB, 2002: 17). While the council was mandated to serve as an advisory body to the government on issues affecting women, the National Women's Bureau, headed by an executive secretary, was set up in the same year to execute its policy decisions (GOTG, 1998: 7), although its role is now shifting from one of implementation to coordination (SPACO, 2003c: 39). In accordance with Vision 2020 which 'calls for partnership between women as men, as well as mutual respect and understanding of issues pertaining to gender and development' (GOTG, 2000: 53), a National Policy for the Advancement of Women (NPAGW) was launched in 1999 which aims to reduce gender inequality and to promote greater well-being and participation among Gambian women (see Box 4.3).

BOX 4.3   OBJECTIVES OF THE NATIONAL POLICY FOR THE ADVANCEMENT OF GAMBIAN WOMEN (1999–2009)

GOAL: To improve the quality of life of all Gambians, particularly women, through the elimination of all forms of gender inequality by concrete gender in development measures.

OBJECTIVES:

1. To ensure that by 2006, all government policies are gender sensitive.
2. To promote women's equal access to and control of productive resources.
3. To continue building up knowledge of the actual and potential role of women in national development, and ensure by 2004 that gender concerns are integrated fully at all levels of development.
4. To strengthen the National Women's Council and Bureau so as to better address the needs and concerns of women.
5. To ensure that women have access to decision-making positions.
6. To ensure an enabling work environment and increase access to training facilities for all categories of female workers.
7. To increase budgetary provisions for addressing women's issues in all government departments and NGOs to more appropriately address women's issues.
8. To enhance grassroots women's participation in the implementation, monitoring and evaluation of the National Women's Policy.
9. To eliminate all forms of discrimination and violence against women and girls.
10. To encourage the participation of women in the promotion of peace.
11. To ensure that at least 90 per cent of girls have access to basic education (grades 1–9) as a fundamental human right by 2007.
12. To reduce illiteracy among women by 40 per cent by 2007.
13. To improve the quality of and access to healthcare services for women and children by the year 2009 and also reduce infant mortality by 25 per cent by the year 2009.

14. To increase the income earning opportunities and potential of Gambian women.
15. To enhance the capacity of Gambian women in environmental and human resource management.
16. To enhance the participation of disabled women and girls in the national socio-economic development process.
17. To promote positive images of women in the media.
18. To enhance the capacity of communicators to address gender issues.

Source: Vice President and Secretary of State for Women's Affairs (1999).

Despite the establishment of national machinery for women, The Gambia's first report to CEDAW has been outstanding since 1994, and it has not yet signed up to the Optional Protocol which provides for women whose rights have been violated to seek redress through the relevant UN Committee. Budgetary inadequacy may have a part to play here, with a notable tendency for the NWB to rely heavily on external sources for capacity-building and gender mainstreaming. Between 2000 and 2003, for example, the NWB depended on a US$1.5 million grant from the Department for International Development (DFID), UK, to mainstream poverty reduction and gender equality strategies into the planning and implementation of public services, especially health, education and financial and economic affairs (see DOSFEA, 2002; NWB, 2002). Yet although one important outcome was the introduction of 'gender focal points' in these and other state departments, the generally disappointing performance on gender in the PRSP process tends to justify the claim of NGOs that the state has done very little in respect of sustained commitment to gender equality.[22]

One notable exception, however, is education, with a discernible trend not only to attempt to correct long-standing gender biases in educational attainment, but for this to translate into outcomes (see earlier). Over and above the waiving of girls' school fees, there is now a dedicated Girls' Education Unit within DOSE which administers a Scholarship Trust Fund. One respondent in my institutional survey who had formerly been a Director of Schools in The Gambia, also noted how the creation of 'girl-friendly' schools had been vital to increasing female enrolment.[23] Prior to 1982, toilets had not been gender-segregated, for instance, which dissuaded many parents from sending their daughters to school. In addition, the 1993–2003 National Education Policy attempted to improve female enrolment and completion ratios in other ways, such as by training more female teachers (Njie-Saidy, 2000).

Other interventions such as workshops to encourage girls to go into less conventionally 'female' subjects such as science, mathematics and technology (APRC, 2001) have been complemented by NGOs. Since its formation in 1997, for instance, FAWEGAM (Forum of African Women Educationalists – The Gambia) which forms part of a larger African network – FAWE International – founded in 1992, has made a major contribution to women's education through co-financing agreements. These have provided grants for girls in secondary and higher education, and established income-generating schemes for mothers in selected areas of the country in order that their daughters are under less pressure to abandon schoolwork (see Box 4.4).[24]

BOX 4.4   THE GAMBIA: MOTHERS' CLUBS INITIATIVE

As part of their mission to promote the education of girls and women, FAWEGAM with the support of the United Nations Children's Fund (UNICEF) launched a 'Mothers' Clubs' initiative in 2000 in the three most easterly divisions of the country: Upper River Division, Central River Division and Lower River Division. The scheme started with 23 clubs, and presently there are 81. In the supporting documentation for this project, FAWEGAM observes that in these areas:

> Poverty is endemic and the populations cling very strongly to their traditions and cultural practices, rarely valuing western education, especially the education of girls. In most instances it is the boys rather than girls who attend school. Girls are left at home to help with the domestic chores. Even though primary education is free, most times families operate at subsistence level and hardly have any extra income to support the education of their children. The main reason for this is the other hidden costs associated with attending schools such as uniforms, writing materials and school lunch that pose considerable financial strain on families. It is this reason, as well as other cultural and traditional practices that lead to low net enrolment rates, especially for girls, often as low as 19 per cent in these communities.

One of the main aims of the scheme is to increase women's income-generating capacity so that they become less dependent on their daughters' assistance and can also afford to send and keep them to school, and enhance their performance. Under the umbrella of promoting community participation, additional objectives are:

- to empower mothers to take full responsibility for the education of their girl children as well as providing them with the opportunities to do so
- to facilitate mother–child/parent–parent peer counselling on sensitive matters such as early marriage, teenage pregnancy and other aspects of reproductive health
- to provide opportunities for mothers to sensitise communities on the importance of girls' education and become strong advocates for girls' education at both family and community levels.

After consultation with mothers at the local level, a decision is reached on appropriate income-generating activities under the guidance and leadership of their own elected executive members. Income-generating activities include batik, tie and dye, soap-making, pomade-making and farming activities. Opportunities are also given to women to learn banking and accounting skills. A one-off grant of around US$150 from UNICEF gets the schemes started after which the clubs are expected to be self-sustaining.

Not only in villages which have Mothers' Clubs are women much more active economically than previously, but the Mothers' Clubs have served as entry points for other interventions including in relation to reproductive health, sanitation and the environment. For example, the dipping of mosquito nets in the insectide Permithrin by mothers has helped reduce malarial-induced absenteeism among their daughters, as well as boost levels of school enrolment.

For girls who have dropped out of school due to lack of family resources, or because of teenage pregnancy, there are an increasing number of organisations, including the Simma Vocational Training Institute, the St Josephs Adult Education and Skills Centre, and the Gambia Home Economics Association Skills Centre, which, for modest fees, provide women the opportunity to pursue vocational training and to improve their literacy and business expertise.

Although women's NGOs in the country are relatively few in number and are often plagued by financial insecurity, one or two are undertaking radical, agenda-setting activities to improve women's position and to advance equality. One such organisation, GAMCOTRAP, mentioned earlier, for example, has worked tirelessly not only to garner popular support for the elimination of FGM, but other harmful traditions such as son preference, nutritional taboos, wife inheritance and early marriage, at the same time as attempting to promote health practices which improve the status of women and children.

GENDER AND GENERATIONAL DIMENSIONS OF POVERTY IN THE GAMBIA

Having presented an overview of the broad parameters of gender, development and poverty in The Gambia, the focus now turns to the views on gender and poverty of professionals in relevant institutions, and to the opinions of people at the grassroots.

The Views of Professionals

Even if deficiencies in income and basic needs featured prominently in most consultations with representatives from a total of 13 state, NGO and international organisations in The Gambia, it is clear that poverty is seen as more than scarcity of income – commonly comprising, for example, 'social exclusion', lack of confidence and self-esteem, lack of political voice, and lack of knowledge. As one respondent, Baboucarr Bouy, the Director of PROPAG, put it, 'information poverty' is as critical as 'income poverty'.

The majority opinion was that poverty has been increasing since the mid-1990s due to a combination of external factors (such as international terms of trade), and poor financial management, with a generally jaundiced view of government efforts to alleviate poverty. While it was recognised that urban poverty was growing, rural poverty was deemed to be worse, and considerably more visible. That said, some people identified growing polarisation in urban areas.

Although informants often claimed how intra-family resource flows made it difficult to determine which age and gender groups are most vulnerable to poverty, a number indicated that unemployed youth (mainly male), who had migrated to urban areas but were unable to find employment, constituted a new risk group. Yet while it was recognised that young men faced lack of opportunities, respondents also emphasised that this was also because they were 'lazy' and to some extent bringing poverty upon themselves. As it was, the vast majority highlighted women as the key victims of poverty, attributing this primarily to ongoing gender gaps in literacy, education and employment, restricted access to land and property, limited opportunities for obtaining and/or controlling loans and credit, lack of 'voice' and decision-making power at household and community levels, vulnerability to summary divorce, and discrimination within the family. Female poverty was felt to be particularly rife in rural areas, especially where the out-migration of youth had deprived women of immediate family support, and/or in cases where women were illiterate or had few skills other than in cooking or vegetable gardening. Only one interviewee (Sebastian Njie, the Director of GNYSS), ventured that in some senses women could be regarded as richer than men. While, on the surface, women might appear to be materially poor and it was hard to see their wealth because it was usually invested in others, and in ways where the paybacks were not immediate or readily obvious, the cultivation of close emotional ties with children, and efforts on their behalf (for example, in relation to schooling), guaranteed returns. Indeed, while most Gambian children do not question the idea of helping parents, they often have a special reverence for mothers because they know they 'suffer for them'.

This, in turn, conceivably helps to explain why most respondents identified women in their thirties and forties as suffering most from material hardship. This group have not benefited from the educational advantage their daughters have had, but are also not yet in a position where their children are old enough to 'give back' in any substantial way, especially given progressively protracted educational trajectories. Older women, by contrast, are beginning to reap benefits from the increased earning capacity of sons, and especially daughters. In turn, although some professionals regard young women as being best-off, not only because of higher levels of education and opportunity, but on account of these affording more scope to pursue personal goals, findings from the grassroots suggest that the situation may be otherwise, with the claims on some young women often advancing faster than their actual accumulation of achievements (see later). Indeed, in respect of carrying the biggest burdens of expectation, obligation, labour and time, some identified little to choose between women in their young or middle years.

Interestingly not one respondent in the institutional survey mentioned female household heads as a particularly vulnerable group. This is possibly because until 1998, at least, official data pointed to female household headship as higher among better-off groups, and because unpartnered women usually live in extended arrangements where the absence of a spouse does not count for very much, especially where women receive extra- as well as intra-domestic transfers from children and other kin.

Grassroots Perspectives on the Meanings, Manifestations and Corollaries of Poverty

Consonant with official reports of self-rated poverty (see earlier), most men and women at the grassroots saw themselves as belonging to the 80 per cent of the population they deemed to be in poverty.[25] Almost without exception, this was regarded as an extremely negative state, centring mainly on lack of money for food, shelter, clothing, and education. One 14-year-old boy, Ebrima, from Bakau, for example, said he felt poor when he had no footwear to go to school. One of his classmates, Amat (16), a Senegalese who from the age of 4 has lived in The Gambia with his grandmother and brother, says he feels poor because he does not have the money to visit his parents who further discourage him on grounds of it being 'too expensive'. A 26-year-old trainee teacher, Isa, complained about not having 'three meals a day and or . . . free choice in what you eat', as well as emphasising that: 'Poverty is about not being able to support oneself, not being able to fulfil your own needs, and having to depend on parents.' Dependency and lack of autonomy were also emphasised by older respondents, such as Garba (41), who heads a transport union in Serrekunda: 'There is no freedom for a man who lives in another man's house. Poverty stops you from having better living conditions, better clothes, better health facilities, for your family and for your very self, better education level and quality, pocket money, travelling expenses and a bank account.' Garba and his colleagues in the transport union were among the most politically sensitised groups I interviewed, and deplored the lack of means to make a living in The Gambia. As Hassan, a 43-year-old long-distance commercial and passenger driver stated: 'Everyone goes on about human rights this, human rights that, but you can't have human rights without a job.'

The idea that this situation might improve was generally felt to be out of the question. While some respondents perceived there to be slightly less hardship than in the past, and that it was now easier to obtain food as a result of increased commerce and transport links, recent price rises in many basic goods and utilities had hit the poor very hard. One woman, Nyima (53), who led a FASE-funded smoked fish project in Old Jeswang, complained that at one time she could buy a cupful of rice for 6 bututs, but the cost was now 3 dalasis. Mariama (54) from Bakau, also pointed out that inflation had produced a situation where 'all women's earnings go on a bag of rice and there is hardly anything left over'.

Leading on from this, lack of decent employment was one of the main factors identified as integral to rising poverty in The Gambia. This was seen to be a more general problem in sub-Saharan Africa, with Sfax (27), an assistant in a palm rhun firm, responding to the question as to why he thought 95 per cent of Gambians in general were poor: 'I have no idea about that. You just have to work hard. This is Africa.' Sfax felt his plight was compounded by the fact that 'I come from a poor family', and because he grew up in a rural area in North Bank Division, where 'the situation there much worse in than in "industry"' (that is, tourism). Some individuals also identified the country's colonial heritage and lack of 'good institutions' left by the British, high dependency on imports, the growing external debt, restricted funds for social investment, depreciation of the dalasi, and 'economic sabotage' on the part of the business community who hoarded goods, created scarcity and/or sold them when the value of the dalasi had gone down. Yassime, a 27-year-old waitress not only attributed growing economic hardship in The Gambia to low salaries, but, like many other respondents, to the fact that people have 'a lot of family'.

Musa, a 27-year-old newspaper seller, declared that many people also *feel* poorer nowadays because much more emphasis is placed in modern times on having cash and goods, whereas in the past people used to be content with less, citing the example of his father who was only a groundnut trader but never complained about hardship. Yet hardship is a daily fact of life for most respondents in the sample. For example, in order to save money on transport, people often make protracted home–work journeys at both ends of an 8–10 hour day. While this often affects women as much as men, most women in their middle and senior years emphasise that the worst aspect of poverty is the constant need to think and plan, especially in respect of feeding the family. They also complained of profound feelings of pain and guilt at being unable to give their children enough to eat. Similar sentiments were echoed by Musa (27) the newspaper seller who claimed that without income one could not 'prepare for most eventualities, to be secure', as well as mentioning that he most disliked poverty because it prevented him from fulfilling obligations to his extended family, as well as leading to a lack of 'face' and 'respect', and feelings of 'inferiority' and 'voicelessness'.

Leading on from this, 'lack of face', as exemplified by not being able to turn up at important social gatherings such as baby-naming ceremonies due to inability to afford gifts or appropriate attire, was taken very seriously. As the trainee teacher, Isa (26) put it: 'Poverty means you can't get actual respect in society, you can't fulfil your desires.' A group of eight schoolgirls aged between 14 and 16 years also talked about experiencing shame and embarrassment at their poverty, their fear of being mocked by others for not being able to pay school expenses, as well as jealousy at others having what they did not, and guilt at making their mothers struggle on their behalf.

Other dispirited psychological and emotional states emphasised by respondents included anger, angst, depression and sadness. As one female fruitseller, Teeda (35), stated: 'You feel "I want to do it, I want to have it", but you can't. There's a lot of suffering for that . . . You feel you are suffering so much that you feel "I don't want to talk about it". You are angry for yourself.' Another woman vegetable grower and seller, in her sixties, interviewed in Bakau, emphasised that: 'After working hard in the (vegetable) garden, and you're still poor, obviously you're going to be sad.'

One or two of the younger respondents emphasised that poverty could bring out the best in people and lead them to help one another, and said that being poor makes one less vulnerable to attack because no one will bother to rob you. The Transport Union men also talked admiringly of the willpower and imagination shown by some poor people in order to avoid 'malpractices' such as stealing, including taking demeaning jobs. However, they also noted that sometimes crime was inescapable in situations of extreme hardship. This was echoed by a focus group of adolescent boys in Bakau who pointed out that the desperation attached to poverty may lead youth to rob, become 'bumsters' (hustlers/layabouts), smoke ganja (marijuana), drink alcohol, and even to prostitute themselves.

When asked how the lives of better-off people compared with the poor, respondents often emphasised material differences, noting that the wealthy 'build their houses in very expensive compounds' and 'they drive wonderful cars'. In turn, wealth was identified as affording people the opportunity to assist extensive networks of relatives, whereas poorer people 'can only help their own sons' (*sic*). On inquiring what one group of GNYSS participants in their early twenties would do if they woke up and found 10 000 dalasis under their pillow (about US$340 at the rate of exchange in November 2003, and equivalent to nine months' wages for an average low-skilled occupation), one young man said 'You could plan your whole life on that', which reinforced a common observation that poverty mired people into short-termism, and constant preoccupation with how to get from one day to the next.

Others said if they suddenly saw an upturn in their fortunes that they would invest in bigger businesses to make more money and to care for others. As Suntu, a 40-year-old batik-maker asserted: 'If I was a rich girl, I would build a house for my family and relatives. I would support my relatives and close relatives, and I would have a small shop' (as opposed to a stall). Yassime (27) would not give up work, but instead of continuing as a waitress, would open a business and 'work very hard to get more money' in order to better enable her to help her natal family. Banjugou, a 13-year-old schoolboy from Bakau, stated: 'I would be helping the poor people – I would be going to their houses and giving them contributions.'

On hitting hard times, most respondents declared they would turn to their bosses or relatives, although the latter could be tougher since reciprocity is often limited when many people are long-term unemployed and inability to pay back can lead to strained relations (see Chapter 3 in this volume). By the same token, people in need of help are unlikely to be refused given the strong pressure on Muslims to give alms to those who are worse off. This is especially the case with food and shelter, with some truth in the popular stereotype that no Gambian turning up on any compound will be denied a meal or space to sleep for the night. However, when the stakes are bigger or involve longer-term commitment, this is a rather different matter, especially for those who are just above the breadline. Satou (38), for example (Box 4.5), who runs a batik stall at Cape Point, makes only a modest profit ('I am not rich, I am just trying') and her income drops drastically during the low season, but the fact that she has her own business means that people perceive she is well-off and come to her for assistance. While noting that men tend to turn people down because they spend their money 'enjoying themselves', Satou like most women, maintains that she cannot refuse, and in fact has been highly proactive in helping others. Not only does Satou have four children of her own, but has also made space in her rented apartment for three adoptive daughters and a grandchild. One adoptive daughter, aged 15, is a relative of Satou's who had become pregnant 'up country' by a schoolteacher who denied rape. Satou invited her to come so that she could escape community gossip and opprobrium. Another adoptive daughter, named after Satou herself, is a 'family friend' of 13 and came to Satou when her mother suffered a disease which left her handicapped and could no longer look after her. The third adoptive daughter, a 'little girl' of 10, came to Satou when her father died. Her mother had seven other children to educate, so Satou took her off her hands and is paying for her schooling.

Grassroots Perceptions of Gender and Generational Aspects of Poverty

Leading on from the above, many women feel that they are more victimised by poverty than men precisely because they have to spend their meagre incomes on others. As the female fruitsellers and batik-makers group concluded: 'If you are a woman you always have to think about having to spend it (money) on everyone else, whereas men will just use any surplus income to secure a second wife' (see also Sear et al., 2006).[26] One of the members, Teeda, complained that 'Men are not doing anything – if they pay for breakfast, it's women who pay for lunch and dinner. Women pay for school lunches. You see the festivals, and it's the women who are selling.' Teeda also added that 'some men are not working, and some men refuse to work, or if they work they don't do it for that (the family)'. A fellow respondent echoed that men are different to women and prone to spend any cash they have on their own gratification or enlarging their reputation among male friends: 'Men follow money, then they start to follow little girls.' Similar views came through in other discussions, such as in a residential compound in Bakau, where the women pointed out that it is they who are mainly responsible for sending children to school and for feeding them. In another predominantly female group of participants aged between 20 and 53 in Old Jeswang, women commented that men can just put on their '*haftan*' (kaftan) and go out, whereas women have to stay behind to answer their children's needs. Although Musa (27) felt that poverty could bring women and men closer to one another on account of having to struggle together in the face of adversity, most women feel that poverty causes tensions and unhappiness, especially given feelings of injustice and being hard done by when men do not provide and there is not enough to feed and clothe the children. For this reason, despite the Senegambian proverb 'A bad husband is better than an empty house', some women profess that they prefer to remain alone, especially if they have already had children and/or their children are grown up (see Box 4.5).

BOX 4.5   POVERTY, GENDER AND FAMILY FROM THE PERSPECTIVE OF SATOU

Satou is 38 years old and was born in Bakau. She identifies herself a Serahuli and a Muslim, and, in addition to her native tongue, is conversant in Wolof, Fula, Mandinka, Jola and English

Partly because she was born in an urban area, Satou was fortunate enough to be sent to school which allows her to read newspapers and write letters, but once she had completed her six grades of primary school at the age of 15, 'they sent me to marry'. Her father decided to give her away to his sister's son, Ebrima, who at the time was 40. Satou, who had been circumcised as a baby, was a virgin at the time. She recalls how she was fixed up in a white loincloth by an old woman before consummating the marriage, and that her mother was especially proud when the bloodied garment was paraded before the wedding guests

Although Satou's husband was a first cousin, the blood connection did not spare her from extremes of humiliation and cruelty. Ebrima customarily beat her up, and she still has scars on her forearm and breasts where he hit her with the buckle of his belt. One bout of violence was so bad that she lost their first baby seven months into its term. Often Ebrima would set upon her out of jealousy – for example, if she happened to smile at any male guest he brought back to the house. Satou had no recourse to any protection because her husband was a peripatetic migrant and in the early years of their marriage took her far from her natal family to live in Sierra Leone. After five years of marriage, by which time

Satou had borne three of Ebrima's children (one son, now 20, a daughter aged 19 and a daughter of 16), he packed her bags and told her to get out. This was mainly because he had decided to take a second and younger wife, whom he declared would keep the son, and if she maltreated him, then so be it. So desperate was Satou to keep her child that she hung on in the marriage where she felt like 'furniture', for another couple of years. Then, when they moved back to The Gambia's Upper River Division, and Satou was pregnant by him for the fourth and last time, she managed to obtain the necessary support of her parents to exit the marriage, eventually obtaining the divorce she had long aspired to.

While Satou's personal life has been chequered in other ways (for example, she was not reunited with her eldest daughter until the latter was 14 and about to become an unmarried mother), she has drawn a lot of strength from her success as a businesswoman. Satou has been batik-making and selling for the last seven years, prior to which she had sold fruit for 15 years. Her transition to crafts trader came about as a result of training and funding provided by the SDF grant to the Sunwing Association at Cape Point market. Batik-making is more profitable than fruit-selling, although Satou claims that there is so much competition that she may need to diversify further. One idea is to try to sell the co-op's goods at international trade fairs. With this in mind, she managed to engineer state-funded trips to Germany in 2000 and the UK in 2003. She has also registered her business with the Chamber of Commerce. Satou claims that the best period in her life, however, came in 2000, when she was elected President of the market association and was chosen by the UNDP and Government of The Gambia to participate in the committee directing operations. This committee was full of 'big men' and foreigners, yet although Satou was offered translation facilities, she insisted on speaking in English and they were impressed with what she had to say. Given her humble background and relative lack of education she is amazed that she has ever got to this position, and has met the President and Vice President of the country. Sunwing recently won a prize for the best women's project in The Gambia, and is regarded as a model, where everyone pays rent for their stall, but the proceeds are reinvested in the cooperative and are used for services and new equipment.

While Satou is generally quite successful, during the 'off season', which begins in mid-April, she sometimes goes two to three weeks without selling anything which makes it extremely difficult to pay the monthly 1500 dalasi (US$45) rent for her serviced apartment, not to mention feeding her extended family and paying her contribution to the association. However, given her previous history Satou has no desire to join forces with another man. Although Satou claims that 'No woman can live without a man', and has had a boyfriend for the last three years who is currently working in a factory in the USA, she prefers to keep the relationship strictly non-cohabitational and informal. The only problems are that Satou has had to keep it a secret to avoid gossip, and that in Serahuli culture, as with other ethnic groups in The Gambia, to be 'sitting without a husband for 15 years' is frowned upon.

The majority view at the grassroots that women are poorer than men was also attributed to the fact that women have to work harder than men to earn comparable money, with their earning capacity compromised by housework, childcare and labour force discrimination. In addition, because their lives in general are harder, marked by more stress, suffering and responsibility. As in the institutional survey, women in their middle years who are supporting children, and often older adults such as their parents or parents-in-law, are often regarded – and regard themselves – as the worst off, although many younger women are also observed to be in a similar position.

Young women, in turn, are the most outspoken about gender inequalities at the domestic level, resenting the fact that many men eschew work in order to spend time at the *bantaba* (sitting area often under a large tree), where they get together to talk, to drink '*ataya*' (green tea), to share '*manis*' or '*taba*' (tobacco), and to play draughts or card games, sometimes with small bets. Indeed, a focus group of eight schoolgirls in Bakau was virtually unanimous about men's pursuit of self-gratification and unwillingness to work being a prime cause of poverty in The Gambia, many of the girls themselves being in part-time employment in order to help their mothers and compensate for the idleness of their menfolk. Sophie (15), for example, declared that while women should be sitting and watching after the children, they have to work because 'some fathers just used (that is, are accustomed) to sit and chat, drinking *ataya* (green tea)'. Such sentiments are not restricted to this particular group of young women, as evidenced in selected writings of women in their late teens and twenties attending a centre for skills training and literacy (Box 4.6).

BOX 4.6 VIEWS ON GENDER AND WORK FROM YOUNG WOMEN IN AN ADULT SKILLS AND LITERACY PROJECT

'Women's Work' – Harriet Ndow

Looking at a picture I can see a woman carrying some wood. She is carrying a baby and holding a baby boy too. The other children are coming to her.

There are some men seated at the bantaba drinking green tea and probably talking about the woman with her children.

There are trees around the compound. The houses are mud houses. There are fences around the compound and a door between the fences.

The men are at the bantaba talking about all kinds of things and the woman is walking. She has looked for wood and is coming to cook. She is with her children too.

Men of today never help women. They just sit talking about some things all the time. I see this happening all the time. We must try to change it.

'Women Have More Work than Men' – Mary Mendy

Women always do more work than men in many ways. Sometimes they will be working and at the same time, carrying their baby on their backs.

A lot of work at home is being done by women, and you see most of the women doing work that belongs to men, such as paying school fees for children and buying clothes for them. The women also do work such as washing clothes, cooking, cleaning, bringing water, going for shopping, and taking care of children at home, such as disciplining them, and also going to find wood.

Whilst some men are sitting at the bantaba chatting and drinking attaya, the women are working hard because they have children to take care of. The men are lazy and refuse to go and work.

Division of Work in the Home – Mariama Conteh

My observation on the division of work in The Gambia is that women work more than men. You can see a woman, when she wakes up in the morning, she will sweep inside and outside the compound. Whilst doing that she will be cooking breakfast for the family whilst her husband will still be in bed.

She will fetch water for the family to bathe. When her husband wakes up he will take his bath, eat his breakfast and go to his place whilst the woman will go to the market to sell the fruit she has planted in the garden. After selling it, the little money she has she will use to buy food for the family and soap to wash the clothes.

A woman will be doing two things at one time such as cooking the lunch and washing the clothes, and after that she will have to rush to the garden till the evening.

Then she will come home to wash the plates, sweep the floor, take care of her children, fetch water for the family, and prepare the family dinner whilst her husband will be with his jobless friends thinking about how to marry another wife!

Source: Saint Joseph's Adult Education Centre (2003).

Some men acknowledged these gender inequalities, such as Edrisa (21) who observed that even if women are now being encouraged to study and work, they still have 'less education and less liberation'. Sfax, the palm rhun worker, was of the same opinion, pointing out that women's access to employment is more limited because they do not have the same freedom to migrate to the coast, where wages are higher. Musa, the newspaper-seller, also declared that while poverty was a struggle for both women and men, women probably suffer more because they have so many obligations to others and therefore less opportunity to address their personal plight.

Yet despite considerable evidence that women often sacrifice their own needs in order to spend on others, one observation, made by two young male bicycle repairers of Guinean extraction, was that women often did less well than men in business because they tended to 'sit on their savings' and be too risk averse. Men, by contrast, often plough all their profits back into their business and make it grow.

Another rather different view, was that the value of women's 'saving powers' would often be cancelled out by expenditure on 'luxury' personal items such as clothes, oils and skin-bleaching products. On top of this, some men commented that married women were potentially better off than their husbands because in addition to receiving money from them, they are entitled to keep any money they make themselves. These men, who felt that women and men were '50-50' these days, also identified that projects for women, together with female encroachment into politics and paid labour represented a major change from the past when 'our fathers exploited our mothers'. Indeed, some felt women are in an even *stronger* position than men because 'the government is concentrating more on women' and exercising policies of positive discrimination. For example, Isa (26) noted that to get into the college where he is training to be a teacher, the passmark out of 200, is 100 for males, but only 93 for females.

Yet among women themselves, there are rather more mixed opinions as to the state of gender equality. On the one hand, some advances identified included the fact that tourism had created more livelihood opportunities for women and strengthened their economic capacity. In addition, institutional initiatives were celebrated as having brought some benefits. This was especially evident among women interviewed in the context of SDF- and FASE-supported projects, who felt official support for women's enterprises had increased their sense of empowerment. In turn, Jammeh's rhetoric about the vital role played by women in Gambian economy and society had made them feel more valued. Satou (Box 4.5) for example, stated that 'Fortunately, things are getting better – we have a good government – it considers women', continuing: 'President Jammeh loves women, he wants to empower them. He sees that women are striving hard. He says that women work harder than men. Nowadays women have "voice", and they are taught about their rights.'

Aside from this rhetorical acknowledgement of women's contributions, and the several micro-credit schemes which have been introduced during Jammeh's period in office, women also feel that the president has drawn attention to the need for protecting women in the event of divorce by at least keeping a shelter over their heads. As Satou declared: 'I can remember that he once said to men, if you are married, and have four wives . . . you are free to choose (to divorce) but you have to go out of the compound' (that is, leave the compound to your wife, making it harder for men to divorce). Yet although more women these days have their name on compound ownership papers than in the past, the majority do not, and, in practice, many women end up with nothing when their marriages break down. This is partly because the bulk of the population are Muslim, and in the Cadi courts, Shari'a law prevails. As Fatou in her fifties declared, most women have to leave their compounds when their husbands are no longer interested in them. Similarly, although the DOSSW nominally helps women to take husbands to court when they are left with young children to care for, many do not pursue child maintenance in the interests of 'having a quiet life'. On top of this, major brakes on gender inequality are posed by women's virtually exclusive responsibility for reproductive labour, and the pattern for men to continue thinking that 'they are the boss'.

Intersections between Poverty, Gender and Household Transitions

Although many women complain about the hand dealt to them in marriage, this continues to be a social expectation for all women (and men) in The Gambia. However, for women who have been widowed or divorced, it is slightly easier to stay alone, and often attractive economically, with some noting that male partners often contribute too little – or, worse still, rely on women's earnings. As voiced by Satou, who had a particularly bitter marital history (Box 4.5): 'It's not a problem for a woman to be without a husband – she can be free and independent if she has no husband. There is no one to condition you, no beating, no fighting. A woman needs a man but she can still have a boyfriend.'

Some mentioned that as long as women have other men in their lives – lovers, sons, other male relatives and so on – they could probably survive just as well if not better. Indeed, one 14-year-old male focus group participant declared that women probably only needed a husband to have a son, who could provide help and security in later life. This was also mentioned by Hadi (37), an unmarried mother of a 23-year-old daughter, who had managed to survive on her own account for a very long time and had no need of a spouse for anything other than pleasing her parents (see Box 4.7).

BOX 4.7 POVERTY, GENDER AND FAMILY FROM THE PERSPECTIVE OF HADI

Hadi is a 37-year-old Jola Muslim Shiite who speaks Jola, Mandinka, Wolof, Fula, a little English and a little French. Jola Shiites have their heritage in the Casamance region of Senegal (both Hadi's parents come from here), although Hadi herself was born in Sifor, Kombo South, in The Gambia. All the Jolas from her region have a club to which they make small, but regular, donations of around 20 dalasis (*c*. US$0.60) a month, and these are used to help each other out in times of need such as medical emergencies, funerals and marriages. Hadi commented that Jola women are very hard-working ('man work, lady works'), unlike Fula and Mandinka women who tend to stay at home while husbands provide, and Wolofs who generally 'do not like to work', particularly the women. Although this is clearly a stereotype, it was one which Hadi lived up to, having worked as a full-time housemaid without a break for over 20 years.

Hadi, who has never married, has one daughter, Mariama, 23 years old, who is currently completing high school (senior secondary). Hadi and Mariama live with Hadi's younger sister, who is also a housemaid, and her sister's son who is a student. The four-member household resides in a small rented unit on a large compound in Churchill Town, Serrekunda, for which they pay 300 dalasis (*c*. US$9) a month. All share the domestic labour, although Hadi's sister, who works shorter hours, tends to do the sweeping of the compound, goes to the market and does the cooking, while Hadi fetches the water first thing in the morning and makes the beds.

Hadi, who was the second eldest in a family of six children (five girls and one boy), had no schooling at all because it was 'too expensive'. Her father, a small farmer, had said 'I've not got the money to educate so many children, so I will just pay for the education of that boy. You girls, you will be married and work for the home.' Hadi started working on the family farm (a multi-purpose plot growing rice, cous [cous-cous], corn and groundnut) when she was about 11 years old, at the same time as helping out with domestic labour, such as pounding rice, 'catching water', sweeping, washing clothes, and cooking food.

Despite these inauspicious beginnings, Hadi has managed to work as a housemaid since adolesence and, fortuitously, mainly for Europeans who, she claims, pay much better than native Gambians. Hadi currently earns 1000 dalasis a month (US$34) for a six-day week, which is more than most of her fellow workers. Hadi has worked with her present employer, an expatriate hotel owner, for seven years now and has had seven employers in all, with one European tending to recommend her to another when they leave. Although Hadi is by no means well-off, she told me she intended to retire after the rainy season in 2004 because 'I am tired, and my bones ache'. She hopes to put her savings into opening a small restaurant or shop in a new rented house.

It is hard to see how Hadi actually has accumulated any reserves since aside from contributing her share of the rent, she and her sister spend 550 dalasis (*c.* US$16) between them each month for a bag of rice (the staple food), and an additional US$26 for 'fish money'. Moreover, Hadi has to find nearly US$1 a day for transport for herself and her daughter, and every two months, she and her sister try to scrape together around 200 dalasis (just under US$6) to send to their parents (their other sisters and brother also taking a turn in this).

In respect of Hadi's personal history, she fell pregnant by a Fula boy at the age of 15. Although her parents and sisters had advised her against seeing him because he was from a different ethnic group, Hadi was in love, and also encouraged by the fact that the tradition for first cousins to marry was breaking down by this time – mainly because of too much pressure on families when couples split. Unfortunately the boy's parents were against him marrying a Jola, so Hadi ended up raising Mariama on her own. She said she was lucky that many of her employers did not mind her bringing the baby along. This allowed her to work and to put Mariama through school. After finishing, Mariama will probably go on to do law, and

Hadi hopes this will enable her to look after Hadi when she's older. In fact Hadi was so worried that this plan would be foiled when her daughter got pregnant at 20, that she begged money from her employers to pay for an abortion in a private clinic. Hadi claims that Mariama's pregnancy was probably her darkest hour given that she had invested so much in her for so long. Indeed, because 'mothers suffer for their children', Hadi feels that women have much a tougher time than men.

Although Hadi has had two boyfriends since Mariama's father, whom she came close to marrying, she was let down. Hadi feels so bitter about these experiences that she professes she would rather never be in love again: 'I have my eye open, and my brain open. I don't like it . . . I suffer, I close.'

This said, Hadi's main mission at the moment is actually to get married, not because she herself wants or needs a man in any way (financially, emotionally or sexually), but because her father would like her to do so to bring 'respect' to the family (and to Allah), before he dies (he is presently in his early 50s). Hadi's daughter will also have 'more respect' if Hadi is married herself. Ideally, Hadi would like a man who has already got two wives, so that she can continue to live in her own place with her daughter, sister and nephew, and not be bothered too often. She does not want his money (and certainly does not want to give him money), although she would like a son because there's more assurance that a son will be able to look after her in old age. If Mariama marries someone who forbids her to support her own parents, Hadi fears 'When I'm old I may be poor . . . so better to get a son as well'.

For the moment, however, Hadi claims to be enjoying her life. She is not rich, but she says that she manages to 'have nice, healthy food, and nice fish', and always lives in the hope that 'God will give' – for example, by finding someone who will take her daughter off to Europe.

Hadi's success as a lone parent arguably is owed in part to the fact that she has been able to pool resources with her sister, although not all cases of household extension are deemed positive by individuals, as evidenced in the case of Sfax who had to give up his highly valued independence when he fell on hard times (see Box 4.8). This said, while Sfax is in what he regards as the unfortunate position of having to share with relatives other than his parents (who had since passed on), household extension with one's natal family is a different matter. Indeed, older women and men alike are taken

BOX 4.8   POVERTY, GENDER AND FAMILY FROM THE PERSPECTIVE OF SFAX

Sfax is 27 years old, lives in Bakoteh, and is currently working in a 'palm rhun' firm which supplies palm timbers used as roof beams in building construction.

Referring to himself a 'provinces boy', Sfax was born in No Kunda, North Bank Division, in 1977. He is a Mandinka and Muslim, but had broken his month-long Ramadan fast within five days when I last met him, saying that it was 'too much to fast on Fridays' (the traditional Gambian 'half-day'). Sfax's 'born mother' died when he was only 7 years old, so he was raised by his father and a stepmother, and shared a home with several half brothers and sisters. Their main source of income was the family groundnut farm.

Sfax claims to have started his primary education when he was 'too small' (=young), but did not get his primary leaving certificate until the age of 15, at which point he came with his father to Western Division, where he did one year of high school. Since lack of funds prevented him continuing, he dropped out and started going down to the beach to look for work, sometimes sleeping in a tent overnight 'like a soldier'. Reasonably soon he managed to get a job as crew on a Dutch fishing boat running trips for tourists, for whom he worked 'for three good years and eight months'. A recommendation from the ship's owner then landed him with his first job as a pool attendant at a small luxury hotel. Although the main reason Sfax got the job was because he was vouched for by his employer, another point in his favour was that being literate enabled him to read the chemical specifications of the cleaning products. Although things went well for two years, however, Sfax made a mistake with the quantities one day which caused a mass break-out of skin complaints among the guests and resulted in his immediate dismissal. Although Sfax went on to clean other pools, including for a foreign embassy, when his contact left he lost his job, which forced him to turn to his friend in the palm timber firm for help. Sfax does not like his present job because it pays so little, and does not really see it as a 'real job', only a stopgap. His earnings have also been slashed by about 50 per cent to about US$26 a month. The advantage with pool cleaning work is that it is low intensity but highly paid, and as Sfax says: 'I like to earn big money.' When he had been doing the pools, Sfax had been sending at least a sack of rice back to his father and stepmother, but this has stopped due to his declining fortunes, and he declares: 'I miss sending money to my father.'

During his time as a pool cleaner Sfax had shared rented quarters with another young man, but at present he lives in a single room on a compound in Bakoteh, which belongs to an uncle who is currently in France. Sfax's aunt does the cooking and everyone eats out of the same bowl – usually rice, domoda (peanut soup/sauce) and bungo fish, but Sfax does his own cleaning and washing (having previously paid a maid to do it).

Sfax sees himself as 'very poor' at the moment, and 'not comfortable'. This is mainly because he does not have a proper job and is reliant on others for his accommodation. Neither does Sfax like living with so many relatives, one reason being that whenever he has money he is obliged to spend it on them. 'This is Africa! You can't afford to have too many relatives. You spend too much!' Sfax also deplores the lack of independence and privacy attached to living in such crowded circumstances. Indeed, aside from lack of income, material goods and his own home, having no choice and no personal space is a big part of poverty as Sfax construes it.

If Sfax was better off he would do many things. He would not be forced into 'hustling' for credit or handouts. He would like to rent, 'without disturbance' and have 'more peace', or buy land and then rent out rooms on part of the plot. Another alternative would be buy a boat and hire it out for fishing. He would carry on working though, since 'without work I cannot live', and this is certainly the only way he is likely get himself out of his current predicament, unless he is lucky enough to find a 'white lady' who can buy him all this, as well as a car!

Aside from aspirations to marry a rich foreigner at some point in the future, Sfax's ideal partner would be – someone educated, beautiful, 'good habit', 'heart clean' – someone who is amiable and is liked by everybody, someone who will reflect well on Sfax and that he can take pride in. He declares he dreams of people saying: 'That is Sfax's wife – isn't she nice, isn't she beautiful?'

By the age of 32 he would also like to be back in high school to finish his education and thereafter specialise in management and diplomacy, perhaps moving into a government post. From there, and perhaps within ten years from now, when he is 37, Sfax jokes about aspiring to be the President or 'King' of The Gambia!

care of by their children. Thus, regardless of having little education or money of their own, elderly people are often not the poorest, the majority view of the men in the Serrekunda Transport Union being instead that they are the best-off 'because we care for them all the time'. Adding that 'It is customary in Gambian society for children to help their families – all are vocationally involved helping parents', the Serrekunda men concluded that it is actually more of a struggle for the younger members of society to keep up these obligations.

These burdens on the young are recognised by some parents too, and for this reason Satou (38) said 'I always tell my son "I will not force you to marry. I don't want you to have two wives. I want you to marry an educated girl, and I don't want to stay with you"' (to be dependent in any way).

However, just as most parents expect support from their children, children do not necessarily see this as a burden. Being raised in a culture in which there is considerable respect for elders, and where young Muslims commonly articulate the belief that the more one does for one's parents, the more 'blessings' one will have in life, the notion of working out of duty and obligation is rarely questioned (see Taal, 2003: 24). This said, it is important to note that such duties may fall unevenly within households, such that girls and elder siblings often take on more than their fair share of domestic and paid labour, often from an early age (Chant and Jones, 2005), and continuing after marriage too.[27] Yet, while Yassime (27) represents a classic case of this syndrome (see Box 4.9), she observes that people are increasingly living apart where they can, and relying on their families less at the same time as helping them out less too.

BOX 4.9   POVERTY, GENDER AND FAMILY FROM THE PERSPECTIVE OF YASSIME

Yassime is 27 years old, was born in Banjul, and currently works as a waitress in Fajara. She is a Jola, and Muslim, with a Gambian father (aged 75), and Senegalese mother (50), both of whom are retired. Although both had jobs in the past, her father as a cook, her mother as a housemaid, they had such difficulty bringing up their children that to alleviate the pressure they sent Yassime to Senegal to live with a childless aunt. Here Yassime did six grades of primary education, graduating when she was 16 years old. Having missed her family profoundly, Yassime returned to The Gambia as soon as she had completed her studies. Her first job back home was to work as a hair and beauty therapist at an exclusive salon, which she did for seven years between the ages of 17 and 24, securing this through a personal contact with the Gambian Lebanese business community. Then, however, through the same contact, she obtained her current job as a day waitress at an upmarket hotel, where she earns about US$60 basic wages a month, and about the same again in tips. Yassime gives 75 per cent of wages over to her parents, who completely depend on Yassime and her three sisters. Indeed, as a daughter, Yassime regards her main role (and that of her sisters) as being to support her parents, and even when she is married, she professes that she will continue to do so from the 'fashion shop' she intends to open.

Despite the fact that most of Yassime's money goes to her parents, she still manages to save a little in a joint account with her sisters, and also participates in work-based and neighbourhood-based '*osusu*' (informal rotating credit schemes). Yassime's sisters are all working: the eldest is a cook, the second a hairdresser, and the fourth (younger than Yassime at 24) is a gallery and shop attendant. The sisters also have a 14-year-old brother whose education is funded entirely out of their contributions. On top of their economic role in the household, the girls are also responsible for the cooking and cleaning, and, even though they pay a washerwoman to do the laundry, Yassime has very little time to herself at all: when she comes home after her eight-hour shift at the hotel (she works six days a week as is common for most hotel and catering employees in The Gambia), she does at least two hours' housework. This leaves only a small amount of time to watch television before she sleeps, and visits to her fiancé (see below) are limited to Sundays. Yet Yassime takes pride in the fact that 'I help my parents too much' ('too much', meaning 'a lot').

This seems unlikely to change much when she marries Mohamed, her 38-year-old fiancé, who is an electrician, and is relatively comfortable financially. They will move, in accordance with custom, to his compound in Barra, which is quite far from her natal home in Abuko, but Yassime will visit her parents regularly and continue to provide economic support. Indeed, throughout their four-year courtship Mohamed has often handed gifts to her parents of up to 7000 dalasis a month (US$210).

Yassime reckons that 'before' women were poorer than men, because only the men used to go out to work, and the woman just stayed at home. Nowadays, however, as life is getting harder in The Gambia, 'women are pushing themselves to get something; women are getting their own money'. This is mainly driven by the fact that most families cannot survive on just the man's income, so in some senses women's relative decrease in poverty is driven by an increase in poverty in general. Although not explicitly linked here, Yassime led on from this part of the discussion with the observation that for women 'it is very important to have your own money'. Why? Because then you can use it as you wish, and not be dependent – one has more discretion over how it is spent. 'Before, you used to have to ask your husband for each thing, like 50 bututs (half a dalasi, or less than one cent) for a match.'

In response to the question as to whether there is any difference in status between men and women including men having more respect, power, privileges and so on, Yassime responded yes, that if you are married 'you have to follow the man too much' – what he says, goes, especially if you are a Jola (like she is) or a Mandinka.

Yet Yassime's lengthy courtship with Mohamed represents a marked change from the experience of her parents who hardly knew each other and had their marriage arranged for them. As Yassime reported: 'The man's parents would tell the lady's parents, I would like your daughter to marry my son – and that was that!' In turn, their long courtship has allowed them to plan something of how their married life will be. Most significantly Yassime has told him 'you can't take away my right', and he has declared his consent to her having her say, which she hopes will follow through in practice. This includes allowing Yassime to open a 'fashion shop', to have only two children (even though he would like more), and to hire a maid for childcare and housework. The reason Yassime wants to have a small family (and will use family planning to make sure it stays that way), is because she sees children as expensive on account of their nutrition needs, health needs, school fees and so on. 'If you want your child to be somebody, then you have to give them something.'

In light of the above, one question I asked Yassime was how she felt about gender-biased systems of inheritance. This was motivated by learning that Mohamed's recently deceased father had left his four properties to each of his sons, leaving the daughter disinherited, and also, that Yassime's own father had already put his son's name down to inherit the entire compound, despite the fact that he and the rest of the family had been supported by Yassime and her three sisters for so many years. As indication of an area where there seems to be little scope for negotiation between the sexes or generations, Yassime simply opined 'We're used to it, so we don't see it as something very bad'.

Conjugality, fertility and inter-generational transfers
Although most young women I interviewed are unlikely to remain single,
many profess to be very much on their guard to avoid a bad marriage. The
teenage schoolgirls in Bakau, for example, claimed to be constantly
fending off the efforts of boys and men to seduce them, cynically talking
about men coming out with the same hackneyed phrases to any woman
they fancied such as, 'I love you. I see something from you. I like you. I will
care for you. We will have a beautiful child.' This is often accompanied by
men taking out a wad of dalasi notes (which they have borrowed from
friends or purloined from their sisters) and thumbing through them in
front of girls to give the impression that they are marriageable and responsible, when in all likelihood they are not. Indeed, many women (and some
men) talk about the fact that nowadays a man looks for a woman who is
earning money and can therefore make their own lives easier. Satou (38)
added that even 'small boys' (of 13–14 years) pursue women old enough
to be their grandmothers in the street, calling out 'I love you', and always
with their eye on the main chance – sex and, if the woman in question is
white, money.

The prospects that women may fare better in marriage than in the past
may be slightly stronger as a result of changing patterns of courtship and
parental intervention in recent decades. For example, among the senior
generation, women were often 'married off' early, sometimes without
knowing their spouses, and perhaps within three months of the arrangement being sealed by the ritual payment of kola nuts by the groom to the
bride's parents. Although parents can still exert an influence, many women
stressed that 'love marriages' are on the rise and you can choose your own
spouse. One of the reasons for the increase in more companionate marriages is the possibility of meeting the opposite sex at school and growing
up with them. In addition, courtships are longer, giving couples a better
chance of getting to know one other. For example, Teeda (35) spent three
years 'going up and down' with her husband, and Hadi (30) divulged that
she had 'played with her husband' for nine years, including having children
with him, before they got married. Yet although young single women often
stressed that they would not marry until the age of 20–25, they would not
delay it much further because men are usually only interested in 'little girls'.
This was endorsed by Juldeh, a 38-year-old Fula in the Serrekunda union
group who declared, that whereas in the past Fula girls would be married
off as young as 10 or 11, 'the school system has jeopardised this' such that
now they are 15 or 16, or even 18 before they marry. The worry here, according to Juldeh and many other of his colleagues, is not only that non-
marriage might encourage lesbianism, but that 'maybe the girls have been
tampering with men and have got pregnant'. Isa (26), also a Fula, claimed

that he would probably marry a woman much younger than him because most women his age have already been taken by older men. Another advantage here would be the likelihood that she would still be a virgin. With her sexual propriety being of the utmost importance, Isa talked of wanting a 'serious girl' for a wife – one who can control her sexual desires – 'one who has respect for elders and a good manner of dressing' (hijabs [headscarfs], veils, long robes and so on).

In choosing their own husbands, the kinds of criteria women take into account are 'good habits' (such as regular prayer) and 'decent'/ 'respectable' family background. If the man's family is 'good', then there's a chance that marriages will last longer, which is critical given that with short unions women are prone to lose everything, including their children. Indeed, in cases where women and men get divorced, women say it is better not to pursue the husbands for maintenance through the courts, because then men feel they have the right to come and take the children away. Indeed, even if women do not, this may still happen, as is the intention of Sahou, who has recently left his wife and two young children (see Box 4.10). This said, women stressed that men tend to ignore children when they are young, and often only show an interest when the children are older, working and have something to offer! As articulated by Satou: 'When your children become a Minister or a Director, that is when the men start to get interested.'

BOX 4.10   POVERTY, GENDER AND FAMILY FROM THE PERSPECTIVE OF SAHOU

Sahou, now 30, considers himself poor mainly because he never had an education and remains illiterate. This said, he is in a stronger economic position than many of his peers because he has recently been able to purchase his own taxi with the financial help of an uncle. He has painted it green (rather than its original yellow) which has converted its status from 'bush taxi' to 'tourist taxi'. This allows him to exploit the most favourable fares in the country such as in the Senegambia tourist area. Although Sahou does not have a clear idea of his profit, after paying for fuel and upkeep, he probably clears 8000 dalasis a month, which at 2003 rates of exchange is equivalent to US$210, and five times more than the average salary of a hotel waiter. For this he works from 7 a.m. to 10 p.m. each day, often seven days a week.

Sahou, a Fula and Muslim, was born in a small village in Upper Nyumi, North Bank Division, in 1974. Sahou started full-time work at the age of 14, having been brought up with an older sister and younger brother by a widowed mother. There was no money for him to go to school, so he spent his childhood helping his mother and siblings on a farm growing groundnuts, potatoes, pepper, cassava and grains such as corn and cous. Since there was no money in farming, he decided to take off for the coast around Bakau where he learned English by talking with locals and tourists. He had no money to open a shop, so, knowing that taxi-driving was better remunerated than other activities and would give him more independence in the long run, he latched on to a taxi driver as an apprentice.

By the age of 22, after an eight-year apprenticeship, Sahou managed to obtain a taxi driver's licence in his own right, although the terms of his trade were not as he wished. He had to 'rent' the taxi from a boss who paid him a weekly salary of about US$23, but required Sahou to hand over his earnings from rides. Although Sahou desperately wanted to buy his own taxi, his ability to save up the necessary sum of US$300 was held in check when at the age of 25 he married a 13-year-old girl called Adama, who bore him a son within nine months of knowing him, and a daughter following three years later.

Despite the fact that he and his wife put up with considerable hardship in the early years of their marriage, in 2003 Sahou finally succeeded in buying his own taxi (16 years after he first started getting into the business). At this stage he left Adama and their two young children (aged 1 and 4 at the time) in a rental compound in Serrekunda and moved to a single room in Bakau. The reason given by Sahou was because his wife insisted on having two of her brothers living with them, and they were not contributing any money to household expenses. With Sahou earning better money, he reckoned they would have even less incentive. Since leaving them all in Serrekunda, Sahou has also informally divorced Adama. However, he still goes back to see the children periodically, and provides a little food money, although his master plan is to take the children away from his wife within the year and 'put them with my sister in Barra'. While Sahou claims he misses his children, he will actually probably see less of them in Barra than he does at the moment, because of the distance and fuel costs. This is likely to be even more the case if Sahou fulfils his wish to travel and work abroad.

Monogamous marriage was another trend identified, and tends to be more favoured by women than men. While a number of men declared that they preferred monogamy, even among younger age groups, where economic hardship and lack of property conspire against this, as well as leading to postponement of marriage (Taal, 2003: 16), aspirations to polygamy are not uncommon. For example Isa (26), as yet still single, professed that in addition to wanting any wife of his to stay at home and perhaps only run a 'doorside' business selling bananas, coconuts, groundnuts and water melon, he would actually like four wives because this would mean that if one is pregnant or indisposed then he could gratify himself sexually without resorting to 'the sins of adultery and fornication'. An additional perspective, aired by the female fruitsellers, was that men feel that with one wife they have a 'headache'. With two wives, however, there is peace, because the women compete with one another to gain favour and give the husband an easier time. The fact is, however, that most men, even if married only to one woman, engage quite extensively in informal polygyny. As Satou noted, many men just want to have sex with you and then finish and 'change women'.

While recognising the importance of children in providing economic security in old age, a number if not the majority of women wish to limit births, deeming quality to be more important than quantity. Teeda (35) from Bakau who has four sons opined: 'With fewer children you can enjoy your family. There are too many families, they are suffering, nobody to help you (with so many children), better to enjoy.' A number of young girls claim only to want between two and four children. This is mainly for reasons of cost but also because they believe that having too many children is ageing, and 'if you age quickly your husband will leave you!'

Whatever the case, access to contraception is generally regarded as a 'good thing' and has made life decidedly easier for married women. Teeda, for example, receives hormonal injections from the family planning clinic, and Haddy (32), also from Bakau, stressed how impressed she was with the choice on offer including the loop, the pill and condoms. For young single women, by contrast, use of contraception is associated with their being seen as 'rampant' or 'prostitutes' and there are few outlets where they can actually access them. This places them at risk of out-of-wedlock pregnancy which arguably has worse consequences. Schoolgirls in Bakau, for example, talked about this inviting serious scolding from mothers ('I told you, sit down and work until you have a husband and maintain with abstinency'), and fathers going the extra mile, saying 'I will kill you, and I will kill the one who makes it to you'.

As for most women, and particularly men, however, large families are still desired, mainly because they are perceived to be positively correlated with security and wealth, in addition to which planning can go against the 'will of Allah'. As one 27-year-old single mother of two put it, 'Children are God's gift'. Among the five men in the Serrekunda transport union, most of whom were in their middle years and had between two and eight children, most would have preferred to have had more – for example, Juldeh (38) declared he would have liked a 'whole football team', but poverty restrained him. Garba (41) added that there is considerable pride attached to having a large family in Gambian culture. It creates more relationships, leaves someone after you when you die, and is also economically more advantageous: 'more people to look after you'.

Younger men, too, often expressed the wish for a large family. Alagi, for example, a 21-year-old GNYSS participant said he wanted five children because they could help him when he is old. Isa, 26 years, a trainee teacher, who reckoned on having four wives, hoped that each would have seven which would give him a total of 28 (like many of the older respondents in the survey).

Grassroots Views on Poverty Alleviation Initiatives

Direct experience of anti-poverty programmes among many respondents had produced quite high awareness of poverty alleviation initiatives, as in the case of the women from FASE- and SDF-funded projects, and GNYSS participants. In many cases, the training and/or credit people had received (or were receiving) was viewed as having given them an important helping hand as well as going some way to 'empower' them, as reported earlier for women members of the Sunwing Association. Young people from GNYSS also talked about how their training and skills would strengthen their capacity for running their own businesses such that they might not be so poor in later life. Men in the transport union, who had been consulted for the PRSP, also felt that this has been important groundwork for more effective combatting of poverty, although they were doubtful about how the implementation of pro-poor development strategies would actually come about.

Indeed, many saw that poverty was so endemic to The Gambia that little short of a miracle would solve the problem, especially given cynicism about government and political accountability more generally. As articulated by Yassime (27): 'They're (agencies) involved in this politics too much – I see that as wasting my time . . . I have this card to go to vote but I prefer to work hard to earn money. They (the politicians) don't know me' (and by implication, they do not care).

CONCLUSION: IS THERE A 'FEMINISATION OF POVERTY' IN THE GAMBIA?

Notwithstanding some discrepancies between official and grassroots views, there is actually surprising consistency in terms of how people in The Gambia define and conceptualise poverty, especially in respect of material difficulties, such as lack of income, food, education, health and shelter, and for women in particular, multiple privations and demands on their time and labour.

One of the most interesting findings relating to poverty's gendered and generational dimensions is that while it might have been expected that elderly women would be more vulnerable than others, especially given their lack of basic capabilities, long-term formal sector employment and absence of pension entitlements, the culture of children supporting parents is so entrenched among The Gambia's predominantly Muslim population that elderly women are rather better off than women in their middle years and even young women (see also below).[28]

Second, female-headed households in The Gambia do not seem to be regarded, or to be in practice, worse-off than their male-headed counterparts. Because ties with extended kin remain strong and resources flow both within and between households, household headship seems to make little difference to people's well-being, especially where women have fathers, brothers, uncles and sons who can fill the breach left by absent husbands. Indeed, the only compelling reason for female heads to (re)marry seems to be out of the desire to please parents, to minimise speculative gossip about their sexual behaviour, and/or gain the community's respect. Yet while accepting that it is socially difficult for female heads of household to be without men, the pressure on women to relinquish their autonomy can be extremely detrimental materially. Women in male-headed households are consistently compromised in earning by demands that they should fulfil all reproductive duties, and if they do have remunerated work, then they are likely to have to take on major responsibility for household expenses too. As such, expanded roles among women often simply serve to feminise labour efforts in households, and afford men even more scope to enjoy freedom and entitlements which are completely out of proportion to their investments in family life.

Third, and in a similar vein, it cannot be denied that young women are benefiting in many ways from gender equality initiatives, including increased access to education, vocational training, and an emerging culture of female professionalism and independence. Yet, while all this, in principle, puts them at less risk of poverty than their mothers and grandmothers, they also frequently find themselves with even more obligations to support others. Although young women rarely complain about this situation, the familial demands placed upon them clearly act to diminish some of the personal benefits prospectively offered by their increased human capital. This relates not only to expectations of transfers to natal kin but to husbands' relatives, with men often looking to marry women with earning potential. Yet since women's social status and 'respectability' derive primarily from having children in the context of marriage, even men with little to contribute to household livelihoods themselves effectively have women in a situation where they have limited room for manoeuvre. As such, while it may be inappropriate to talk about a 'feminisation of poverty' as an ongoing trend in strictly money-metric terms, it could be said to apply if poverty is conceived more broadly as constraints on personal freedom and time, and as associated with heavier inputs of labour under increasingly exploitative conditions.

Leading on from this, while poverty has accorded women more space to be independent (for example, by pushing them into situations where they are earning their own income), it has also had adverse effects in respect of women bearing the burden of poverty-combatting programmes. Although women often celebrate their involvement in these, it could also be levelled that their female bias simply reinforces the idea that women should uphold obligations to others. More disturbing still is that among young women there is little in the educational curriculum which appears to be fostering notions of greater gender equality in family responsibilities. Empowering women of all ages to negotiate their way out of self-sacrifice and subordination is clearly something which will require more than micro-credit, vocational training or education as these currently stand.

NOTES

1. In 2003, fruits and vegetables accounted for as much as 22.8 per cent of total domestic exports (DOSFEA, 2004: 16).
2. Although in June 2004 Sierra Leonean refugees faced a deadline for UNCHR-assisted repatriation, and the end of special benefits for those remaining in The Gambia, many have stayed behind.
3. Following the return to civilian rule in 1997, primary education in The Gambia became officially designated as 'lower basic' education and junior secondary as 'upper basic'. In 1998, the Department of State for Education (DOSE) declared the intention not only of achieving nine years' basic education for every Gambian child (starting at the age of 6 or 7), but at least a 50 per cent transition rate to (senior) secondary education (DOSE, 1998; see also GOTG, 2000: 107). In order to smooth the transition from lower to upper basic, 'Basic Cycle' schools in which the complete nine years of basic education is taught are presently being established (Martin, 2003: 12–13).
4. The 'Education For All – Fast-Track Initiative' 2004–15 came into being with the World Forum on Education in Dakar in 2002 which reaffirmed calls for the provision of primary education for all children and the reduction of adult illiteracy with support from

multilateral and bilateral agencies (see Uchida and Ogawa, 2002). The EFA-FTI was devised as a 'development compact' offering donor financing for countries willing to prioritise universal primary education and to embrace policies aimed at improving the quality and efficiency of the primary education system. The Gambia was added to the list in 2003.

5. From the age of 20 years upwards, the male economic activity rate is higher than the female, as discussed later.

6. TANGO is the umbrella organisation for 95 registered NGOs in The Gambia.

7. The most recent poverty survey (Integrated Household Poverty Survey/IHPS) was conducted in 2003, but as with the Census which was undertaken in the same year, data entry has been impeded, *inter alia*, by irregular electricity supply, and full results have not yet been made available to the public.

8. The Gini coefficient produces a score between 0 and 1, with a figure nearer to 1 meaning a more unequal distribution of income.

9. Personal communication, Abdou Touray, Director, SPACO, Banjul, November 2003.

10. I am grateful to Alu Sarr of the CSD for providing 2003 data on household headship, as well as for speculative discussions as to why the poverty incidence among female-headed households had undergone such a pronounced increase in the period between 1998 and 2003. Regrettably, Mr Sarr, along with Falu Njie, the director of SPACO, admitted to being as baffled as me as to why this should have occurred. Clearly, the possibility of error in the data cannot be discounted, although as of August 2006, this remained impossible to determine.

11. Poverty Reduction and Growth Facilities were established by the IMF in 1999, and, as of March 2005, 78 countries were classified as eligible for assistance under this initiative. The PRGF lending is conditional on approved PRSPs, and on demonstrable commitment to higher social expenditure, especially pro-poor spending. Loans are awarded with an interest rate of only 0.5 per cent per annum with repayment due within ten years, beginning 5.5 years after the start of the loan.

12. *Kafos* are traditional community organisations, usually gender or peer groupings, which are mostly engaged in sociocultural activities (FASE, 2003: 20).

13. The GEM is omitted from Table 4.7 because it has not been calculated by the UNDP for all 3 countries.

14. One typical article – 'Don't Shout at Husbands' by Musa Saidykhan – was published in *The Nation* (22 June 2004: 1–2). Reporting on the views of the Imam Camara of Tabokoto Mosque, the article describes how he declared at a wedding: 'It's a pity to know that housewives in Tabokoto deliberately behave ungodly towards their husbands. I wonder why they keep shouting at their husbands at the peak of their voice. The menace has become rampant and it appears women don't even bother about it. Islam has given rights to women but they have gone extra-mile and as a matter of fact they behave shamelessly on their spouses. They succumb to Satanic tides thus abdicating their marital responsibility.' The Imam continued: 'it has come to my notice that most housewives keep creating endless problems for their husbands. If men had not been tolerant, a lot of homes would have been shattered by now'. Appealing to wives to avoid being cursed in this world and the hereafter, Camara exhorted: 'Please distance yourselves from disrespecting your husbands. A woman is duty-bound by Allah to be obedient to her husband. Those who shout on their husbands cannot be termed as good housewives.' At the same ceremony, the Iman also advised women to treat the children of their co-wives fairly, and an old woman in attendance added that while women should not be bullied, 'Womanhood goes with a lot of weaknesses that's why men should at all times guide us . . . Culture and religion teaches us that men are always on top of us which is why they marry us.' Another article, published in *The Independent* (28 June 2004: 5 – 'Women and Domestic Violence' by Fatou Badjie), talks about traditional beliefs of many being that women need to be 'kept in line by their husbands', and should not 'try to wear the pants in the household'.

15. *Daily Observer*, 16 June 2005: 10 – 'The Home and Education', by Omar Sanneh.

16. The legal system in The Gambia comprises Received English Law (Common Law and Equity), Shari'a (Muslim) Law, and Customary Law (GOTG, 1998: 10).

17. *Forayaa*, 28–31 April 2005: 5. Letter to the editor from Yankuba Jaiteh, Grade 10 student.
18. A Matrimonial Bill proposing that marriages should only be polygamous with the express consent of the first wife at the time of contracting the marriage has been sitting in the National Assembly since 2000. Some argue this is due to lack of a critical mass of feminists in parliament to drive the proposal.
19. The paramount social and symbolic significance of ties with kin – even distant or fictive – is evidenced in the frequent and ongoing cross-over of kin-based terminology to describe people with different kinds of relationships. For example, good friends and even acquaintances and strangers are often referred to as 'brothers' and 'sisters', and father's younger brothers are sometimes called 'stepfathers' or 'small fathers' instead of uncles because often they act as second fathers, indicating the way in which kinship is often shaped through function. In addition, signs of respect are to call older men – even just by a few years – 'Dad' or 'Uncle'. The importance of relatives in general rather than as specific individuals is such that people often enter 'My family' in the Next-of-kin box on their identity cards.
20. Despite the high incidence of poverty in The Gambia, an increasing number of people possess mobile phones (often second-hand ones brought into the country by relatives or friends from abroad as gifts, or recycled and bought cheaply in markets). This is mainly because of the dearth of landlines, although it should also be noted that mobile phone ownership is higher among men who regard this as a status symbol.
21. *Forayaa*, 28–30 April 2005: 10, NGO Report on Women's Affairs in The Gambia.
22. *Forayaa*, 16–19 June 2005: 10, NGO Report on Women's Affairs in The Gambia.
23. Personal communication, Adelaide Sosseh-Gaye, Director, Worldview The Gambia, November 2003.
24. In April 2005, FAWEGAM held its first ever week, comprising exhibitions and lectures, to make the Gambian public aware of their achievements in girls' education. Among these are a total of 1066 scholarships awarded to girls by FAWEGAM since its founding in 1997 (see *Daily Observer*, 19 April 2005: 10, article 'SoS Faye opens FAWEGAM's exhibition', by Ramatoulie Charrek and Saffiatou Bah.
25. Although there was considerable ethnic variation among my respondents, all but one was Muslim.
26. While seemingly confident and outspoken in one-on-one interviews and in single-sex groups, women are much less likely to be so with men, adopting more passive strategies such as sulking instead.
27. See also Punch (2001; 2002) on the importance of birth order, as well as other factors such as sibling composition and gender in determining the work experiences and strategies of young women and men in rural Bolivia.
28. This confirms John Caldwell's (1976; 1977) classic arguments about wealth flowing from children to adults in West Africa, whereas in other contexts in the Global South, such as Latin America, resource transfers tend to be from parents to children (see Escobar Latapí, 2003).

5. Gender, generation and poverty in the Philippines

INTRODUCTION

Following the same format as the previous chapter, the first section of this chapter sketches in a broad overview of development and gender in the Philippines, reviewing the extent and characteristics of poverty on the basis of official documentation. In the second half of the chapter attention shifts to the views of professionals and people at the grassroots, with particular regard to their perceptions of a 'feminisation of poverty'.

My grassroots fieldwork in the Philippines was conducted in Metro Cebu, the country's second biggest urban agglomeration after Metro Manila (see Figures 5.1 and 5.2). Situated in the province of Cebu, Metro Cebu's population of nearly 1.8 millions is made up of Cebu City itself (718 821 inhabitants), and ten smaller cities and/or municipalities, the second and third largest respectively being Mandaue City (269 728) and Lapu Lapu City (217 019). Cebu City itself was the point where Ferdinand Magellan disembarked on the archipelago in 1521, and was the site of the first permanent Spanish settlement in 1565. Cebu has long been an important industrial, shipping and commercial centre, not only being the Philippines' second major port after Manila, but since the 1980s, a major hub of international tourism (NEDA, 2002: 30). Visitors to the Central Visayas (otherwise termed 'Region VII' – see Figure 5.3), where Cebu is the principal destination, numbered 824 498 in 2000, with over one-quarter being from overseas (mainly Japan, Korea and the USA) (NEDA, 2002: 75).

Cebu City is also a national leader in rattan furniture and wood products, fashion accessories such as shellcraft jewellery, and, increasingly, IT production, with Central Visayas being the first region to be connected to the Internet (NEDA, 2002: 23). In turn, Lapu-Lapu City is home to the first Export Processing Zone (EPZ) in the metropolis (MEPZ/Mactan Export Processing Zone). Specialising in electronics and garment production, it has over 100 companies, mainly Japanese, with overspill having led to the establishment of MEPZ II in 1997, which contains 24 firms, principally electronics and automotives. Although the latter tends to recruit more

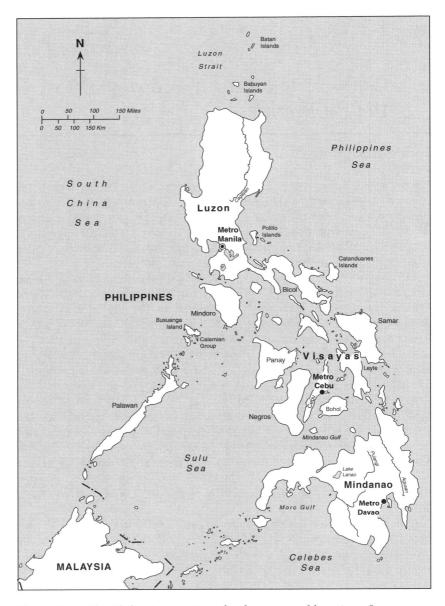

*Figure 5.1   The Philippines: major island groups and location of
           Metro Cebu*

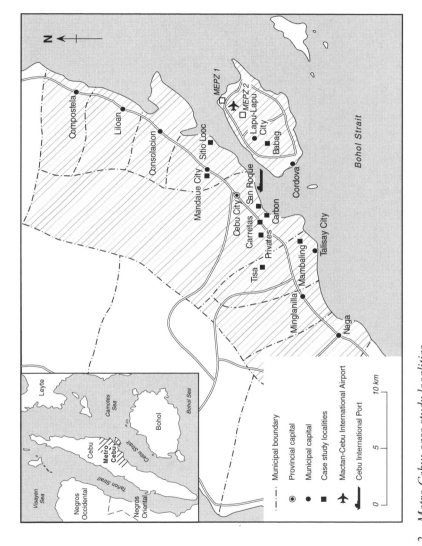

Figure 5.2   Metro Cebu: case study localities

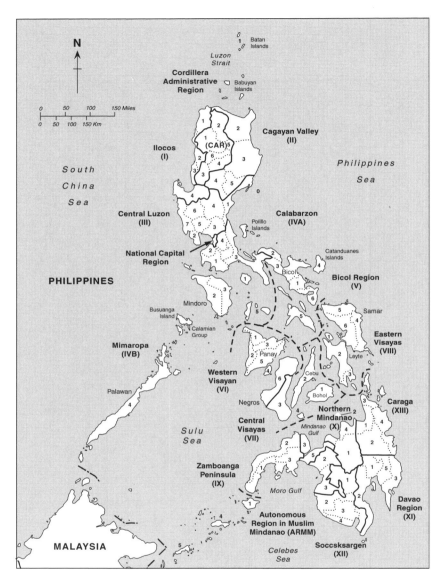

Figure 5.3 The Philippines: regions and provinces

REGION/PROVINCE

National Capital Region (NCR)

Cordillera Autonomous Region (CAR)
1 Abra
2 Apayao
3 Benguet
4 Ifugao
5 Kalinga
6 Mountain Province

Ilocos (I)
1 Ilocos Norte
2 Ilocos Sur
3 La Union
4 Pangasinan

Cagayan Valley (II)
1 Batanes
2 Cagayan
3 Isabela
4 Nueva Vizcaya
5 Quirino

Central Luzon (III)
1 Aurora
2 Bataan
3 Bulacan
4 Nueva Ecija
5 Pampanga
6 Tarlac
7 Zambales

Calabarzon (IVA)
1 Batangas
2 Cavite Laguna
3 Quezon
4 Rizal

Mimaropa (IVB)
1 Marinduque
2 Occidental Mindoro
3 Oriental Mindoro
4 Palawan
5 Romblon

Bicol (V)
1 Albay
2 Camarines Norte
3 Camarines Sur
4 Catanduanes
5 Masbate
6 Sorsogon

Western Visayas (VI)
1 Aklan
2 Antique
3 Capiz
4 Guimaras
5 Iloilo
6 Negros Occidental

Central Visayas (VII)
1 Bohol
2 Cebu
3 Negros Oriental
4 Siquijor

Eastern Visayas (VIII)
1 Biliran
2 Eastern Samar
3 Leyte
4 Northern Samar
5 Samar
6 Southern Leyte

Zamboanga Peninsula (IX)
1 Zamboanga Sibugay
2 Zamboanga del Norte
3 Zamboanga del Sur

Northern Mindanao (X)
1 Bukidnon
2 Camiguin
3 Lanao del Norte
4 Misamis Occidental
5 Misamis Oriental

Davao Region (XI)
1 Davao
2 Davao del Sur
3 Davao Oriental
4 Davao del Norte
5 Compostela Valley

Soccsksargen (XII)
1 North Cotabato
2 Sultan Kudarat
3 South Cotabato
4 Saranggani

Muslim Mindanao (ARMM)
1 Basilan
2 Lanao del Sur
3 Maguindanao
4 Sulu
5 Tawi Tawi

Caraga (XIII)
1 Agusan del Norte
2 Agusan del Sur
3 Surigao del Norte
4 Surigao del Sur

male operatives, the traditional emphasis on light assembly has not only favoured a plant-based but also a subcontracted workforce dominated by women with Region VII having the highest proportion of all homeworkers nationally (31.8 per cent) (Hornilla, 1995: 2).

The incidence of poverty among families[1] in the Central Visayas dropped from 59.9 per cent in 1985, to 39.9 per cent in 1997, but, given the heavy dependence on Cebu and on multinational manufacturing and international tourism, the Asian crisis of 1997–98 provoked a rise to 43.1 per cent in 2000, which was greater than the national level of 33.7 per cent (Reyes, 2002: 7, table 6; also later). This said, poverty in rural parts of the region in 2000 (51 per cent) was more than twice as prevalent in urban areas (23.6 per cent), and my own survey suggests that some of Metro Cebu's poor count themselves fortunate compared with other parts of the country. This is partly due to sustained efforts to address poverty by Local Government Units (LGUs) and NGOs, the latter having 40 per cent representation in Cebu's city government compared with 20 per cent elsewhere. Cebu was also chosen as the UN Habitat's 'Women Friendly City' in 2004 owing, *inter alia*, to it being the first Philippine city to adopt a Gender Code, and, due to the efforts of a local NGO, Lihok Pilipina, to have pioneered a flagship programme against domestic violence – '*Bantay Banay*' (see Figure 5.4; also later).

DEVELOPMENT AND POVERTY IN THE PHILIPPINES

Philippine Economy and Society in Brief

The Philippines gained independence in 1946, after 50 years of US control, a brief interlude under Japanese occupation (1941–44), and prior to that, over 300 years of Spanish rule. The country consists of 7107 islands (although only 2773 have been named), which fall into three main groups: Luzon, the Visayas and Mindanao (Figure 5.1). Lying between 4 and 21 degrees north of the equator and spanning a total area of 300 000 km², the Philippines has a tropical equatorial climate in Mindanao, and a tropical monsoon climate in the two more northern island groups, marked by a five-month rainy season from late May to early December. Administratively the country is divided into 16 regions (Figure 5.3), which as of 2003 comprised a total of 79 provinces, 115 cities, 1495 municipalities and 41 945 *barangays* (administrative villages) (NSO, 2003).

In 1986, the 'People Power Revolution' wrested the country from over two decades under President Ferdinand Marcos which had included a

Note: Photograph by Sylvia Chant.

Figure 5.4 Lihok Pilipina poster on women's unvalued labour, Cebu City

highly unpopular nine-year regime of martial law. This ushered in a new constitutional democracy led by Corazon Aquino, the widow by assassination of one of Marcos's major rivals, Benigno Aquino. Aquino's administration was succeeded by that of Fidel Ramos (1992–98), and then by Joseph ('Erap') Estrada who was deposed three years into his regime in January 2001 on grounds of corruption by the 'People Power II Coup'. Estrada's Vice President, Gloria Macapagal Arroyo completed his term which ended in June 2004, and was then re-elected until 2010. Arroyo belongs to Lakas (Lakas ng Edsa – National Union of Christian Democrats), the chief entity in the People's Power Coalition (PPC), which, despite a reasonably vibrant range of opposition parties, has dominated national politics since the ousting of Marcos.

The Philippine president, under normal circumstances, is constitutionally limited to a term of six years with no re-election, and heads the executive branch of national government aided by a Vice President and a 24-member Cabinet. A legislative branch is made up of a bicameral Congress of the Philippines which has 24 senators and over 200 elected district representatives, while a judicial branch comprises the Supreme Court and other special courts. At provincial and municipal levels, officials are elected and serve a three-year term.

After the demise of the Marcos regime during which poor economic performance led the Philippines to be regarded as 'the sick man of Asia' (Balisacan and Fuwa, 2004: 2), an aggressive neoliberal growth strategy was introduced as a means of bringing the country up to speed with its more successful neighbours. A process of trade liberalisation, which commenced in 1986 with the relaxation of import restrictions, accelerated during the 1990s, with further tariff reductions and a Foreign Investments Act (1991) which removed barriers to foreign direct investment (FDI) over a three-year period (Lim and Bautista, 2002: 12–13). Foreign capital inflows reached their highest level in 1996, constituting 5 per cent of GDP. This liberalising trajectory continued under Ramos who introduced an unprecedented programme of privatisation (see Perez-Corral, 2002a: 196–7).

Whether these measures have benefited the Philippines is widely contested, not least because of their adverse effects on distribution and exposure of the country to greater financial risk (see for example, Illo, 2002a; NCRFW, 2004d: xvi). However, during 1994–97 the country managed to sustain an average GDP growth rate of 5 per cent (Lim and Bautista, 2002: 14). Although the Asian crisis of 1997 and the El Niño drought of 1998 engendered setbacks, real GDP growth in the Philippines rose from 3.4 per cent in 1999 to 6.3 per cent in the first half of 2004 (NEDA, 2004: 3, table A), the main driver of growth since 2000 being services, especially the telecommunications sector (EIU, 2005b: 2).

While there may be some cause for optimism in respect of GDP, however, other aspects of contemporary economic development in the Philippines are less positive. Although inflation was only 3.1 per cent in 2002 (NSO, 2003: 38), for example, it climbed to 7.6 per cent in 2005 (EIU, 2006b: 11). Other disturbing factors are that the Philippines has not succeeded in bringing down its foreign debt, a substantial amount of which was inherited through the profligacy of the Marcos family and its cronies. While in 1988, the total external debt was US$29 million, by 2004 it had increased to US$69.4 billion, with the debt service ratio standing at 15.7 per cent (EIU, 2005b: 5). Moreover, despite ongoing attempts to stimulate and diversify the economy, GNP per capita (at 1995 prices) was virtually the same in 2000 (US$12 871), as it had been in 1981 (US$12 643) (Lim and Bautista, 2002: 46, table 3). In addition, investment in the Philippines (at *c*. 20 per cent of GDP) is now the lowest in South-East Asia (where it averages 30–35 per cent), due, *inter alia*, to peace and order problems, weak confidence in the government's enforcement of contracts, and the high costs of setting-up business in the country (UNDP Philippines, 2004: 11).

Concerns have also been aired about the country's increasing reliance on the export of a relatively small range of manufactured goods (Illo, 2002b: 20). Although the Philippines has a broader export base than The Gambia, comprising machinery, transport equipment, coconut products and chemicals, the largest share is made up by garments (which dominate traditional exports) and electronics (non-traditional exports) (Lim and Bautista, 2002: 26). As of 2002, for example, electronics alone generated as much as 68 per cent of the Philippines' export earnings (Aganon, 2003: 140).

Another problem with manufacturing in the Philippines is that its major products are heavily import-intensive. While in 2002 exports generated a total of US$70.6 billion, imports cost as much as US$35.4 billion (nearly half this amount being consumed by electronics and components), mostly from the USA and Japan (NSO, 2003: 39). In addition while the manufacturing sector contributes more than 20 per cent of value-added in the country, it generates only half as much in respect of employment (UNDP Philippines, 2004: 11). Another problem is that the Philippines' leading sectors face increasing competition from other countries in South-East Asia. During 2003, stagnation in exports (posting a decline of −4.5 per cent) was largely due to the poor performance of electronics exports which faced mounting competition in OECD markets from China (EIU, 2004b: 11 and 29).

One sector which looks relatively healthy, however, both in respect of employment and foreign exchange generation, is international tourism, which has been growing fairly steadily in the last decade. In 2002, visitor arrivals totalled 1.9 million which was around double 1990 levels (WTO,

2005). Only 4 per cent of visitors in 2002 were overseas Filipinos, with just over 1 million coming from other countries in Asia (NSO, 2003: 36). Receipts from tourism in this year amounted to US$1.7 billion (compared with US$1.3 million in 1990), with the average spend being US$102.9 a day for foreign visitors, and US$53.7 for visiting overseas Filipinos (NSO, 2003: 37). In the first half of 2004, there was a 32.4 per cent increase in international tourists from the same period in 2003, and a 40.6 per cent increase in visitor receipts, and the hope is that by 2010 annual international arrivals will reach 5 million (NEDA, 2004: 70 and 73). This said, over and above its long-standing association with 'sex tours' (see later), the Philippines only attracts one-quarter of the tourists visiting Thailand and Malaysia (WTO, 2005). In order to rectify this it is planned to inject more government investment into 'gateway cities' such as Manila, Cebu, and Davao (NEDA, 2001: 22).

Another major source of foreign exchange, and one which is often regarded as the Philippines' prime export commodity, is labour (Alcid, 2002a: 86). Overseas deployment of Filipinos by local and foreign agencies is regulated through the Philippines Overseas Employment Administration (POEA) which in 2002 processed a total of 891 908 land- and sea-based overseas workers (NSO, 2003: 28). Overseas contract work (OCW) is generally undertaken by one or two members of a household, and the level of dollar remittances is high (see Table 5.1). Indeed, as of 2002 the Philippines ranked third globally among all remittance-receiving countries with a total of US$7.4 billion, or 9.5 per cent of GDP (IOM, 2005). While overseas migration boosts the economy with repatriated dollar earnings and helps the Philippines to work around its shortage of domestic employment (Orbeta, 2002: 11), the tendency for more skilled people such as teachers and nurses to leave the country results in something of a 'brain drain' or 'de-skilling' of national resources. In turn, overseas Filipino workers (OFWs) themselves often end up working in menial occupations in destination areas (NCRFW, 2004a: 7; Parreñas, 2001: 245; also Ball, 2004: 121). With the tightening up of immigration controls in many countries, especially in post-crisis Asia, there are fears that the mismatch between qualifications and opportunities will intensify, with Filipinos limited to jobs that are 'SALEP' ('shunned by all nationals except the very poorest'), or '3D' ('dirty, demeaning and dangerous') (Alcid, 2002a: 84). This not only includes domestic employment but jobs in the 'entertainment' industry – a euphemism for 'sex work' (ibid.: 85). Yet notwithstanding the often inferior and/or underground nature of their work it is claimed that women remit just over 70 per cent more than their male counterparts: indeed, in the first two months of 1995, Filipina workers in Hong Kong (mostly in domestic service) sent home US$36 million compared with just $1.2 million by the more numerous and largely male workforce in Saudi Arabia (Mission,

Table 5.1   The Philippines: remittances from overseas workers, 2001–03

Sending region	Remittances in millions of US dollars		
	2001	2002	2003*
Africa	3.6	3.9	9.6
Oceania	21.2	33.3	25.5
Europe	406.2	659.6	472.1
Middle East	711.9	725.2	654.6
Asia	1049.6	1092.4	676.8
Americas	3300.3	3609.7	2808.2
Others	742.1	805.9	416.4

Note: Data pertain to the months up to and including August 2003.

Source: NSO (2003: 29).

1998). The importance of OFWs to the national economy is such that Aquino referred to them as 'the new heroes' (*'mga bagong bayani'*) (see Chen, 2005: 48; Lutz, 2002: 100), with Arroyo coining the strategic term 'Overseas Filipino Investor' (OFI) (de Guzman, 2003, cited in Chen, 2005: 49). This said, given the prevalence of skilled workers among overseas migrants, the benefits of remittances tend to be skewed towards richer families who can afford the costs of a recruiter.[2] For example, in the early 1990s, the richest 20 per cent of the population obtained 11.5 per cent of their income from overseas remittances, whereas this was only 1 per cent among the poorest 20 per cent (World Bank, 1996: 45).

As part of a drive to reduce reliance on OCW and to create skilled domestic opportunities, one important initiative discussed at length in the country's main planning instrument – Medium-Term Philippine Development Plan (MTPDP) – which is coordinated by the National Economic and Development Authority [NEDA]), as well as enshrined in the country's technology plan ('IT21'), is to develop Philippine expertise in information and communications technology (ICT). In 2000, the Philippines had 1.5 million internet users, up from 1.1 million in 1999, and as many as 1.2 internet hosts per 10 000 people, compared with only 0.8 in Indonesia, and 0.1 in India. The country has also developed a number of 'IT Zones' or 'ICT Parks', which offer a variety of incentives for ICT businesses. As noted by NEDA (2001: 32):

> The Philippines enjoys significant comparative advantages in ICT – an English-speaking, highly educated, easily trainable, and skilled workforce with a growing track record of successful ICT work; a basic policy environment that is right for business; government commitment at the highest levels, with strong private

sector support in pursuit of a common ICT agenda; and rising entrepreneurial
abilities suitable for a globalising economy. With its rich human resources, and
strategic location in Asia and the Pacific, the Philippines has the potential to
fully benefit from an ICT-driven development strategy.

Despite this optimism, many poorer Filipinos are not only unable to buy a
computer, but lack the electricity to run one, Moreover, the Philippine
Long Distance Telephone Company (PLDT) charges as much as P2500
(US$44) monthly for broadband connection, which is a month's wages for
some lower-paid workers.[3]

Population and demographic dynamics

The Philippine population grew almost fourfold between 1948 and 2000,
from 19.2 to 76.5 million, and by 2005 was 87.5 million (EIU, 2006b: 5).
The population comprises a diverse range of ethno-linguistic groups,
including the Tagalog (28 per cent), Cebuano (13 per cent) Ilocano (9 per
cent), Bisaya/Hilgaynnon/Ilongo (7.6 per cent), Bicol/Bikol (6 per cent),
and Waray (3.4 per cent). Over 80 per cent of Filipinos profess to be Roman
Catholics, a further 5 per cent Muslims (or '*Moros*') (concentrated mainly
in Mindanao), and 2.8 per cent Evangelical, with the remainder, various
Protestant sects such as the Aglipayan, Iglesia ni Cristo, Seventh Day
Adventists, Jehovah's Witnesses, Born Again Christians, and the United
Church of Christ in the Philippines.

   Although population growth in the Philippines declined from about 3
per cent per annum in the 1960s, to 2.3 per cent in the 1990s, the rate is still
almost twice that for Thailand and Indonesia, owing mainly to high fertility levels (NEDA, 2001: 109; Orbeta, 2002). While the TFR has dropped
from a peak of 6 at the beginning of the 1960s, Filipino women still give
birth to an average of 3.2 children (see Table 1.2). Given that half the
female population is currently in the reproductive age group (15–49 years),
and 37 per cent of the population as a whole is 14 years or under, growth
is likely to remain high for the foreseeable future.

   One reason for high fertility is that despite progress in bringing down
infant mortality in recent years (from 45 to 29 per 1000 between 1990 and
2001), data suggest the trend is very uneven, being only 20.9 per 1000
among the richest quintile of the population but as much as 48.8 per 1000
among the poorest (Herrin et al., 2003: 18, table 17). Despite a decline in
maternal mortality rates from 190 to 172 during the 1990s, these also
remain among the highest in Asia (ADB, 2004: viii), part of the reason
being that only 60 per cent of births in the Philippines are attended by
skilled personnel (WHO, 2005a: annex table 8).

   Another reason for high fertility is that while contraceptive use has
tripled since the introduction of family planning in the 1970s[4] the Catholic

Church exerts a powerful influence over the bulk of Filipinos, and its advocacy of restricting birth control to 'natural methods' seems to have been particularly persuasive among the poorer segments of society (Lakshminarayanan, 2003: 97). In turn, poorer women seem to have less access to, and more limited choice in, contraceptive methods (Orbeta, 2002; UNDP Philippines, 2004). In 2003, for example, contraceptive prevalence among the poor was only 42.9 per cent compared with 51.5 per cent among the non-poor, and in respect of modern contraceptive methods, levels were 29.5 per cent and 37.6 per cent respectively (Herrin et al., 2003: 8, table 6). While the non-poor have a TFR of only 2.1, the corresponding rate for the poor is 6.5 (ibid.). Fertility differentials according to socio-economic status are even more marked among the young, with 1998 data revealing that the fertility rate for the 15–19-year age group among the poor was ten times that of the rich (ibid.: 11).

An additional factor constraining high birth rates in the Philippines is that abortion remains illegal except in the most extreme circumstances and has traditionally met with such opprobrium, mainly on religious grounds, that clients needing post-abortion care have often been denied treatment in public health facilities (see Shire and Pesso, 2003). Despite indications of an increasing number of abortions being performed by medical and paramedical personnel, women who cannot afford the luxury of travelling overseas often have to induce terminations themselves through the use of prostaglandins such as Misoprostol, or by seeking the aid of traditional practitioners whose techniques include deep abdominal massage (Singh et al., 1997). Population Commission (POPCOM) figures indicate that poor women are the likeliest candidates for abortion, with one of the three main reasons given being 'economic difficulty' (UN/UNIFEM, 2003: 71). Since an estimated 400 000 unsafe abortions take place annually it is no surprise that these constitute the fourth leading cause of recorded maternal deaths in the country (Singh et al., 1997; UNDP Philippines, 2004: 27). This is unlikely to change given the Philippine government's reluctance to include emergency contraception as a 'preventive measure' (NCRFW, 2004a: 8).

Among the consequences (and concerns) of continued high fertility in the Philippines is that youth dependency will remain high, with 43 per cent of Filipinos being under 18 (NORFIL, 2004). Certainly, the Philippines does not yet have a problem with elderly dependency, with only 5.9 per cent of the population being over 60, and 3.8 per cent, 65 years plus (NSO, 2003: 5). In turn, the dependency ratio of the elderly on the 'economically productive' population (aged 15–64 years) in 2000 was a mere 6.5 per cent, compared with 62.6 per cent for youth (NSO, 2003: 6). Nonetheless, this still makes for high dependency overall, especially in relation to neighbouring countries where only 40 per cent of the population are estimated to need support from others (ADB, 2004: 7). Since high dependency ratios tend to depress savings, and physical and human capital investments, the Philippines has missed out on the 'window of opportunity' or 'demographic bonus' which has occurred in other parts of South-East Asia as lower fertility produces a temporary bulge in the economically active population before elderly dependency sets in. Instead, the Philippine situation has been described as one of a 'demographic onus' (Orbeta, 2002: 3).

With regard to the spatial distribution of the population, there has been a virtual doubling in the urban population since the 1970s, to 60.2 per cent in 2002, with natural increase now being more important than migration (DOLE, 2002: 3). Although there has been some filling out of the urban hierarchy in the last 30 years and some diminution in the dominance of Metro Manila, the latter has 10 million inhabitants, which along with the 1.8 million residing in Metro Cebu and 1.7 million in Metro Davao, means that the country's three metropoli contain one-quarter of the urban population between them.

Overseas migration, as touched upon earlier, has also been a distinctive feature of Philippine population dynamics, especially since the country launched its overseas employment programme in 1974. In 2000, it was estimated that a total of 7.4 million (*c.* 10 per cent) of Filipinos lived abroad, with around one-third of these (2.6 million) being permanent migrants (DOLE, 2002: 5). Although earlier in the twentieth century most went to the USA, from the 1970s onwards destinations have diversified to the Middle East and other parts of Asia, such as Japan, Korea and Taiwan (see Table 5.2).

Traditionally, overseas migration was dominated by men, with women as recently as 1975 being only 12 per cent of the total (Milagros et al., 2004: 203). By 1987, however, they constituted 47 per cent, and from 1992 onwards, women have exceeded men among first-time and land-based workers contracted by a foreign employer through a licensed placement agency. In 2000, as many as 69.1 per cent of OFWs registered by the POEA were female (Morada, 2001: 2, table 1).

In 2001, the dominant occupations among male OFWs were as plant and machine operators and assemblers (29 per cent), and trade and related workers (27 per cent). As for female OFWs, 57.4 per cent were in sales and services (predominantly as domestic workers), with the category of 'Overseas Performing Artists' (OPAs) being predominantly female (UN/UNIFEM, 2003: 39). Although women may not embark on migration with a view to sex work, many are tricked or forced into the 'entertainment industry'. Japan is the biggest single recuiter admitting entry to *c.* 80 000

Table 5.2   *Land-based overseas Filipino workers (OFWs) deployed*
2001–03 by region of destination

Region of destination	Number of deployed OFWs		
	2001	2002	2003*
Oceania	2 061	1 917	910
Trust Territories	6 823	6 075	2 775
Africa	4 943	6 919	4 874
Americas	10 679	11 532	7 641
Europe	43 019	45 363	24 191
Asia	285 051	288 481	166 924
Middle East	297 533	306 939	176 814
Unspecified	11 530	10 882	6 144
Total	661 639	678 108	241 618

Note: * = Data pertain to the months up to and including July 2003 and, as with other years, include only those migrants contracted through licensed placement agencies.

Source: NSO (2003: 28).

Filipina entertainers a year, who may find themselves having to service 30 clients a night (Alcid, 2002a: 85). Even where women do actively seek work as entertainers, however, their main objective is usually to gain access to a 'transnational field' (see Yea, 2004; also NCRFW, 2004d). Many hope to stay in destination countries through marriage, despite the fact that Taiwan, Singapore and Malaysia have banned marriage to local men, and in the latter, even foreigners working in the country (Alcid, 2002b: 101; Chen, 2005: 55; Zlotnik, 1995). Despite this, as summarised by Pineda-Ofreneo (2002a: 61): 'The feminisation of migration continues unabated as women pour out of the country to become domestic helpers, entertainers and factory workers abroad even as they encounter worsening work conditions and more abuse in their host countries which are threatening to send them home.'

Employment

In 2003, the Philippine workforce numbered 34.6 million, 30.4 million of whom were actively employed, with 37 per cent being in agriculture, fisheries and forestry, 16 per cent in industry (comprising manufacturing, mining, construction, electricity, gas and water),[5] and 42 per cent in services (BLES, 2004: 5; see also Tables 5.3 and 5.4). Nearly half the workforce (48 per cent) are in the 'formal sector', with government

Table 5.3   Employment in the Philippines

Branch of employment	% of workforce
Agriculture, fishery and forestry	36.7
Mining and quarrying	0.3
Manufacturing	9.5
Electricity, gas and water	0.4
Construction	5.7
Transport, storage and communications	7.5
Wholesale and retail commerce	18.5
Hotels and restaurants	2.3
Finance and real estate	2.8
Public administration, defence and compulsory social security	4.8
Education	3.0
Health and social work	1.2
Other community, social and personal services	3.0
Private households with employed persons	4.1
All	100.0

Source: BLES (2004: table 2).

Table 5.4   The Philippines: employed persons by major occupation group

Major occupation group	% of workforce
Officials of government and special interest organisations, corporate executives, managers, managing proprietors and supervisors	11.6
Professionals	4.3
Technicians and associate professionals	2.8
Clerks	4.2
Service workers and shop and market sales workers	9.1
Farmers, forestry workers and fishermen	19.7
Trade and related workers	9.2
Plant and machine operators and assemblers	7.5
Labourers and unskilled workers	31.2
Special occupations	0.4
All	100.0

Note: Data pertain to October 2003.

Source: NSO (2003: 27–8).

employees, who numbered around 1.4 million in 1999, making up the biggest single group in this category. However, it should also be noted that as many as 91 per cent of formally employed persons as a whole are in firms with fewer than ten workers, which has tended to result in rather uneven coverage by unions, and a fragmented labour movement (Fashoyin, 2003: 1–2). Weak union power is compounded by the fact that even workers in large firms may only be employed on temporary contracts (Aganon, 2002a: 119). The latter also has implications for wages (temporary workers, for example, being eligible only for 75 per cent of minimum pay rates), and for social security coverage and fringe benefits (Fashoyin, 2003: 42; see also below). Indeed, in 2000 it was estimated that only 28 per cent of the Philippine labour force was covered by the Social Security System (SSS), over one-fifth of whom belonged to the Government Service Insurance System (GSIS) (ILO, 2001: 10). As for the informal sector, which has occupied around 50 per cent of the labour force for the last 20 years (ADB, 2004: viii), approximately half are self-employed, a further 14 per cent employ others, and as many as 35 per cent are unpaid family labourers (Fashoyin, 2003: 2).

Although, as noted earlier, the post-Marcos period has been characterised by significant diversification and growth in the Philippine economy, recovery from 'bust' periods has not been sufficient to save jobs, especially in agriculture and industry (Fashoyin, 2003: 1). The Asian crisis, for example, forced some firms to make staffing cuts of up to 20 per cent (Aganon, 2002b: 127), and unemployment in April 1998 stood at 13.3 per cent compared with 10.4 per cent in April of the previous year (Laopao, 1998: 3). That relatively little labour absorption has occurred during times of recovery owes partly to efforts to improve labour productivity in the wake of ever-increasing competition from abroad (Lim and Bautista, 2002: 41–2). Another factor is the growth of the labour force relative to demand. During 1999–2000, for example, there was 'jobless growth' as GDP registered a 4 per cent increase, but employed persons a decline of 4.24 per cent (UN/UNIFEM, 2003: 33). Between 2003 and 2004, again, despite an upturn in demand for industrial workers in connection with the presidential election campaign, employment expanded by only 3.6 per cent, compared with 5.4 per cent growth in the labour force (BLES, 2004: 1). In turn, of the little growth in employment in 2001, 87.7 per cent was constituted by part-time work (Fashoyin, 2003: 3), and between 2001 and 2004, there were rises both in unemployment – from 13.3 per cent to 13.7 per cent[6] – and underemployment – from 17.5 per cent to 18.5 per cent (see Morada and Manzala, 2001: 1). The casualisation of labour has been on the increase since the early 1990s, with regular employees displaced in favour of short-term contract workers who, by virtue of working for less than six months, forego benefits and are particularly vulnerable to summary dismissal. Between 1990 and 1994, for example, an estimated total of 14–15 per cent of workers in enterprise-based employment were contractual, casual or part-time workers, and by 1997 this figure had increased to 21.1 per cent (CWR, 2003: 2). The growing prevalence of subcontracting in labour-intensive manufacturing industries such as textiles and wood also plays a major part in casualisation (Hornilla, 1995: 4). Even if most homeworkers (68 per cent) have traditionally been active on a year round basis (ibid.: 7–8), trade liberalisation seems to have affected these almost as adversely as plant operatives, especially in garments, with less work being put out to traditional embroidery communities since the mid-1990s, and the same applying to fashion accessories outwork in Cebu (see Pineda-Ofreneo, 2002b: 72–3). The above makes it difficult to see how the Philippines will be able to honour its commitment to promote the ILO's 'decent work' agenda, which advocates, *inter alia*, opportunities for work, freedom of choice of employment, work that enables livelihoods, fair and equitable treatment in work, security, protection and dignity (DOLE, 2003: 3; ILO, 2003b; Tidalgo, 2004).

As for child labour, technically speaking under-15s cannot work unless they are assisting parents or guardians or working in public entertainment, such as television, and then only for a maximum of 20 hours a week (ADB, 2002: 64; BWYW, 2003). Following the Philippines' ratification of ILO Conventions 138 (Minimum Age Convention), and 182 (Prohibition and Immediate Elimination of the Worst Forms of Child Labour), a National Programme Against Child Labour (NPACL) was launched in 2001 comprising a package of welfare, education and rehabilitation services. This has since given rise to the Philippine Time-Bound Programme (PTBP) which involves a social partnership committed to putting an end to the labour exploitation of children (see BWYW, 2002). Yet, although levels of child labour are lower than in The Gambia, a survey undertaken by the National Statistics Office (NSO) in 2001 indicated that 4 million children aged 5–17 (or 1 in 6 of that age group) were engaged in remunerated labour, and 36.5 per cent were not attending school (NORFIL, 2004).[7] On top of non-attendance, two out of every five working children drop out of school, and one-quarter of those who are in education report difficulties in catching up with their lessons (Del Rosario, 2002b: 183). Because many work in family enterprises only three in every five child workers are paid (BWYW, 2002). Some of this is dangerous (for example pyrotechnics, deep-sea fishing), which together with prostitution, mining and quarrying, has led to an estimated total of 59.4 per cent of child labourers being engaged in hazardous activity (NORFIL, 2004).

Although, as in The Gambia, the majority (63.5 per cent) of child workers are boys, girls are much more likely to be engaged in reproductive labour (BWYW, 2002; Del Rosario, 2002b: 183). In turn, since much of girls' work is confined in the home, or is in underground activities such as prostitution, it is 'hidden from scrutiny, accounting and programmes of advocacy . . . (and) . . . neglected' (Del Rosario, 2002a: 170).

Education

Despite poverty, many parents invest in their children's education, motivated in part by the expectation that they will give back in later life. In light of early state expansion of basic education, literacy compares favourably to The Gambia (not to mention many other developing countries) being 92.3 per cent in terms of simple literacy (basic reading and writing skills) among the 10–64-year age group, and 83.8 per cent for functional literacy (numeracy and ability to use literacy skills for specific purposes in the community or workplace) (NSO, 2003: 16).

Basic education covers six years of elementary schooling, plus four years of secondary (high school), and was made a major priority when the education system underwent restructuring in 1994 (DOLE, 1998: 23). Yet, although participation in elementary education grew from 85 per cent in the school year 1991–92, to 97 per cent in 2001–02, enrolment does not signify completion, and indeed, the cohort survival of those enrolling in Grade 1 actually deteriorated from 68.4 per cent in 1985 to 67.1 per cent in 2000 (NEDA, 2001: 15). Moreover, as noted by UNDP/UNFPA (2001: 2), only 43.4 per cent of the poor complete their elementary schooling compared with 72 per cent of the non-poor.

As for secondary education, access was expanded by Republic Act (RA) 6655 of 1998 which provided for free public secondary education. This contributed to a rise in the GER from 68.4 per cent in the school year 1991–92, to 76.2 per cent in 2000–01 (ADB, 2004: 12, table 2.1), although only 70.6 per cent of students who enrol in the first year of high school actually complete (NORFIL, 2004). One reason for the latter is that private schools dominate the secondary sector, which means higher costs. For example, at a national level, only 60 per cent of secondary schools are in the state sector (WEDO, 2005: 101), and in Cebu City there are only 17 state secondary schools as against 42 private institutions (NEDA, 2002: 67). Quality of teaching is also an issue along with large pupil–teacher ratios, which is part of the reason for the current drive to introduce computers into state secondary, and some primary schools, as specified in President Arroyo's '10-point agenda' (see Box 5.1).

BOX 5.1 THE PHILIPPINES: TARGETS OF PRESIDENT ARROYO'S '10-POINT AGENDA', 2004–10

LIVELIHOOD
1. Creation of 10 million jobs
Create 10 million jobs by 2010 through government programmes and projects, and private sector investments. Support to 3 million entrepreneurs through tripling of loans to micro, small and medium enterprises, thereby enabling business expansion and greater employment generation. Development of 2 million hectares of agribusiness land.

EDUCATION
2. Quality education for all
Ensure quality education for all through resource provision, including the construction of at least 3000 additional school buildings and the hiring of 7500 new teachers in 2004. Provision of computers in all state high schools by 2010, and about 20 per cent of state elementary schools. Granting of scholarships to members of 5 million poor families under the *Iskolar para sa Mahirap ng Pamilya* programme.

FISCAL STRENGTH
3. Balanced budget
Attain balanced budget by 2010 to restore health of the fiscal sector and ensure funding for priority programme on a sustainable basis.

DECENTRALISED DEVELOPMENT
4. Decentralisation of development
Develop transport network such as the 'ro-ro', and interconnect whole country through digital infrastructure.

5. Power and water supply nationwide
Provide clean water to areas where 50 per cent of the population or more are not covered by water supply – translating into three towns and cities per month for six years.
Energise all potential *barangays* by 2006 at a rate of 1500 *barangays* a year.

6. Decongestion of Metro Manila
Develop new government centres, businesses and housing in Luzon, Visayas and Mindanao to decongest Metro Manila.
7. Development of Clark and Subic as the best international service and logistics centres in the South-East Asian region

NATIONAL HARMONY
8. Automated elections
9. Long-lasting peace pacts with rebel groups in Mindanao and other insurgency areas
10. Closure of wounds of EDSA 1, 2, 3

Source: NEDA (2004).

Tertiary education, which comes under the jurisdiction of the Commission on Higher Education (CHED), also created as part of the 1994 restructuring process, consists mainly of degree programmes, while vocational education and training fall into two main categories: 'formal' technical vocational education which offers integrated post-secondary tuition geared to middle-level occupations, and 'non-formal' education and training which caters to primary and secondary school drop-outs, the unemployed, and 'marginalised and vulnerable' groups (DOLE, 1998: 23). The latter are the responsibility of the Technical Education and Skills Development Authority (TESDA), whose general mandate is to promote and strengthen technical education and skills to better equip the Philippine population for qualified middle-level employment in an increasingly globalised market (ibid.). Since its creation in the mid-1990s TESDA has come to supervise 60 technical and vocational training institutes, 16 regional training centres and 45 provincial training centres (Fashoyin, 2003: 46). This, in turn, has given rise to the Philippines boasting the second highest number of training facilities for computer programming and related courses in the whole of Asia (NEDA, 2001: 38).

Despite some success at all segments of the educational spectrum, however, the poor continue to be particularly disadvantaged in further and higher education, with only 19 per cent of tertiary establishments being government run (WEDO, 2005: 101). This is unlikely to rectified given the Philippine government's intention to 'encourage individuals and families to allocate their own funds for education and training' (NEDA, 2001: 97). Indeed, while between 1999 and 2000 there was an increase in public expenditure on education in absolute terms, and by the latter year this amounted to 20.6 per cent of government expenditure (Table 4.4), the share of total spend on education actually declined (NEDA, 2001: 98).

Health and Other Social Services

Although better-off to some degree in respect of basic services and infra-structure than The Gambia, the Philippines does not boast anything approaching universal coverage. While the proportion of the population with access to safe sanitation purportedly increased from 69 per cent to 83 per cent between 1985 and 2000 (Reyes, 2002: 21), only 50 per cent of households have legal electricity, and a 2001 survey indicated that only one-quarter of households nationally availed of a piped domestic water supply, leaving the remainder of the population to collect water from wells, springs and public standpipes (NCRFW, 2002a: 12).

Housing conditions are also poor, with around 40 per cent living in over-crowded and frequently makeshift informal settlements, which is higher than in other countries with comparable levels of per capita income. While income poverty is one factor prompting the proliferation of informal set-tlements, another is competition over land from commercial interests (Yu and Karaos, 2004; also Sajor, 2003). One of the main mechanisms through which the poor have been housed to date is through the Community Mortgage Programme (CMP) launched in 1987 by Aquino, which gave the state the role of 'enabler' and 'facilitator' in housing provision. The CMP allows communities to borrow government funds at subsidised rates of interest for land purchase, development and regularisation of tenure (Ragragio, 2003; Yu and Karaos, 2004). This said, out of 66 per cent of the population who are owner-occupiers, a mere 3 per cent of those on low incomes have obtained their dwellings through formal housing or finance programmes (UN/UNIFEM, 2003: 55). Despite a new national shelter programme introduced by Arroyo, the government itself has admitted that most of its packages are out of reach of the poor (NEDA, 2004: 60; Ragragio, 2003: 19). This is perhaps no surprise given that only 3 per cent of the national budget is dedicated to health, housing and community development, and only 1 per cent to the main welfare agency – the Department of Social Welfare and Development (DSWD) (see UN/UNIFEM, 2003: 50).

These deficiencies, coupled with inadequate nutrition, undoubtedly help to explain why 'diseases of poverty' are still rife in the country. For example, pneumonia is the third leading cause of death nationally, after heart disease and other vascular conditions (NSO, 2003: 8–9), and the incidence of tuberculosis in the Philippines is four times greater than in Singapore, Indonesia and Thailand (ADB, 2004: 23).

While Filipinos have greater access to health services than their Gambian counterparts, many of the poor are excluded on account of cost and inaccessibility (NEDA, 2001: 123). This is often attributed to low state investments in health care: while average public spending on health in developing countries is 2 per cent of GDP (Pineda-Ofreneo and Acosta, 2001: 14), in the Philippines in 2000 it was only 1.5 per cent (Lakshminarayanan, 2003: 99). According to 2002 figures, per capita state health expenditure is only US$28 (WHO, 2005b), and an estimated 48 per cent of costs on health services come from 'out of pocket' expenditure (UN/UNIFEM, 2003: 14). Out of the country's 1739 hospitals in 2002, only 662 were public (NSO, 2003: 10). The number of physicians per 100 000 people in 2002 was only 124, and an estimated 20–50 per cent of the population lacked access to essential drugs.

In addition to limited investment in the health sector, government spending has traditionally been biased towards personal curative services rather than public health, and only a minority of the population are covered by social insurance (Lakshminarayanan, 2003: 99). As noted by the World Bank (1996: 35), a mere 25 per cent of the health budget goes to primary or preventive care, the rural poor seem to be especially 'short-changed'.

One attempt to address inequalities in health care has been decentralisation, especially since the passing of the Local Government Code (LGC) in 1991 which called for devolution of significant service functions, responsibilities and resources (Lakshminarayanan, 2003: 7).[8] This led to the establishment in most *barangays* of a health station staffed by a midwife and locally recruited health workers. Yet while decentralisation can often bring health benefits, especially to poorer non-urban groups, different responsibilities at national and local level seem to have compromised the effectiveness of referrals (ibid.: 97). This pattern is aggravated by inadequate funding and administrative efficiency at the local level (NEDA, 2001: 163).[9]

Another gesture towards improving the poor's access to healthcare was the setting-up of the Philippine Health Insurance Commission (PhilHealth) in 1995, which, in partnership with LGUs, subsidised the annual health insurance contributions of over 500 000 poor families in the year 2000 (NEDA, 2001: 123). This said, coverage is rarely enough to extend to more than a few days in hospital and basic medicines. More complicated procedures, such as operations require the shortfall to be made up privately.

Fortunately the incidence of HIV/AIDS is classified as 'low', affecting only 9400 persons in 2001, which is less than 0.1 per cent of all Filipinos.[10] Moreover, although the primary route of transmission is heterosexual contact, in June 2001 women were only 39.1 per cent of those who tested seropositive. Among the reasons for the low incidence of HIV/AIDS are male circumcision, a 'culture of sexual conservatism', low levels of intravenous drug use, and routine health checks on registered 'hospitality workers'. Another potentially important factor is the existence of an AIDS Prevention Programme since 1988, steered by the Philippines National AIDS

Council (PNAC) comprising stakeholders from government agencies, NGOs, and people living with HIV/AIDS. Among the programme's achievements are the introduction of HIV/AIDS education in schools, including in theological education, and the provision of basic health and social services for HIV-positive individuals. This said, while the 'low and slow' HIV/AIDS prevalence rate is to be applauded, the potential for epidemic is there, especially due to increasing rates of infection among sea-based OFWs and the country's ongoing 'hospitality' (sex) trade (UNDP/UNFPA, 2004: 3).

Last but not least, provision for the elderly is also relatively limited, with most of the care resources for senior citizens coming from households themselves (UN/UNIFEM, 2003: 54). Since 1992, however, for those on low incomes, or retirees from public or private office, the Senior Citizens Act (RA 7432) has granted discounts on transport and lodging, exemptions from income tax (if below the poverty line), and free medical and dental treatment in government facilities (ADB, 2002: 67). It also provided for the establishment of an Office of Senior Citizens' Action (OSCA) and a Senior Citizens' Centre (SCC) in all cities and municipalities. By the same token, the number of facilities and centres for the disabled nationally fell from 19 in 1997 to only 6 in 2001 (UN/UNIFEM, 2003: 51).

Poverty Levels and Trends

The first official statistics on poverty in the Philippines were collected in 1985 and released in 1987. Since this time a diverse array of figures have been generated at national, regional and local levels, including the Annual Poverty Indicator Survey (APIS) and the Family Income and Expenditure Survey (FIES) (see ADB, 2005b; Pascua, 2003; UNDP Philippines, 2004; Virola, 2002).

Traditionally the poverty threshold has been set by the National Statistical and Coordination Board (NSCB) as the income necessary to meet basic food and non-food needs (the food or 'core' poverty threshold being determined by capacity to afford basic food requirements, amounting to an average of 2000 calories for energy and protein and other essential nutrients – Reyes, 2002; Virola, 2002).[11] Yet as in The Gambia, determining trends in poverty is complicated, amongst other things, by inconsistencies in methodology. For example, the 'old methodology' (dating from 1992) suggests that between 1985 and 1997 the incidence of poverty dropped from 44.2 per cent to 31.8 per cent of families, but by 2000 had climbed again to 33.7 per cent (Table 5.5; also note 1). The 'new methodology' (introduced in 2003), which revised pricing methods for items making up the poverty line, also records an increase between 1997 and 2000, though at a lower level – from 28.1 per cent to 28.4 per cent (see

Table 5.5   Poverty in the Philippines, 1985–2000

	Households in poverty (%)					
	1985	1988	1991	1994	1997	2000
Total	44.2	40.2	39.9	35.5	31.8	33.7
Urban	33.6	30.1	31.1	24.0	17.9	19.9
Rural	50.7	46.3	48.6	47.0	44.4	46.9

Source: Reyes (2002: table 7).

ADB, 2005b: xii and app. 1). Moreover, according to the new methdology only 24.7 per cent of families were in poverty in 2003, equating to 30.4 per cent of the population (compared with 33 per cent in 2000) (SEPO, 2005). Yet as ADB (2005b: xii) observes, given the Philippines' massive population growth, the magnitude of poverty in absolute terms is significant, with as many 4 million people being added to the ranks of the poor between 1985 and 2000. As further noted by NEDA (2001: 118): 'The poor now save very little of their income, spend two-thirds of their money on food, rely more on public and private income transfers, and are less likely to belong to a cooperative or even a people's organisation.' Indeed, it is arguably significant that when poverty is defined by people themselves in respect of whatever they associate with the word '*mahirap*' (difficulty) (self-rated poverty – SRP) – it is regularly higher than the incidence of poverty as determined by income (WEDO, 2005: 98). Even if self-rating tends to follow official estimates (World Bank, 1996: 62), in 1983, SRP in the Philippines was 55 per cent, in 2000, 58 per cent, in 2001, 66 per cent, and in 2003, 62 per cent (ADB, 2005b: xiv; Reyes, 2002: 50; SWS, 2001).

On top of this, despite a slight decline in the Gini coefficient from 0.4881 to 0.4814 between 1997 and 2000, in 2001, the richest 20 per cent of the population enjoyed 52.3 per cent of national wealth, compared with 5.4 per cent among the lowest quintile (UNDP, 2004: table 2), making the Philippines one of the most unequal countries in Asia.

In terms of groups most vulnerable to poverty, rural households have a higher incidence than their urban counterparts (at 47 per cent versus 20.5 per cent – Table 5.5). This is mainly owing to lack of income-generating opportunities in agriculture, whereas in urban areas poverty is argued to be more associated with deficiencies in housing, transport and basic services such as water supply and sanitation (UNDP Philippines, 2004: 8).

Again, as in The Gambia, poverty in the Philippines is also higher among large households (see Table 5.6), with average family size among the poor being 6 versus 4.67 among the non-poor.

Table 5.6   The Philippines: poverty incidence by household size, 1985–2000

Household size	Poverty incidence (%)					
	1985	1988	1991	1994	1997	2000
National	44.2	40.2	39.9	35.5	31.8	33.7
1	19.0	12.8	12.7	14.9	9.8	9.8
2	20.0	18.4	21.8	19.0	14.3	15.7
3	26.6	23.2	22.9	20.7	17.8	18.6
4	36.4	31.6	30.1	25.3	23.7	23.8
5	42.9	38.9	38.3	31.8	30.4	31.1
6	48.8	45.9	46.3	40.8	38.2	40.5
7	55.3	54.0	52.3	47.1	45.3	48.7
8	59.8	57.2	59.2	55.3	50.0	54.9
9 or more	59.9	59.0	60.0	56.6	52.6	57.3

Source: Reyes (2002: table 11).

Poverty is also more prevalent among households with limited schooling (NEDA, 2001: 118). Moreover, in 2000, poverty only affected 2.5 per cent heads with a college degree, compared with 6.5 per cent in 1985, whereas the incidence of poverty among households whose heads had no grade of schooling underwent an increase from 55.9 per cent to 60.5 per cent, suggesting that 'it is becoming more difficult for those with no schooling to earn enough to become non-poor' (Reyes, 2002: 9).

Unlike in The Gambia, however, elderly households do not show up as a high-risk group in official poverty statistics, possibly because the extended households into which elderly Filipinos are incorporated have more income earners and/or higher earnings relative to their Gambian counterparts.

As regards gender and poverty, this is difficult to determine in the absence of a nationwide headcount breakdown (NEDA, 2004: 151). Although the NSCB are currently collaborating on this with the UNDP[12] the dearth of sex-disaggregated poverty statistics is owing in large part to the fact that the APIS of the NSO is 'family based, treating the household as a homogeneous unit rather than one where there may be competing gender-based interests' (Pineda-Ofreneo and Acosta, 2001: 18).[13] Following this, there are no reliable time-series data on the interrelationships between gender and poverty. The only studies which exist are descriptive, weak in respect of analysis of intra-household distributional factors, and reveal little vis-à-vis the 'feminisation of poverty' (ibid.: 8 and 19).

More data are available on household headship and poverty, however, and interestingly, as in The Gambia until its recent apparent about-turn, poverty does not seem to be greater in female-headed households, or at least consistently (Angeles, 2001: 15; World Bank, 1996: 7).[14] Although male-headed households had higher average incomes in 1991, in 1985 those of women-headed households were over 10 per cent of men's, in 1997, almost 12 per cent greater, and in 2000, 4 per cent greater (UN/UNIFEM, 2003: 44). Given that the mean size of female-headed households is only 4, compared with 5.2 among male-headed households, crude per capita income differentials are even more marked. On top of this, the proportion of female-headed households classified as poor in 2000 was only 17.7 per cent, compared with 30.7 per cent of male-headed households.

Reasons for this apparent anomaly could include the fact that highly successful lone women feature among female heads of household. Although a greater proportion of female heads (6.9 per cent) have less than a year's schooling compared with their male counterparts (4.1 per cent), more female heads have college degrees than men (21.4 per cent versus 18.2 per cent). Moreover, since the majority of female heads (62 per cent) are widows, and have an older average age than male heads (54 versus 45.4 years), they have had time to accumulate assets as well as being at a stage where their children are old enough to support them (Morada et al., 2001: 8 and 16). Indeed, a 1996 survey of Filipinos aged 60 plus revealed that contributions from children and other relatives accounted for as much as 40.6 per cent of the income of female-headed households, compared with only 23.9 per cent among their male counterparts (see Ofstedal et al., 2004: 179–80). Female-headed households are more likely to be extended than male-headed units. Even though unemployment rates of co-resident members in female-headed households are higher (15.5 per cent) than in male-headed households (10.2 per cent), there are also relatively more co-resident members in female-headed households who are employed (37.6 per cent) than in male-headed households (30.4 per cent). The above factors have led Morada et al. (2001: 16) to assert that:

> In several dimensions, female-headed households appear to be at a greater advantage. They have smaller household membership which means lesser cost to maintain; reside in urban areas which means greater access to amenities and resources; more educated household members which means greater employment and income potential; and more importantly, more members that are economically active which means more income and financial support.

Yet even if female household heads do not seem to be unduly disadvantaged in terms of incomes, and women in general are more educated than men, the fact that they tend to be in less prestigious jobs is undoubtedly an important reason why women are identified by the Philippine government as one of the most vulnerable groups 'who must be protected from the debilitating effects of poverty' (NCRFW, 2002a: 11). In turn, it is recognised that a 'rising trend towards the feminisation of poverty' (ibid.) is also a function of women being 'the ones mainly responsible for the welfare and survival of households under conditions of increasing poverty' (ibid.). As echoed by UNDP/UNFPA (2001: 3): 'Although women play an active part in politics and the economy, in terms of "gender equality", they continue to bear a disproportionate burden of effects of poverty.' Indeed, as one example, a lot of press coverage during my time in the field in late 2004 was given to evidence that women were bearing the brunt of food cutbacks, sacrificing their own nutritional needs in the interests of feeding husbands and children.[15]

Poverty Reduction Initiatives

Poverty reduction has been an important, if not central component, of Philippine development planning since 1987. This has been realised through the MTPDPs as well as by stand-alone poverty programmes (see Orbeta, 2002; 2003; UNDP, 2000a). Over time, Reyes (2002: 40) argues that it is possible to discern a trajectory in government rhetoric from 'alleviating' poverty, to 'reducing' or 'eradicating' it, even if all these aims have been compromised, *inter alia*, by the 'short term-ism' of different programmes (ibid.: 44), and by periodic economic crises attached to the country's weak global position. Indeed, even if economic growth had a bigger role in accounting for declining poverty incidence than redistribution between 1985 and 2000 (Reyes, 2002: 53), UNDP Philippines (2004: 11) contends that 'The growth of the Philippine economy has not been strong or equitable enough to contribute to a reduction in poverty'.

Aquino's ascent to power in 1986 led to the setting of the first national target for poverty reduction, which was mainly to be achieved through assisting the rural poor via an employment-based rural development strategy and Comprehensive Agrarian Reform Programme (CARP) (Reyes, 2002: 37; see also Guardian, 2003; Mundlak et al., 2004). On assuming the presidency in 1992, however, Fidel Ramos switched the focus to rapid industrial-led growth. He also took the unprecedented step of introducing an integrated anti-poverty programme known as the 'Social Reform Agenda' (SRA), which was drawn-up with the participation of NGOs and grassroots organisations, some of whom were represented on its coordinating body, the Social Reform Council (SRC) (see World Bank, 1996). Working with a multidimensional perspective on poverty, the three pillars of the SRA were access to quality services, asset reform and institution-building, and participatory governance (Bennagen, 2000: 2–3). The SRA targeted 20 provinces with particular priority for 'flagship' poverty alleviation programmes, which, in line with neoliberal orthodoxy, was seen to be a more effective way of reaching the poor than universal programmes (see Reyes, 2002; World Bank, 1996).

In 1997 the SRA was institutionalised through the Social Reform and Poverty Alleviation Act (RA 8425), which disbanded the SRC and created in its place the National Anti-Poverty Commission (NAPC) (Bennagen, 2000). The NAPC was set up as a policy advisory body with a mandate to coordinate poverty reduction programmes (Reyes, 2002: 47). Guided by the notion that popular participation is vital to promote change within government and to advance anti-poverty agendas, the NAPC not only comprises representatives from 22 relevant national government agencies, together with presidents of the four local government leagues, but also civil society representation from 'basic sectors', including women, workers, youth, small farmers, NGOs and so on, the bulk of whom also feature as client groups (see below).

Targeting continued during Estrada's three-year term, in which the NAPC was retained but a new anti-poverty strategy was introduced – the *Lingap Para Sa Mahirap* (Caring for the Poor Fund) which provided the 100 poorest families in each municipality with medical assistance, livelihood opportunities, socialised housing, drinking water, and food subsidies (Angeles, 2000a: 9; Clarke and Sison, 2003; Virola, 2002). This was complemented by the Comprehensive and Integrated Delivery of Social Services (CIDSS) programme, which also focused efforts on the poorest communities in the country and involved the participation of beneficiaries in meeting Minimum Basic Needs (MBN) through the delivery of support services to enhance socio-economic development. By 1999–2000, just before Estrada was deposed, the CIDSS programme had benefited just under 5 million of the poorest families in the Philippines, which was only 17 per cent short of target (NEDA, 2001: 119).

Both the MTPDPs introduced in Arroyo's terms of office have also singled out poverty as the main challenge facing the country. The latest of these, MTPDP 2004–10, which is guided by Arroyo's '10-point agenda' (Box 5.1), commences with a statement of the need to 'fight poverty by building prosperity for the greatest number of the Filipino people' (NEDA, 2004: 1), and aims to reduce poverty by half (to 17 per cent) in its six year period (ibid.: 8). In order to achieve this, five main anti-poverty measures are identified: enhanced livelihood capacity through credit support and capacity-building, asset reform (including agrarian reform), improved accessibility and affordability of essential services such as health care and sanitation, protection of vulnerable groups such as children, the disabled, and women in difficult circumstances, and 'empowerment of the poor' through programmes such as KALAHI-CIDDS (ibid.: x).

Kabit Bisig Laban sa Kahirapan (Linking Arms to Fight Poverty – KALAHI), was launched in 2003 and is coordinated by NAPC in conjunction with Regional KALAHI Convergence Groups (RKCGs), comprising a broad range of representatives from government, the private sector and civil society who attempt to address poverty as determined through a basic set of local poverty indicators (LPIMS) (see Box 5.2). In the interests of targeting the poorest, a total of nine basic sectors have been prioritised, namely, the urban poor, informal sector workers, children, farmers and landless rural workers, persons with disabilities, women, senior citizens, victims of disasters and calamities, and indigenous peoples, for whom different core issues are addressed, such as affordable housing and land tenure for the urban poor, and credit assistance and protection from police harassment for informal workers (see NAPC, 2003). Geographical as well as group targeting is also pursued, with the KALAHI-CIDSS programme highlighted as a key strategy in the latest MTPDP, entailing the residents of poor communities targeting the infrastructure and services they need to enhance local livelihoods and well-being, albeit with the onus on villagers and LGUs to provide around 40 per cent of the costs. Between 2003 and 2004, the number of communities benefiting from the KALAHI strategy rose from six to 700, with World Bank funding for KALAHI-CIDSS between 2003 and 2007 anticipated to provide focused assistance to 'catalytic' community projects in over 5000 *barangays* (NAPC, 2003: 3).

Also in the spirit of poverty reduction more responsive to local needs, in 2003 LGUs were mandated to formulate their own Local Poverty Reduction Action Plans (LPRAPs). To enhance capacity, the Department of the Interior and Local Government (DILG) undertook to train Local Poverty Reduction Action Officers (LPRAOs) in poverty diagnosis, planning and monitoring at provincial, municipal and *barangay* levels (NAPC, 2003: 3). The involvement of NGOs in these are likely to improve success rates, given the experience of Cebu City where there is a long history of engagement between civil society and government thanks to the creation in 1988, by Mayor Tomas Osmeña,[16] of the City Commission for the Urban Poor (CCUP, now DWUP, the Division for the Welfare of the Urban Poor) (see Etemadi, 2004).

Some of the biggest concerns remain about the gender dimension of NAPC interventions however. While Administrative Order No. 21 of 2001 stipulated that: 'The SRA shall pursue a gender-responsive approach to fight poverty' (Pineda-Ofreneo and Acosta, 2001: 20), and in 2002 introduced a GAD focal point, guidelines as to how NAPC is to address gender remain limited, even though the organisation works in conjunction with the National Commission on the Role of Filipino Women (NCRFW, 2004a: 5).

BOX 5.2 THE PHILIPPINES: LOCAL POVERTY INDICATORS MONITORING SYSTEM

Thirteen Core Indicators

1. Proportion of child deaths in 0–5 year age group
2. Proportion of children aged 0–5 years who are malnourished
3. Proportion of households without access to safe water
4. Proportion of households without access to sanitary toilet facilities
5. Proportion of households who are squatting
6. Proportion of households living in makeshift housing
7. Proportion of households with members victimised by crime
8. Proportion of households with income less than the poverty threshold
9. Proportion of households with income less than the food poverty threshold
10. Proportion of households who eat fewer than three meals a day
11. Unemployment rate
12. Elementary school participation rate
13. Secondary school participation rate

Source: Social Development Division, NEDA Region VII office, Cebu City, November 2004.

This said, a number of government agencies have striven to alleviate poverty among women. These include the People's Credit Finance Corporation (PCFC), a state owned and controlled organisation which is the main vehicle of micro-finance delivery to the poor, and in the period 2001–03 had catered to 864 965 borrowers, 98 per cent of whom were female (NCRFW, 2004a: 5). Another programme for women – Women Workers' Employment and Entrepreneurship Development (WEED) – is run by the Department of Labour and Employment's (DOLE's) Bureau of Women and Young Workers (BWYW). This aims to enhance the activities of women in the informal sector through skills training and assistance in self-employment, entrepreneurship and cooperativism (DOLE, 1998: 34). In 2004 alone, the programme had released US$22 180 to fund 24 Training Cum Production programmes (TCPs) submitted to DOLE regional offices benefiting 709 women members. Similar programmes are administered by the DSWD including the Community Participation Skills Development, Practical Skills Capability Building for Disadvantaged Women (PSCB), and Special Project for Women in Especially Difficult Circumstances (Angeles, 2000b). Between 1995 and 1999, a total of 166 923 women were able to access skills training through DSWD programmes, of whom 82 per cent were later incorporated into the workforce, and in 2001 a further 31 827 women, which led to gainful employment for 87 per cent (NCRFW, 2004a: 4). Many interventions of this nature are replicated by NGOs, although as Illo (2003b: 155) cautions, micro-finance should not be regarded as an unqualified success given that most borrowers are expected to repay nearly 100 per cent, which forces women to work harder and longer hours. Moreover, many women complain that gaining access to micro-finance can be overly bureaucratic and demanding (Pineda-Ofreneo, 2002b: 77).

GENDER IN THE PHILIPPINES

Despite uneven progress in poverty reduction, the Philippines is often held up as a case where great strides have been taken in respect of gender. From being one of first nations in Asia to grant women the vote (in 1937), and to have a woman member elected to parliament (1941), gender equality became inscribed as a key tenet of the new 1987 Constitution (ADB, 2002: 40; see also later). The Philippines also ranks as one of the leaders in South-East Asia in respect of ratifying the largest number of international treaties relating to women's status, and to have done so without reservation, including the Optional Protocol to CEDAW (NCRFW, 2004a: 3). Government initiatives for gender equality have long been complemented and strengthened by the country's vibrant and diverse women's movement, with Pineda-Ofreneo (2003: 13) noting that many of the gains in women's status are 'largely a result of civil society/women's movement initiatives and their effects on state policies, structures and processes'.

Not only does the Philippines have a high GDI score (see Table 4.7), but in respect of the GEM has made particular progress in raising women's representation as senior and managerial employees, and professional and technical workers in the last decade (Table 3.7). The Philippines also has more women in politics than many other Asian countries, not to mention two female presidents to date. Even if women are seldom more than one-quarter of elected politicians (CIDA, 2001: 7), and in 2002 only three out of 24 senators were female, and 33 out of 208 legislators (NCRFW, 2004a: 14), the situation may well improve with the prospective passage of the

Women Empowerment Act, which aims to reserve for women at least 30 per cent of appointed positions in national and local government (WEDO, 2005: 98).

Culturally, the Philippines has long been renowned for its absence of 'consolidated patriarchy', which 'provides women and men greater room for manoeuvre and flexibility in negotiating their gender roles and identities' (Angeles, 2001: 9). Yet while on the surface, the 'public image is that women have high status' (Hindin and Adair, 2002: 1386), the NCRFW (2004d: xvii) cautions that: 'Gender inequality or discrimination persists, despite illusions of gender parity and anti-discrimination legislation. Unequal gender relations are manifested in violence against women and girl children, while gender discrimination has been noted in the distribution of and access to resources, and participation in politics and decision-making.'

This rather contradictory state of affairs is mirrored by competing views on gender in the Philippines. At one extreme, some claim there is 'near equality' in gender relations (see Medina, 1991), as reflected in women having a purportedly commensurate status with men in society at large, and a central role in domestic affairs – often being referred to as '*ilaw ng tahanan*' (the light of the home), or even as (albeit jokingly, by their husbands) as 'boss' or '*kumander*' (commander) (Angeles, 2001: 11). Women exert an influence over budgeting, for example, that renders them 'co-managers' rather than 'implementers of their husbands' wishes' (Castillo, 1991: 250; also Illo, 1989), notwithstanding that the money they manage may only just cover basic household needs (see Aguilar, 1988; Angeles, 1990; Illo and Veneracion, 1988).

The nominal egalitarianism of Filipino spouses also is seen to have a positive impact upon the entitlements of younger generations, with education and 'favours and privileges' tending to be meted out equally (Medina, 1991: 24; also Licuanan, 1991: 15; Villariba, 1993: 8). Paid work among women has also long been accepted (see Bucoy, 1992; Hollnsteiner, 1991a) even if 'the wife's work is considered only as temporary or supplemental to her "real" job at home', and she gets little relief from household chores (Morada and Llaneta, 2000: 5; see also DOLE, 1998: 1). Indeed, although some studies note that men may put in almost one-third of the time women do into housework and childcare (see Aguilar, 1991; Illo and Polo, 1990; Pavia-Ticzon, 1990), others, such as that of Dumont (1994: 177) observe that during much of the limited time men actually spend in the home, they tend to sleep as a means of 'disengaging from any domestic responsibility' (see also UN/UNIFEM, 2003; 45). That men may also let their wives assume the major responsibility for generating income (see Chant and McIlwaine, 1995), has led to the charge that the gender division of labour remains skewed in favour of men, with women working longer hours and having less time for themselves or to engage in 'leisurely activities' (Pineda-Ofreneo and Cabanilla, 2003; see also Varua, 1999).

Leading on from this, while women may be *a* if not *the* dominant member in Filipino households (Chen, 2005: 70), another viewpoint emphasises difference and inequality between women and men: 'In the ideology of the Filipino family, the roles of wife/mother and husband/father are sharply differentiated, with the wife/mother cast as manager, nurturer and moral pillar, and husband as resource provider and titular head' (ibid.: 81; see also Morada and Llaneta, 2000: 1). Some even go as far to describe the Filipino family/household as a conflictive, hierarchical unit (see Eviota, 1992: 113). One important issue over and above divisions of labour and responsibility, is that men often spend a disproportionate amount of time and money (including that of their wives) on extra-domestic activities, including socialising with their '*barkadas*' (literally gang, or group of male friends), and/or engaging in '*bisyos*' (vices) such as betting on cockfights, drinking, and taking '*queridas*' (mistresses) (Angeles, 2001; Chant and McIlwaine, 1995; PROCESS, 1993: 510). Men may also be violent towards women, which is identified as one of the principal factors contributing to the latter's low productivity and vulnerability to human and income poverty (ADB, 2004: vii).

Recognising that many women do not report violence to the authorities, in 2003 alone, the Philippine National Police (PNP) handled 8011 cases of domestic violence (ADB, 2004: 24). Out of 2500 married women respondents in a Longitudinal Health and Nutrition Survey in Cebu, 13 per cent reported experiencing physical abuse from their husbands, the main reasons given being 'talking back', 'nagging', jealousy and drunkenness (Hindin and Adair, 2002: 1389–90). Women earning more than 50 per cent of household income, or women whose husbands did not turn over all their income to wives were at most risk (ibid.: 1392). While Hindin and Adair (2002: 1396) point up something of a contradiction in that women with a substantial degree of economic and decision-making power are still subject to abuse, the notion that domestic violence is 'ordinary' or 'normal' within the context of marriage has long held sway in Philippine society, as evidenced by several other studies, such that of Israel-Sobritchea (1991: 102) on Kalayaan in Laguna province, where 'reprimands and an occasional beating are considered necessary for the wives', especially in cases of infidelity and 'wilful disobedience'. Research elsewhere in the country shows that domestic violence often arises out of conflicts over men's (often unfounded) sexual jealousy, their wives' decisions to separate, money shortages, unwanted pregnancies, male drinking or womanising (de la Cerna, 1992: 54; Nagot, 1991: 118). Indeed, wife-beating is so common in some low-income communities that domestic abuse is construed by some women as a sign that their husbands love them (Hollnsteiner, 1991a: 263).

Marriage, Family and Sexuality

However varied the views of gender dynamics within Filipino households, the family continues to be regarded as a fundamental social institution.

Although average family size has begun to decline (from six in 1970 to five in 2000), and households are increasingly adopting a nuclear form, extended arrangements comprising relatives and sometimes non-kin continue to make up 13–16 per cent of the total (see Clarke and Sison, 2003: 219; Pedro, 2003). Moreover, links with wider kin networks are so prevalent that even if the Filipino household is 'residentially nuclear', it is better characterised as 'functionally extended' (Castillo, 1991: 245; Medina, 1991: 14–16; Peterson, 1993: 571–4). This applies even across the Philippine diaspora, with Milagros et al. (2004: 204) pointing out that 'While transnational migration is reshaping the contours of the Filipino family, it has in no way diminished the importance of being, or the desire to be, "family"'. Strong kin linkages are often seen to derive from a combination of bilateral kinship, the historical and cultural importance of affective ties, and shortfalls in institutionalised social security, not to mention legal stipulations, as typified by Article 194 of the Family Code, which requires not only that parents, but grandparents and other extended family members should support children (CWC, 2000: 51).

Leading on from the above, marriage and childbirth are integral elements of Filipino family life with the ADB (2003: 9) noting that: 'Filipino women and men are culturally expected to marry and have children regardless of socio-economic class, ethnicity and geographic region.' This said, greater social stigma descends on women who remain unmarried (ibid.), and as articulated by Hollnsteiner (1991a: 254): 'the possibility that a woman might voluntarily choose to perpetuate her single state rarely enters the Filipino mind'. In 1998 the crude marriage rate (marriages per 1000 population) was 15.0 for women, and 14.8 for men, and out of 1268 respondents in the Filipino Family Survey (FFS) of 2003, as many as 84.5 per cent of adults were married, only 3.3 per cent lived in concensual unions and a mere 2.5 per cent were never married (Pedro, 2003: 23). Religious unions also continue to hold sway. Although there has been a decline in Catholic marriage over time, falling from 55.7 per cent of the total in 1976 to 43.6 per cent by 2000 (Pedro, 2003: 21), a further 20.8 per cent of ceremonies in this latter year were Muslim or Evangelical, and only just over one-third (35.5 per cent) were civil (NSO, 2003: 7). Relative to The Gambia, however, Filipino women have quite a late marrying age, and this has risen in the last few decades – from a mean of 22 years in 1960, to 24 in 1998 (the corresponding ages for men being 25 and 26.7 years) (Pedro, 2003: 20), even if marriage among those with limited education continues to be common under the age of 20 (UN/UNIFEM, 2003: 35).

Excepting the minority Muslim population, the emphasis placed by state and church on lifelong monogamous marriage is so strong that divorce remains illegal. As stated by the ADB (2004: 9): 'Divorce is not allowed and Catholic beliefs promote marriage not just as a social contract between two individuals but more fundamentally as a union that is divinely ordained.' In turn, the Philippine Civil Code describes marriage as an 'inviolable social institution and the foundation of the family' (ADB, 2002: 47).

Absence of divorce, combined with religious opprobrium, and exacting bureaucratic and financial costs of legal separation, are undoubtedly significant in contributing to exceptionally low (reported) rates of marital breakdown. Other factors which seem to play an important role in maintaining marriages 'in-tact' include the common propinquity of extended family which can attenuate marital tensions or put pressure on people to stay together (see Chant, 1997a: 143; Varua, 1999). Separation is also discouraged by socially conditioned norms of not 'losing face' or bringing shame upon one's kinfolk, as summoned up by the concept '*hiya*'. Added to this, the Philippines is widely regarded as a child-centred culture where the importance attached to love and duty towards children constrains parents' pursuit of personal interests and desires (see Chant, 1997a: ch. 6; Enriquez, 1991: 99; Ramirez, 1984: 30; Shimuzu, 1991: 118).

Although poverty is seen to exert greater tendencies to conjugal breakdown among lower-income groups (Gonzalez, 2003: 3), female-headed households are not especially common in the Philippines. Notwithstanding likely underestimation on account of the informal nature of marital separation (Chant and McIlwaine, 1995: 18), levels of female household headship increased only marginally – from 10 per cent to 12.2 per cent between 1970 and 2002. In turn, a mere 5.9 per cent of children in the Philippines live only with their mothers, compared with a mean of 10.9 per cent for 41 countries in Asia, Africa and Latin America and the Caribbean (Delamonica et al., 2004: 9, table 1). This may not only be accounted for in part by the fact that widows make up two-thirds of female heads (see earlier), but that a further 21 per cent are married (corresponding in the main to de facto heads whose husbands may be migrant workers), and only 10.5 per cent are single.

Despite the economic advantages documented earlier for female-headed households, socially they have been subject to stigmatisation, particularly where the heads concerned are young single or separated women (see Chant and McIlwaine, 1995). Indeed, in cases where young women become 'unwed mothers' they often attempt to minimise their visibility by remaining as 'embedded' families within the homes of their parents, or even move to other cities in order to spare them from gossip ('*tsismis*') (Chant, 1997a: 144).

Leading on from this, despite a pre-colonial history of relative tolerance for sexual freedom among both women and men (Carba, 2003: 4), sexual double standards dating from Spanish colonialism seem to have been remarkably persistent, encouraging restraint and fidelity among women, and licence among men to engage in casual sex and extramarital affairs (see for example, Chant and McIlwaine, 1995: 12–13; Eviota, 1991: 166; Hollnsteiner, 1991a: 252–3; Medina, 1991: 99; Ramirez, 1984: 32). As summarised by Goodno (1991: 259):

> Women in the Philippines find themselves in an odd position. Many doors are open to them and they can enter virtually every profession and responsible position in the public and private sectors. Yet society expects them to manage a house, maintain their virtue and provide their men with sexual gratification. Along Catholic Filipinos, who are not allowed to divorce, there is a flourishing macho tradition in which men pursue their sexual fantasies, have extra-marital relations, and often keep two families.

Although as in other countries of the world, pre-marital intercourse is increasing among both sexes, in 2002 the reported incidence was only 15 per cent among girls in the 15–24-year age group (up from 11 per cent in 1994), compared with 31 per cent among boys (up from 25 per cent in 1994) (Carba, 2003: 3).

The fact that there has long been an established sex industry in the country, is viewed by some authors as resulting not only from poverty and the historical presence of foreign military personnel, but from a situation in which sexual access to 'ordinary' women is not condoned. 'Ordinary' women often distance themselves from sex workers not only in respect of contact, but also in the manner in which they act and dress (refraining from smoking or drinking, or from wearing revealing clothes), and in their open disapproval of women with 'loose' morals. Sex workers themselves also frequently have low self-esteem as a result of failing to live up to the moral standards prescribed by culture and religion, which seems to be one reason why they often look to enter into long-term partnerships with and/or marry their male clients (see Chant and McIlwaine, 1995; also Yea, 2004). Despite the general strictures around heterosexuality, however, homosexuality, especially among men, seems to be reasonably widely tolerated.

Gender Dimensions of Education

The Philippines is one of a handful of developing countries where gender disparities in education are minimal, and even biased in favour of women.

As far back as 1989 women and men's literacy was on a par at 89.8 per cent, and by 2000, the female rate among the population aged 10 or more was higher (92.5 per cent versus 92.1 per cent) (NSO, 2003: 16). In turn, women's educational enrolment now outnumbers men's even at tertiary level (NCRFW, 2004: 6). Substantial efforts have also been made to eliminate gender biases in textbooks and to introduce gender into school curricula, including sensitisation to ideas such as joint parenting, reproductive rights and non-violent forms of conflict resolution (NCRFW, 2004a: 2 and 7). In addition, in the academic year 2001–02, 57 per cent of CHED scholarships for higher education went to women (ibid.: 7). However, there remains some gender tracking in respect of degree choice; while women still tend to avoid subjects like engineering, architecture, and science and technology, they outnumber men in business education, teaching and education, and health-related courses (CIDA, 2001: 6; DOLE, 1998: 8; NCRFW, 2004a: 7).

One attempt to diversify women's vocational skills has been the 'Women in New Trades' project (WINT), launched by TESDA in 1998. This trains women in non-traditional areas such as technology, industry, and entrepreneurial skills (DOLE, 1998: 31), with one outcome of the initiative being the establishment of a National Vocational Training and Development Centre for Women, funded by grant aid from Japan.

Another important factor when considering gender and education is that parents often prioritise daughter's schooling because of the likelihood that they will end up working in non-farm jobs where educational qualifications are an important criterion for entry (see Quisumbing et al., 2004). However, just because Filipino girls may get more education than boys, or many of their counterparts in other countries, does not mean that they are spared reproductive or income-generating work during their school years or beyond.

Gendered Divisions of Labour and Employment

As noted above, although gendered divisions of labour are not as marked in the Philippines as in many other societies, women are still more tied to the home than are men, which impinges on their involvement in remunerative activities. In turn, employers often regard women as 'secondary workers' who are merely supplementing their husbands' wages (CWR, 2003). This said, female labour force participation in the Philippines has traditionally been among the highest in developing countries, especially in urban areas, with women's share of the overall labour force during the last 10–15 years hovering at round 38 per cent. Although there are only two economically active women for every three men (ADB, 2004: 30), the growth of the labour force in the last decade has seen absolute numbers of women escalate from 8.7 million in 1988, to 11.4 million in 1997, and to 13.4 million in 2003 (NCRFW, 2004a: 11). Moreover, between 1987 and 1997, the labour force participation rate of women climbed from 28.3 per cent to 48.9 per cent (DOLE, 1998: 4), and by 2002 to 51.7 per cent, although this was still lower than men's (80.8 per cent) (ADB, 2004: viii).

Recent increases in female labour force participation have mainly occurred in older age groups. While in 1997 women aged between 25 and 34 constituted the largest single group within the female workforce (at 23.7 per cent), by 2001 they had been overtaken by 35–44-year-olds (22.5 per cent), who back in 1987 had been less that one-fifth of female workers (19.8 per cent) (DOLE, 1998: 4; UN/UNIFEM, 2003: 34). Associated with this trend, the percentage of married women working more than doubled between 1988 and 1997, from 9.9 per cent to 20.5 per cent (Morada and Llaneta, 2000: 2), which is generally attributed to changing social and cultural patterns, as well as to the growing economic difficulty of supporting an average household of five persons on less than two incomes (ibid.: 5). Indeed, Aganon (2003: 129) contends that: 'Caught in an economic crisis which has beset the region since 1997, more and more Filipino households rely on women not only to bring in extra money, but to be the main breadwinners of the family.' This is partly due to the disproportionate loss of male jobs in manufacturing and construction in the aftermath of the Asian crisis, with Illo (2003a: 35) asserting that many women's 'sideline' incomes became the household's 'final line of defence' as mainline sources collapsed.

A 'sideline' is a term which Filipino women often use, somewhat self-deprecatingly, to refer to income-generating activities which may be taken on in conjunction with other jobs (see Chant and McIlwaine, 1995: 85). The likelihood of sidelines being informal in nature increased during the period 1997–2003 when the number of women engaged in own-account ventures grew by 22 per cent, compared with 18 per cent in numbers of women employed overall (NCRFW, 2004a: 11). Women are currently estimated to be half of the informally employed, mainly engaged in petty commerce, domestic service, laundry work, beauty culture, animal raising and home-based subcontracting (NCRFW, 2002a: 13; Pineda-Ofreneo and Acosta, 2001: 11). In turn, women in the informal sector are more likely than men to be own-account and subcontracted workers (three-quarters of all home-workers are female), rather than owner-operators or paid workers in informal enterprises (ADB, 2004: viii; see also Pineda-Ofreneo, 2003: 4–5). Around 19 per cent of employed women are also unpaid family workers vis-à-vis 10 per cent of men (UN/UNIFEM, 2003: 37).

Leading on from the above, although the Asian crisis led to greater displacement of male than female workers (Lim and Bautista, 2002: 34), men continue to have a higher share of formal sector employment (61.8 per cent)

Table 5.7   The Philippines: male and female employment by sector

	Men% of male employment		Women% of female employment	
	1980	2000–2002	1980	2000–2002
Agriculture	60	45	37	25
Industry	16	18	15	12
Services	25	37	48	63
All	100	100	100	100

Source: World Bank (2004b: table 2.3).

Table 5.8   The Philippines: gender distribution of employment

Branch of employment	% of male workforce	% of female workforce
Agriculture, fishery and forestry	45.3	24.5
Mining and quarrying	0.6	0.0
Manufacturing	8.4	12.7
Electricity, gas and water	0.6	0.2
Construction	8.1	0.3
Transport, storage and communications	11.1	1.0
Wholesale and retail commerce, trade	9.2	28.4
Finance, insurance, real estate and business services	2.2	2.8
Community, social and personal services	14.4	29.9
Industry not adequately reported	0.0	0.0
All	100	100

Source: ADB (2004: table 3.4).

(NCRFW, 2002a: 13). Notwithstanding some diminution in gender segregation and segmentation over time (see Morada and Santos, 1998), women are mainly concentrated in commerce and services, while men dominate agriculture, fishing transport, storage and construction (Tables 5.7 and 5.8). That there is a reasonable mix of men and women in manufacturing, with women constituting 43.8 per cent of workers in this sector, is argued to be a function of their preponderance in the export industry, which attaches high value to women's flexibility, lower wage costs, and lesser militancy (Illo, 2003a: 29; also CWR, 2003: 2).

Despite the fact that women also preponderate in government employment, and that they have entered more administrative and managerial jobs over time, UN/UNIFEM (2003: 18) observe that their rising engagement in the 'formal' labour market has occurred 'amidst a progressive decline of wages combined with wage differentials between women and men'. Indeed, despite the fact that more women than men have college degrees in the Philippines, women's average earnings are still only 50–60 per cent of men's (Lakshminarayanan, 2003: 97; see also Table 2.2). Moreover, the gender gap in management indicates bias in favour of men 'not only in placement but in on-the-job training and promotion practices as well' (CIDA, 2001: 6). It is also noted that the coverage of women by social security is declining as they are increasingly taken on as temporary rather than permanent workers.

These patterns stand in glaring contrast to numerous provisions nominally protecting against sex discrimination in the Philippine Labour Code. Aside from prohibition of discrimination on grounds of sex or marital status, with regard to recruitment, pay and/or promotion (see ADB, 2002: 59), for example, women who have contributed to SSS at least three times in the year preceding childbirth (or abortion or miscarriage),[17] are nominally entitled to maternity leave for 60 days on 100 per cent salary plus routine benefits (for a normal delivery), and 78 days for a Caesarian (DOLE, 1998: 12). There is also legislation in place governing women's health and safety at work (ADB, 2002: 63), and the Philippines is the first country in Asia to have passed an Anti-Sexual Harassment Act (1995), mainly targeted at the workplace and in places of instruction. Yet although a recent ILO Gender Audit reported being impressed by the level of awareness of gender concepts and mainstreaming in relevant agencies such as DOLE (ILO, 2004c), the same organisation only three years previously described women as 'the largest sector of unemployed, under-employed and underpaid people in the Philippines' (ILO, 2001: 1). Indeed, it is important to consider that the unemployment rate in 2003 was still marginally higher for women (10.3 per cent) than for men (10 per cent), as it has been since the 1980s (ADB, 2004: 30), and that during the last ten years female unemployment has been particularly marked among younger age groups, affecting 25.4 per cent of those aged 20–24 years compared with 20.6 per cent of their male counterparts (UNDP Philippines, 2004: 23).

The potential inefficacy of gender-aware legislation is perhaps most marked in respect of prostitution, which continues to be a preponderantly female sector, catering both to local men and to foreigners. Despite efforts to 'clean-up' core centres since the early 1990s, street prostitution has proliferated in the Philippines' three main metropolises, with a disturbing rise in child workers (Collins, 2003; Del Rosario, 2002b: 185–6). Data from 'social hygiene clinics' at a national level, for example, estimate that while approximately 43 000 women are registered commercial sex workers in the country, around 300 000 women are engaged in prostitution overall, with about 75 000 of these being under age (UN/UNIFEM, 2003: 73). As noted by Pineda-Ofreneo (2002a: 61): 'Women and girls who have nowhere else to go engage in the flesh trade, and their numbers are rising. The sex industry is growing, feeding on the desperation of the unemployed.'

While the tourism industry may have conformed with the call to outlaw the 'blatant promotion of sex tours', as noted by Illo (2002a: 2), it still finds ways to offer women and girls to male tourists, both within and beyond national boundaries. Moreover, although an Anti-Mail Order Bride Act was passed in 1990 (RA 6955), the rise of cyber technology has made the law easier to circumvent, requiring new measures to enforce this legislation (NCRFW, 2004a: 17). One recent response been the 2003 Anti-Trafficking in Persons Act which provides legal aid to victims and survivors of trafficking, and tougher penalties for violators of the law, redefining prostitution as a crime committed by any person involved in the exchange of sexual services for money or profit, and thereby stipulating penalties for 'users' and 'clients' as well as the women themselves (NCRFW, 2004a: 3). This represents a major sea-change given that the old law on prostitution was widely regarded by feminists as 'the most archaic and discriminatory against women', prostitution being classified in the Revised Penal Code as 'a crime against decency and good customs'. Aside from the fact that the Code did not acknowledge male prostitutes, female prostitutes could be punished with fines or prison sentences, but not their pimps and procurers (ADB, 2002: 85).

Policy Responses to Gender Inequality

The National Commission on the Role of Filipino Women (NCRFW) was formed in 1975 (originally under the name of the National Commission on Women [NCW]), at the start of the UN Decade for women, although it arguably only began to have a major impact ten years later at the end of the Marcos era, when it first began attempting to mainstream women's concerns in national government agencies (CIDA, 2001: 7).

The NCRFW is a policy advisory rather than implementing body, yet although it has no executive or legislative powers, it has played a major role in promoting women's empowerment and gender equality, often supported by grants from overseas agencies such as the Canadian International Development Agency (CIDA) (see Angeles, 2003). The NCRFW's activities encompass policy advocacy, the monitoring of laws pertinent to women, and guidance to national and local government agencies and NGOs, including gender-training of staff (Angeles, 2000a: 7; NCRFW, 2004a: 21). There is also profound 'interconnectedness' between state and civil society as representatives from a current total of around 200 NGOs dedicated to women's concerns and rights are frequently recruited into the NCRFW as officers, staff and consultants. As noted by Angeles (2003: 285): '*"Bibingka"* (rice-cake) strategy – the equivalent of sandwich strategy in English – is the local idiom used by the NCRFW and women's NGOs to refer to this critical collaboration between state and civil society.' Another effort in this regard has been the NCRFW's establishment of GAD Resource Centres (GRCs) in five regions of the country which bring together academics, policy-makers and programme implementers for the purposes of sharing information and best practice (NCRFW, 2004a: 21).

To uphold commitment to CEDAW, and latterly to the BPFA, the NCRFW has produced two major development plans since 1990: the Philippine Development Plan for Women (PDPW), 1990–95, and the Philippine Plan for Gender-Responsive Development (PPGD), 1995–2025 (see Box 5.3). The second of these was for a 30-year time span in recognition of the fact that it would take 'at least a generation to wear down resistance, redefine policies, and carve out a culture where gender issues become mainstream issues' (NCRFW, 2004c: 11).

BOX 5.3   THE PHILIPPINE PLAN FOR GENDER-RESPONSIVE DEVELOPMENT, 1995–2025

Core objectives

- Promote gender equality
- Help women and men to actualise their potential
- Mainstream gender and development (GAD) in government
- Encourage gender-sensitive industry and employment planning
- Increase women's involvement in politics
- Promote women's political and legal education
- Empower women through strategies which uphold their rights in the context of structural changes for development

Source: DOLE (1998: 20).

Since the early 1990s, monies for gender budgeting have gradually increased and diversified. From the passing of the Women in Development and Nation Building Act (RA 7192) in 1992, which mandated government agencies to set aside part of their official development assistance for programmes and activities for women, in 1995 NCRFW succeeded in lobbying for a provision in the General Appropriations Act (GAA) (RA 8174) for government agencies (including government owned and controlled corporations [GOCCs] and state universities and colleges [SUCs]) not only to reserve at least 5 per cent of their respective budgets, but 30 per cent of ODA (Angeles, 2000a: 9; DOLE, 1998: 19; NCRFW, 2004c: xv). This was deemed to be a critical 'milestone in the promotion of gender equality in the Philippines', even though it clearly had to be assisted by capacity-building, gender training and technical assistance (NCRFW, 2004c: v).

In 1998 the mandate for a 5 per cent GAD budget extended to LGUs (see Flor and Lizares-Si, 2002: 98). By 2001, 214 of these had submitted GAD plans to the NCRFW, at which point 41 per cent of 334 national government offices had complied with the GAD Budget provision (NCRFW, 2002a: 21). By 2004, there were also GAD focal points in 100 out of 341 government agencies (NCRFW, 2004a: 22).

Yet despite these achievements compliance among GOCCs, SUCs and LGUs has been somewhat uneven, with gender budget experiments often being hampered by lack of cash, capacity and political will (see Flor and Lizares-Si, 2002, on Bacolod City; also WEDO, 2005: 98). Moreover, evaluation of GAD plans often reveals only superficial commitment, and even failure, to address any clearly defined gender issue. As summarised by NCRFW (2004c: 15): 'After several years of implementation, the GAD Budget policy continues to struggle with issues of interpretation and implementation.' This may in part be due to the fact that LGUs, who are bearing increased responsibility for service provision without a commensurate increase in resources often see national initiatives as an unwelcome imposition from the centre and/or a threat to local autonomy (ibid.: 21). Also, while the Philippines started gender budgeting earlier than most countries and to date is the only country which actually specifies what percentage of the budget should go to GAD (ibid.: 2), there is still no penalty for non-compliance, nor significant incentive for compliance (ibid.).

In an attempt to remedy some of these problems, one goal of the NCRFW's Framework Plan for Women for the period 2001–04, referred to as 'time-slice of the PPGD' and intended to complement Arroyo's new MTPDP, was to provide guidelines for LGUs in their preparation of GAD plans. Other current concerns of NCRFW are to 'arrest the growing feminisation of poverty, the increasing vulnerability of those in the informal sector and the unabated rise of female overseas labour' (NCRFW, 2002a: 9). In line with the views of many other governments and international agencies: 'The agenda to eradicate poverty through the economic empowerment of women is intricately tied to the ability of government to protect, and more importantly, advance their human rights' (ibid.).

Despite this rhetoric, it is important to take on board the argument that many programmes oriented to improving women's economic status – some of which have already been detailed – might more accurately be described as WID rather than GAD interventions and to have had relatively little impact on account of focusing on women in isolation, in providing only small amounts of credit, or limiting vocational training to conventional female skills (see for example, Angeles, 2000a: 11; Pineda-Ofreneo and Acosta, 2001: 28). In many respects, there is also a somewhat disappointing record in relation to social and family interventions.

At one level there is little doubt that more state attention in the Philippines has been given to women's roles and rights within the family than in The Gambia. Even if divorce remains illegal, major revisions to the Family Code as far back as 1987, for example, included removing the need for women to have spousal approval to engage in paid work, the re-casting of household management (financial and otherwise) as the joint responsibility of husband and wife, requiring the family home to be the joint possession of couples, and recognition of physical violence as a criterion for legal separation (see Chant, 1997a: 146; Hindin and Adair, 2002: 1387; Morada and Llaneta, 2000: 1).

On top of this there have been some potentially far-reaching interventions of a more practical nature, albeit with rather qualified outcomes.

In order to alleviate some of women's domestic burden, for instance, RA 6972 of 1990 mandated for a day-care centre to be set up in every *barangay*, and by 2003, the DSWD had established 34 979 centres, which was an estimated 83 per cent of the target (Illo, 2003a: 33). This said, the centres are usually open for only a few hours a day and are wanting in facilities for pre-school learning, which constrains women's possibilities of working full time (see Pineda-Ofreneo and Acosta, 2001: 15).

Another potentially radical step to alleviating women's reproductive labour came about with the Empowerment and Reaffirmation of Paternal Abilities programme (known as ERPAT, which is an abbreviation that doubles up as a colloquial Tagalog term for 'approachable father'). Launched in 1995 by the DSWD, though not operational until 1999, ERPAT aims to increase fathers' contact with and responsibilities for children through group training lasting up to 27 hours at the *barangay* level. Once a 'core group' of 20–25 fathers have undergone this process, they are expected to sensitise and train others in the community (CWC, 2000: 47).

Yet although it is stated in the programme literature that there is 'no right way/recipe to be a father', the perceptibly heavy Catholic emphasis may be alienating to non-Catholics, besides which, from a gender perspective, statements such as 'fathers are the head of household' are hardly likely to unseat patriarchal stereotypes (see Box 5.4). Moreover, it is estimated that only around 2 per cent of fathers have actually participated in the programme.[18]

BOX 5.4   THE PHILIPPINES: EXCERPTS FROM THE TRAINING MODULES OF THE EMPOWERMENT AND REAFFIRMATION OF PATERNAL ABILITIES PROGRAMME (ERPAT)

FROM MODULE V: FATHERS AS ADVOCATES IN THE PREVENTION OF FAMILY VIOLENCE

Session 2: Preventing violence in the home

Preamble
Fathers as male species are naturally aggressive and easily provoked to anger. When you are angry you are in stressed – that means you lose balance in your thinking and emotional state. To prevent the consequence of that imbalance feeling and thought, one needs to manage his/her feeling so he/she can devise way to control one's feelings particularly when one is in anger state. Otherwise the strong feeling of anger will have to be released to the people around him/her particularly his/her family and hurt the people she/he loved.

Key learning points

- Anger requires so much attention. It brings chaos into familial relationships and hurt people's lives even worse destroy the family's or marital's bond, unity and stability
- When conflict occurs particularly between a couple we experience feelings such as frustration, defeat, embarrassment, guilt or insecurity. A secondary feeling of anger usually follows these feelings. And when this occurs, it must be given attention. It must not be ignored, avoided and kept secret or suppressed otherwise it will be deepen and one may resort to negative and unhealthy ways

- Anger though can be controlled and managed. It is within our means to do something about it. Hence when you are angry, you may do the following:
    - Understand the roots of your anger by focusing less on the person but on your feelings and ponder on the situation that caused your anger
    - Recognise your anger style by determining whether your act is aggravating more to your feeling or anger and whether you are hurting more yourself or the people around you
    - Learn tools and techniques to control your anger positively such as walking away from the situation for a while and letting things cool down. Positive self-talk such as 'I know I am angry but I will calm myself down'
    - Redirect your feeling of anger to positive or productive tasks such as listening to music, cutting the grass or washing the dishes
    - Release your feeling of anger internally through visualisation
    - Release your anger in a safe and supportive environment
    - Face and resolve the anger of your past. If an issue occurs never go to sleep or never let one day pass without resolving the conflict. You may cool down for a while but work on your conflict as soon as you can.

FROM MODULE VIII: PROMOTING FAMILY SPIRITUALITY

Session 1: Fathers as spiritual leaders

Preamble
Try to look back at your past and look at your present situation. Do you think you can be proud of yourself for the rest of your life? Do you have that inner confidence, inner love, peace and trust emanating from your enduring faith in God? What have you done to yourself as spiritual being in the context of your role as father? And just what do you think does it take for you to be the kind of father we need to be in order to provide the most wholesome and spiritually rich home in which your children's souls might be unfolded?

Key learning points

- The father is the spiritual leader in the community
  - The family is a small church and is governed by the Almighty. The father heads it and he serves as the spiritual leader. His main goal is to re-inspirit every member of the family and family life as a whole to be able to raise spiritual children.
- Family spirituality
  - Here is the synergistic byproduct of all the interpersonal dynamics between parent and child, child and sibling and spouse and spouse. This can be characterised by a strong bond among family members – healthy relationships with love, support, guidance and a sense of shared identity. It generates and energises spiritual power making us become more trustful and hopeful to pursue things despite occurrence of obstacles. It gives us a clear vision of life and its meaning. It gives sympathetic understanding to a nagging wife, domineering husband, troublesome children and meddling neighbours.
- Family life
  - Is your spiritual life – seeking together, ritualising together, learning and teaching peace?

Note: Excerpts are verbatim.

Source: DSWD/UNICEF (2003).

The Solo Parents Welfare Act (RA 8972) of 2000, while again quite radical in principle, especially in a context in which lone parents have traditionally suffered stigmatisation, seems to have fallen short of the mark in practice. Nominally this provides a comprehensive package of support services such as educational scholarships, skills development for livelihoods and self-employment, health services and help in psychological, emotional and social issues, where the 'nuclear family is not available or cannot be restored' (CWC, 2000: 48; DSWD, 2004; see also Box 5.5). Although the DSWD coordinates the programme, access to various benefits need to be negotiated with a bewildering array of agencies. This entails considerable bureaucracy and endorsement by social workers, as well as some rather moralistically slanted eligibility criteria for some programmes such as having a 'good reputation in

BOX 5.5 THE PHILIPPINES: HIGHLIGHTS OF THE SOLO PARENTS WELFARE ACT

Republic Act No. 8972 (2000)
- An Act providing for benefits and privileges to solo parents and their children

Declaration of policy (Section 2) – It is the policy of the State to promote the family as the foundation of the nation, strengthen its solidarity and ensure its total development. Towards this end, it shall develop a comprehensive programme of services for solo parents and their children to be carried out by the DSWD, Department of Health (DOH), Department of Education, Culture and Sports (DECS), DILG, CHED, TESDA, National Housing Authority (NHA), DOLE and other related government and non-government agencies

Definition of terms (Section 3)

a) A **'solo parent'** is an individual who falls under any of the following categories:
   i) A woman who gives birth as a result of rape or other crime against chastity, and keeps and raises the child
   ii) Parent left alone with responsibility of parenthood due to death of spouse
   iii) Parent left alone due to imprisonment of spouse for at least one year
   iv) Parent left alone due to certified physical or mental incapacity of spouse
   v) Parent left alone due to legal or *de facto* separation
   vi) Parent left alone due to annulment of marriage
   vii) Parent left alone due to abandonment by spouse for at least one year
   viii) Unmarried mother or father who has kept and is raising children
   ix) Any other person who solely provides parental care or support to a child
   x) Any family member who assumes responsibility of head of family as a result of the death, abandonment, disapparance or prolonged absence of parent(s)
b) **'Children'** refer to those living with and dependent upon the solo parent for support who are unmarried, unemployed and not more

than 18 years of age, or over 18 years of age in case of inability to self-support due to mental and/or physical incapacity

c) **'Parental responsibility'** with respect to children shall refer to the rights and duties of parents as per the Family Code of The Philippines

d) **'Parental leave'** shall mean leave benefits enabling solo parents to perform parental duties and responsibilities where physical presence is required

e) **'Flexible work schedule'** is the right granted to a solo parent employee to vary his/her arrival and departure time without affecting the core work hours as defined by an employer

Criteria for support (Section 4) – Any solo parent whose income falls below the poverty threshold as set by NEDA and subject to assessment by local DSWD worker. *Note:* Non-poor solo parents are also entitled to flexible work schedules, parental leave and freedom from employment discrimination.

Comprehensive package of social development and welfare services (Section 5) – To be developed by an interagency committee comprising a range of relevant agencies headed by the DSWD (see above), initially including: a) livelihood development services, b) counselling, c) parent effectiveness services, d) critical incidence stress debriefing (for example, stress management to enable solo parents to better cope with situations of crisis or abuse), e) special projects for individuals in need of protection (for example, temporary shelter)

Work discrimination (Section 7) – No employer shall discriminate against any solo parent with respect to terms and conditions of work on account of his/her status

Parental leave (Section 8) – In addition to leave privileges under existing laws, solo parents are entitled to no more than seven days parental leave after a minimum period of service of one year

Educational benefits (Section 9) – The DECS, CHED and TESDA shall provide scholarship programmes for qualified solo parents and their children in institutions of basic, tertiary and technical/ skills education, as well as non-formal education as appropriate

Housing benefits (Section 10) – Solo parents shall be given allocation in low-cost housing projects on liberal terms of repayment

Medical assistance (Section 11) – DOH to develop a comprehensive health-care programme for solo parents and their children

Additional powers and functions of the DSWD (Section 12) include:

a) Conduct of research to develop a new body of knowledge on solo parents, to define executive and legislative measures needed to promote and protect the interests of solo parents and their children, and to assess the effectiveness of programmes designed for disadvantaged solo parents and their children
b) Coordinate government and NGO activities oriented to solo parents and their children
c) Monitor the implementation of the provisions of the Solo Parents Welfare Act

Implementing rules and regulations (Section 13)
Interagency committee led by DSWD to consult on these with LGUs, NGOs and people's organisations

Appropriations (Section 14) – The amount necessary to execute the provisions of the Act shall be included in the budget of concerned government agencies in the General Appropriations Act of the year following enactment into law and thereafter.

Repealing clauses (Section 15) – All laws, decrees, Executive Orders (EOs), administrative orders or parts thereof inconsistent with the provisions of the Act to be repealed or amended accordingly.

Source: Republic of the Philippines (2000).

the community' (DSWD, 2004). Also, employers can be exempted from the clause in the act requiring flexible work schedules (ibid.: 22).

Rather more success, perhaps, has transpired with efforts to reduce violence against women, which at a national level started in 1993 with the opening of 'women's desks' in police stations. Following the establishment of a number of family courts in Philippine cities through RA 8369 of 1997, the 1998 Rape Victim Assistance and Protection Act (RA 8505) set up a rape crisis centre in every province and city, and stipulated that at least 10 per cent of new recruits to the police force should be female. This quota has been surpassed in all years since, and in 2002, reached 17 per cent (NCRFW, 2004a: 15). In 2004, came the Anti-Violence Against Women and their Children Act (AVAWACA, RA 9262) whose objective is to protect women and children from violence in all types of close relationship (including legal and common-law marriage, and courtship) (NCRFW, 2004a). Taking an impressively broad perspective on violence, the law covers physical, sexual, psychological and economic abuse, with the latter including the withdrawal of financial support or prevention of the victim from engaging in any legitimate occupation, deprivation of the right to use and enjoy common assets, the destruction of household property and control of victims' money (NCRFW, 2004b: 2–3).

Such initiatives have not only been complemented but sometimes spurred by local government action, with Cebu City Council having passed various ordinances penalising domestic violence prior to the 2004 national law, such as a '*barangay* protection order' (BPO), which permits local officials to temporarily remove abusers from the home, regardless of in whose name the conjugal property is registered (Javate de Dios, 2003: 6). Another major Cebu-based initiative is the programme '*Bantay Banay*' launched by the NGO Lihok Pilipina in the early 1990s, and which has now been replicated in numerous other Philippine cities. *Bantay Banay* (Cebuano for 'Family Watch') brings together *barangay* officials, male and female and residents, local doctors, health workers, and police with the intention of sensitising communities to identify and eliminate gender-based violence. In some neighbourhoods this has been so successful that battering by husbands has fallen from affecting 60 per cent to 20 per cent of the female population.

GENDER AND GENERATIONAL DIMENSIONS OF POVERTY IN THE PHILIPPINES

The Views of Professionals

Although 'new' official figures suggest a downturn in poverty from 2000, most of the 15 respondents in my institutional survey in the Philippines as of late 2004 felt that poverty was on the increase, and that the gap between rich and poor was widening. Poverty was construed by many as a multidimensional phenomenon comprising deficiencies in assets such as secure land tenure and social capital. Powerlessness was also emphasised, as well as cultural, intellectual and spiritual poverty, although income remained central, with the poor deemed to be particularly hard hit by declining purchasing power and job opportunities. The latter situation was attributed to strategies such as liberalisation, deregulation and privatisation, and lack of political will to redistribute wealth. One respondent, from the Asian Development Bank, claimed that increased numbers in poverty between 1985 and 2000, especially in rural areas, was due, *inter alia*, to weak macroeconomic management, insufficient employment, high population growth, incomplete agrarian reform, and security issues, especially in Mindanao. Another respondent, also from an international development agency, drew attention to lack of state accountability: 'Each new administration is a complete replica of the former. Graft and corruption are getting worse each year, under each new president. Political, social and economic insecurity are constant factors which prevail in each administration.' This corroborates a survey carried out by Clarke and Sison (2003) with 57 members of the elite, among whom the majority argued that poverty is primarily a political problem arising from 'the inequitable distribution of resources, the prevalence of corruption and the persistence of "traditional" (semi-feudal or oligarchic) politicians' (ibid.: 225).

Not all respondents laid the entire blame at the feet of government or the global economy however. One cause frequently mooted was the persistence of high birth rates. Another was that people's priorities at the grassroots were misdirected – for example, they spent on video cassette recorders and mobile phones at the expense of basic consumption and services. One respondent, however, felt that overspending on 'non-merit goods' at the domestic level was a result of poverty itself, for example, by pushing people into drugs or drink.

The majority of interviewees, especially from NGOs and international agencies, do not feel that the Philippine government is approaching poverty reduction in the most appropriate manner. For example, one respondent, who had actually migrated from the state sector, highlighted the fact that measures tended to be 'palliative' rather than 'preventive', also emphasising how difficult it is to implement plans due to lack of financial and human resources, especially at the local level. A substantial number also feel that despite reference to gender and/or the identification of women as a 'vulnerable group' in the MTPDPs, the translation of this rhetoric into policy leaves a lot to be desired. Indeed, some are also rather cynical about 'empowerment', commenting that with terms like this and 'marginalisation' the only tangible benefit of state poverty interventions has been an enrichment of the poor's vocabulary! Worryingly, too, many professional respondents had not heard of the KALAHI programme, or if they had, had seen no evidence of it in practice and had little idea as to what it entailed.

Even if many feel that intra-household transfers make it difficult to determine income gaps between women and men, it was widely claimed that women are disproportionately affected by poverty, especially if thinking about poverty in a broader sense and as comprising 'access', 'opportunity', 'time' and 'effort'. Even where women had made inroads into arenas such as the labour market where they stood to improve their socio-economic status, for example, gains are often cancelled out by limited change in domestic regimes and the rise in heavy 'double-shifts' for women. For example, Tessie Fernandez, the founder of the Cebu feminist NGO Lihok Pilipina, observed that while local women have increasing access to employment (as in MEPZ, where 80 per cent of workers are female), this is sometimes used as an excuse by men not to work, and they rarely compensate by doing more domestic labour. Another NGO director pointed out that women's mounting labour force participation can lead to male 'backlash' in the form of non-cooperative behaviour or violence.

Leading on from this, most respondents emphasised that women had no choice other than to fend for their families because men in situations of hardship tend to resort to 'escape routes' such as drugs and drink. One perceived upshot is that poverty makes women even more industrious, imaginative and capable. As a spokesman for NEDA Region VII articulated: 'this is why we tend to direct poverty alleviation programmes to women'. While in some senses focusing on women is clearly a sensible option, it was also recognised that women are also pushed in many cases into extremes of self-sacrifice. This not only extends to going without food (see note 15), but starving themselves of time. As one (male) respondent from Cebu's Division for the Welfare of the Urban Poor put it: 'Men work eight hours a day, but for women the working day is endless.'

When identifying the age groups at greatest risk, one or two people suggested that children were the most vulnerable to income poverty, basically because if their parents were poor they could do little other than to scrape income from street work or begging. However, majority opinion was divided on whether women in their middle or senior years were hardest hit. Interestingly too, the emphasis was not so much on income, but on bearing the burden of coping with poverty. As in The Gambia, some identified women with young children (generally in the 25–40 age group) as carrying the heaviest load. Others, however, noted that women in their later years are not just having to extend their working lives past retirement age but are also having to look after grandchildren. This is sometimes because young couples are unable to live apart, especially if unemployed, but in other cases because daughters migrate overseas leaving their mothers to look after their children. In addition, trends towards the increased extension of households, while in some respects beneficial to the poor, are also rendering households 'over-extended',[19] with the main burden of care, support and daily provisioning falling to adult and/or senior women, and economic support to their younger counterparts. Although there were also perceived rises in lone parenthood, significantly no respondent mentioned that women-headed households were disproportionately afflicted by poverty.

Ways suggested out of the Philippines' 'poverty trap' included reduction of fiscal imbalance, an improved investment climate, enhanced infrastructure, the strengthening of institutional capacity (particularly that of LGUs to deliver services to the poor), the improvement of assets, land and resource management, and the reduction of geographical inequalities. However, most emphasis was placed on the generation of more jobs, and stimulating entrepreneurialism through credit and skills training, although as one NGO interviewee cautioned, even these would be doomed to failure if government continued to toe the line of economic liberalisation promoted by the WTO, the International Monetary Fund (IMF) and the World Bank.

Grassroots Perspectives on the Meanings, Manifestations and Corollaries of Poverty

As in The Gambia, the majority of low-income people interviewed at the grassroots in the Philippines felt that around 80 per cent of the population were poor, which is substantially higher than official estimates and even self-rated poverty as recorded by Social Weather Stations (SWS) surveys (see earlier). As Joel, a 69-year-old pensioner described: 'The Philippines is a desperately poor Third World country.'

Poverty is conceived mainly as a lack of income – arising from high prices, and low earnings – with poor people condemned to leading 'daily lives of hardship and grind'. One 23-year-old trisikad driver, Landing, saw himself as poor 'because we are always eating foods which is not delicious'. Leoncia, 61, a part-time washerwoman echoed: 'Being poor is about being unable to save money. Sometimes we have no *viand* (meat or fish). Sometimes we skip meals.' Conrada, a 24-year-old shell-craft pieceworker declared her family was poor 'because we eat food which is not nutritious – we used to snack on bread, and now have rice porridge – and have no money to buy appliances'. Similar views were expressed by Manilfa (14) and Delia (25) in a focus group in Looc, who concurred that poverty is about 'no money, no food, having dirty dresses as if they are a fool. Somebody who just eat leftover foods, such as leftover foods from Jollibee' (a modern fast-food chain). Genita, a 36-year-old vendor of *utap* and *ampao* (sweet pastry and rice cake respectively) who lives in an 11-member extended household, declared: 'I consider myself as poor because I don't have a helper, not like the rich people. And I don't have a better job, and also I don't have electricity in the home.' Alfredo, a 56-year-old construction worker, identified further dimensions of poverty as 'no time for leisure, can't afford to send children to school, very low in status, shy type of person'. Some respondents, such as Elizabeth (47) who supports a husband and five children on her meagre earnings as a laundrywoman and part-time masseuse, emphasised shelter conditions: 'Being poor is very pitiful, when you live in a dilapidated house and have no food to eat.'

The main reasons given by respondents for high rates of poverty were government economic mismanagement and corruption, such as spending more than it earned and lining its own pockets. Commonly mentioned additional factors were the lack of job opportunities, the increase of contractual work relative to permanent employment, and low wages. Michelle (28), for example, explained that her family was poor because her husband's job as a porter was only 'off and on'. A male trisikad driver, Sherwin (24), is in a similar predicament: his average wage (of around 150 pesos – just under US$3 – a day) is less than the minimum wage of US$3.78, and even when combined with his wife's income from a small food stall at Cebu's port, 'can only buy food, not enough for clothing'.

Although most pointed the finger of blame at the state or the economy, some also talked about poverty in Cebu being aggravated by the influx of migrants from poorer parts of the country such as Mindanao. This was thought to have contributed to saturation of the city's labour market and to have been responsible for a rise in begging and stealing. Others felt that heredity played a big hand, that they were poor because they had been born into poor families lacking the means to educate them and with no assets to pass on. Others felt that the state was divinely ordained, such as Leoncia, a 61-year-old Catholic: 'Poverty is God's will. If you are born destined to be poor no matter how hard you work to earn a living, still you are poor.' Yet converts to Evangelism, who, like Benedicta (68) in Babag had become a 'Born Again Christian', attributed poverty not to God, but to people's own 'low personal values and *bisyos*' (vices). Even though Juanita (Box 5.6) represented a cast-iron case of someone who had tried to break out of poverty and in many respects failed, she also claimed: 'Seldom do ambitious people end up poor. For example, hard-working people do the sensible thing by trying to seek "greener pastures" rather than sitting around waiting for graces to come.' The idea that some people remain poor because they never aspire to anything more was frequently seen to be compounded by high fertility, even if they all saw benefits in having children (see later).

BOX 5.6   POVERTY, GENDER AND FAMILY FROM THE PERSPECTIVE OF JUANITA

Juanita is 41 years old and lives with her husband and four children in Sambag 2, a low-income settlement in Cebu City. She and her husband are in the process of buying their house with the aid of a state-subsidised mortage from the Community Mortgage Programme (CMP).

Juanita was born in Ronda, a village in the south of Cebu Province near Moalboal in 1963. Her parents had a small farm raising animals and growing crops. They only had two daughters, but made sacrifices to educate them both, such that Juanita was able to finish high school, which potentially gave her a much better start than many other girls in her community. However, by the time Juanita graduated from high school, her parents could not afford to pay for further studies, besides which they were getting on in years and needed help themselves. So, at the age of 15, Juanita migrated to Cebu City where she got a job in a beauty parlour alongside her elder sister, and to pay for her keep in her sister's home, acted as cleaner and general helper to her sister, husband and their young family. Concerned to 'get on in life', and to carve out a profession for herself, Juanita decided to put herself through college. With the money she received from the beauty parlour, and living 'rent-free' (if not 'work-free'), she not only sent remittances back to her parents in Ronda, but also registered for a Bachelor of Science degree in commerce at a local college, majoring in accounting. So determined was Juanita to conclude her studies, that for four years she worked around the clock, averaging only four hours' sleep a night. However, at the age of 20 she met and married her husband, and gave up her course when she became pregnant. She regrets not having got to the stage where she would have been able to practise a profession, but aside from having raised four children, she has at least played a major role in supporting her family economically. This has been especially critical since 2001, when her husband (now 43 years old) lost his job in a wood and stonecraft export company after the September 11 terrorist attacks on New York and Washington, DC. Orders plummeted and he was made redundant. With the small amount of redundancy money he received he set up a 'dressed chicken' business which Juanita helps him with. The work is fairly intensive, involving the taking on of 47 new-born chicks at a time, keeping them under electric light and feeding and watering them constantly for 34 days until they weigh 1 kilo without feathers, and are then ready to be cooked and sold.

In addition to this, Juanita has been very active in community and civic affairs, with her voluntary activities in Sambag 2 having led to becoming a part-time *barangay* employee in receipt of a small honorarium. As a volunteer for the city's major feminist NGO, Lihok Pilipina, and as a member of the Cebu City Women's Coalition, Juanita was well-qualified for the job of *barangay* GAD advocacy person, although she is now concentrating on a *barangay* solid waste management scheme. In addition to this, Juanita capitalises on the expertise acquired in her years in the beauty parlour by operating a 'sideline' in pedicures, manicures and haircuts from home or by visiting clients in their houses.

Having long regretted the premature termination of her own studies, Juanita has always made the education of her children a big priority in the hope that they will have good careers. However, nowadays the stakes are a lot higher. While her 8-year-old daughter and 16-year-old son, are in elementary and high school respectively, her two eldest sons (aged 18 and 20) despite having finished high school, are unable to find jobs and may return to study if the situation persists.

The worst aspects of being poor according to some respondents were not being able to buy what they wanted, lacking opportunities, having little scope to exercise any rights, and being underestimated and put down. Although, unlike in The Gambia, where basics such as food, elementary education and everyday clothing such as shoes are often people's major aspiration, a number of Filipino respondents expressed frustration about not having luxury consumer goods such as 'beautiful dresses', jewellery, make-up, cars, television, refrigerators, and karaoke and video machines. However, for women, one of the major issues was 'not being able to satisfy our children's needs and desires'. As reported by Prima (42), for example, a mother of seven:

> Being poor makes me feel sad; have worries of getting sick because we have no money. Like the past All Souls Day, we have no rice to eat. Instead we eat boiled banana for lunch, and in the evening we just drink water and go to bed. Looking through to my children sleeping, I couldn't take the pain of being poor.

Angelina, a 35-year-old houseperson and mother of five also declared she felt worst when 'my children are asking for milk and I have nothing to give. I feel so miserable and I can hardly sleep at night thinking about the situation'. Angelina felt that if she were better off: 'There would be no more headaches about what we're going to cook for this meal. You will not be roaming around looking for where to borrow money to buy food. No more feelings of emptiness inside our hearts.' Another issue commonly mentioned was the lack of resources to allow children to pursue tertiary education, which is increasingly essential for a career in the Philippines. One 57-year-old woman, Lilia, who participated in a focus group of 11 women in Barangay Carretas, also observed from her work as a 'fixer' (see Box 5.7) that lack of educational qualifications among the poor were compounded by the fact that applications for any half-decent job required costly typed-up 'bio-data', copies, and photographs, as well as references.

As indicated above, the emotional states accompanying poverty were overwhelmingly negative, such as anxiety, fear, fatigue, jealousy, irritability, anger, conflict, sadness and desolation. Maricris, an 18-year-old ambulant vendor, reported of her family that 'we always keep on quarrelling because of no money'. This was echoed by Delia, a 37-year-old buyer and seller of firewood, and mother of seven: 'Poverty makes me feel emotional, sad, irritable, face keeps on frowning, especially when somebody in the family get sick and we don't have the money to buy medicine. Very, very sad.' Desolation had also afflicted Romelito, a 32-year-old lone father with 3-year-old twin sons, who reported: 'During the pregnancy of my wife, she had toxic goitre, but at the time I felt so sad because I could not afford all the medicine she needed. And the saddest moment for me was when my wife passed away. I have no helpmate in raising my children.'

As in The Gambia, some people also saw poverty provoking 'underground economic activities', 'anti-social' behaviour and crime, ranging from begging, to theft ('fiddling'), violence, and even assassination. For example, Bernie, a 20-year-old NGO volunteer, stated that 'Because of poverty, many people will resort to kill somebody to steal things'.

Drugs are also seen as a major corollary of poverty, with the bulk of respondents reporting that between 50 and 90 per cent of their neighbours engaged in substance abuse. Parents (especially fathers) would often turn to taking drugs such as 'shabu' ('poor man's cocaine), 'rugby' (glue-sniffing), marijuana or cough syrup, for solace or to curb hunger pangs. Sometimes they would also take to selling drugs, and even use their children as go-betweens. However, peddling drugs was seen to be particularly rife among unemployed male youth, whose parents were too busy to supervise them and/or did not show them enough love. Referred to as 'rugby boys', many of these young males formed gangs who became involved in other types of illegal behaviour.

BOX 5.7   POVERTY, GENDER AND FAMILY FROM THE PERSPECTIVE OF LILIA

Lilia is 57 years old and has been head of her own household since 1984 when her husband died of a nervous breakdown. Although technically speaking, widowed people can remarry in the Philippines, Lilia claimed in front of 10 other participants in a focus group meeting that 'with one dead husband, I don't want another one!'

Lilia had four children in total, of whom three are now married and living apart. She still has one unmarried son of 22 years living at home, who works as a volunteer for a local NGO, and one 18-year-old granddaughter who came to stay with Lilia when her mother was separating from her first spouse, and carried on doing so when the mother took up with someone new.

When first asked about her employment, Lilia commented modestly that she only had 'sidelines' – a term many women use for activities which may be poorly remunerated and/or not identifiable as 'proper' salaried employment. It turned out, however, that these sidelines were fairly substantial as well as diverse. First, Lilia is an owner-occupier, benefiting from a 25-year subsidised mortgage from the Community Mortgage Programme, and is thus able to run her own *sari-sari* store from home. In addition, using skills acquired through a project organised in her community by a local NGO, Lilia is now a practising reflexologist which she does on an 'on demand' basis. Finally, having been active in the community as member of her women's association and the like, Lilia has gathered many contacts over the years and has set herself up as a 'fixer', which is something of a hybrid between a personal assistant, courier and Citizen's Advice Bureau representative. This is a job which involves arranging payments and/or paperwork for other people, usually at the City Hall, ranging from electricity bills, to permits, to job applications. For the service she charges a small fee and relies for expansion of her business on word of mouth.

Although, as in The Gambia, people felt there was not much to commend poverty, the female focus group in Barangay Carretas commented that their Catholic faith strengthened their belief in the poor being 'righteous' and once dead would be 'lifted up' to heaven. Genita (36) added that: 'poor people are more prayerful, and they have a peaceful mind'. Connie a 63-year-old *sari-sari* store owner and *barangay* health worker, opined that the poor manage to live simply and are not materialistic. Even though Connie talked about the suffering experienced on the many occasions where she had had to mortgage her dresses just to buy food, 'still my faith in the Lord never change'. In addition, although the poor may not be well-off in material terms, some professed that they were rich spiritually and emotionally, and pulled together to help each other. As one woman articulated: 'When poor, people share more, You do not see the rich sharing a meal.' In addition, a more practical advantage of being poor was that the poor rarely left much debt behind them because no one would lend them large sums of money in the first place. Some also felt that being poor encouraged people to be hard-working, even if this was only because they had to be.

Leading on from this, when asked about what people would do when they hit hard times, some, such as Angelina (35), talked about turning to God: 'Strive hard and ask Grace to God because He is our great provider'; or as Deliia (37) professed: 'I pray to God that I can sell more firewoods so I can have money.' More pragmatically, however, most respondents said they would turn to family (especially children) first. For example, Germina (65), an 'on-and-off' laundrywoman, declared: 'I will go to my children and ask for money or food. I won't ask anyone else for money because I cannot pay (repayment is usually required with interest), and nobody will lend me money because I have no permanent work.' While some stop short of going beyond their immediate family, others resort to associations in their *sitios* (settlements) and *barangays*, ranging from neighbourhood networks ('*bayan ihan*'), to rotating credit and savings schemes ('*biray*'), which require a modest contribution of about 10 pesos (*c.* US$0.20) a month, and are there for emergencies. People also emphasised the need to work harder during difficult times. For example, Joel, the trisikad driver declared that when money was really lean he 'doubled efforts in fetching passengers for trisikad'. Another type of sacrifice was made by Maricris (18) who had given up school at 14 to start work as a vendor in order to conserve house-hold resources. Indeed, women are often those who make the biggest sacrifices, with Johnace, a 19-year-old marine engineering student and his unemployed father and housewife mother, depending totally on remittances sent by Johnace's older sister from Japan, where she reportedly worked as a singer.

Grassroots Perceptions of Gender and Generational Aspects of Poverty

When asked about their perceptions of which groups (according to gender and age) were most vulnerable to poverty, there were (as in the institutional survey), mixed views. Indeed, in respect of age and income poverty there was probably most consensus on who was at *least* risk, namely, youth (both male and female), primarily on account of their having more education, skills and access to employment than their elders. Even then, and somewhat surprisingly in light of high demand for female workers in Metro Cebu, it was often stated that women in general face more difficulties gaining employment than their male counterparts. As articulated by Alfredo, the 56-year-old construction worker: 'Men easily get jobs compared to women because they can do any kind of work, and heavier work.' Gerilyn (20), a home-based shell-craft worker, echoed: 'Men have a bigger salary because they do hard work compared with women. Men can easily get a job because they have more job opportunities, whether they are old or young, while the woman needs back-up.' This said, whether gender discrimination in the labour market actually translates into income disparities at the household level is another issue. While employment can clearly provide women with their own income, the Barangay Carretas female focus group claimed that it is actually very difficult to see income differences between women and men within the family. Virgie, a 44-year-old firecracker-wrapper married to a trisikad driver in Babag added that: 'Women have to work now like men, so they all know what it is like to labour hard for low wages.'

Notwithstanding some divergence of opinion around gendered gaps in income poverty, a major point of correspondence among respondents at the grassroots (and again dovetailing with the views of professionals) was that women bear the heaviest burdens as far as *dealing* with poverty is concerned. This affects women at all life-course stages in so far as young women often play a much bigger role in economic support to parents than their brothers. However, women in their middle and senior years are generally regarded as the worst off in terms of time and effort. For example, although one or two people noted that senior citizens without family or pensions were potentially at risk of income poverty, there was also the acknowledgement that where they live with relatives (as so many do), they do not have an easy time – older women in particular often being required to help out with the care of grandchildren while their daughters work. The middle generation of women (especially from their forties onwards) are also squeezed by the simultaneous demands of childcare and elderly care, as well has having to hold down jobs. Moreover, as pointed out by Baby (55), women not only work harder, but also 'suffer emotionally from the stress of poverty'.

In the process of coping, however, and echoing an idea iterated by one or two Filipino professionals, some talked about the way in which poverty often sent men on a path to escapism, vices and ruin, but women to self-improvement. While male and female participants repeatedly stressed men's proclivities to indulge in 'ABS' – the three stereotypical vices of male Filipinos, notably, *alak* (alcohol), *babae* (women), and *sugal* (gambling) – because women usually have no choice other than to take responsibility for their children they can often expand their skills and sense of achievement. As articulated by Linda, a 44-year-old hospice worker from Barangay Carretas:

> It is better to be a poor woman than a poor man. Say a poor man will say 'I do not have a job, I do not have some things', and usually most will resort to gambling or drinking . . . vices . . . to try and compensate them for what they don't have. Whereas a poor woman will carry her responsibilities. She will create something in order to have earnings. I have to have a *sari-sari* store to have earnings. I have to cook to eat to sustain ourselves, different to a man.

As echoed by Conrada (24):

> Nowadays men spend little time with the family. They are fond of getting out with their '*barkadas*' (gang/group of male peers), drinking beer just around the neighbourhood. Women and children are just left behind at home . . . Women have a brighter future than men because nowadays more men indulge in vices like drugs, '*shabu*', mistresses, card-playing and drunkenness. Though there are women in these vices, it is not as much as men. Maybe because men are the source of income and have money anytime they can do what they want to do?

Nelia (46) feels that these differences owe to the fact that 'Men don't take problems as seriously as women. Men don't worry much even when there is nothing to eat or no food to be cooked. They only depend on women.' Indeed, even where men are less 'irresponsible' and do uphold their economic obligations, most feel it is their right to to sit down when they get home from work and be 'attended to' by wives. Part and parcel of this is the idea that reproductive work is something which women should primarily be responsible for even when they are also earning. For example, as expressed by Cris, a 41-year-old father of six who cannot get by on his income as a trisikad driver without the money his wife makes selling fruit: 'Women should do all the household chores while men are the ones in charge of looking for work to raise his family.' Such views reflect the continued undervaluation of the labour of women, who, even when they have a number of remunerative 'sidelines', are often just referred to (and refer to themselves) as 'plain housewives'.

Leading on from the above, there are major gender disparities in leisure time. For example, Juanito, a 57-year-old trisikad driver, who heads a six-member extended household, has about 5 hours off in an average day. This includes a long lunchbreak, a nap when he comes home from work, and at least 2 hours 'roaming around' in the evening with neighbours and friends. In contrast, Maricris, an 18-year-old single woman living at home with her mother and two younger sisters (her father is in jail on charge of murder), gets no rest at all. For the last four years she and her next youngest sister of 15, have sold snack foods from a pushcart in Carbon Market (the centre of vegetable trading in Cebu), between 6 p.m. and 6 a.m., seven days a week, earning just US$1.75 a day, and committing half the proceeds to their mother. Despite catching up on some sleep during the day, Maricris maintains: 'we still have time to do the household chores, including the laundry'. More disturbing still, perhaps, than these actual examples of gender difference, is that many people do not see fit to comment, simply accepting this as the 'natural' order of things. This in turn, arguably helps to account for the fact that there are relatively few signs of change in respect of the disproportionate engagement of young women in reproductive work, and their relative lack of freedom compared with men, to 'roam around' whenever and wherever they like.

Yet in spite of this, some respondents feel there are advances towards greater gender equality. Because women now have more employment opportunities, for example, some feel that they are less likely to fall into poverty than in the past, and that the gap between women's and men's poverty is closing. As respondents in one focus group of middle and senior women declared: 'Before women were more likely to be poor, because men were above women. Now women are getting empowered and often having their own earnings.' The efforts of the government and NGOs to promote gender equality have also not gone unnoticed. For example, while arguably somewhat overstated, and bearing all the trademarks of her own involvement in gender training at *barangay* level, Alma, a 42-year-old NGO worker, spoke enthusiastically of the fact that: 'Women are no longer poorer than men because we have women's empowerment. We are mainstreaming gender, and we have 5 per cent of the LGU budget reserved for GAD activities such as gender sensitisation.'

Intersections between Poverty, Gender and Household Transitions

One indication that changes are taking place on the ground, however, is that female household headship seems to be more viable than in the past, both economically and socially, and in the popular imagination. Although there were only a few lone parents among respondents, rarely did they or others stress that they were particularly victimised by poverty. While one or two people such as Alfredo (56) made the point that in households 'in which the breadwinner is the wife, it is not an easy task that you are mother at the same time as father who is raising the family', if anything, large households with lots of children and few workers are regarded as more vulnerable, as attested to by official data.

In terms of the reported experiences of female heads themselves, Germina, the 65-year-old head of an extended household saw her role has having been one of great responsibility, not to mention 'tiresome': 'I am the *tatay* (father) and the *nanay* (mother) in our household. So all the household work, earning a living, and taking care of the children was done by me – very difficult.' Yet this situation was deemed eminently preferable to the experience of living with her husband:

> My husband was only good during the early years of our marriage, Later on he was very irritable, always drunk, and when he arrived home he would quarrel with me. My husband when he was yet alive, when he came home from work, he will not help me in doing household chores. He even battered me. Instead he kept on drinking and when he didn't like the food I gave him he would quarrel with me. He got angry with me when I asked him why his earnings were so small. More money was allotted to alcohol than food . . . For me, men should help women even fetch water, gather firewoods, repay the house, and even wash clothes and do the cleaning.

A similar marital history had plagued a mother of two Milagrosa (35), who now runs a very successful *sari-sari* business at the port, has both children (aged 11 and 15) in school, and claimed that without a husband, she had found it easier to make a life for herself and her children. She could make her own decisions and there was less conflict. Milagrosa also claimed not only that she was personally proud, but that the community is proud, that she has survived on her own and raised her children.

Even some men stated that women were better off unmarried, especially if young and well educated. According to Rudy a 42-year-old trisikad driver, for example: 'In this situation a woman can buy anything she wants with no one who will stop you in doing so.'

Conjugality, fertility and inter-generational transfers

Despite the foregoing, marriage continues to be widespread among the poor, and in many cases unions endure, even if there is considerable infidelity on the part of men, and as in The Gambia, women claim that any excess income is spent on mistresses. While many respondents – especially in the older age groups – had married young, however, the ideal age was now deemed to be about 25 for women, and 28 for men. Maricris (18), for example, declared:

> I plan to get married at 25 because by that time I am already mature enough to have my own family and probably I already finished my schooling by that time. This is an older age than my mother when she got married. Age at marriage keeps on changing depending on the situations that you consider. Even if you are young and you think you are financially stable, then you can get married and have a

family of your own. For as long as you are responsible enough to raise your own
children whether you are young or old then you have the right to get married.

Children are seen as an integral part of married life, and, as opposed to The
Gambia where son preference persists, both sons and daughters are highly
valued, with most people expressing the ideal of having one of each. A lot
of stress was also placed on the emotional and spiritual rewards of parenthood, with Alfredo (56) declaring: 'Children are a gift from God. They are
our pacifier whenever there is conflict between couples. They are an inspi-
ration and joy to parents, somebody to lean on in times of hardship.'

That children might be 'leaned on' when they are growing up is, in principle, generally disfavoured by respondents who stress that ideally children
should not work until they are around 18, or at least have finished their
studies. The practice, however, is often rather different, with many people
of all ages in the survey having started work themselves in their early- to
mid-teens. Moreover, in some cases, respondent's own children had commenced working very young. For example, Lucia (65), recalled how her
family was so hard-up at times that she had to send her children garbage-
scavenging. For the most part however, children's value as an economic
resource is something which realises itself primarily in adulthood. As participants in a mixed focus group in Looc claimed, children will take care of
you when you were old and/or sick and as such require investment when
they are young (see also Ofstedal et al., 2004: 174), and below).[20]

While the idea of children being a long-term source of security was
widely shared, exactly how many to have was more contested. The vast
majority of young people expressed a preference to have just two. While this
was also the case with a large number of middle and senior adults, some
had only had two or three children because of straitened circumstances. As
reported by Germina (65), for example:

> Well, having children is good. There is somebody who will look after you when
> you are old, and when you are sick they are there for you to attend to. There is
> somebody to run to when you are in need financially. They are there to support
> you morally, but frankly I didn't want to have many children because I didn't
> have the money to raise them. Two children is enough.

Alfredo (56) also saw the pros and cons in small families stating that 'Three
is already a lot of children . . . Lots of children is disadvantageous and at
the same time advantageous economically because if they are still young
you have to educate them well. But when they grow up and they have
finished in school and they have a job of their own, they can help you.'
At the other end of the spectrum, and possibly with a hint of *post hoc*
rationalisation, Delia, a 37-year-old mother of seven, declared: 'Children

are blessings to you from God. Very advantageous to have many children. Many will look for work to earn a living. Many will look after you when you are old already, when you get sick. Many will plan how to overcome poverty. Seven children is fine with me, but more than that is too many.'

Grassroots Views on Poverty-Reduction Initiatives

Echoing Illo's (2003a: 25) observation that despite the vitality of women's movements in the Philippines, many poor women remain ignorant of state, civil society or community-driven initiatives, most respondents in Cebu are extremely uninformed about national or even local initiatives to reduce poverty, unless they have had direct contact with an NGO in their own communities. Where respondents have been involved in programmes, as is the case of participants in '*Bantay Banay*', or as with the women in Barangay Carretas who had been given employment-related training by an NGO, including skills they had not previously possessed such as reflexology, there was a decided emphasis on benefits.

People also emphasised how NGOs, particularly church-based organisations, and even LGUs, were more accountable to the poor and less prone to corruption than national government, which many respondents felt could do a great deal more. Edward, a 22-year-old factory hand, felt that completely cost-free education would be one thing which would help the poor move out of poverty. Others felt that the state should create more jobs, for example, by investing in infrastructure projects which would generate opportunities for poorer people. Joel (23) also felt that a reduction in cronyism would facilitate this process: 'Our government officials should not only give work to their own relatives and close friends, but give work to those who are poor.'

Reflecting the common view that people themselves have a part to play in combatting poverty, some respondents stressed the need for people to be more industrious and less indulgent in wasteful vices. Angelina (35), also felt that more collective effort would help. 'At least we Filipinos should be humble enough to work hand in hand for a better future. You know, Filipinos are "high pride" (very proud people), not like the Chinese who help one another, working as one, hand in hand. If people do like the Chinese maybe there is a chance to progress.'

CONCLUSION: IS THERE A 'FEMINISATION OF POVERTY' IN THE PHILIPPINES?

Evidence that women are poorer than men in the Philippines, or becoming poorer, at least in income terms, seems to be more limited than that for The

Gambia. This applies as much to statistical evidence as to professionals' views as to the opinions of people at the grassroots. This said, institutional and grassroots respondents highlighted that women are playing an ever-expanded role in household livelihoods and, as in The Gambia, are finding few ways to offload or even share their responsibilities for coping with poverty with men. This is endorsed by other research such as that of Varua (1999: 2) on Iloilo City in the Western Visayas:

> Poverty affects women directly because women are responsible for meeting the basic needs of the family on a daily basis. Cutbacks on (*sic*) social services mean that women have to provide the difference in care, expenditure or both. Women have to make trade-offs among different needs in the use of resources such as their labour time, land, cash income and other resources over which they have some control. But often, women's labour time becomes the only resource over which they have any control. This means that in order to cope with poverty, women have to extend their working day thus increasing their work burden.

In light of this, it is important to respond to the call that 'Women's capacity to renegotiate the distribution of unpaid work caring for family needs is crucial' (ILO, 2003b: 7).

One major difference between the Philippines and The Gambia, however, is that although Filipino men are reported as not taking poverty 'so seriously' as women, and spending on 'vices' (including other women), wives can generally expect to receive more spousal support. The lack of formal polygamy tends also to mean that whatever resources men do devote to their wives and children, these are generally bigger than in The Gambia where co-wives effectively have to support their own children.

In turn, while in The Gambia elderly women are reportedly the most protected from hardship by virtue of upward inter-generational resource transfers, in the Philippines, women in both their senior as well as middle years, seem to be bearing the brunt of sacrificing their time and effort for household needs. This is partly because rising needs for secondary and indeed tertiary education in a more elaborate job market raises the costs of children, requires more investment, and postpones the stage at which sons and daughters are able to start 'giving back'. As such, while young Filipinas do not escape from taking on domestic chores, or indeed from providing economic support when they do get employment, they also seem to have scope to pursue their studies for longer, and to delay marriage until a later stage.

More generally, although family ties are strong in the Philippines, and many households are extended in composition, there does not seem to be the diversity of claims on Filipino women (or men) from such large networks, nor is the idea of looking after kin quite so engrained, as evidenced perhaps in the stress placed by Filipinos at the grassroots about how greater wealth would enable them to fulfil their obligations to immediate family, or even desires for consumer goods, rather than play benefactor to relatives. In short, Filipino women (and men) seem to be able to exercise greater discretion in who they provide for and what they provide, which, as far as younger generations of women are concerned, may carry some prospect of greater autonomy, as well as a narrowing of gendered poverty gaps.

NOTES

1. Interestingly, tables on poverty incidence in the Philippines refer to 'families' rather than 'households', although the household is actually the unit of measurement, and not all households are exclusively composed of family members.
2. Some firms offer a 'go now, pay later' package whereby earnings are deducted (with interest) over varying lengths of time from migrants' earnings in destination countries. Such a package usually costs US$8000–10 000 and not only involves salary deductions for up to two years, but considerable upfront payments as well, often involving families selling their houses in order to fund a member's migration. An alternative is moving alone on a tourist visa and working illegally, although this usually involves 'show money' at the point of disembarkation. One masseuse I interviewed had managed to work in Sydney, Australia, for the length of her three-month tourist visa on a 'TNT' (or *tago ng tago*/illegal) basis. While she was there she had to be particularly careful not to reveal her tourist status to Filipinos she did not know and trust, since the Australian government offers a financial reward to those who inform on people working illegally.
3. *The Philippine* Star, 20 November 2004, p. 15: 'Digital divide' by Ana Marie Pamintuan.
4. Although Marcos launched the country's first major family planning programme in the 1970s with the aim of reducing births to two per couple (Chant and McIlwaine, 1995: 66–7), in 2000, only 40 per cent of total expenditure on family planning came from government, with the remainder coming from donors, NGOs and the private sector (Herrin et al., 2003: 3). As noted by the ADB (2004: 20), reluctance to adopt family planning and a slight decline in contraceptive use in recent years can in part be attributed to 'the vigorous stance of the Catholic Church against the use of "artificial contraceptives", and the negligible budget and political support for family planning and population management services'. Indeed, as of 2004 the government declared its intention not to provide any further support for family planning (NCRFW, 2004d: xxi).
5. The electronics industry alone employs more than 300 000 workers (Aganon, 2003: 140).
6. Average unemployment in the period 1997–2003 was 10.6 per cent and almost half the unemployed (44.8 per cent) are in the 15–24-year age group (ADB, 2004: viii).
7. There are estimated to be 240 000 streetchildren in the Philippines' 22 biggest cities, although most return home each night (Racelis, 2005).
8. Now that LGUs have more autonomy, they also have increased financial responsibility for programmes, as well as having to a play a lead role in promoting a favourable climate for investment (NEDA, 2001: 130; Sajor, 2003: 729).
9. This seems to be symptomatic of a more general concern noted by UNDP/UNFPA (2001: 3) about the 'weak link' between policy, legislation, planning and budgeting in the Philippines. For example, for 23 laws passed between 1991 and 2001, only 40 per cent of funding was forthcoming.
10. Website http://www.youandaids.org, accessed 13 August 2004.
11. National estimates of poverty on the basis of food menus produce a far higher rate of poverty than international dollar-a-day measures (see Table 5.5 and compare with Table 1.3).
12. Personal communication, Bernadette Balamban, NSCB, July 2004.

13. A 'household' is officially defined as an aggregate of persons generally, but not always, bound by kinship, who reside under the same roof and share in common the household food (Morada et al., 2001: 2).

14. A household head is defined in the Philippine census as the adult who is primarily responsible for the organisation and care of the household, and/or who is regarded as such by other household members. Although technically this person could be male or female, cultural bias tends to result in the reporting of men unless adult women are unpartnered (see Illo, 1989). In cases where households consist of two or more *unrelated* individuals, the household head is generally considered as the eldest male or person recognised as head by other members.

15. *The Philippine Star*, 29 November 2004, pp. 1 and 4: 'The face of hunger in RP is female', by Vina Datinguinoo.

16. Tomas Osmeña served two consecutive three-year terms as mayor between 1988 and 1995. Following two terms by his former ally, Ramon Garcia, Osmeña made a comeback in the period 2001–04, and was voted in again for the period 2004–07. Mayoral re-election is prohibited after three consecutive terms.

17. The Asian Development Bank (2002: 61) points up the irony in abortion being a condition of maternity leave in a predominantly Roman Catholic country in which abortion is illegal except on severe medical grounds. This said, since the passing of RA 8187 in 1996 all legally married fathers are entitled to seven days paternity leave to assist in child care for up to four legitimate children by their legal wives, and also to lend support in event of a miscarriage (ibid.; CWC, 2000: 51).

18. Personal communication, Ben Baruc, DSWD Region VII Field Office, Cebu, November 2004.

19. I am grateful to Tessie Fernandez, Executive Director, Lihok Pilipina, Cebu, for this term.

20. These views correspond closely with the findings of the FFS of 2003, where aside from the idea that children made marriages complete and stable, and were 'gifts' or 'blessings' from God, there was a strong notion that they helped assure the future security of the family (Pedro, 2003: 29). Indeed, as many as 29 per cent of FFS respondents also expressed the hope that their children would be able to work abroad (ibid.: 31).

6. Gender, generation and poverty in Costa Rica

INTRODUCTION

Costa Rica is the wealthiest of the case study countries, scores highly on human development, and is on track to achieve most MDGs by 2015 (CSG et al., 2004: 116–17).[1] However, while international estimates suggest the incidence of monetary poverty is under 5 per cent (Tables 1.2–1.4), national data indicate that poverty has affected one-fifth of the population since 1994 with no obvious sign of reduction (Barquero and Trejos, 2005; Monge and González, 2005). Moreover, unlike in The Gambia and the Philippines, official statistics point to women being more vulnerable to income poverty than men, both as individuals and as heads of household, with the share of poor and extremely poor households headed by women having risen since the early 1990s. In many respects this is puzzling given Costa Rica's high-ranking scores on the GDI and the GEM, and unprecedented targeting of social expenditure on women in the last decade.

These apparent paradoxes are explored in the context of a broad review of development and gender in the country, followed by the findings from my institutional and grassroots surveys. The grassroots interviews were conducted in a total of six urban localities in Guanacaste, one of Costa Rica's seven provinces, also known for planning purposes as the 'Chorotega Region' (see Figures 6.1–6.3).[2] The main reasons for selecting Guanacaste were threefold, the first being that it is one of the poorest parts of the country, with the lowest coverage of social services, and the highest consolidated deficit in housing (see IFAM, 2003; WVCR, 2004). Indeed, in 2004, when 21.7 per cent of households nationally were classified as poor, the incidence of poverty in Chorotega was 33.1 per cent compared with only 17.1 per cent in the Central Region (corresponding with the capital, San José – see Figure 6.2). Moreover, respective levels of extreme poverty were 10 per cent and 3.6 per cent (INEC, 2004b: cuadro 11). Along with other peripheral provinces such as Limón and Puntarenas, Guanacaste also scores low on the HDI (IDH/Indice de Desarrollo Humano Cantonal) calculated for Costa Rican cantons by the UNDP (see

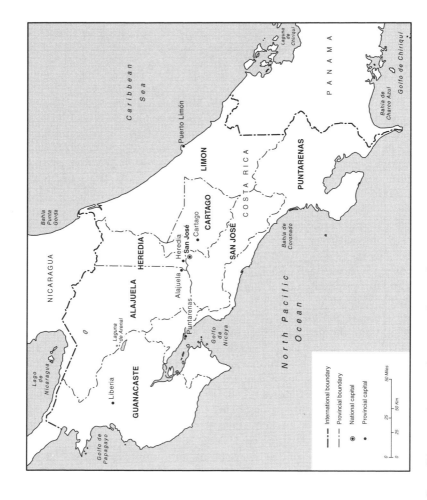

Figure 6.1   Costa Rica: provinces and provincial capitals

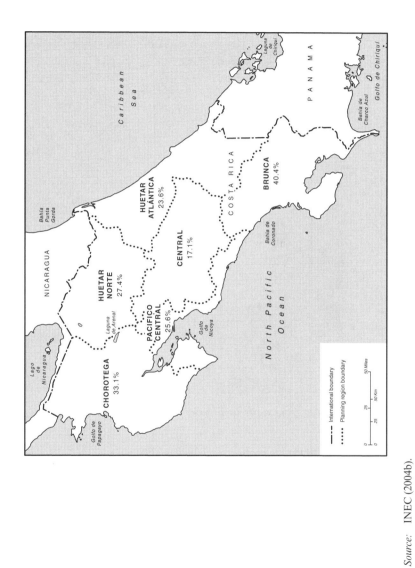

Source: INEC (2004b).

Figure 6.2 Costa Rica: planning regions and proportion of households in poverty, 2004

265

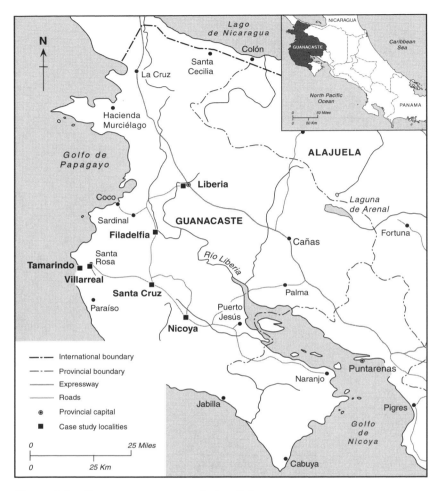

Figure 6.3   Guanacaste: case study localities

PNUD, Costa Rica, 2005). A second reason for choosing Guanacaste is that like Cebu in the Philippines, and the GBA in The Gambia, it is a growth area for international tourism, making for some correspondence in respect of labour markets. Third, the bulk of my research in Costa Rica since the late 1980s has been based in Guanacasteco towns, providing ready access to contacts.

DEVELOPMENT AND POVERTY IN COSTA RICA

Costa Rican Economy and Society in Brief

Costa Rica was first 'discovered' by Christopher Columbus in 1502 on his fourth and final voyage to the Americas. Colonisation got underway in 1522, although not in any dedicated manner until 1560. Even then the process was slow because, unlike other countries in the region such as Mexico and Peru, a dearth of precious metals, minerals and labour[3] made it relatively unattractive to Spanish settlers other than poor farmers and homesteaders. Geographically, however, Costa Rica had advantages that later turned the country into a major producer of export crops. Lying between 8 and 11 degrees north of the equator, and flanked by both the Pacific and Atlantic Oceans, Costa Rica's 51 000 km² territory is marked by a mountainous interior, rich volcanic soils, and substantial climatic diversity. While the country as a whole experiences a seven-month rainy season, from May to November, conditions range from tropical in the south to subtropical in the north, and a cooler more Mediterranean climate in the highland interior. The latter proved ideal for coffee-growing and, after Independence in 1821, the first head of state, Juan Mora Fernández, gave out free land and seeds in an attempt to encourage production (Gudmundson, 1986). This led to a 'coffee boom', which was followed at the end of the century by the establishment of bananas as a second major export crop.

While Costa Rica enjoyed unprecedented prosperity between the mid-nineteenth century and the late 1920s, decline associated with the Great Depression brewed into social upheaval and political conflict in the 1940s (see Barry, 1991; Daleng, 1998: 14). This culminated in a brief (40-day) Civil War in 1948, and, in 1949, a New Constitution which, *inter alia*, abolished the army and gave political rights to women and residents of Afro-Caribbean origin. It also laid the foundations of Costa Rica's distinctiveness as a social democratic regime with a strong welfarist orientation, earning it the title of a 'managerial' or 'benefactor state' (Brenes Camacho, 2005: 4). Supported by sturdy public intervention and expenditure (in part facilitated by the absence of military investment, and in part by the existence of 'quasi-Weberian civil service' marked by meritocratic recruitment and routinised decision-making and promotion – Sánchez-Ancochea, 2005), subsidised health care, low-cost housing, child welfare, minimum wage laws, nationalised banking, and free and compulsory education (including a university system), stood out as important hallmarks of Costa Rica's post-war 'modernisation' (see Lara, 1995: 4–5; Vargas, 2002: 1540). Distinguished by social indicators surpassing many richer countries in Latin America, Costa Rica is described by the World Bank (1997: i) as having 'an exceptional record of providing social benefits for all its citizens'. Assisted by an average GDP growth rate of 6.6 per cent per annum between 1950 and 1970, and major injections of US foreign aid (to prevent communism), sustained building of Costa Rica's welfare regime during the second half of the twentieth century was arguably a major reason why the country escaped the internecine political conflicts common among many of its Central American neighbours.[4]

From the late 1970s onwards, however, following the hike in world oil prices, a widening trade imbalance, budget deficits, hyperinflation, and balance of payments problems, Costa Rica's social democratic model came under threat (Brenes Camacho, 2005). The early 1980s saw the country's worst recession since 1930, with real GDP plummeting by 9.2 per cent, open unemployment doubling from 4.5 to 9.4 per cent, and purchasing power reducing by one-third (ibid.: 5). By 1985 the country had little choice but to succumb to its first phase of Structural Adjustment Lending (PAE/Programa de Ajuste Estructural). Consonant with neoliberal orthodoxy, the IMF and the World Bank put pressure on the government to reduce public expenditure and employment, to privatise public institutions, to liberalise trade, and to promote and diversify exports (see Green, 1995: 128–9; Ulate, 1992). One of the most significant outcomes was the switch from an economic model based on agricultural exports and Import Substitution Industrialisation (ISI), to one dominated by non-traditional exports and tourism (Brenes Camacho, 2005: 2; OECD, 2004: 9). The 'opening up' of the economy since this time has seen exports (now numbering 3000) come to contribute 50 per cent of GDP compared with 30 per cent in 1980 (Carstens, 2004; World Bank, 1997), with non-traditional exports rising from 53 per cent to 85 per cent of this total between 1990 and 1999 (MIDEPLAN, 2002: 12; OECD, 2004: 112). Given the granting to foreign companies of generous tax incentives and the same rights as domestic firms, FDI has also posted massive increases. In 1990, FDI flows into Costa Rica were US$168 million, but by 1999, stood at US$619.5 million, and in the period 1997–2001 financed as much as 82 per cent of the country's current account deficit (OECD, 2004: 68 and 72). Most FDI originates in the USA and is directed into manufacturing, followed by tourism and financial services. With the likely, if contested, accession of Costa Rica to the Central American Free Trade Agreement (CAFTA),[5] trends towards further economic diversification and foreign investment will undoubtedly continue.

Costa Rica is a democratic republic, with an Executive branch consisting of the president (and head of state) elected for a four-year term,[6] two vice presidents, and a 15-member Cabinet (one of whom is also vice president)

(USDS, 2004). The Legislative Assembly consists of 57 deputies, each of whom is elected for four years, with the Judicial branch comprising the Supreme Court of Justice, with 22 magistrates elected by the Legislative Assembly for eight-year renewable terms. As part of the Costa Rican state's extensive system of 'constitutional checks and balances', the offices of the Ombudsman, Comptroller General and Procurator General exercise an 'autonomous oversight' of the government (ibid.). There has also been in place a long-standing tradition of consultation and consensus-building on policy reform, which, although making decisions rather long drawn out, has contributed to social and political stability, and 'helped to maintain the credibility and accountability of public institutions' (World Bank, 2004c: i).

Since 1949, political power has tended to move fairly regularly between the countries' two main parties: the Social Christian Unity Party (Partido Unidad Social Cristiana/PUSC), which is slightly to the right of centre, and the National Liberation Party (Partido Liberación Nacional/PLN), which is slightly to the left. Although there are a further six political parties these have never held presidential office, although in both the most recent elections (of 2002 and 2006), the centrist Citizen's Action Party (Partido Acción Ciudadana/PAC) came close to winning. Moreover, Oscar Arias whose last period in office had been 1986–90 and who is heading-up a new PLN administration until 2010, beat the PAC candidate, Ottón Solís, by only a narrow margin in this latter year. While the PLN is less in favour of CAFTA than PUSC, it is far more so than PAC, and Arias has declared this to be one of his foremost priorities.

The Central American Free Trade Agreement may well boost the fortunes of one of Costa Rica's leading economic performers – the tourist industry – which has found a distinctive niche in the international 'ecotourist' market on account of its huge diversity of flora and fauna (especially birds), and the fact that one-quarter of national territory is dedicated to national forests. Growth has been especially marked since the mid to late 1980s, when special tax exemptions were granted as part of a campaign by the Costa Rican Tourism Institute (ICT/Instituto Costarricense de Turismo) to promote the country overseas, especially in the USA and Canada. While foreign tourists in 1987 totalled only 278 000, they had risen to 700 000 by 1995, and to 1.43 million by 2004, and in this latter year generated a total of US$1436.9 millions in revenue – more than double that of ten years earlier (Pacheco de la Espriella, 2005: 21; WTO, 2005). Foreign direct investment in the tourism sector quadrupled between 1990 and 2000, with a substantial amount of Spanish origin (OECD, 2004: 78). This has added to the situation whereby 65 per cent of hotels belong to foreigners, with one unfortunate outcome being the marginalisation of Costa Rican investors.

A similar international presence characterises industry, which since 1998 has generated an average of 23 per cent of GDP and in 2002 accounted for nearly three-quarters of total exports (OECD, 2004: 82 and 93). Consonant with the shift from ISI to EOI (Export-oriented Industrialisation), a major element in Costa Rica's post-1980s manufacturing boom has been establishment of '*zonas francas*' (Free Trade Zones/FTZs), which now number 17, and house about 300 firms, mainly assembly plants, which directly employ around 34 000 people. Owing to its stable and transparent government, geographical proximity to the USA, sound environmental record, and appeal to expatriate settlers, Costa Rica's highly educated workforce has played a major role in attracting leading transnational corporations such as Intel. The country's main manufactures are high-technology goods such as computer and electronic components, with microprocessor exports alone now accounting for around 15 per cent of Costa Rica's foreign earnings (EIU, 2004c: 10). Although medical equipment, processed foods, clothing and textiles also play their part in generating foreign exchange, given Costa Rica's comparatively high wage rates (at US$1.62 per hour in 2000), there is some concern about sustainability of the latter in the wake of cheaper competitors such as China (ibid.: 22). Moreover, the appeal of the FTZs to foreign companies more generally may well diminish given the WTO's ruling that tax and other benefits should cease by the end of 2007.

Even if agriculture has receded in importance relative to industry and tourism, the sector is still able to generate just over 10 per cent of GDP (CSG et al., 2004: 4). Indeed, after four years of decline, earnings from Costa Rica's biggest primary export, bananas,[7] went up by 16.9 per cent in 2003, and a similar trend was observable for coffee, notwithstanding that pineapple has now usurped its former rank as the country's second biggest agricultural export (EIU, 2004c: 20–21).[8] As a result of diversification (which has also included such products as ornamental plants, watermelons and tubers), Costa Rica's four traditional primary export products – coffee, bananas, sugar and beef – accounted for only 14.3 per cent of total exports in the nine-month period ending in September 2002 (OECD, 2004: 112–13).

Thanks to the volume of exports, real GDP growth has been relatively favourable since 2000 at an annual average of around 5 per cent (EIU, 2005c: 5). Compared with The Gambia and the Philippines, which are classed by the World Bank as 'severely' and 'moderately' indebted respectively, Costa Rica is described as 'less indebted', with a total external debt in 2004 of US$5.6 billion, equal to a per capita debt of US$1333, and a debt service ratio of 9.7 per cent (ibid.). Yet external debt rose from around 6.2 per cent of GDP in 1990 to 20 per cent in 2000 (World Bank, 2003d: 4), and total public debt is on the rise, currently representing 55 per cent of

GDP. Moreover, annual inflation in 2004 was running at an eight-year high of 13.1 per cent (PEN, 2005: 26), in large part driven by rising oil prices and weakening of the US dollar (EIU, 2005c: 10). Indeed, while CAFTA is heralded by the IMF as a positive move towards 'new trade opportunities' and 'further structural reforms' (Carstens, 2004), many believe that deeper integration into the global economy may expose Costa Rica to greater vulnerability (see MIDEPLAN, 2002; also note 5).

Whatever the case, continued investment in education is likely to be vital to the country's future, having proved critical in absorbing the labour force in the past (World Bank, 1997). A drive to introduce computing into general education dates as far back as the late 1980s (see Trejos, 1995), and computer literacy could well favour further ICT developments necessary to fulfil Costa Rica's aim of becoming a knowledge-based economy (Pacheco de la Espriella, 2005: 17). Another stated priority, relevant to this and to the tourism sector, is to foment greater proficiency in English (OECD, 2004).

Population and demographic dynamics
Costa Rica is frequently described as a 'multi-ethnic pluri-cultural society' (CEDAW, 2003: 15). Although nearly 95 per cent of its 4.2 million population are white/*mestizo*, around 3 per cent are Afro-Caribbean, 1 per cent Chinese and 1 per cent indigenous Amerindian. Moreover, a sizeable number of white/*mestizos* are of Nicaraguan descent with 2000 census data pointing to a total of around 300 000, or 6–8 per cent of the country's population (Sandoval-García, 2004a). Although there had long been cross-border migration from Nicaragua into Costa Rica for casual employment in cane-harvesting and cotton-picking, political conflict leading up to and during the Sandinista regime and the Contra War gave rise to an unprecedented exodus of refugees in the 1970s and 1980s. In the 1990s, further flows from Nicaragua were propelled by post-socialist structural adjustment measures, and displacements caused by Hurricane Mitch (see IOM, 2001; Mojica Mendieta, 2004). Although return migration, and irregular migration continue to be common, a migratory amnesty in 1999 gave rise to the total of documented Nicaraguans with permanent residence or regularised status growing to 250 000, with the gender balance being slightly feminine, and age skewed towards the young and/or economically active (IOM, 2001: 11–13). By the same token, further migration may well be curtailed by a new law approved by the Legislative Assembly in October 2005 which imposes fines on employers who recruit 'undocumented aliens'.[9]

The majority of Nicaraguan migrants who have settled in Costa Rica have done so in established 'enclaves' in the north of the country. Indeed, prejudice against Nicaraguans continues despite increasing integration in the shape of '*tico-nica*' households which are now estimated to constitute 5 per cent of all households nationally (IOM, 2001: 36; see also Sandoval-García, 2004a; 2004b), and that Nicaraguans feature prominently among the three-quarters of the population who declare themselves Roman Catholics. Nicaraguans also make up some of the 13.7 per cent who are Evangelical, 1.3 per cent Jehovah's Witnesses, and 0.7 per cent 'other Protestant'.

Despite a higher birth rate among the Nicaraguan as well as indigenous population, Costa Rica's TFR is now only 2.4 (see Table 1.2). This has con-tributed to a drop in population growth from an average of 2.3 per cent per annum between 1993 and 2003, to a current level of 1.5 per cent (WHO, 2005b). Declining fertility reflects *inter alia*, the low child mortality rate, which in 2004 was down to 9.25 per 1000 and is largely attributable to the fact that as many as 98 per cent of births are attended by skilled personnel – something which has also had positive impacts on reducing maternal mor-tality (currently only 25 per 100 000 live births – WHO, 2005a: annex table 8). Also responsible for falling fertility has been the rising use of contracep-tion, with recipients of social security entitled to free condoms, as well as sterilisation. Indeed, between 1964 and 1999, the proportion of women in marriages or consensual unions who had been sterilised (most in public health-care institutions) rose from 6.1 per cent to 21 per cent (Carranza, 2003).[10] Although the Catholic Church maintains a hostile stance towards artificial birth control, and abortion continues to be a criminal offence except in extreme circumstances, the main public health provider, the Costa Rican Social Insurance Institute (CCSS/Caja Costarricense de Seguro Social), has started to make concerted efforts to disseminate family planning advice, and there has been some opening up of debate on abortion, as well as emergency contraception.[11] As in many other countries, responsibility for family plan-ning tends to lie with women, which, as pointed out by a Costa Rican Commissioner for Women, is rather contradictory given that women rarely have more than one pregnancy a year, whereas one man can make several women pregnant in that time (CEDAW, 2003: 114; see also later).

Although the bulk of Costa Ricans (65 per cent) are in the 15–64 age group, 8 per cent are 60 or more, and 5.5 per cent are 65 years plus, with the elderly constituting the fastest-growing population segment (WHO, 2005a: 174). The 'ageing index' (persons of 60 or more per 100 children under 15) stood at 24.1 in 2000, which is one of the highest in Latin America (PAHO/MIAH, 2004: 2). This owes not just to declining fertility, but to exceptional gains in life expectancy – from a mean of 42 years in 1930 to 78 in 2000 (Brenes Camacho, 2005: 5).

While there are roughly equal numbers of women and men in the population, given that the former have a higher life expectancy (80 versus 75 years) (WHO, 2005a: annex table 1), the sex ratio is feminine in the 65 year plus age cohort, at only 90 men per 100 women (CELADE, 2002: 60). In common with other countries in Latin America and beyond, a greater proportion of Costa Rican women aged 60 or more are widowed (13.5 per cent) in comparison with men (3.5 per cent) (INEC, 2001: cuadro 9).

Unlike The Gambia and the Philippines, where there is a marked orientation to overseas migration, only 2 per cent of Costa Ricans (c. 90 000 people) are estimated to live overseas, mainly in the USA (IOM, 2001: 7), with the bulk originating in the province of Limón (see McIlwaine, 1993). Overall, however, Costa Rica is a net importer of population, with a positive annual migration balance of around 20 000 (Barquero and Trejos, 2005: 7). While Nicaraguans predominate, a substantial number are European or US citizens, the latter tending to have high incomes and to be retired or semi-retired.

Despite low levels of external migration, however, migration within Costa Rica is extremely common, both on a temporary and long-term basis. A survey I conducted with 350 households in two Guanacasteco towns in the late 1980s, for example, indicated that 80 per cent of adult women had a history of mobility, with most tending to settle on a long-term basis in urban areas, while their menfolk engaged in extensive temporary rural migration (Chant, 1991b). The latter has traditionally been dictated by the seasonality of labour requirements in cane-cutting, coffee-harvesting, and pasture clearance. Rural migration of a more long-term nature was also favoured at one time by the existence of an agricultural 'frontier' whereby peripheral lands were available for colonisation. However, declining availability, coupled with expansion of employment, education and services in towns and cities, has resulted in progressive urbanisation (see Camacho Zamora, 1985; Oduber Quirós, 1987). Between 1963 and 2003, the urban population of Costa Rica almost doubled from 31 per cent to 61 per cent, with over half the national population as a whole residing in the San José Metropolitan Area (SJMA), which comprises the city of San José itself and the capitals of its three neighbouring provinces, Alajuela, Cartago (the original capital of Costa Rica) and Heredia (see Figure 6.1). The only major urban settlements outside the SJMA are Puntarenas and Limón, with around 100 000 inhabitants apiece. Given few signs of diminution in urban primacy, Hall's (1985: 208) description of non-metropolitan Costa Rica as a country of 'predominantly small towns' still largely holds true today.

Education

Costa Rica was one of the first countries in the world to proclaim in its Constitution that education should be free and compulsory for all (Daleng, 1998: 41). This rhetoric has been backed up by significant state expenditure in education, at around 5 per cent of national income, which is 1 per cent higher than the level recommended by United Nations Educational, Scientific, and Cultural Organization (UNESCO) (Lara, 1995: 67). Expenditure has not only been directed to primary and secondary schools, with a basic nine years of education deemed 'compulsory', but also to further and higher education, with Costa Rica boasting four public universities (ibid.). At the other end of the spectrum, a programme called '*De la Mano*', launched in 2000, has tried to improve the targeting of existing Early Childhood Development (ECD) programmes, and in its first year succeeded in raising the number of poor children under 5 attended to in Comprehensive Child Attention Centres (CEN-CINAI/Centros Integrales de Atención Infantil), Community Homes (Hogares Comunitarios), Ministry of Education and other programmes from 27 600 to 44 600, representing nearly one-tenth of children in this age group (ibid.: 46).[12]

Even if the Philippines outranks Costa Rica by a small margin in some dimensions (see Table 4.4), Costa Rica's high levels of literacy and school enrolment continue increasing, with the GER in primary education in 2004 being 109.9 per cent, and in secondary education 84 per cent (Pacheco de la Espriella, 2005: 3–4).

Yet although Costa Rica has the best public education in Central America, the number of private schools has been increasing in recent decades. While in 1975 the ratio of public to private high schools was 7:1, in 2000 this had dropped to 3:1 (Palmer and Molina, 2004: 362), even if 88.2 per cent of secondary school students still attend state establishments (PEN, 2005: 17). At the tertiary level, Costa Rica's four public universities now compete with 50 private universities (some being specialist institutes in medicine, law and so on), and 46 private institutes of higher education offering diplomas, technical and non-university degrees (OECD, 2004: 102–3).

Despite the fact that enrolment in the state sector remains relatively buoyant, the average level of schooling in the country increased only from 6.4 years to 7.5 years between 1980 and 2000 (Brenes Camacho, 2005: 11), and in deprived areas in the north (including Chorotega), drop-out rates in the primary sector are as much as 4.2 per cent for girls and 5.2 per cent for boys, and at secondary level, 10.2 per cent and 13.2 per cent respectively (WVCR, 2004: 62). More generally, completion rates in primary education are only 62 per cent in the lowest income groups compared with 92 per cent in the highest income groups, added to which 10 per cent of all primary school students repeat at least one grade, and 16 per cent of those in secondary schools (World Bank, 2004c: annex C, 5). Only 15 per cent of the poorest children finish secondary education (around one-quarter of the rate for the wealthiest 25 per cent), which is deemed to be the minimum threshold for breaking inter-generational poverty cycles in Latin America

(World Bank, 2003d: 36; 2004c: annex C, 3; also Barquero and Trejos, 2005: 6n). Indeed, as of 2001 the average monthly salary of people with a university degree (US$800), was about four times greater than for those without education (World Bank, 2003d: 78n), indicating the polarising effects of educational divisions.

Shortage of household income is one reason for low educational achievements among the poor, despite the granting of several annual tuition scholarships (around US$30 per student), and subsidies for school transportation and lunches. Beyond this, the quality of education for people in deprived areas is hardly conducive to children's development. Class sizes are prone to be large (at 40 pupils or more), school rooms basic and overcrowded, and resources limited. While teachers are often posted to poor communities on graduation, they usually leave after their obligatory year of service. High turnover is compounded by absenteeism, with as many as one-third of teachers at any moment in time off work owing to the stress associated with heavy work burdens and low pay (Daleng, 1998: 42).

Unlike in The Gambia and the Philippines, where there seem to be more pressures upon children to earn income, official figures suggest that only 3.9 per cent of 10–14-year-old Costa Ricans were engaged in employment in 2001 (down from a level of 8.2 per cent in 1995), and that the proportion of 12–17-year-olds in work halved (from 21.5 per cent to 10.2 per cent) between 1988 and 2004 (EIU, 2006c: 21). Moreover, as many as three-quarters of working children attend school (ILO, 2005). This partly reflects the fact that even though 15 is set as the minimum age of employment, under-18s need a special permit. This said, school drop-out rates are almost seven times higher in households in which adolescents are working (Ministerio de Trabajo, 2002). Boys aged 10–14 tend to have higher rates of employment (5.8 per cent), than girls (2.1 per cent), although the latter's participation in unpaid reproductive work is usually far greater, especially in low-income households. Research in Santa Cruz, Guanacaste, for example, reveals not only that 8.2 per cent of school-age boys and 2.4 per cent of girls are engaged in income-generating activities, but that girls' education is particularly compromised by housework, with one-third of teachers in the canton reporting that all girls help out in the homes as against 43 per cent of boys (WVCR, 2004: 64). Following the creation in 1998 of a National Council for Infancy and Childhood (Consejo Nacional de la Infancia y la Niñez), there have been renewed efforts to reduce child labour within and beyond the home, especially in the worst-affected provinces such as Guanacaste (Pacheco de la Espriella, 2005). By the same token, even where children do not work, poverty is still reported as interfering with their education through compromising the purchase of essential items such as uniforms and learning materials (WVCR, 2004: 63).

Employment

Economic diversification in Costa Rica over the last few decades have seen massive shifts in employment. In 1950, 55 per cent of the population were engaged in agriculture and mining, but only 15.3 per cent by 2003 (CSG et al., 2004: 4). In contrast, services grew from occupying 30 per cent of the labour force in 1960 to 59.9 per cent in 2003 (ibid., see also Table 6.1). Growth in the tertiary sector has partly been driven by the expansion of tourism (see Table 6.1), which alone generated as much as 24.3 per cent of domestic employment in 2002 (OECD, 2004: 94). As for employment in industry, this has remained stable in terms of numbers – at around 200 000 since 1990 (PEN, 2005: 22), occupying 28.7 per cent of the labour force in 2003 (CSG et al., 2004: 4).

While economic diversification has generally been accompanied by an employment growth (OECD, 2004), unemployment has been rising since the turn of the century, from 5.2 per cent in 2000, to 6.7 per cent in 2004 (ILO, 2005). This is partly because jobs at the lower end of the labour market have been filled by Nicaraguan migrants (IOM, 2001: 18 and 27).

Table 6.1   Employment in Costa Rica

Branch of employment	% of workforce
Agriculture, fishery and forestry	14.8
Mining and quarrying	0.1
Manufacturing	13.9
Electricity, gas and water	1.3
Construction	6.9
Transport, storage and communications	5.5
Wholesale and retail commerce, vehicle repair, and personal services	19.4
Hotels and restaurants	5.8
Finance and real estate	8.3
Public administration and social security	4.5
Education	5.7
Health and social work	2.9
Other community, social and personal services	4.3
Private households with employed persons	4.9
Miscellaneous	1.9
All	100.0

Note: Percentages provided by INEC do not add up exactly to 100.

Source: Instituto Nacional de Estadísticas y Censos (2003a), cited in http://www.inamu.go.cr/indicadores/TrabEmpleo.html, accessed 19 April 2005.

However, that the highest levels of open unemployment (17.2 per cent) are in the 16–20 age group (PEN, 2005: 21), has also been attributed to the fact that the social and employment expectations of Costa Ricans have risen in recent years against a decline in the quality of opportunities on offer. For example, the 'new economy' based on tourism, services and export-manufacturing is held responsible for a proliferation of informal occupations such as street vending, parking attendance and pirate taxi-driving, and an 'informalisation of the formal sector, which includes the lowering of labour standards in EPZs, and a general decline in unionisation (from 21.4 per cent of waged and salaried workers in 1995 to 14.6 per cent in 2002 – ILO, 2005). According to the ILO Subregional Office for Central America (ILO, 2005), which classifies the informally employed as comprising non-professional and non-technical own-account workers, unpaid family workers, domestic workers, and employers and employees in firms with fewer than five people, a total of 42 per cent of the Costa Rican labour force is engaged in the informal sector (but only 36.8 per cent in urban areas).

Informal workers make an average of US$200 a month, which is about four-fifths of the basic legal minimum wage (Gindling and Terrell, 2004: 14). While in general terms the Costa Rican state has also endeavoured to maintain protection for workers (see Itzigsohn, 2000), and social security now covers 77.7 per cent of the labour force (ILO, 2005), in 2004 real wages (adjusted for inflation) among employed Costa Ricans fell for the third year in a row (PEN, 2005).

Health and Other Social Services

Compared with The Gambia and the Philippines, basic service coverage in Costa Rica is good, with 93 per cent of the population having access to safe sanitation, and 85 per cent access to an improved water source (UNDP, 2004: table 7). Since 1987, assistance for housing has also been provided through a Family Housing Voucher (BFV/Bono Familiar de Vivienda) administered via a specialised Housing Subsidies Fund of the National Housing Bank (BANHVI/Banco Hipotecaria de la Vivienda). Vouchers aid vulnerable groups such as the poor, the elderly and disabled, and female household heads to purchase land or housing, and/or to improve construction, and undoubtedly helped to expand the asset base of Costa Ricans during the 1990s (World Bank, 2003d: 14 and 152). Although the numbers of people living in precarious settlements grew by 6.2 per cent between 2002 and 2004 (PEN, 2005: 14), by 2010, it is intended that no more than 1.8 per cent of dwellings nationally will be built of makeshift materials, and no more than 10.7 per cent of the population will have insecure tenure or depend on others (CSG et al., 2004: 109).

Over and above this basic infrastructure, investments in healthcare undoubtedly play a part in the fact that life expectancy in Costa Rica is not only higher than in the other two case study countries, but also in relation to the rest of Latin America (see ECLAC, 2004a: 19). Expenditure on health care in 2001 stood at 20.1 per cent of all public spending, and 8.7 per cent of GDP (WHO, 2000: annex table 8). In 2002 the latter rose to 9.3 per cent, amounting to a per capita spend of US$383 (WHO, 2005a; 2005b). Costa Rica currently has 29 hospitals, boasts over 100 doctors and 150 nurses per 100 000 population, and there is virtually universal immunisation against measles, mumps, rubella, diphtheria, tetanus and polio (PAHO, 2002).

Costa Rica's health system is described by Londoño and Frenk (2000: 30–31) as a variant of a 'unified public model', whereby despite the availability of private options, public health care is virtually universal. Since 1990, when health sector reforms stripped down the role of the Ministry of Health to that of a regulatory and policy-making body only, the bulk of public health-care financing and services in Costa Rica have been provided by the CCSS (World Bank, 2003d: 39). The latter was set up in 1943 as an autonomous agency of the state, and traditionally required employees to pay 8 per cent of their salary, and employers a further 10 per cent. As from 1971, when health care was extended by law to the entire population, the scheme has included the voluntarily insured, and nominally the coverage of non-earning as well as earning family members (Daleng, 1998: 40).

Although the traditional centralisation of major public healthcare facilities in urban areas has disadvantaged rural residents (OPD et al., 1999: 71), the WHO's call for PHC in the late 1970s led to the establishment of Basic Teams for Integral Health Care (EBAIS/Equipos Básicos de Atención Integral en Salud, now numbering 871) in 90 'health zones' across the country (Pacheco de la Espriella, 2005: 6; World Bank, 2003d: 39). Each team comprises a small number of doctors, nurses and technicians, and is responsible for a catchment of *c.* 45000 individuals, offering first-level health care and referrals to higher-order services. In the interests of drawing on local expertise and increasing accountability, each team is supported by a local community-based committee. Yet although there appear to have been demonstrable effects in reducing infant mortality, many health centres are only open one or two days a week, and access is often difficult and costly especially during the rainy season (WVCR, 2004). As noted for the health system more generally, people are prone to suffer long waiting lists, poor service, limited access to essential drugs, and inability to pay for 'extras' (World Bank, 2004c: annex C, 6).

An additional challenge for the health sector is Costa Rica's mixed epidemiological profile (World Bank, 2003d: 38). Reflecting the generally advanced state of human development, life expectancy and health care, the major causes of mortality among the population are non-infectious conditions such as cancer and cardiovascular disease (PAHO, 2002). While demographic ageing coupled with the cost and complexity of treatment, is a cause for concern (PEN, 2005: 15), at the other end of the spectrum, the health system has also had to cope with the reappearance of infectious diseases such as dengue, which affected nearly 30 000 people in 2005, and requires other types of measure, such as early warning systems and basic public health measures. At least, however, the incidence of HIV/AIDS is on the low side with an adult prevalence rate of only 0.6 per cent, which partly reflects the early introduction of prevention campaigns. Moreover, as of 2001, women were only 12 per cent of all HIV cases confirmed since 1983 (CEDAW, 2003: 117).

Partly as a result of universal health care, and partly due to the targeting of special assistance to vulnerable groups, the elderly and disabled tend to fare better economically in Costa Rica compared with The Gambia and the Philippines. In 1999, for example, a Comprehensive Act for the Older Adult (Law no. 7935) created the Consejo Nacional para el Adulto Mayor (CONAPAM/National Commission for the Older Adult) and established rights of persons aged 65-plus years to health, education, housing, work, social security and recreation. Between 2002 and 2004, a total of 9396 new pensions were granted to older adults in extreme poverty under the CCSS non-contributory pension scheme (Bertranou et al., 2004: 11; also Nitsch and Schwarzer, 1996).[13] In the same period, several new pensions were granted for incapacity, and a total of 16 348 families with one or more members suffering from disability were given attention by the Instituto Mixto de Ayuda Social's (IMAS's) programme of basic services for disabled people (Pacheco de la Espriella, 2005: 3). This followed up the provisions of the 1998 Equal Opportunities for Disabled Persons Act (Law no. 7600) which obliged public and private institutions to guarantee rights and responsibilities in relation to physical space, transport, housing, access to information and communication, culture, sport, leisure, health, education and work.

Poverty Levels and Trends

Costa Rica has traditionally relied on a poverty-line approach whereby 'poor households' are those whose per capita income falls short of that deemed necessary to meet basic survival needs such as housing, education, clothing and transport, and 'extremely poor' households being those unable to afford a basic food basket (see Barquero and Trejos, 2005: 2; Brenes Camacho, 2005: 6; INAMU, 2005: 4). Data on poverty are mainly collected through the National Household Survey (ENH/Encuesta Nacional de Hogares) and the Multi-Purpose Household Survey (EHPM/Encuesta de Hogares de Propósitos Múltiples), which are conducted by the Costa Rican Institute of Statistics and Censuses (INEC/Instituto Nacional de Estadísticas y Censos). The first ENH was carried out in 1966, and since 1987, when the first EHPM was launched, basic social, economic and demographic data have been gathered for a 1 per cent sample of the population on an annual basis (see Brenes Camacho, 2005: 6).

Although differences in the calculation of the 'basic basket' of goods and services over time undermines the veracity of longitudinal comparisons (see Brenes Camacho, 2005: 6–7), there is little doubt that considerable achievements in poverty reduction have been made over the last few decades. In 1961, for example, 51 per cent of Costa Rican households were living in poverty. Despite some fluctuations, this declined to 40 per cent by 1984, and to 18.5 per cent by 2003. Although as of 2005 poverty had crept up to 21.2 per cent (see Figure 6.4 and Table 6.2), the level of around one-fifth of households (equating to just under one-quarter of the population – Barquero and Trejos, 2005: 6n), is considerably less than the average poverty rate for Latin America (44 per cent) (ECLAC, 2004b: 18). Moreover, extreme poverty in Costa Rica halved from 11.7 per cent in 1991 to 5.6 per cent in 2004, which is again much lower than the regional mean (20 per cent) (World Bank, 2004c: 10). Compared with the other case study countries the level of inequality as measured by the Gini coefficient is also low, standing at 0.488 in 2002 and rendering Costa Rica the second most equitable country in Latin America (ECLAC, 2004a: 12), even if inequality has risen since the early 1990s (Montero and Barahona, 2003: 13).

Despite the fact that Costa Rica's success in reducing extreme poverty puts it in the position of achieving MDG 1 (CSG et al., 2004; see also note 1), concern has been expressed at the lack of decline in poverty in general from 1994 onwards. Notwithstanding the observation that individual households can move in and out of poverty quite frequently (see Castro, 2004: 11; also Slon Montero and Zúñiga Rojas, 2005),[14] reasons offered for stasis in Costa Rica include the fact that economic growth has not improved real wages across the board, that continued immigration has tended to increase competition for unskilled jobs, and that a dip in secondary school completion rates during the crisis of the 1980s has depressed human capital achievements (Barquero and Trejos, 2005). Another proposition is that the growth of the over-60s, who have enjoyed relatively less in the way of state social investments than younger generations, form a caucus of 'hard core' poor who have been poor throughout their lifetimes and not just as a result of old age (Brenes Camacho, 2005: 17; see also below).

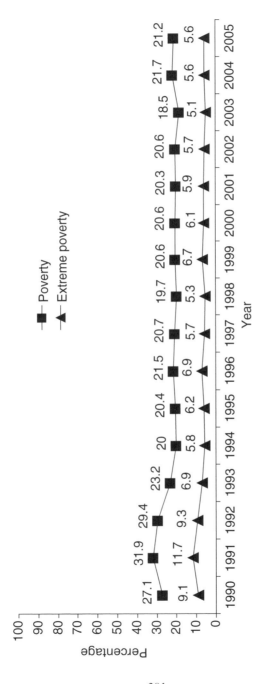

Source: INEC (2005a: figure 1).

Figure 6.4 Costa Rica: percentage of households in poverty and extreme poverty, 1990–2005

Table 6.2   Total, urban and rural poverty in Costa Rica, 1987–2004

	Households in poverty (%)						
	1987	1990	1994	1997	2000	2002	2004
Total	29.0	27.0	20.0	20.7	20.6	20.6	21.7
Urban	22.9	23.6	15.5	16.3	17.1	17.3	18.9
Rural	34.4	32.8	25.9	24.1	25.4	25.4	26.0

Note: Data pertain only to households with known or declared incomes.

Sources: INEC (2004b: cuadro 1); MIDEPLAN (2005).

Leading on from this, it is no surprise that, as in The Gambia and the Philippines, freedom from poverty is unevenly distributed. The incidence of poverty is greater in rural than in urban areas (see Table 6.2), even if growing urbanisation of the population means that in 2004, for the first time the majority (52 per cent) of poor households were urban (PEN, 2005: 11). Ethnicity and migrant status constitute another set of factors, with Afro-Caribbean and Nicaraguan households disproportionately represented among the poorest 5 per cent (World Bank, 2004c: 11).

People in the 60-plus age group have a greater incidence of poverty (18.2 per cent) than those aged 10–59 (17.2 per cent) (CELADE, 2002: 66), especially in rural areas where the probability of poverty among those aged 60 or over is almost 50 per cent greater than for 10–59-year-olds. This may help to explain why the mean age of heads of poor households (as of 2002) was 48.2 years, compared with 45.3 among the non-poor (Monge and González, 2005: ch. 4). Even though the Costa Rican elderly are better off than many of their counterparts elsewhere in Latin America, only half the 65-plus age group have pensions (World Bank, 2004c: annex C, 4), and social security coverage of those aged 60 or more in poor households is 50 per cent less than in non-poor households (Monge and González, 2005: ch. 4).

Although pensions have helped to temper old-age poverty to some degree (Bertranou et al., 2004), another factor qualifying a disproportionate concentration of poverty in old age is that larger households, which tend to be younger, and generally comprise dependent children, are also at greater risk of poverty (Barquero and Trejos, 2005: 6; Montero and Barahona, 2003: 12) – poor households having an average size of 4.5 and 1.4 children under 12 years (compared with 3.8 and 0.8 respectively among the non-poor). Indeed, in 2003, the average number of children younger than 12 years of age in poor households was 75 per cent greater than in non-poor households (Monge and González, 2005: ch. 4).

Another group at particular risk of poverty are women, with CEDAW's (2003: 103) assertion that 'the disproportionate representation of women among the poor is steadily increasing – the feminisation of poverty is a process, not simply a state of affairs that exists at a particular historical juncture' seeming to borne out by official data. Male and female head-counts in poor and non-poor households in 2002, for example, show that while there are only 97–98 women per 100 men in non-poor house-holds, there are 108 among the poor (see Figure 6.5). There are also indications that older women are more deprived relative to men and to their younger counterparts (see Table 6.3), which, given that they have grown as a proportion of female household heads in recent years, may go part-way to explaining why the latter feature disproportionately among the poor.

A general link between female household headship and poverty is sug-gested by the fact that since the 1970s their representation among house-holds in poverty and extreme poverty has steadily increased (see Figure 6.6).[15] Indeed, in absolute terms the number of poor female-headed house-holds nearly doubled between 1997 and 2005 (from 37 584 to 73 941), whereas the growth in poor male-headed households was only by about half that amount (from 101 102 to 146 780).

However, one very interesting factor is that despite the progressive increase in the share of female-headed households among the poor, the probability of poverty among female-headed households actually declined from around one in three in the late 1980s and early 1990s, to one in five in the mid-1990s, possibly as an effect of the general decline in poverty between 1991 and 1994 (see Figure 6.4). Moreover, even if there was an upturn in the likelihood of female-headed households being poor from 1997 onwards, differentials in the probability of poverty according to household headship have remained about the same since this time – at around one in four among female heads, and one in five among male heads. This points to the growing share of women-headed households in poverty in Costa Rica being mainly a function of a near tripling in numbers of female-headed households between 1990 and 2005 (more than doubling between 1997 and 2005 alone – from 138 823 to 280 776), whereas between 1990 and 2005, male-headed households only grew by a factor of 1.4 (from 519 914 to 759 137).

Extreme poverty figures from the EHPM arguably reveal a more worry-ing trend. Although, overall, extreme poverty dropped from 9.1 per cent to 6.1 per cent of all Costa Rican households during the 1990s, and to 5.6 per cent by 2005, the proportion of female-headed households in this category rose from 25.7 per cent in 1990, to 31.4 per cent in 1997, and to 43.5 per cent by 2005 (see Slon Montero and Zúñiga Rojas, 2005: cuadro 2; also

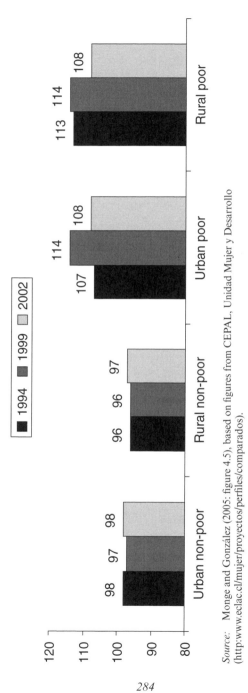

Source: Monge and González (2005: figure 4.5), based on figures from CEPAL, Unidad Mujer y Desarrollo (http:www.eclac.cl/mujer/proyectos/perfiles/comparados).

Figure 6.5 Costa Rica: index of femininity in households by year, urban/rural residence and condition of poverty, 1994–2002

Table 6.3   Gender, age and poverty in Costa Rica

	Total	Age groups (years)				
		0–6	7–12	13–19	20–59	60+
Urban						
Males in poverty (%)	16.8	25.9	26.3	19.6	11.3	15.2
Females in poverty (%)	19.2	26.8	25.2	21.5	15.1	20.4
Rural						
Males in poverty (%)	20.8	29.7	29.5	16.8	15.3	24.3
Females in poverty (%)	23.8	29.3	31.5	22.3	19.2	29.0

Source: CEPAL (2002: table 6a).

Figure 6.6). While the probability of being extremely poor among female-headed households has hovered around the same level, at around 1 in 11 since 1994, among male-headed households the likelihood has diminished: from 1 in 19.9 in 1994, to 1 in 20 in 1997, to 1 in 23 in 2005. While the increase in the relative share of female-headed households among the extremely poor is again probably largely attributable to the growth in numbers of female-headed households overall, it is clear that gender gaps in poverty have remained stubborn.

How this has occurred in the wake of unprecedented state assistance in the last decade is difficult to fathom, except that there have been slightly higher concentrations of female heads at extreme ends of the age spectrum during this time. According to the census of 2000, for example, 10.4 per cent of all female heads were in the 14–29-year age group compared with 9.3 per cent in early 1990s, and over the same period the proportion of those aged 70-plus grew from 14.9 per cent to 17.8 per cent. While the proportion of male heads aged 14–29 has also grown – from 15.7 per cent to 16.7 per cent – those in the 70-plus age group have declined from 7.5 per cent to 7 per cent.

On one hand, the growth of lone motherhood among younger groups of the population has been seen as a major concern in policy circles, with Olsen de Figueres (2002: 2) declaring that:

The increase in births reported by minor mothers in 2000 greatly limits the present and future possibilities of both the young single mother and the female child who will grow up in the midst of serious needs. Single parent homes headed by women are the most poor and precarious. With the increase of poverty and misery, the feminisation of poverty is self-evident and growing. The percentage of poor households headed by women has increased in recent years and presents a profound and damaging structural obstacle to women.

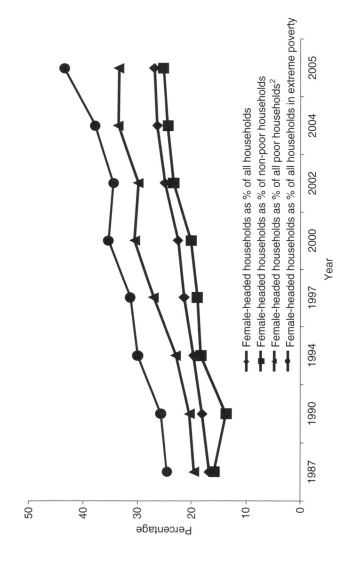

Notes:
1. Data relating to poverty categorisation relate only to those households with known or declared income.
2. Percentages for poor households include those in extreme poverty.

Sources: http://www.mideplan.go.cr/sides/social/09-02.htm; INEC (2005b: cuadro C03).

Figure 6.6   Female-headed households as a proportion of all households, and according to poverty status, 1987–2005[1]

As for the growing proportion of older female heads, lower pension coverage, coupled with the fact that only 7 per cent of women aged 65 or over are economically active, compared with 33 per cent of men, could be important reasons accounting for greater poverty among female-headed households as a whole. These factors are also flagged up by Monge and González's (2005) detailed study which further identifies that female-headed households are at greater risk on account of lower earnings, lower levels of education, and more dependence on income from others.

Indeed, while the labour force participation rate of poor female household heads increased overall – from 31.2 per cent to 33.6 per cent – between 1990 and 2000, this was not to the same extent as among non-poor female household heads (from 48.2 per cent to 55.8 per cent). In turn, when considering the greater likelihood of female heads being in informal employment (see Cunningham, 2000), and that in 2000 nearly one-quarter (24.8 per cent) of working female heads earned in the bottom two deciles (more than double that of male heads – 11.4 per cent), and that only 18.7 per cent of female heads earned in the top two deciles (as against 24.8 per cent of male heads),[16] it is no surprise that poor female household heads generate on average only half the income of their male counterparts (Monge and González, 2005). Although heads are by no means the only workers in households, and the proportion of other household members working actually rose in poor female-headed households – from 26.7 per cent to 38.4 per cent between 1990 and 2000, as against a decline from 59.9 per cent to 54.4 per cent in those headed by men – not all households benefit from the labour supply of others, with another conceivable reason for rising poverty incidence among female-headed households being that the proportion of one-woman units of the total of grew from 11.3 per cent to 14.3 per cent between 1990 and 2000, and lone-parent households from 44.5 per cent to 49.9 per cent, meaning that fewer female-headed households contained other household members (for example, children or other relatives) who could bolster well-being (Monge and González, 2005). Interestingly perhaps, the civil status of female heads seems to bear little relationship to poverty, with only marginal differences in the proportions of female heads between poor and non-poor categories in urban areas (see Table 6.4).

Poverty Reduction Initiatives

Yet despite evidence for gender gaps in poverty, with its long history of redistributionism and high social expenditure, it is perhaps no surprise that Costa Rica is noted as having had 'remarkable success in reducing poverty and improving the social welfare of its population' (World Bank, 1997: i).

Table 6.4   *Costa Rica: civil status of women and men in urban households according to poverty status, 2002*

Civil status	Poor (%)		Non-poor (%)	
	Women	Men	Women	Men
In couple	11.4	90.6	13.4	90.7
Single	20.7	3.8	22.9	4.0
Separated or divorced	42.9	3.1	41.0	3.8
Widowed	25.0	2.5	22.6	1.6

Source: Monge and González (2005: cuadro 4.2), elaborated from data from CEPAL, Unidad Mujer y Desarrollo, http://www.eclac.cl/mujer/proyectos/perfiles/comparados.

During the 1990s public spending grew by 70 per cent in real terms, and the share spent on the social sectors rose from 59 per cent to 63 per cent – the most rapid growth being in education and pensions (World Bank, 2003d: 3). On average, between 1.5 per cent and 1.8 per cent of GDP (*c.* US$250 millions) is expended annually to protect vulnerable groups (World Bank, 2004c: 13), although in real per capita terms, social spending was actually 20 per cent less in 2004 than in 1980 (PEN, 2005: 15).

The most dedicated attempts to reduce poverty started in the 1970s, with 1971 seeing the creation of the Social Welfare Institute (IMAS/Instituto Mixto de Ayuda Social), and 1974, the Social Development and Family Assignation Fund (FODESAF/Fondo de Desarrollo Social y Asignaciones Familiares) (Castro, 2004; Trejos, 1995). These entities worked on initiatives for vulnerable groups relating to food and nutrition, health, education, training, housing, and income-generation, which, along with universal social programmes, have helped to provide a buffer against destitution. Generally speaking universal social programmes have been funded out of direct and indirect taxes, whereas targeted programmes have mainly been financed from FODESAF moneys which are mandated by law (Montero and Barahona, 2003: 16–17). This said, the tendency for the state to retain universal programmes under its 'broadly based welfare concept' has attracted criticisms about leakage to the non-poor (see World Bank, 2004c).

Partly in response to such criticisms, a shift towards a more targeted approach began in 1995 with the launch of the National Plan to Combat Poverty (PNCP/Plan Nacional de Combate a la Pobreza) by President José María Figueres (1994–98). The PNCP was designed to foment greater coordination of the social sector, the involvement of a broader range of actors in poverty reduction (including autonomous agencies as well as different ministries), the closer linking of social policies with economic policy, and the integration of poverty reduction within the National Development Plan (see Castro, 2004; Montero and Barahona, 2003: 20). Its five targeted areas were: '*Proinfancia y Juventud*' (Pro Childhood and Youth), '*Promujeres*' (Pro Women), '*Protrabajo*' (Pro Work), '*Solidaridad*' (Solidarity), and '*Desarrollo Local*' (Local Development) (see Chant, 2002a). The National Solidarity Plan (PNS/Plan Nacional de la Solidaridad) introduced during the administration of President Miguel Angel Rodríguez (1998–2002), and 'New Life Plan' (PVN/Plan Vida Nueva), launched by Pacheco (2002–06) followed similar lines, combining social assistance components with those of social development and poverty alleviation, including some degree of geographical and group targeting, in which women have featured prominently – at least in rhetoric (see Castro, 2004: 34). Yet given the failure of the last two programmes to achieve their desired poverty reduction targets, Arias has expressed the intention to make poverty alleviation a key focus of his administration through the re-prioritisation of universal social programmes (EIU, 2006c: 14–15).

While the state has been the biggest player in poverty reduction initiatives, especially since the late 1990s when donor funding began to wane in the wake of Costa Rica's mounting prosperity (CEDAW, 2003: 127), it has often been assisted in its efforts by international agencies and NGOs, as in the case of health and education programmes for Nicaraguan migrants (see Mojica Mendieta, 2004).[17] Non-governmental organisations have also played an important role in initiatives for low-income women. For example, the NGO CREDIMUJER has provided credit to numerous female micro-entrepreneurs, complementing an initiative to orient credit to women by the National Bank of Costa Rica (BNCR/Banco Nacional de Costa Rica) (CIDA, 2002: 41). Non-governmental organisations of a religious nature, such as the Pastoral Social in Guanacaste, also try to help the 'poorest of the poor', especially women and youth, to start small businesses via educational and vocational training in subjects such as English, dressmaking and computing.[18]

GENDER IN COSTA RICA

As of 2002, Costa Rica was one of three developing countries (the others being Argentina and South Africa) with the highest levels of gender equality and 'women's empowerment' according to the selected indicators for MDG 3 (UNIFEM, 2002: 13; see also Box 1.3). Costa Rica has also long surpassed the Philippines and The Gambia in terms of its GDI score and rank (see Tables 3.2 and 4.7). In respect of its GEM components, Costa

Rica has made especially good progress in more than doubling the seats in parliament occupied by women between 1994 and 2004, as well achieving similar strides in women's representation as legislators, senior officials and managers (Table 3.6). Moreover, on the WEF measure of women's empowerment (see Chapter 2), Costa Rica ranked eighteenth (and highest of all 28 countries in the South), occupying an especially elevated position (ninth) in political participation, if only forty-ninth in economic participation. This mirrors a more general situation in Latin America whereby women have negotiated major advances in terms of political rights and citizenship, but lag behind in respect of economic, social and cultural rights (Arriagada, 2002: 158).

Women in Costa Rica have technically been entitled to the same rights as men since the New Constitution of 1949. However, it was not until the ratification of CEDAW in 1986, and the creation of the country's first 'national machinery' for women, the Centro Nacional para el Desarrollo de la Mujer y de la Familia (CMF/National Centre for the Development of Women and the Family), that efforts to advance gender equality really got under way. One major step was the enactment of the far-reaching Law Promoting Social Equality of Women (Law no. 7142) of 1990, which aimed not only to promote, but to guarantee, women's equality with men (see Chant, 1997a: 136–7). Specific provisions of the law included compulsory joint registration of property in marriage (or in consensual unions, registration in the woman's name), prohibition of dismissal from jobs on grounds of pregnancy, greater powers to evict perpetrators of domestic violence, increased funding for daycare centres, and more opportunity for women to decide on the custody of children (see Badilla and Blanco, 1996; IJSA, 1990; Vincenzi, 1991). The Social Equality Law paved the way for more than 20 new legislative initiatives in the 1990s with important implications both for women's personal rights and entitlements within and beyond the household (see Pérez Echeverría, 2005). For example, reform of the Electoral Code (Act No. 7635) in 1996 set quotas for women's participation in parties and in candidate lists for popularly elected posts at a minimum of 40 per cent (see Table 6.5). Although there is some debate about the value of quotas (see Chant with Craske, 2003: ch. 2; Jones, 2004; WEDO, 2005: 182), this undoubtedly contributed to the proportion of elected women councillors rising from 12.4 per cent to 45.8 per cent between 1990 and 2002. Women have also occupied at least one of the two vice-presidential positions since the start of the Rodríguez presidency in 1998. In that same year, Act 7801 upgraded CMF to INAMU (Instituto Nacional de las Mujeres/National Institute for Women) (Table 6.5). This gave INAMU its own legal status and an enhanced budget, as well as raising its political ranking by appointing as director a Minister for

Table 6.5   Costa Rica: key reforms to general and specific laws relating to gender approved by the Legislative Assembly, 1995–2005

Act no	Title of legislation	Year of approval
7476	Act on Sexual Harressment in the Workplace and Educational Establishments	1995
7491	Reforms to Article 95 of the Labour Code (followed by 7621 (1996) (establishing right to paid leave for maternity and child adoption)	1995
7499	Approval of the Inter-American Convention on the Prevention, Sanctioning and Eradication of Violence Against Women	1995
7532	Regulation of *De Facto* Unions	1996
7586	Act on Domestic Violence	1996
7600	Comprehensive Act on Persons with Disability	1996
7653	Reforms to Electoral Code (to ensure 40% female participation)	1996
7735	Services for Teenage Mothers	1997
7739	Code on Childhood and Adolescence	1998
7769	Act on Services for Women Living in Poverty	1998
7794	Municipal Code (creation of permanent commission on the situation of women in municipalities)	1998
7801	Act creating the National Institute of Women	1998
7817	Act creating the *Amor Jóven* and *Construyendo Oportunidades* programme	1998
7880	Reform of article 33 of the Political Constitution replacing the term 'man' with 'person'	1999
7899	Act on Sexual Exploitation of Minors	1999
7935	Comprehensive Act on the Older Adult	1999
7940	Authorisation for IMAS to grant total and partial forgiveness of mortgage loans on social housing	1999
7954	Creation of the Women's Gallery (to celebrate achievements of outstanding women)	1999
7950	Reform of the National Housing Finance System Act	2000
8017	Comprehensive Childcare Centres	2000
8089	Optional Protocol to the UN Convention on the Elimination of All Forms of Discrimination Against Women	2001

Table 6.5   (continued)

Act no	Title of legislation	Year of approval
8101	Responsible Paternity Law	2001
8107	Reform of the Labour Code (incorporation of principle of non-discrimination in the workplace)	2001
8128	Creation of the Domestic Violence Court in the Second Judicial Circuit of San José	2001
8129	Creation of Domestic Violence Courts in the Circuit of Heredia, in the First Judicial Circuit of Alajuela and the Initial Circuit of Cartago, and a Criminal Court in the Canton of La Unión, Cartago Province	2001
8184	Act on Services for Women Living in Poverty (creation of a trust fund)	2001
8261	Act on Young Persons	2002
8312	General Act on Protection of Teenage Mothers (reforms)	2002

Sources: CEDAW (2003: table 1); CR (2004: 2–4 and 44–5);
http://www.inamu.go.cr/derechos/.

Women's Affairs, which, in accordance with the goals of the National Policy on Gender Equality and Equity, nominally helps to mainstream gender (CEDAW, 2003: 41; see also Box 6.1). In 2001, Costa Rica also became one of the first signatories to the Optional Protocol to CEDAW (CR, 2004).

While the above led the fourth periodic report submitted to CEDAW to identify Costa Rica's significant progress for women in respect of education, employment, health care, political participation and legal resources (CEDAW, 2003: 9), it was also noted that 'deep structural problems remain, which maintain and intensify gender gaps in a variety of areas', and that 'profound social, economic, political and cultural changes are needed if the country is to consolidate and build upon the progress achieved thus far' (ibid.).

Marriage, Family and Sexuality

The so-called 'traditional' nuclear-family unit – comprising a male bread-winner, female housewife, bound by marriage and their biological children – has arguably not been as long-lived nor as numerically dominant in Costa

BOX 6.1   COSTA RICA: MAIN GOALS OF THE
NATIONAL INSTITUTE OF WOMEN
(INAMU) – NATIONAL POLICY ON
GENDER EQUALITY AND EQUITY

• Formulation and promotion of national policy on gender equality and equity
• Protection of women's rights
• Promotion of gender equality
• Coordination to ensure that public institutions establish and excecute national policy on gender equality and equity
• Promotion of full social, political, cultural and economic participation by women
• Promotion of public policies for equity (this area coordinates programmes for gender-equity mainstreaming in the state apparatus)
• Active citizenship, leadership and local management
• Women's legal status and rights protection
• Construction of identities and life projects (this area aims to influence processes of socialisation, identity construction and life projects in childhood and adolesence)
• Stimulation and promotion of a state policy to eradicate gender violence, including domestic violence, sexual harassment, sexual exploitation and forced prostitution, and sexual violence outside the family
• Specialised information area, consisting of the Offices of Communication, Documentation, Research and Information Technology

Source: CEDAW (2003: 41–2).

Rica as it possibly has been in other parts of the world.[19] In Guanacaste, for example, '*uniones libres*' (consensual unions) have historically prevailed in a context of temporary male out-migration associated with serial monogamy among women, and tendencies among men to form two (or more) households simultaneously, leading, *inter alia*, to a high incidence of 'blended' households comprising step- and half-siblings (see Chant, 1991b; 2000). In recent decades, however, as elsewhere in Latin America, there has been a general trend towards a decline in nuclear households (Arriagada, 2002; ECLAC, 2004a: 35; Lavinas and Nicoll, 2006). A decline of 6 percentage points since 1987 leading to just under 50 per cent of households conforming to a nuclear model (Barquero and Trejos, 2005: 28, fig IV.1), has led to the observation that 'The traditional nuclear family is no longer the standard' (CIDA, 2002: 2; Monge and González, 2005). In turn, Costa Rica has experienced an increase in people living alone (from 5 per cent to 7 per cent of households between 1987 and 2002), a rise in extended or complex households, which now constitute around 20 per cent of the total and sometimes comprise non-kin, and mounting numbers of one-parent units nearly all of which are headed by women (Fauné, 1997: 92; Pereira García, 1998: 187; Monge and González, 2005: ch. 4). Along with the decline in birth rates (see earlier), these tendencies have contributed to a shrinkage of mean household size from 4.4 in 1990 to 3.8 in 2004.

The decline in male-headed nuclear households is partly driven by increasing conjugal instability: while only 1 in 11 marriages ended in divorce in 1984, by 2001 the proportion was four in ten (Palmer and Molina, 2004: 361). Another factor is falling rates of marriage, the number of marriages per 100 persons being only 5.5 in 2004, compared with 7.4 in 1990, and 8 in 1984. This seems largely accounted for by a lower incidence (or at least postponement) of marriage among young people, since although as many as 73.7 per cent of the population in conjugal unions in 2000 were formally married, the level was only 57 per cent among under-30s as against 79 per cent among those aged 30 or over (INEC, 2001: cuadro 11). As part and parcel of these trends, official figures also indicate that the proportion of births outside marriage in Costa Rica doubled between 1960 and 1999 (from 23 per cent in 1960, to 51.5 per cent) (Budowski and Rosero Bixby, 2003; INAMU, 2001: 8), rising further, to 59 per cent, in 2004. Despite mounting awareness of and access to contraception, and the fact that the average age of first birth for women has risen from 21 to 23 years between 1990 and 2004, teenage pregnancy remains common, especially among lower-income women and predominantly outside formal marriage or consensual unions. Indeed, while rates of adolescent fertility (the number of births per 1000 women aged 15–19) declined from 106 per 1000 in in the first half of the 1970s, to 81 in 2000–2005, Costa Rica's current level remains higher than the pan-Latin American average of 72 (Monge and González, 2005: gráfico 4.24). Moreover, the proportion of girls aged 17 or under who had given birth slightly increased during the inter-censal period 1984–2000, from 11 per cent to 12 per cent with the probability of motherhood at this age being four times higher among the poorest third of the population than the wealthiest (Rodríguez Vignoli, 2004). In 2000, as many as 33 per cent of mothers in the 15–19 age group were lone parents, compared with an average of 28 per cent among the population as a whole (INEC, 2001: cuadro 16), and two-thirds of births from 'unknown' or 'unreported fathers' ('*padres desconocidos*') occurred to women under 19 years of age (INAMU, 2001: 8). Currently births to teenage mothers in conditions of social risk number 14 500 per annum (CR, 2004: 18).

In many ways familial alternatives to the patriarchal nuclear model have been better supported in Costa Rica than in many other countries (see Chant, 2002b). For example, aside from the fact that Costa Rican women have long had much readier access (in principle) to divorce and legal separation than their counterparts in The Gambia and the Philippines (see Chant, 1997a: 137), the material and social viability of 'non-standard' households has been bolstered in various ways by the 1990s' amendments to the Family Code such as recognition of children born outside marriage and the legal validity of consensual unions (see CMF, 1996: 22; CAL, 1997; IMAS, 1998; also Table 6.5). Subsidised childcare (see note 12), has also been of assistance.

Other significant developments in respect of family flexibility (and protection) have included the passing of a Law Against Domestic Violence, the Law for the Protection of Adolescent Mothers, the Law for Women in Conditions of Poverty, and the Law for Responsible Paternity (IMAS, 1998; INAMU, 2001; see also Table 6.5 and later). Yet, notwithstanding these developments, there is still far from being widespread endorsement of family plurality. For example, many government (and academic) publications continue to use the term '*familia completa*' (complete family) to denote units comprising two parents and their children, whereas one-parent households are consigned to the category of '*familia incompleta*' (incomplete family) (see Sagot, 1999: 101). There is also common reference to '*desintegración familiar*' (family breakdown) with one of the principal evocations being the absence or irresponsibility of one or both parents, normally fathers, as encapsulated in the term: '*paternidad irresponsable*' (irresponsible fatherhood), which tends to reinforce the idea that 'family' is synonymous with the 'in-tact' male-headed unit and is the standard from which other arrangements deviate (Chant, 2002b).

In turn, there is a discernible tendency to draw links between the decline of 'the family' and other social ills, such as 'prostitution, alcoholism, drug addiction and violence' (Loaíciga Guillén, 1994: 10 [my translation]), with the NGO World Vision regarding the Costa Rican family as a 'weak, defenceless structure', and children as 'victims of a society that lacks a solid basis of moral and spiritual values' (WVCR, 2004: 5). The claim that there is 'strong censure of unmarried mothers in general, and young single mothers in particular' (Muñoz, 1997: 44; see also CEDAW, 2003: 59), is also no surprise given a culture of sexual double standards which tends to accept, if not exalt, men's womanising, but disapproves of overt or extra-marital sexual activity among women (see Goldenburg, 1994: 204–5; Krauskopf, 1998: 103; Sandoval-García, 1997: 180–82).

Hostility towards non-marriage and illegitimacy is strikingly apparent in religious quarters, with the Catholic establishment having been the most outspoken constituency in the country about rises in lone motherhood and births unacknowledged by fathers, deploring these as the outcome of 'sinful behaviour', and as highly threatening to the moral and social order (Budowksi, 2003; also Schifter and Madrigal, 1996: 62). Additional concerns about prostitution and the mounting visibility of homosexuality have provoked numerous Church appeals for adults to set good examples to the young by eschewing the evils of libertinism and modern consumerism, and conserving 'family traditions', as promulgated through its *Movimiento Familiar Cristiano* (Christian Family Movement).[20]

In turn, despite Costa Rica's long-standing reputation for 'democratic values', and the fact that a bill proposing same-sex unions is currently under discussion by the Legislative Assembly, research conducted under the auspices of the Central American Programme for Sustainability, discovered that Costa Ricans were much less tolerant of 'minority' groups than their neighbours in the region, ranking homosexuals top of the list of 'most disliked groups', Nicaraguans second, and atheists third (Chant, with Craske, 2003: 154; see also Lumsden, 1996: 165; Thayer, 1997).

Gender Dimensions of Education

In light of the above, it is no surprise that the Catholic Church has attempted to resist efforts to introduce sexuality 'centred on persons and not restricted to reproduction' into the school curriculum (CEDAW, 2003: 63), although it has been slightly easier to eliminate sexism in educational materials, prinicipally through the Hacia el Siglo XXI (Towards the Twenty-First Century) series of textbooks.

In turn, and as in the Philippines, Costa Rica presents a situation in which women are now performing as well as, if not better than, men, with higher average levels of schooling and greater enrolment in university institutions (Table 4.8; also CEDAW, 2003: 19). This represents a far cry from the relatively recent past, since, according to the 2000 census, as many as 51.5 per cent of women aged 60 or over had received no education or had not finished primary school, compared with only 15.5 per cent of 40–49-year-old women, and a mere 8.2 per cent of women in the 20–24 age group (the corresponding figures for men were 47 per cent, 13 per cent and 10 per cent respectively) (INEC, 2001: cuadro 7).

Yet women's rising education has not eliminated gender discrimination in the labour market (Pérez Echeverría, 2005). This is partly a function of gender segregation in subject choices, with more than three times as many women as men graduating from the University of Costa Rica in education in 2001, but a reverse ratio in engineering (CSG et al., 2004: 33). It is also important to note that low levels of education among poor women means that a substantial segment of the female population have little chance of accessing any kind of formal employment. In 2003, for example, nearly two-thirds (62 per cent) of poor women had only attained a maximum of primary school completion (six years), and only 12 per cent had finished or gone beyond secondary education (12 or more years). The latter is deemed critical for women to substantially increase their employment and income prospects, given that while just over one-third of women with incomplete primary schooling were poor in 2003, the rate was one-quarter for those with complete primary schooling, and only about one-tenth for those with completed secondary schooling (Monge and González, 2005: 24, gráfico 4.10). While education and poverty generally show an inverse relationship, the particular importance of education in breaking the gender–poverty link is also indicated by the fact that while women's and men's labour force participation alike is lowest when they have incomplete primary schooling, gender gaps are much greater among those with one to six years' education than with post-primary schooling (ibid.: gráfico 4.11). Disappointingly, however, recent attempts on the part of the Costa Rican state to increase their access to education and training have had negligible effects, with the average years of schooling among poor women aged 15 or over rising only from 5.2 to 5.4 between 1994 and 2003 (Sauma, 2004, cited in Monge and González, 2005).

Gendered Dimension of Labour and Employment

Aside from the role of poor women's educational deficits in depressing their labour force involvement, another critical factor is an uneven burden of labour between women and men, with the former taking on considerably more unpaid work, especially in the home. The seeds of this start early in people's lives, with gender socialisation encouraging independence, freedom and detachment of domestic tasks among boys, but grooming girls to 'take on home responsibilities, to care for others – even above the satisfaction of their own life needs – to be submissive and dependent' (WVCR, 2004: 55). One study for example, revealed that regardless of socio-economic status, teenage girls put in nearly 20 times as many hours as their male peers in domestic tasks (Ramos, 2001). The Convention on the Elimination of Discrimination Against Women (2003: 20) further notes that the unpaid nature of women's domestic work and subsistence production invisibilises a major contribution to national development, which, according to INAMU, may amount to 17 per cent of GDP (by CSG et al.: 45).

As for paid work, and notwithstanding that this is often under-recorded given many women's involvement in part-time, informal and/or seasonal income-generating activities (see CEDAW, 2003: 12), between 1980 and 1995, official data document the share of the Costa Rican workforce made up by women as rising from 24.3 per cent to 30.5 per cent (Fauné, 1997: 58). Between 1980 and 2000, female labour force participation had risen by 143 per cent overall, and by 2002 38.5 per cent of women were in the labour force (as against 73.3 per cent of men) (CIDA, 2002: 3). Urban women are more likely to be employed than their rural counterparts, with the gross urban participation rate of women in 2003 being 35.2 per cent (as against 55.9 per cent of men), and the rural rate was only 22.4 per cent (as against 56.7 per cent men) (CSG et al., 2004: 35).

As in the other case study countries, mounting female employment has not only been been driven by education, but declining birth rates, and by neoliberal-driven pressures on households to expand and diversify their income sources. In the Costa Rican case, the decline in, and casualisation of, agricultural employment, which has traditionally been a male sector, has played a major role here. Women's main openings have been in the service sector, in which they comprise 50 per cent of workers, and which occupies as many as 84 per cent of the economically active female population (INEC, 2001: cuadro 13; see also Table 6.6). The expansion of light manufacturing in Free Trade Zones has also opened up industrial opportunities for women (see Sandoval-García, 1997).

Table 6.6   Costa Rica: gender distribution of employment

Branch of employment	% of male workforce	% of female workforce
Agriculture	26.8	4.9
Manufacturing and mining	15.4	16.7
Electricity, gas and water	1.3	0.3
Construction	9.6	0.2
Transport, storage and communications	7.5	1.7
Wholesale and retail commerce, trade	17.6	27.0
Financial institutions	5.1	4.7
Community and social services	15.6	42.4
Not specified	0.6	0.5
All	100.0	100.0

Note: Figures taken directly from source, but may not add up exactly to 100 due to rounding.

Source: CEDAW (2003: table 9).

*Table 6.7   Costa Rica: mean monthly earnings of men and women
according to branch of activity*[1]

Branch of employment	Mean male earnings (colones, 2004)[2]	Mean female earnings (colones, 2004)	Female earnings as proportion of mean male earnings (%)
Agriculture and stock-raising	98 143	77 280	78.7
Fishing	110 639	90 600	81.9
Mining and quarrying	198 140	144 255	72.8
Manufacturing	184 438	119 462	64.8
Electricity, gas and water	240 379	309 127	128.6
Construction	150 499	149 799	99.5
Commerce	167 805	115 202	68.7
Hotels and restaurants	161 035	103 246	64.1
Transport, storage and communications	190 873	215 079	112.7
Financial services	365 982	250 626	68.5
Business and real estate	209 867	184 914	88.1
Public administration	259 645	250 945	96.7
Teaching	265 865	224 486	84.4
Health and social welfare	305 255	239 106	78.3
Community and personal services	181 174	113 049	62.2
Domestic service	72 859	51 982	71.6
Extra-territorial organisations	358 812	322 433	89.9
Unclearly specified activities	318 362	130 000	40.8
Total	173 921	142 358	81.8

Notes:
1. Excludes non-remunerated workers.
2. Exchange rate July 2004: US$1 = 430 colones.

Source: INEC (2004a: cuadro 18).

Yet despite the fact that slightly more of the female labour force is in man-ufacturing than men, the latter seem to have access to a broader range of sectors and at higher levels. Beyond women's concentration in tertiary activi-ties, for example, they have a greater tendency to be employed on a part-time basis (15.5 per cent of the female workforce versus 6.5 per cent of males), and to be informally employed (46.4 per cent versus 39.6 per cent). On top of this, women are also more likely to be unemployed than men (8.2 per cent versus 5.8 per cent respectively) (ILO, 2005). Even if increases in male unemployment in both the 15–25-year and 45–70-year age cohorts have been noted as problematic (Arias, 2000: 26, table 1), as many as 18 per cent of women aged 15–24 years are unemployed versus 12.9 per cent of men (ILO, 2005).

It is also important to note that women who have entered the labour force in the last decade have done so in the context of deteriorating conditions (CEDAW, 2003: 22; CIDA, 2002: 3). While women now account for almost half the employees in specialised professional, technical and managerial posts, and there has been some narrowing in wage gaps (see Table 3.6), 28.3 per cent of women workers in 2001 earned less than the minimum wage compared with 20.4 per cent of their male counterparts (ILO, 2005; also Table 6.7).

In order to address gender inequalities in the labour market, the Ministry of Labour and Social Security with assistance from INAMU and international funders, has started training women to become labour rights promoters, launched a media campaign on women's labour rights, and set-up an '*800-Trabajo*' phone line which affords women the opportunity of reporting on violations of their labour rights (CEDAW, 2003: 45). Indeed, although women are entitled to four months' maternity leave with 50 per cent paid by the employer and 50 per cent by social security, and men are given 15 days paternity leave, including for adopted children (CIDA, 2002: 5; ECLAC, 2004b: 96), measures to strengthen the rights of pregnant workers would seem particularly crucial in view of the volume of complaints from mothers-to-be who seem to be at particular risk of losing their jobs, especially when employed on temporary contracts (CEDAW, 2003: 100). Interventions are, arguably, also necessary to foment greater acceptance among men of women's employment (see Chant, 2000).

Policy Responses to Gender Inequality

Despite the financial contraints faced by INAMU and its predecessor (CEDAW, 2003: 9 and 28),[21] we have already seen evidence of a wide range of initiatives introduced to advance the situation of women. One of particular relevance to poverty was a programme for lone mothers/female household heads, coordinated by IMAS and introduced in 1995 under the auspices of the '*Promujeres*' (Pro-women) branch of the PNCP (see earlier). Going under the title of the 'Comprehensive Training Programme for Female Household Heads in Conditions of Poverty' (Programa de Formación Integral para Mujeres Jefas de Hogar en Condiciones de Pobreza), this offered women a modest stipend ('*asignación familiar temporal*') for up to six months during which they were expected to take courses in personal development (including the building of self-esteem) and in employment-related training (Chant, 1997a: 151; Marenco et al., 1998: 52). Although there were problems with the training component and with general coordination, a total of 25 000 women benefited from human training between 1995 and 1998 (Marenco et al., 1998). Following the 1998 Act on Services for Women Living in Poverty (Table 6.5) it became a state obligation to assist women in poverty. This led to the Comprehensive Training Programme being revised and re-launched under the name of *Creciendo Juntas* (Growing Together), the nomenclature reportedly spawned by the fact that women at the grassroots felt that 'women in conditions of poverty' was too degrading.

The basic format of the original programme, emphasising a combination of personal development and vocational and technical skills was retained, but *Creciendo Juntas* became a major inter-agency venture and was extended to all women in poverty, albeit with priority to female household heads (see below), as well as being broadened to include completion of basic education, and housing benefits (see IMAS, 2001; Jiménez, 2002). The stipend was set at 30 per cent or more of the minimum wage of a general worker, and in January 2002, another article was added to Law no. 7769 to provide for micro-enterprise initiatives as part of the objective of promoting greater labour force insertion (Jiménez, 2002). Selection for the programme was made through data from the Information System of Target Information (SIPO/*Sistema de Información de la Población Objetivo*)[22] and although only reaching an estimated 17 per cent of all female household heads classified as poor between 1999 and 2001, female heads were around half the overall total of 15 290 beneficiaries covered during this period, which exceeded the target of 25 per cent (Jiménez, 2002). The cumulative total of women who benefited in the period 1998–2002 was 19 106 (INAMU, 2005: 12), and in the period 2002–04, 13 640. An estimated 43–50 per cent of the latter were female heads, and in those same years nearly 24 000 female heads in poverty and extreme poverty also received housing subsidies (CR, 2004: 7).

Two other programmes complementing the above, and motivated largely by alarm at persistently high rates of teenage motherhood, were introduced in 1999: *Amor Jóven* (Young Love), and *Construyendo Oportunidades* (Building Opportunities). *Amor Jóven*'s main objectives are to encourage healthier and more responsible attitudes among young people towards sexuality, thereby preventing early motherhood. *Construyendo Oportunidades* seeks to (re)integrate teenage mothers into education, and to equip them with personal and vocational skills to enhance their own lives and those of their children (see Chant, 2002a; IMAS, 2001; PDR, 2001). The annual target is in the region of 2400 teenage mothers.[23]

Despite the provisos mentioned earlier, some progress also seems to have been made in respect of reducing domestic and sexual violence, which is viewed as a major corollary of poverty (see PNUD, Costa Rica, 2004). Traditionally women have been 60 per cent of homicide victims, mainly resulting from break-ups with abusive partners – totalling 25 women in 2000 alone, and ranking alongside perinatal complications and HIV/AIDS as the principal cause of female mortality around the 30-year age mark (CEDAW, 2003: 128–9). Under the National Plan for Attention and Prevention of Domestic Violence (PLANOVI/Plan Nacional para la Atencion y Prevención de la Violencia Intrafamiliar), a 911 help line has been established for women, along with provision for legal, social and psychological assistance in the Office of Women's Affairs, the setting up of specialised courts for domestic violence, care facilities in state hospitals and clinics, and government refuges in three different parts of the country (CEDAW, 2003: 47; also Table 6.5). The latter are complemented by a nationwide system of shelters and self-help groups set up by the NGO, CEFEMINA, under the auspices of the '*Mujer, no estás sola!*' (Woman, you are not alone!) programme, which started in 1988. Such initiatives seem to have put a brake on the phenomenon, with denunciations made by women in 2004 declining markedly from previous levels (Pacheco de la Espriella, 2005: 23).

Costa Rica's interventions in respect of gender and the family have also included the 'Law for Responsible Paternity' ('*Ley de Paternidad Responsable*') of 2001. Momentum for this radical legislation came, *inter alia*, from the rising number of children without 'named fathers' who were unable to use their fathers' surname or receive financial support. In order to uphold children's rights, and to alleviate the financial, social and emotional costs of lone motherhood, the law requires men who decline voluntarily registration on their offspring's birth certificates to undergo a compulsory DNA test at the CCSS. If the result is positive, they not only have to pay alimony and child support, but are liable to contribute to the costs of the pregnancy and birth, and to cover food expenses for at least one year (INAMU, 2001; Menjívar Ochoa, 2003). This initiative is heralded as a 'historic landmark in the struggle by women's organisations and the National Mechanism to eradicate offensive discrimination in the field of filiation and family responsibilities' (CEDAW, 2003: 181). Whether it will be sufficient to transform long-standing patterns of paternal neglect, however, is another issue since even where men live with children, they do not always commit much emotional or financial investment in family life (see Chant, 2003a). Indeed, as evidenced by previous research in Guanacaste, men often prioritise themselves as the main recipients of care, looking for partners who can fulfil the role of '*segunda madre*' (second mother), or '*madre-esposa*' (mother-wife) (see Chant, 2000: 209).

GENDER AND GENERATIONAL DIMENSIONS OF POVERTY IN COSTA RICA

The Views of Professionals

Despite stasis in poverty levels according to official figures since the late 1990s, the majority of persons interviewed in government agencies, NGOs and international organisations felt that poverty was on the increase, and that there was growing polarisation between rich and poor. As in the other countries, institutional personnel emphasised that poverty was more than a material phenomenon, encompassing insecurity, vulnerability, and lack of training, capacity, information and political power. One spokesperson for a religious NGO based in Santa Cruz also talked about poverty being about a lack of values and spirituality.[24]

In identifying causes of increasing poverty most interviewees stressed price liberalisation and, in particular, recent rises in the costs of food, fuel, transport and basic utilities. Another issue was employment shortages especially at the lower end of the labour market, and driven partly by migrant competition, Other reasons iterated included the ageing of the population, the running down of social programmes, and no effective policy for vocational training or for the retention of lower-income groups in education. These, in turn, were attributed to political corruption, financial mismanagement, and pressure to restructure the economy on the part of IFIs.

Despite the national plans to combat poverty launched during the last three administrations, these were not deemed to have had major impacts. Indeed, a number of people were not even aware of Pacheco's PVN, and the few who had heard of it described it as a piece of rhetoric without any substance. In turn, the post-1990 shift towards greater targeting of the poor in social policy met with mixed reactions. One respondent from the NGO, Procesos, felt that targeted programmes were necessary if only to bring the poor into universal programmes, and that various schemes such as housing subsidies had been particularly beneficial to low-income groups. Others, however, drew attention to adverse outcomes when targeting had come at the cost of universal programmes, and that the undermining of the latter had played a part in increasing poverty. As one IMAS spokesperson declared: 'Creating selective programmes to "plug a hole" is a mistake.' There were also complaints that the majority of government programmes were 'paternalist' and 'welfarist', and despite growing emphasis on '*corresponsibilidad*' (co-responsibility), this was mainly to get people on board in implementation, while design remained 'top-down'. As a respondent from the feminist NGO CEFEMINA pointed out, programmes to help women get out of poverty were often devised with no input at all from the women they were intended to serve.

Despite dedicated programmes for women and the nominal 'mainstreaming' of gender more generally, institutional commitment to gender equality goals was not felt to be as widespread in practice as in rhetoric. Many saw resistance to implementing programmes which departed from women's traditional social roles. Another problem identified was that with the increasing fashion for inter-agency collaboration which tended to undermine if not lead to the evaporation of gender mainstreaming on account of poor coordination.

These issues in turn, may well have played a part in the fact that virtually all respondents in the institutional survey deemed women to be poorer than men. Frequent reference was made to a 'feminisation of poverty', with the very definition of poverty used by CEFEMINA, being that of *'pobreza con cara de mujer'* and INAMU *'rostro de mujer'*, both of which mean 'poverty with a woman's face'. This, in turn, was linked with women's ongoing disadvantage in access to credit, property ownership, and employment, despite numerous (and some successful) initiatives aimed at eliminating discrimination against women, especially in relation to education, politics, and domestic violence. Women's lower rates of economic activity and lower wages were attributed in large measure to the intransigence of traditional gender roles, especially the normative ideal that men should be the principal breadwinners, and women the homemakers and unpaid care workers. As an interviewee in the NGO, Centro Pro-Derechos Humanos (CPDH) articulated: 'in the private sphere there has been no redefinition of roles within the family, and women continue carrying major responsibility for domestic activities, which gives them a double or triple day, as well as taking on communal work'. A consultant from UNICEF added that: 'In terms of daily life, the burden of poverty for women is greater because of their additional work in the home. We are a long way from the notion of co-responsibility.' This was highlighted by some not just as resulting from gender divisions of labour, but from polarities in power and privilege. As an interviewee from a religious NGO declared, poverty affects women more than men 'because women are still excluded in a society in which men rule'. A respondent from the UNDP emphasised that another problem for women in poverty was domestic abuse, often exacerbated by rising female labour force participation and the progressive introduction of women-friendly legislation which have made men feel threatened and marginalised.

When asked to specify which age groups were most at risk, the bulk of respondents specified senior citizens on account of their labour market disadvantage, but almost always added that senior women were worse afflicted on account of their lower pensions and retirement benefits. In turn, one

UNDP spokesperson claimed that women suffered more than men throughout the life course, albeit in different ways. For example, while young women are subject first and foremost to discrimination in employment, women in their middle years carry multiple labour burdens at the same time as lacking control over household assets (*bienes gananciales*), and older women, who may have assets, are often forced to relinquish these to other family members. Older women were also seen to experience age-based discrimination earlier than men, with one NGO respondent declaring that prejudice against women in the job market (often on grounds of their physical appearance), set in as early as 30 years.

Although age was an important criterion of differentiation among women, most felt that heading households made them more vulnerable still. This was attributed to the fact that poor female household heads are unable to generate as much income as their male counterparts, especially if they have low levels of education, and that absent fathers usually manage to evade paying maintenance. The spokesperson for the NGO, Pastoral Social, in Santa Cruz added that women have little choice to live up to survival challenges given men's retreat into alcohol and other forms of escapism. This view, as with many of the others summarised above, was shared by a substantial number of people at the grassroots.

Grassroots Perspectives on the Meanings, Manifestations and Corollaries of Poverty

One striking feature of the grassroots interviews in Costa Rica was that while around half the respondents felt that the majority of the population were poor, unlike in The Gambia and the Philippines, the remainder did not estimate the proportion of the national population living in poverty as that much higher than official statistics (that is, around one-quarter of the population). Moreover, although many respondents were in difficult circumstances – for example, they worked in menial and/or casual jobs, were unable to enjoy more than a basic diet, or could not afford independent accommodation, they tended to downplay their own poverty and stress that the plight of others was worse. Although some respondents, such as William José, an 11-year-old schoolboy from Liberia with a part-time job as a bottle-recycler complained that he had often experienced having to work on an empty stomach, being unable to buy food afflicts far fewer respondents than in The Gambia and the Philippines, which is possibly one reason why Costa Rican respondents do not regard their own poverty as particularly severe. For example, one female head, Yiselda (32), from Filadelfia said: 'Well, perhaps we don't consider ourselves poor because we're struggling through, and we can buy a bag of beans.'

Beyond the issue of not suffering extreme poverty, conceivable reasons for minimising poverty include, first, that most Costa Ricans have a strong sense of pride in their country and its social institutions, and admitting to privation (especially to a foreigner) could cast the country in a bad light. Second, most enjoy the basic security that comes from widespread coverage of basic services. Moreover, even if incomes do not necessarily stretch to buy all the goods desired, many people, especially with origins in rural areas, have assets such as land, which can potentially be liquidated to fend off destitution.

A further likely reason for unwillingness to admit to poverty is that this might signify that people themselves had been unable to muster the will or fortitude to cope with straitened circumstances, and in this way have 'failed' (see below). Some people, such as Sonia, a 44-year-old female household head from Santa Cruz, claimed not be be a materialist and valued other things. Although Sonia had had an immensely difficult life, recently compounded by a fall at work which had damaged both knees (see Box 6.2) she declared: 'I feel like a millionaire . . . because I have my health, despite my knees. I'm not poor. I am rich in health, I have my children, I can work, I can study.'

BOX 6.2   POVERTY, GENDER AND FAMILY FROM THE PERSPECTIVE OF SONIA

Sonia is 44 years old and lives with her three children, Javier (24), Carina (19) and Ernesto (16), in a low-income settlement in Santa Cruz. Each child has a different father, but only the youngest, Ernesto, has paternal contact. This is mainly because his father, from whom Sonia separated four years ago, lives on an adjacent plot along with two daughters from a previous union. Yet despite this proximity, and the fact that Sonia and Ernesto's father were together for a total of 15 years, the latter provides no regular maintenance, leaving Sonia, with the help of Javier, who works as a waiter in Santa Cruz, responsible for the entire upkeep of the household. At the time of interview Sonia was in receipt of sickness benefit (equating to full pay after tax of about US$40 a week) following an accident at the school where she has worked as a cleaner ('*miscelaneas*') for eight years. She had been on sick leave for two months, and this has represented one of the few occasions in her life where she has not worked round the clock outside as well as inside the home. Although she suffers with the pain in her ankle and knees as a result of her fall, she is hoping that she will be signed off for longer in order to give her more time for her house and family, and, in particular, for her studies, which in the last few years have turned her life around.

In order to help her get over the split with Ernesto's father, in 2001 Sonia took advantage of free adult education in Santa Cruz, and, along with her daughter, who has also returned to study, is just entering the fifth and final year of her high school diploma ('*bachillerato*'). Although this requires a commitment of three hours each evening, and she does not get home until after 9 p.m., Sonia has managed to secure high grades, and is hoping eventually to enrol part-time on a university degree course and to become a teacher. This is a far cry from the types of jobs which Sonia has done previously, and from a very early age.

Sonia was the eldest of seven children born to poor farming parents in one of Santa Cruz's rural cantons, Tempate. Straight after finishing primary school, 11-year-old Sonia was sent by her mother to work as a live-in servant in the capital, San José. Although Sonia felt '*decepcionada*' ('deceived') to have been sent so far away so young, she remitted virtually all her wages to support the family back home for most of the nine years she was in San José. Once she returned to Santa Cruz, by which time she had had her first child, she combined domestic service jobs with home-based activities such as raising hens, pigs, turkeys, which in part generated income and in part provided subsistence.

Sonia never had an opportunity not to work because although she had her first child at 20, and her second at 25, neither father wanted to know about the children, and still less, assume financial responsibility. While Sonia had wanted her first child, she did not intend to get pregnant a second time, and only did so because the man in question insisted he was sterile and that they had no need for contraception. Sonia never pursued maintenance through the courts, preferring instead to maintain her independence. However, a few years ago, at the behest of the daughter who was the product of this second union, she used the recently passed Law of Responsible Paternity to force him to have a DNA test and to give his surname to Carina. While Sonia managed to provide for her first two children through her own work, she conceded to moving in with the youngest child, Ernesto's, father, a bus driver, because she saw in this the possibility of getting her own house: '*un hogar para mis hijos*' (a home for my children). For the first three months they were happy, but thereafter the situation deteriorated, mainly on account of her spouse's drinking and violence which for several years made Sonia feel fearful of leaving him. As a preliminary step to departure Sonia purchased the plot next door in her own name. Once they had not had sexual relations for a year, Sonia felt it was easier to make the break and to divide their living arrangements. If she ever settles down with her current *novio* – a married man of 52 – she says she will need him to provide her with another home in order that she can leave her existing property to the children.

Despite all the difficulties Sonia has had, including Carina having a child at 16, whom she rejected and who is currently being looked after by the father and his parents, Sonia has a strong sense of self-esteem which has come from raising her children with little help from men. Declaring '*Yo puedo sola . . . soy la madre y el padre*' ('I can go it alone . . . I am the mother and the father'), she said she has proved herself to be capable without a man, and that she does not need to ask anyone for assistance. In turn, Sonia does not think that households headed by women are worse off. For Sonia, the idea that women are the '*sexo débil*' (weak sex) is a '*mentira*' (lie). 'A woman doesn't need a man. She has capacity.'

This said, a substantial number of respondents maintained that they were poor (if not the poorest), and in some cases declared that major life decisions had been influenced by poverty. For example, Victorio, a 55-year-old casual labourer from Villareal, and Geovany, a 39-year-old groundkeeper from Liberia, were among a number of men who declared they had never married because their meagre wages would not have been enough to support wives and children. Another person claiming to have been in this predicament was Arsenio (49), from Santa Cruz, who despite working as a sometime musician, was mostly engaged in casual farm work for which his earnings of US$25 a week (less than half the minimum wage) stretched only to cover food and cigarettes. Paulo, a middle-aged undocumented migrant from Nicaragua, claimed that poverty drove him from a country where he says 100 per cent of the population are poor (see Box 6.3), even if he still sees himself in the same state in Costa Rica 'because they don't give me a decent wage'.

Leading on from this, poverty was conceived mainly in material terms. As articulated by Mariela (15): 'Poverty is about not having anything . . . no food, no money to study or to dress oneself.' As echoed by Juan de Dios, a 78-year-old widower from Santa Cruz, poverty is 'not having money to buy things, going hungry. Or people who don't have a house and sleep wherever

BOX 6.3 POVERTY, GENDER AND FAMILY FROM THE PERSPECTIVE OF PAULO

Paulo is 47 years old and came to Costa Rica in 2003 from Nicaragua in the hope of finding employment. He lives with his elder brother, a musician, in rented quarters in Santa Rosa and each month sends 25 per cent of his salary back to his wife and family in his home town of Masaya.

For 20 years Paulo had been fortunate enough to have a stable (and relatively well-paid) job as a driver for a company in Masaya, but when the firm closed, and he was made redundant, he was forced into casual and poorly remunerated agricultural work which was scarcely enough to live on, and took him further from his dream of buying a plot of land for his large and growing family. The land he wants measures $60 \times 200m^2$, and to buy it he will need US$10 000. This land is extremely important to Paulo because he has never had anything to call his own, and no security. When he and his spouse first started living together when he was 15, and she 16, they were so poor that they had to live in a cardboard annex in Paulo's father's house. The situation has not improved much since, especially as all seven of their children (presently aged between 21 and 27) are living at home, and five of these are now in partnerships, each with three children of their own. Paulo often wishes he had not had so many children, but declares 'We "filled" ourselves with kids because there wasn't the means to prevent this'. In the time of Somoza, he had wanted to get sterilised, but was not allowed to do so, but once they had had seven children (by the Sandinista era), his wife got sterilised instead.

According to Paulo, the employment situation is dire in Nicaragua: no one invests, there are few factories, and the country's incipient tourist industry is nowhere near the scale of Costa Rica's. Added to this, Paulo has only had primary education, and has limited experience in anything other than van-driving and manual labour. Since his brother had lived in Costa Rica for several years, had been made a resident, and now had a '*cédula*' (identity card), Paulo decided to try his luck by coming to the country as an illegal immigrant. This was quite a costly process since he had to save up US$30 for his passport, and US$50 for 'show-money' at the border. It was also the first time he had ever been out of the country, which he admits to having made him very scared.

The first few months were extremely hard, but eventually Paulo's brother managed to secure him his present job as a security guard in a modest apartment complex in Tamarindo through personal contacts. Paulo works six nights a week, with a shift from 6 p.m. to 6 a.m., for which he earns 35 000 colones (*c.* US$72). He would like to send more than US$70 home a month, but this is impossible. Although he shares accommodation costs with his brother, the rent alone comes to nearly one-quarter of his salary, added to which bus fares cost US$6 a week, service charges around US$3, and food US$20 – he tries to eat twice a day (usually rice and beans), and to have meat two or three times a week. While he also tries to phone his wife at least every seven days, international calls are prohibitively expensive.

Paulo describes his present situation as difficult. First, he lives under constant threat of being deported. On a number of occasions he has been stopped by the police and asked to show his identity card, although to date has been lucky enough to have been let off. This may be less likely now that legislation passed in October 2005 aims to reduce the number of undocumented migrants in Costa Rica, and to fine their employers. Second, although Paulo is with his brother with whom he collaborates in everything such as cooking and the household chores, he misses the comforts of a 'normal' family life, and is sad not to have seen his wife, children and grandchildren for two years now: 'When you love people it's logical that you want to be with them.' Paulo also confessed to feeling worried that he might give way to temptation and fall in love with some one in Costa Rica – the '*nuevo*' (new) often being more enticing than the '*viejo*' (old), especially when one has not been with one's wife for a long time. He says he will try to stop this happening, but has seen many of his compatriots stay in Costa Rica and start a second home, abandoning their families in the process.

the night falls'. Poverty for Arsenio (49) was about having to 'put-up with not being able to afford the things that one wants', and, aside from poverty forcing him to 'have to think ahead to tomorrow all the time', for Paulo (Box 6.3) poverty was about skill deficits which confined one to menial, low-paid jobs.

Even if not everyone confessed to suffering material hardship, the majority of respondents did feel poverty was increasing. This was especially felt in the sphere of basic goods and services. Sonia (Box 6.2), for example, reported that the monthly electricity bill for her three-roomed house in an irregular settlement had recently risen from US$12 to US$19. She also pointed out that increases in the price of basic foodstuffs such as beans and rice meant that there was less money for protein. As such people were killing the hens they commonly breed for laying eggs, or hunting in the bush for animals such as armadillos.

Reasons identified for increasing poverty ranged from the structural to the personal, and often in combination. At the structural level, many pointed the finger at government corruption, the failure of the state to redistribute national wealth more effectively, and the intervening effects of natural disasters such as flooding, which, during the hurricane season in the autumn of 2005 when I was conducting the fieldwork, was particularly severe and caused widespread crop destruction in Guanacaste. In turn, it was strongly felt that the government should do more to arrest poverty – by bringing down the prices of food, petrol and so on or by permitting salaries to keep pace with inflation, by reducing taxes, creating more jobs, and providing more incentives to study. One or two people also mentioned that it might be good for the country to ratify CAFTA, since although there had been a lot of popular resistance to this, there was no way of knowing whether it might be of benefit unless tested.

Some of the older respondents also talked about how modernisation of the economy over the last few decades had eroded people's ability to make a living. Not only had the building of a highway between Belén and Tamarindo in the late 1960s robbed certain communities such as Santa Cruz of their commercial status in the province, but small businesses had often gone under with the opening up of supermarkets and chainstores. The expansion of international tourism was also seen to have made life difficult for locals since those unable to speak English were often excluded from 'decent jobs'. As for more menial occupations such as construction work, gardening and domestic service, the growth of the Nicaraguan population was also seen to have deprived many Costa Ricans of employment. As Geovany (39) declared bluntly: 'The Nicaraguans come and take work from people here.'

Yet while the blame for poverty was frequently attributed to others and/or to events beyond people's control, it was rare that respondents did not mention personal issues as well.

As in the Philippines, some respondents saw poverty as 'hereditary'. When parents had nothing to give or leave behind, then children would start life at a disadvantage. Growing up in a poor family meant little or no education, and work from a young age, which was particularly marked among older respondents. For example, Leandro (81), who had been born in Nicaragua, reported that he had never set foot inside a school and started looking for work as early as the age of 8. Juanita (67) had also had no education, partly because poverty had forced her family to foster her out at the age of 3 to people who treated her as little more than a slave. Although Calicsto (47), had managed to complete primary schooling, at 12 years old he had migrated from the north to the south of the country to work in the banana industry (see Box 6.4; also Box 6.2).

BOX 6.4   POVERTY, GENDER AND FAMILY FROM THE PERSPECTIVE OF CALICSTO

Calicsto is 47 years old and lives in a low-income neighbourhood in Santa Cruz in a single room on his mother's lot. He completed primary education at the age of 12 and immediately left for the *zona bananera* in the south of the country. A brother who worked there helped him get a job even though he was under age.

Since turning 29 Calicsto's main job has been as a musician in a dance ensemble which plays in hotels and bars. His earnings are rather erratic, however – ranging from 60 000 to 70 000 colones (US$124.22–144.92) in a good week in the high season, but dropping to around half this in the rainy summer months. For this reason Calicsto has always had to supplement the income from his musical career with a variety of jobs. These have mainly consisted of casual agricultural work, as well as growing crops for his own consumption such as maize and beans. When he was living with his spouse and children (for eight years before he was ousted on grounds of alleged violence), he had a *'mini-super'* (small supermarket) as well.

Although Calicsto spends less on food during the high season, he finds it difficult to save, mainly because during this time he has to use his earnings for clothes and and other necessities which he cannot afford to buy in the low season.

Calicsto attributes his own poverty to the fact that his parents were poor, and that because he had to start work at a young age he was unable to further his studies. Calicsto also feels that:

> Poverty can affect people's self-esteem. But even if a person is poor, this shouldn't lead to them undervaluing themselves. For me, if one can't get ahead, or feels one can't get ahead, you have to say I am worth something, and 'let's do it', if you want to work that is.

Calicsto does not feel that getting out of poverty is just about pulling oneself up by one's bootstraps however. He also thinks that recent governments have done very little to address poverty in Costa Rica, and have missed the fact that the country is rich in natural resources and agricultural potential. To solve the national poverty problem Calicsto thinks that more subsistence-oriented production is in order:

> I believe that we have to go back to how we were beforehand. I remember when I was a child, that each individual, each family who lived in the countryside, produced at least what they consumed. Viewing the situation from 25 years ago to the present, the rural folk, those who we called the 'people of the mountains', sold their farms to come and search for a better life in the centre (of the country), and it's a disaster, because it hasn't worked. Those who cannot produce have nothing. So the people will have to go back to a subsistence way of life.

Regardless of individuals' backgrounds and childhoods, however, many were of the opinion that poverty was compounded, if not brought on, by people's attitudes – as articulated by Arsenio (49) '*su manera de pensar*' (their way of thinking), or by Ixi (40) '*pobreza de mentalidad*' (mentality/ attitude poverty). People had become lazy and did not '*sabe luchar*' (know how to struggle). As Floribet (49) from Santa Cruz stressed: 'Most people are poor because the problem is that they don't struggle to get out of this condition.' This was echoed by Guillermo, a 32-year-old repairer of electrical applicances from Liberia: 'people also need to change, because there are many who don't want to work. There are wasters just looking for an easy life; they ask and expect everything to be given to them; they are irresponsible and this is not the government's fault.' Lack of personal effort and motivation, in turn, was often seen to be exacerbated by alcohol and drug-addiction.

Among middle and senior adults, poverty induced by lack of motivation, effort and capacity to struggle, was regarded as being particularly rife among male youth, with their female peers associated with another undesirable tendency – premature pregnancy. This was not necessarily the fault of young women themselves, however, who often aspired to marriage – especially with an older man – to provide them with a home and hope for the future. Yet as Deyanira (32) from Villareal, declared: 'Men deceive them and leave them, so that's where poverty comes from most in Costa Rica . . . The majority of the girls go back home because they don't have the support of the men so they have to look for it from their mothers.' Giuliana who was only 10 also observed: 'Men hook up with young girls but when the girls get pregnant they leave them. They just go. So how are they going to be for work if they are pregnant?' Although high fertility was not accorded the same weight in exacerbating poverty as in the Philippines or The Gambia, some respondents, such as Arsenio (49) made the point that: 'The saying that when you raise one you can raise five is a falsehood.'

With regard to the emotional and psychological states accompanying poverty, these were identified as low self-esteem, depression, stress, a sense of abandonment, misery, sadness and envy. Teodora, a 48-year-old housewife and mother of two from Villareal, recalled growing up in poverty thus:

> I remember that I would see other girls well-dressed and I would feel inferior to them. People would give me things, and second-hand clothing, because my parents couldn't afford to buy for me, My parents worked but earned very little. I helped my mother to wash clothes and help in other people's houses where they at least gave us lunch and other things . . .

Unwillingness to compare himself with others was also stressed by another respondent, Victorio (55) who added that poverty made him feel fearful of going hungry, as well as reaching an age when he would be too old to work. Tenure insecurity was also identified by Eida, 52, a separated woman who headed an eight-member extended household in Santa Cruz: since the land she occupied belonged to the municipality, there was always the fear that her house could be 'knocked down at any moment'.

Another important source of insecurity among respondents was crime and delinquency. Arsenio (49), for example, talked about people being prone to 'aggressive activities such as robbing because they have no food', and Juan Gabriel, a 31-year-old apprentice welder from Santa Cruz, went as far as to say that when people have nothing: 'there are people who can even kill because of this'. Carlos Olivier (12) from Liberia professed that: 'because of the bad people you can't go out in the street because they will attack you'. Indeed, Floribet (49) had felt such menace at the conditions in her settlement, Guayaval de Santa Cruz, that she had enlisted the support of neighbours to create a community police force ('*policia comunitaria*'), under the auspices of national scheme set-up to improve the reporting of incidents such as theft, drugs, and anti-social behaviour.[25] Additional responsibilities that the Guayaval force have taken on include the reporting of parents who fail to send their children to school.

In some senses, the stress placed by some on violence and vulnerabilty was at odds with the observation made by a focus group of 11 women in Villareal that being poor probably made one safer because no one would bother to mug or burgle you, which was also identified in the Philippines and The Gambia as one 'positive' aspect of poverty. Here, however, the similarities stop. Whereas in The Gambia there was scarcely anyone who spoke up in defence of poverty, and in the Philippines most stress on the upside of poverty tended to be placed on the fact that it made for greater 'Godliness', in Costa Rica poverty was frequently emphasised as 'character-building', especially among older respondents.

For example, Eida (52), from Villarreal, said that being poor made people 'learn to struggle harder in life', and Elba (66), was of the opinion that with poverty 'one learns to value things'. This view was shared widely by elderly men in a focus group in Santa Cruz, with Leandro (81) going as far as to say that poverty could be '*maravillosa*' (marvellous), because 'you gain experience, right?, and through that, you get on in the world . . . If you don't know poverty, you can't learn the things that poverty teaches you, like working and making a life for yourself'.

Another factor mentioned by Teodora (48), was that poverty could strengthen solidarity, with poor people tending to perform favours for each other for free while the rich tended to charge! Indeed, one 67-year-old resident of Santa Cruz, Juanita, had not only had seven children of her own, but had taken in a further 11 (mainly relatives) and seen them all through school, as well as saving a Nicaraguan adolescent from abduction.

This said, some identified people's lack of cooperation with others in similar straits, stressing that poverty could rob people of basic compassion and 'community spirit'. Sonia (44), for example, claimed that *Creciendo Juntas* had not worked in her neighbourhood because people were not interested in struggling together – they were too preoccupied with their own lives – '*cada quién por su buche*' (which literally translates as 'each for his own' [beak]). This was echoed by Jeannette (50) from Filadelfia who had actually participated in the programme: 'It's really awful when you have to go begging, because not everyone likes to help . . . you feel better when you don't have to depend on others.' Jeannette talked from bitter experience here, since when her husband had a car accident some years ago, which left him permanently disabled, no one came to her aid, despite the fact that she had a young family: 'I nearly went hysterical to see him in that wheelchair, and no one called to ask how we were doing, whether we had money for food . . .'. While Sonia's take on the reasons for limited solidarity may well be a function of scarcity, it is also important, as identified earlier, to note that people are not struggling for basic necessities at the same level as in The Gambia and the Philippines. As such, it may well be that the individualism observed in Costa Rica is more a function of consumerism and accumulation, including people having more 'hard' assets and wanting to protect them. Indeed, when people were asked what they would do if they were better off, many stressed the acquisition of material goods – especially property or a business – rather than helping relatives or others in the community, as had been particularly marked in The Gambia. Many also declared that in times of hardship they would only turn to their immediate family, or perhaps a government institution or the Church, but, out of pride, would not make recourse to their neighbours or more peripheral kin.

Grassroots Perceptions of Gender and Generational Aspects of Poverty

When asked to identify which groups of the population were most vulnerable to poverty, some older people warned that the young generation would be suffering most from poverty in years to come because they were so cosseted and not doing anything for themselves. As a focus group of elderly men in Santa Cruz concurred 'youth don't know how to struggle', and often waste the educational opportunities that are now open to them. For the most part, however, the poorest groups identified were the elderly, women, and female-headed households.

One reason why the elderly were deemed to be at the greatest disadvantage was because of discrimination against them in the labour market. On the surface this applies just as much to men as women. Not only do elderly men feel that they are more at risk of poverty because 'pretty young women' find work easier than them, but because they cannot even establish their own businesses due to lack of commercial credit. As Leandro (81) from Santa Cruz declared: 'Now we are no longer creditworthy, even if we have the vision.'

By the same token, while many men seem to be able to carry on working until formal retirement age (between 60 and 65), and even into their seventies, for women, as indicated earlier, their possibilities often start shrinking dramatically as early as their forties and fifties.

Calicsto (Box 6.4), for example, talked about women over 40 standing little chance of getting a job because 'they don't look good enough' to present a 'good image'. This was corroborated by Ixi, who having just turned 40 had been sacked from her job selling imported Colombian underwear on grounds of what she suspected was ageism. Although some felt that employers were also reluctant to recruit women in this age group because of their family responsibilities, others stressed this was more due to the fact that because most women in the past had tended to stay at home, they had less education, training and job experience.

Another factor identified as having a major bearing on poverty among older women was that they are unlikely to be covered by contributory pensions due to lack of continuous – if any – employment in the formal sector. Even then, one widower, Juan de Dios (78) from Santa Cruz, who had retired on a police pension professed that he was only able to make ends meet because he was sharing a home with two working daughters in their forties, and a granddaughter.

In living with his children, Juan de Dios counted himself fortunate compared with other elderly people in the survey, with as many as six out of eight men aged between 65 and 81 in a focus group in Santa Cruz living alone in rented rooms. Even if in some cases this was because participants had no children on account of of sterility induced by work on banana plantations,[26] the general perception was that older people, especially men, could not rely on care from their families as in the past. From the perspective of Danny, a 13-year-old schoolboy, for example: 'The men most vulnerable to poverty are elderly men because the family doesn't love them and kicks them out.' This corroborated a recent national study undertaken by the National University's Institute of Social Studies in Population (IDESPO),which explodes the notion that the elderly are supported by their children as a 'myth'.[27]

That childless men had not been taken in by other relatives was in part defended on grounds that the men in question did not want to be a burden on others, and in part because they had pensions on which they could subsist. Additional reasons centred on the observation that people were becoming increasingly individualistic with families opting for nuclearisation and independence. This was sometimes attributed to the fact that both spouses tend to work now, meaning that fewer women are around to look after elderly persons, who, as a result of living longer, often have specialist health needs. One of the members of a senior female focus group in Santa Cruz, Antonina (59), reported that she had advised a neighbour of hers that she should put her extremely frail 90-year-old father in a '*hogar de ancianos*' (old people's home) for his own good because she was not there during the day to take care of him.[28]

Although some respondents spoke rather cynically of the fact that some elderly people were only taken in by their families when they had pensions and/or property to leave behind, elderly women in Guanacaste, who usually have neither of note to speak of, are actually more likely to live in extended households. All three single or separated female survey participants in the 'senior' age group, for example, lived with kin, whereas this was the case with only four out of ten men. While these numbers are small, they typify a pattern established by 2000 census data, where only 41 per cent of lone person units among the over sixties in Guanacaste are female, as against a national average of 47 per cent. In turn, even if as many as 31 per cent of female heads of household in Guanacaste are aged 60 or more (compared with 19 per cent of male heads), only 39 per cent of women in this age group head their own households, and a mere 40 per cent of these consist of women living alone. Among their male peers, by contrast, 83 per cent head their own households, and 54 per cent of these are one-man units.

Among the reasons for the greater tendency for older women to reside in extended households in Guanacaste is that they can provide a valuable service in respect of childcare, especially with so many mothers working. In addition, given the widespread practice of child abandonment or neglect by fathers in the province, and because women have usually been the major parenting figure in children's lives, affective ties with mothers are often stronger (see Chant, 2002b).

Yet even if older women are not as vulnerable in practice in Guanacaste as opinion portrays, women in general were deemed to suffer from poverty to a greater extent than men. This was not only on account of income disparities stemming from men's advantage in the labour market, but because of the responsibility women bear for servicing others, with several respondents commenting that men could escape a lot more easily from family obligations and leave women carrying the can for household provisioning. Many, in turn, attributed this to 'men's egoism' and 'women's altriusm'. As articulated by Ixi (40):

> A poor women doesn't only think of herself; she thinks about her family, her children, in getting ahead. In contrast, men are more selfish, only concerned with their own needs, unlike women who are thinking not only about their own necessities but those of her family. When men see a situation getting difficult, they tend to go off and leave the woman alone to assume responsibility.

A similar view was expressed by Geovany (39): 'Women must suffer more because they think about feeding their children, not just about themselves.' William José (11) from Liberia also noted greater suffering among women 'Because women are left alone with their children, and men with alcoholism'.

Owing in part to the persistence of feminine norms of altruism and servility, women not only tend to work hard but in many cases resort to extreme self-sacrifice in order to fulfil children's needs. As stressed by Juanita (67), from Santa Cruz: 'we don't let the kids die of hunger'. And, if food is particularly short, as María Ester (27) from Filadelfia, pointed out: 'you'd rather have the children eat than eat yourself'. In male-headed households, the expectation that women should be servicing husbands as well as offspring means additional obligations. Indeed, although nominally benefiting from having co-resident partners, women in this position may be more exploited on account of men's 'free-riding' on the backs of their labour. Indeed, even where women work outside the home, they can seldom expect assistance from their spouses in housework and childcare. As Juanita (67) commented, when men marry or start living with someone what they really want is an '*empleada*' (domestic servant). Lack of domestic help from men also extends to sons, especially in cases where women have spouses. Although a number of mothers are now encouraging their sons to help out more, and took pride in saying how they had got them to make their beds, help out with cleaning and so on, and as Marielos (42) said, boys will only learn 'if one shows them that you're not a servant', the extent to which respondents are able to enforce domestic responsibilities is sometimes rather limited. This is often due to resistance on the part of spouses who fear their sons will turn out gay.

Corroborating findings from my earlier research in Guanacaste (see Chant, 1997a; 1997b), not to mention studies in other countries (see Chapters 2 and 3), men also demonstrate a propensity to retain earnings for personal use which is frequently injurious for the well-being of their spouses and children. As observed by Yiselda, a 43-year-old participant in a focus group held in Filadelfia and former partner of an alcoholic. 'If men earn 50 000 [*colones*], they give you no more than 25 000, and they spend the rest on drink.' Even where men do help out financially they tend to abrogate responsibility for making their contributions stretch to meet family needs. As Roxana (37), in a focus group in Villareal reported: 'The man gets home with the money he's earned and says to his wife: "take this, and do a miracle with it, pay the electricity, water, food . . . everything!" '

The fact that men's discretionary expenditure often bankrolls indulgence in '*vicios*' (vices) such as alcohol and drugs was repeatedly flagged up as evidence of men's cavalier regard for the well-being of their families. As summarised by Eida (52), a separated female head from Santa Cruz:

> Men are more reckless/wasteful, because when they have money they go to the bar, whereas when women have money they think about buying food for their children . . . men don't worry about anything. They're only concerned about themselves, and it doesn't matter to them whether people are waiting for them at home.

At its logical extreme, men's disregard for family well-being leads to female household headship. Yet while this clearly forces women to struggle against poverty single-handedly, it is recognised that women may also conduct this battle alone even when they live with men, and sometimes under greater constraints. Paulo, the 47-year-old Nicaraguan nightwatchman in Tamarindo, for example, stated that male-headed households were worse off than female-headed units because while women '*piensan en la comida*' (think about food), men are only concerned with *güaro* (liquor).

In light of the above, it is no surprise that most women express bitterness about having to bear the brunt of, if not sole, responsibility for their families while men detach themselves from their obligations. As summed up by one senior respondent, Elba (66): 'Women are compromised with their children, and are those who end up beaten, abused, and without employment.'

Intersections between Poverty, Gender and Household Transitions

Women who head their own households were almost unilaterally identified as the 'poorest of the poor', mainly on account of women's disadvantage in employment and earnings, but also because of men's dismal record of financial contributions following relationship or family breakdown. As Teodora (48) from Villareal stated: 'Poverty is found above all among women who live alone because they also need to work out how to raise the children. The problem is that many don't use family planning and don't look after themselves, then the men leave them with the children.'

Although some young people perceived father absence as problematic, an equal, if not greater number espoused opposing views. For example, Giuliana (10) conceded that while some women who get lonely without a partner may put up with problematic relationships, she also stressed how men did so little about amending their 'bad behaviour' that this was forcing more and more women to opt out of unhappy unions. In her own case, Giuliana expressed relief that her family no longer had to endure her father's drinking, and pride in the fact that even though her 35-year-old mother was only selling sweets and ice cream from home, she was succeeding in raising the children alone.

Leading on from this, there was pretty widespread recognition, as expressed by Juanita (67) from Santa Cruz, that 'even when women are alone, they still manage to survive', and as Elieth, a 51-year-old former school dinner lady from Santa Cruz, echoed that 'women struggle more than men; men can't fight alone against poverty, and because they can't they have to find a woman who will accompany them'.

While these views on female headship tend to run counter to the opinion that this is necessarily a poverty-inducing or exacerbating state, a further paradox is presented by the fact that in actuality many women in Guanacaste find living without partners a positive alternative. Female headship seems to offer women, *inter alia*, more power and independence, greater occupational choice, more control over household finances, enhanced mobility and freedom, less exploitation, less insecurity and greater peace and well-being. For example, Nuvia (49) a female head working as a cleaner in Villareal declared that since splitting with a violent, alcoholic spouse:

> Of course I am happier now, because now I know that I can buy rice and beans, and eat in peace, while when I was with him . . . if he left at 6 o'clock in the morning to work, he didn't come back until 6 o'clock the following morning, drunk and causing me trouble, and me there perhaps without food. Whatever I have had to suffer, I don't wish that on any of my female companions.

Floribet (49) from Santa Cruz, who has had eight children by four different fathers, admitted to having suffered as a lone mother, although she also felt that long lapses between partners had given her a better opportunity to provide for her offspring. This was because she could do any job she wanted without having to undergo protacted and conflictive negotiations. In her various efforts to raise her children Floribet had worked as a waitress, as a cleaning lady, and claims at times to have come near to prostitution. Now she has only two children at home and on top of making a modest living selling '*arroz con leche*' (rice with milk) and '*tejidos*' (knitwear), receives money from an older son and daughter. Although she is far from well-off, she likes the security attached to being the manager of the household income, and draws comfort from the fact that none of it is squandered. That she has managed to give her children a reasonable start in life has also given her a sense of pride in her achievements, added to which she now feels able to put men behind her altogether. Floribet joined the Iglesia Bíblica de Guayaval (a small Costa Rican Evangelical sect) two years ago, and declares not only that she became '*una hija de Dios*' (a child of God), but also that 'the only husband for me from now on will be Jesus Christ!'

Eida (52), from Santa Cruz, whose husband left her six years ago and who heads an eight-member household, was also vehement about not cohabiting with anyone else in future. Observing that young people often seek out the company of older partners in the interests of having an easier life, she affirmed that: 'I prefer to clean houses than to sell myself to young men.' As indicated earlier, Sonia, who has made a major professional breakthrough since she left her spouse, is also extremely reluctant to relinquish her independence (Box 6.2).

As highlighted in Sonia's case, when female heads have assets in their own name this gives them more scope to dictate the terms of their relationships with men. While as recently as 20 years ago separated women would typically seek another partner to enhance their income or to gain access to housing (see Chant, 1997a), serial monogamy of a non-co-residential nature is now more common, partly because rising levels of land and property titling among women have strengthened their ability to survive alone, and partly because the desire to protect assets makes them more wary of letting other men get too involved in their lives. Another factor is that although women do not have the same freedom as men to conduct multiple sexual relationships, there seems to be more tolerance of out-of-wedlock sex among women than previously.

A further critical benefit women identified as a result of heading their own households was eliminating violence from their lives. As Ixi (40) declared:

> In many circumstances it's better [for women] to live alone, for example, in cases of domestic violence, whether this is psychological, physical, or involves any form

of aggression, it's better to be alone. As long as there is violence, the economic or social situation means nothing. If there is violence, it is better to live alone.

Another advantage of being alone stressed by many women is no longer having to put up with men's seemingly compulsive infidelity. This is no empty stereotype. Marian (12), whose father had left her mother for another woman, declared bitterly that 'men only serve to destroy'. Men's proclivity to 'play around' was usually acknowledged by men too, with the rider that this could severely impoverish families. As one focus group of eight adolescent boys in Liberia concurred, the more money men had the more unfaithful they could be, which dissipated resources among all the women and children they were connected with.

While various advantages of female headship have always featured in discussions with women at the grassroots (see Chant, 1997a), I sense that women are even better able to do without men than in the past. One reason is that women in general perceive they are more equal with men, or at least less subordinate. For example, although some women are still forbidden by their husbands to work (which was the case with Ixi [40] before she separated), many do have paid work, which gives them some means of independence.

Aside from the fact that women perceive themselves to be in a stronger position financially to survive without men, greater possibilities of independence have also been furnished by legislation around conjugal assets, and domestic violence. This seemed to be felt even more strongly on the part of men than women. Victorio, 55 years, from Santa Cruz, for example, reported:

> Before many men beat their wives. There was no dialogue. They treated them badly simply because of lack of trust. I remember that my father treated my mother very badly. This was dismal, because even though I was very young at the time, it made me afraid. In contrast, if a man beats his woman now, they send him to prison. They can leave the man without a house, or woman, because afterwards the woman puts another man in the house. I think women rule now because the law supports them rather than men.

Although Victorio's experience as the son of a violent father had made him see some value in new family legislation, Guillermo (32) noted:

> Women today don't put up with anything. If the man doesn't suit her or treats her badly, she leaves him. So, when there are many problems and arguments, I think it's better that people live apart. At times it's the man who causes problems, but at others, the woman. There are women who also maltreat their menfolk, but the law doesn't protect men . . . and there are some men whose wives beat them.

Juan de Dios (78) also observed that: 'Now women rule; the law is on their side. Men can even be left without a roof over their heads, while women are protected. This wasn't the case before.'

While Guillermo's and Juan's opinions were based on perception and hearsay, some men in the survey had come up against the law in practice. This was especially the case among older men who had taken young second or third wives and had been kicked out when they were past it (jokingly referred to as 'finished flying') – usually only after the man in question had built them a house. Rodrigo in his late sixties, for example, reported that although he had never laid a finger on his wife, the mere fact that she had denounced him as threatening her with violence led to his being banned from the home and prevented him from going within 300 metres of the door.

For the most part women too feel that denunciations of domestic violence will get them further, even if in some cases, such as that of Nuvia (49), the police do not always take women's complaints seriously:

> I denounced the man I was with, the father of my two girls. I called the police, but when they came and found I was not black and blue, that there was no mark on me – because I didn't let him hit me – they just let it go. The police only intervene when they actually kill you, and what's the sense in that?

Indeed, despite a recent decline in the level of denunciations, legislation has by no means eradicated domestic violence,[29] and in some respects punitive legislation towards men, coupled with women's new freedoms, is seen to have exacerbated violence and discord within the home. For example, one female head from Filadelfia, Maribel (42) who had recently separated from an alcoholic husband, said that while she had grown up with the idea that women had to give men their food, and men would do nothing around the house:

> nowadays it seems that this is changing because of all this women's liberation. It seems to be changing but I don't know until which point. I know that it's good, but there is a 'but', and that is domestic violence, and because of this many women have died just because we don't want to put up with things like we did before. We want to be equal.

That pro-female laws might drive men to more extreme behaviour was also expressed by their male 'victims', such as Calicsto (47), who felt that new legislation was seriously undermining family cooperation and unity:

> There is more hostility, because, although I don't really want to go into this, the family is becoming divided because of this law – they call – the 'protection of

women', which they apply when women say their husbands have been violent towards them, whether physically or verbally. But no judge or lawyer knows anything about psychology. For example, I've seen cases where there are problems in a family, and neither judge nor lawyer has the solution. Or rather, they don't know anything about what's going on in the home in the first place. So first you need a psychologist, not a police officer or a judge. Then, instead of sorting out the problem, what they do is to split the family up, and I'm telling you this because of my own experience. They applied this law to me, they booted me out of the house, I lost my relationship with my children, and the law was completely wrong . . . If you think about it, it's easy to say so-and-so is guilty . . . saying someone is guilty is easy . . . and because of this families are being split apart. To give you an example, you've seen the hordes of women who have been attacked in Costa Rica, and their husbands are told they cannot go within 300 metres of the house, and the husband is dogged by shame . . . well . . . the first reaction men are going to have is to kill their wives.

Conjugality, fertility and inter-generational transfers

Despite the difficulties in conjugal relationships, most people embark on these, albeit it at a slightly later stage than in the past. For example, while many middle and senior female participants were in their teens when they had their first live-in relationship and/or child, as in The Gambia and the Philippines, younger women feel that marriage and children should not ideally happen until their mid-twenties to give them a chance to finish their studies and get decent work. Indeed, many young women not only express a firm commitment to securing a profession before marriage and children, but, in the interests of not losing power, even reluctance to get married at all. Mariela (15), from Santa Cruz, for example, who has never known her father and lives with her mother and two elder brothers stated: 'I don't like to be ordered around. It's better to study and work so that no one bosses you around and causes problems.' Similar sentiments were articulated by Andreina (11) who resides with her mother and two half-brothers: 'If you get married, the man will not let you do what you want, or go out when you want . . . Men rule women more than women rule men. Women can't do what they want.' Although the prospects of women negotiating any autonomy within the context of a union is still perceived as limited, their stronger 'fallback' position at least makes them feel able to cope with independence if the situation arises. By the same token, Abdías (14) in Liberia, was one of many young people who cautioned that in situations of poverty, women should watch out about becoming too successful economically because men are attracted to women with money for the wrong reasons.

As for the nature of marriage, Guanacaste's long tradition of consensual unions may have contributed to the fact that most respondents see little difference between getting married and living together. Julia (43), from Filadelfia, for example, who had married her spouse only after several years of cohabitation, declared that men treat their legal wives in the same way as they do their common-law spouses. Consuelo (30), from the same focus group echoed 'the law protects married and unmarried women alike'. This said, in practice marriages tend to be more enduring than unions, possibly because as Paulo (47), said, it costs so much more to get out of a marriage, and arguably more '*respeto*' (respect) is attached to a legalised arrangement. In addition, women who are formally married stand to get more financial benefits if husbands leave them for another woman, but fail to divorce, as reported by two sisters in Santa Cruz whose mother had been deserted by the father but was still eligible to receive his pension when he died of cancer.

Whether in marriages or unions, however, having children is strongly favoured, albeit fewer of them than in the past. While many older interviewees had six or more children, the bulk of these, along with their younger counterparts, suggested that the ideal number was two. Despite some concern about artificial contraception being disapproved by the Catholic Church, its growing availability on the national health was welcomed, with Juanita (67), for example, consistently advising her sons, daughters and adoptive children that they should '*planificar*' (plan their families), because with a lot of children 'then comes total poverty'. As Danny (13) echoed: 'It is very nice to have children, but if you don't have much money, better not to have too many.' Part of the desire to limit births is arguably because paid labour among children is relatively uncommon, and it is not until they reach adulthood that they are able to help out financially in any significant way. Even then, there is no guarantee given that 'wealth flows' in Costa Rica tend to be from parents to children, rather than vice versa, as in The Gambia and to a lesser extent the Philippines.

Yet despite desires to limit births, and regardless of the perception that senior citizens should 'go it alone' and not depend on their children in old age, childlessness can be a source of anxiety, especially where people do not have a contributory pension. Victorio (55), a casual labourer with no children, for example, admits to feeling increasingly 'defenceless' and hopes his younger brothers will help him when he has to give up work. It is also conceivably the case that children are seen not only as a source of material insurance in later life, but of social, psychological and emotional security, providing a sense of 'family' in the context of rising conjugal instability and a perceived weakening of extended family ties.

Grassroots Views on Poverty Alleviation Initiatives

Awareness of social programmes is generally much higher among people at the grassroots in Costa Rica compared with their counterparts in The

Gambia and the Philippines. This is probably a function of the fact that most had benefited personally, or through an immediate family member, from government assistance, whether in the form an education scholarship, health care, housing finance, or pension. Although there was often a sense that the government could do more, there was some pride in the country's relatively high level of redistributionism, and a general feeling that the assistance received had been helpful.

Creciendo Juntas had clearly reached a number of women in Guanacaste, and as noted in the Costa Rican report on the implementation of the BPFA:

> The qualitative impact . . . reveals a strengthening of women's personal and collective capacities to defend their human rights, since they have the information and knowledge on the legislation that protects them and the mechanisms available, along with enhanced capacities and skills to demand services and resources for access to the labour market and self-employment. (CR, 2004: 11–12)

In many respects this is borne out by women in the survey such as Yorleny, a 43-year-old food vendor from Filadelfia, who stated that: 'we have learned many things we didn't know before'. A fellow member of this group, Marielos, a 42-year-old temporarily unemployed chambermaid whose last spouse left six years ago for someone else, said: 'Above all, we know who we are now because before the programme we believed we weren't worth anything. And we've been taught things we can do which we didn't know before.'

CONCLUSION: IS THERE A 'FEMINISATION OF POVERTY' IN COSTA RICA?

Quantitative data from official Costa Rican sources point to a 'feminisation of poverty' in so far as the last decade has seen an increase in the presence of women, and particularly female heads of household, among the poor and extremely poor. Yet this seems mainly to be a function of the growth of female-headed households who, as a group, do not seem to face any greater probability of poverty now than they did in the late 1990s. Despite the fact that a slight tendency towards greater proportions of female heads at extremes of the age spectrum may have held in check an overall narrowing of gendered poverty gaps sought through policy interventions, there is ample qualitative evidence from Guanacaste that women who head their own households are increasingly able to negotiate a personally profitable 'trade-off' between lower incomes and greater well-being. While the volume of income entering the household budget may drop, its regularity may increase, and there are other spin-offs including reductions in the unequal resource allocation, violence and exploitation. Indeed, it could well be the case that CEDAW's (2003: 103) assertion that 'in Costa Rica poverty is becoming increasingly "feminised"', with women being 'exposed to forms of poverty that affect men relatively less', is not necessarily a function of an increase in female household headship, but that the burden of coping with poverty is becoming more skewed towards women in male-headed households. As discovered in the other case study countries, trends in the 'feminisation of poverty' are perhaps best characterised as an increasing unevenness of *inputs* to household survival between women and men, rather than widening gaps in the incidence of income poverty.

While gender policy initiatives in Costa Rica have clearly assisted some poor women to negotiate new ways of coping with poverty which simultaneously grant them more opportunity to evade domestic inequalities, there is still some way to go. One major issue that needs to be addressed is that of discrimination in employment and incomes, with the odds continuing to be stacked heavily against middle-aged and older women. Thanks to programmes such as *Creciendo Juntas* which is oriented to women of 'productive age', and, despite having no explicit limits, tends mainly to recruit women between their late thirties and mid-forties,[30] some women in their middle years are able to enhance their vocational skill set. However, for older women, who face most discrimination from employers, who have few alternatives given a dearth of vocational and training opportunities in micro-entrepreneurship for senior citizens, and who also tend to be disadvantaged in respect of pensions, there is clearly an urgent need for action. This is especially so given a context of demographic ageing and declining birth rates, which may force more elderly women to live alone in future.

Also critical in circumventing any future 'feminisation of poverty' will be the incorporation of men in gender programmes. Although women's awareness of gender inequalities is increasing and the state has made attempts to encourage greater paternal compliance with the Law for Responsible Paternity, more attention needs to be directed to changing attitudes. One initiative, '*Apoyémonos*' (Let's Support Each Other) was first discussed by IMAS in 2003. This was mooted as taking the form of gender-consciousness raising among the partners of *Creciendo Juntas* participants who had learned about women's rights only to find themselves unable to exercise them in the home. While still only a blueprint, without an infrastructure of greater male sensibility and commitment to women and their children, women either end up with the lion's share of work in households and communities, or are forced into situations of conjugal dissolution because they are unable to negotiate new deals within the context of two-parent households.

NOTES

1. Progress towards MDG 1, which is to reduce poverty from 21.7 per cent to 16 per cent of households by 2015, and to reduce extreme poverty from 5.6 per cent to 4.5 per cent, are deemed 'satisfactory' and 'very satisfactory' respectively (CSG et al., 2004: 116). Other MDG targets already achieved include that of equalising the ratio of girls to boys in primary and secondary education (encompassed in MDG 3), and halting forest degradation (encompassed in MDG 7) (World Bank, 2004c: 3; see also Box 1.3).
2. Costa Rica's seven provinces are subdivided into 81 cantons and 421 districts. For planning purposes, the country is divided into six regions. Guanacaste corresponds with the '*Región Chorotega*', which is the largest in terms of size (10 140 km²). This represents 19.8 per cent of the country's land area, and 6.9 per cent of the population (IFAM, 2003).
3. Costa Rica's estimated indigenous population at the time of the Spanish conquest was a mere 25 000.
4. Costa Rica has not only earned itself a reputation as a 'haven of peace, but also as peacemaker for the Central American region as whole, especially following the award of the Nobel Peace Prize to President Oscar Arias in 1987 for his contribution to bringing about the Peace Accord in Guatemala.
5. CAFTA is a free trade agreement comprising USA, Guatemala, El Salvador, Honduras, Nicaragua and Costa Rica (EIU, 2004c: 7). Negotiations began in 2004, but have faced continued resistance from trade unionists, intellectuals and public sector workers on grounds that CAFTA will render the country even more vulnerable to US imperialism and erode Costa Rica's sound tradition of social welfare. Costa Rica has been the last country to ratify the treaty which is supposed to become fully operational in 2008 (PEN, 2005: 18).
6. Between 1969 and 2003, Costa Rican presidents were not eligible for re-election. However, in April of this latter year the Constitutional Court ruled that ex-presidents could run for re-election provided they had spent 8 consecutive years out of office (USDS, 2004).
7. Costa Rica produces around 20 per cent of the world's bananas.
8. In 2003 pineapples beat coffee into second place for Costa Rica's export crops, and exports of pineapple between 2004 and 2005 grew by 34 per cent (*Tico Times*, 7 October 2005, pp. 1, 10 and 11, 'Pineapple boom: a mixed blessing', by Robert Goodier).
9. *La Nación*, 27 October 2005, p. 2, 'Canciller Nica Critica Nueva Ley Migratoria'.
10. Carranza's (2003) in-depth study of sterilisation in Costa Rica indicates that mothers often play a very important role in the decisions of daughters to have the operation, often encouraging them to do so given the adverse effects of high fertility in a context of male unreliability. It should also be noted that women's scope to decide on sterilisation was strengthened by Executive Decree 27913-S of 1992 which ruled that women should have the right to surgical sterilisation without spousal consent.
11. The pro-choice association Colectiva por el Derecho de la Mujer (CDM/Women's Rights Collective), is currently lobbying for legal safe abortion in Costa Rica, and elimination of the article in the Penal Code which specifies three years imprisonment for women terminating unwanted pregnancies (*Tico Times*, 7 October 2005, pp. 1, 6 and 7, 'Is abortion debate on the horizon', by María Gabriela Díaz). The CDM is is also concerned about the morning after pill. Although many in the religious and political establishment equate emergency contraception with abortion, which has rendered Costa Rica the only country in Central America to resist its introduction, emergency contraception is only a preventative measure, and, given a loophole in the law, it looks as if this will not only be allowed to go on sale in pharmacies, but also to be provided by the CCSS (*La Nación*, 20 October 2005, p. 16a, 'Píldora del Día Siguiente Puede Llegar a las Farmacias', by Marcela Cantero).
12. The CEN-CINAI centres are run by the Ministry of Health and provide integrated health care for poor children aged 2–5 years, along with powdered milk and food rations,

early stimulation, and pre-school education (World Bank, 2003d: 46). '*Hogares Comunitarios*', which are administered by IMAS, provide subsidised childcare in poor neighbourhoods through the training of local women as 'community mothers' (see Sancho Montero, 1995).

13. The non-contributory pension scheme is deigned to help vulnerable people – such as those aged 65 or more, those with a disability, widows, and orphaned children – whose monthly per capita household income is less than 50 per cent of the minimum threshold for contributory pensions (World Bank, 2003d: 129). As much as 46 per cent of non-contributory pensions are financed by employers' contributions, with the remainder being sourced from general tax revenues and taxes on specific items (Bertranou et al., 2004: 5).

14. In the detailed investigation of Costa Rica's poverty dynamics 2002–04 carried out by Slon Montero and Zúñiga Rojas (2005), three factors demonstrating the strongest association with chronic or repeated poverty were: (1) age of household heads (those over 50 being at particular risk; (2) heads' level of education (those with unfinished primary being especially vulnerable), and (3) sex of household heads, with women being at greater threat than their male counterparts. The latter resonates with a more general observation made by Moghadam (2005) that women are more likely to be persistently poor than men.

15. Household headship in Costa Rica is officially defined as applying to persons 15 years or older who are considered to be the household head by other members, or who earn the largest share of economic resources. When this is difficult to determine headship is assigned to the oldest individual in the household (INEC, 2000: 58). Given patriarchal traditions, headship in family-based households comprising a couple and their children tends to be ascribed to men, and only to women where they lack a co-resident male partner. As pointed out by Monge and González (2005), for example, in 2002 nearly 90 per cent of self-reported female heads did not have a spouse in residence. In non-family households, the head is the person who has most authority or the biggest administrative role, who is the oldest in the household, or who been in the household the longest (INEC, 2000: 58).

16. These figures excluded domestic servants and retired persons which one imagines would have given rise to even greater differentials between women's and men's earnings.

17. Although there are some state funds for Nicaraguans, the law requires that FODESAF programmes should attend only to Costa Rican families (see IOM, 2001: 34).

18. Interview with Hermana Rosalina Serrano Retes, Hogar Cristiano Divina Providencia, Pastoral Social, Santa Cruz, October 2005.

19. Rodríguez (1999) claims that the nuclear household only became a powerful normative concept with the rise of liberalism in Costa Rica in the nineteenth and twentieth centuries, although Catholic marriage was first introduced in the mid-eighteenth and early nineteenth centuries in the Valle Central (see also Budowski, 2003: 61; Rodríguez, 2000).

20. The Latin American Movimiento Familiar Cristiano (MFC), which originated in Argentina in 1948, started in Costa Rica with a small group in 1958 and became a fully fledged regional movement in the 1960s (Rodríguez Cháves, 1999). The objectives of the movement are to promote 'human and Christian values in the family and in the community', and to provide assistance to families (MFC, 1997). These services include a range of programmes designed to strengthen marriage and to help people lead 'Christian family lives', such as prenuptial courses, support groups, matrimonial retreats, 'family integration' weeks, and a marriage advisory service.

21. INAMU's funding is supposed to come from 2 per cent of FODESAF moneys. However, in both 2001 and 2002, the sum actually received by INAMU was only about half this due to government expenditure cuts (CEDAW, 2003: 48; also PEN, 2005).

22. Administered by IMAS since its creation in 1999, SIPO registers potential beneficiaries of social assistance (for example, for school bonds, housing bonds, non-contributory pensions and so on) on the basis of the relative poverty of the region in which they live, statistical analysis of poverty-related variables (for example, income, education, existing coverage by social programmes), and a questionnaire interview with the family in question (see World Bank, 2003d: 50n and 166). It should be noted that definitions of female

headship in SIPO are looser than the census definition (see note 15) referring only to 'a woman who has the responsibility for the household', which can clearly refer to women who are living with men, or who are de facto heads of household in receipt of remittances from migrant spouses, as well as those who are unpartnered.

23. Interview with María Leiton, IMAS, San José, September 2005.
24. I would like to have included full verbatim comments in Spanish in this and the grass-roots section of the chapter, word-length restrictions do not allow.
25. This provides a valuable service given scant policing in low-income neighbourhoods, and that relative to the national population the number of police officers has declined in recent years (see PEN, 2005).
26. Between 1970 and 1985, the pesticide 'Nemagon', manufactured by Dow Chemical, was widely used on Costa Rica's banana plantations. Since many workers did not use gloves, the pesticide was absorbed through their skin and rendered them infertile. In some cases workers were given compensation of US$100, but many claims remain unsettled.
27. According to IDESPO's study more than 1000 of Costa Rica's 300 000 elderly have been abandoned by families in CCSS hospitals, and 56 per cent of the elderly support themselves from retirement funds (see *Tico Times*, 28 October 2005, p. 9, 'Ageing in Costa Rica: a troubling process').
28. In actuality it is quite difficult to get a place in a state run old people's home, unless the elderly person in question has been abused (*agredido*). Personal communication, Enid Jaén Hernández, Universidad de Costa Rica, Centro Regional de Guanacaste, Liberia.
29. Newspaper articles continue to abound with regard to deaths of women at the hands of violent husbands (see, for example, *La Nación*, 11 October 2005, p. 13a, 'Estranguló a su compañera para evitar la separación', by Irene Vizcaino).
30. Personal communication, María Leiton, IMAS, San José, December 2005.

7. Conclusion

This chapter draws out the major theoretical, methodological and policy implications from my explorations of The Gambia, the Philippines and Costa Rica. While I do not intend to reiterate the main findings from each country or the comparisons already noted, synthesising their principal similarities and differences helps to determine whether a 'feminisation of poverty' is in any way perceived and/or discernible as a general trend, and if so, what form this is tending to take. Thereafter, I wish to revisit (and go some way to re-casting) the term's key connotations such that it more accurately depicts trends in gendered privation. Finally, some pointers to future research and policy are ventured.

Prior to teasing out the major findings, it is worth noting in general terms that people's discourses on poverty often bear little relationship to statistical evidence, or to actual circumstances. For example, professional and popular perceptions alike in all three case study countries are that the incidence of poverty is on the increase, even though the only country where official data support this is The Gambia. In turn, dominant views on which groups of the population are most vulnerable to poverty seem often to be shaped more by popular stereotypes than by actual experiences. This was especially the case in Costa Rica, where female-headed households are repeatedly stressed as the 'poorest of the poor' despite frequent improvements in women's income and well-being following conjugal dissolution. Another prominent pattern is for divergence between opinions on advances in gender equality on the one hand, and personal practices and experiences on the other. Although there is no space here to explore the potentially fascinating and important reasons behind these differences (and contradictions), they underline the inherently problematic nature of mapping trends in gendered poverty. They also suggest that any conclusions derived from quantitative or qualitative data, or both, must of necessity be circumspect, an epithet which cannot be ascribed to most discourses on the 'feminisation of poverty' to date.

COMPARING GENDERED AND GENERATIONAL BURDENS OF POVERTY IN THE GAMBIA, THE PHILIPPINES AND COSTA RICA

In policy documents in all three case study countries women are almost always identified as among the most vulnerable groups in the population, usually along with senior citizens and youth. This is despite the difficulties of determining from official statistics how far women are actually affected by poverty, even in a strictly monetary sense. Except in Costa Rica, for example, there are no sex-disaggregated headcount data on income poverty. Moreover, as for trends, which as Medeiros and Costa (2006) remind us are a more accurate measure of 'feminisation' than mere 'over-representation', The Gambia lacks reliable longitudinal data even on aggregate household incomes.

While in Costa Rica there is statistical evidence of a higher incidence of poverty among women than men, as well as among female versus male household heads, in the Philippines and in The Gambia (until recently), official data on poverty and household headship suggest on average that male-headed units are worse off. In general terms, this tends to dovetail with popular perceptions in the different countries. Whereas low-income respondents and institutional personnel in The Gambia and the Philippines do not mark female-headed households as a group at especially 'high risk', in Costa Rica the overwhelming consensus is that they are disproportionately so. Moreover, Costa Rican income statistics not only indicate above-average levels of poverty and extreme poverty among female-headed households, but that the share of households headed by women in these categories has increased in recent years. At first glance this seems anomalous since female heads in Costa Rica have received more support from the state than in the other two countries. As discussed in Chapter 6, however, government gender equality initiatives seem to have increased the viability of female headship, thereby leading to more women opting for this state. That this, in turn, is not as negative in practice as in principle, especially when poverty is conceived as broader than income, begs caution about uncritical readings of money-metric data.

Some caution is also necessary when considering the determination of age groups most vulnerable to poverty, as well as their intersections with gender. Statistical evidence in Costa Rica points to elderly people – and especially the female elderly – being at greatest risk. This largely accords with the views of respondents, most of whom attribute this to lack of employment and inadequate pensions, especially where people live alone. While in actuality elderly women who live alone are a minority, and more are likely to reside in extended households than their male peers, it is possible that income poverty may undergo (further) feminisation if life expectancy continues to rise, and falling birth rates together with a weakening of extended family ties erode prospective bases of support. In The Gambia and the Philippines, by contrast these trends are currently less marked and the elderly appear able to rely to a greater extent on intergenerational family transfers, whether from members within or beyond their households. Indeed, despite the fact that Gambian data point to a slightly higher incidence of poverty among senior citizens, at the grassroots and according to institutional personnel, this age cohort is generally regarded as the most advantaged, mainly because 'wealth flows' tend to be in an upward direction (that is, from youth to elders).

Notwithstanding the existence of three criteria making for higher poverty among households across all three countries (namely, large size, rural residence, and limited education), it is difficult to conclude, let alone generalise, either on the basis of objective measures or subjective views that (a) income poverty is particularly pronounced among women, let alone growing, relative to men, (b) that any particular age group is more vulnerable to poverty than another, or (c) that rises in female household headship are necessarily associated with a 'feminisation of poverty'. In turn, while the Beijing pronouncement that women face a *persistent* burden of poverty is possibly correct – especially in terms of income – when talking about *increases* I contend that this can only be upheld if we adopt a broader take on poverty, my single most striking finding being the virtually universal perception that women seem to be making ever-greater inputs of time, labour and effort in household survival relative to men. A further critical issue is a notable disjuncture in all three countries between what women and men invest in household livelihoods and what they get out, with this disparity showing up most starkly in male-headed units.

Not Incomes, but Inputs: Understanding the 'Feminisation of Poverty' as a 'Feminisation of Responsibility and Obligation'

Bearing in mind that the dearth of relevant statistical data forces me to rely heavily on the findings from my qualitative surveys, my main conclusion from The Gambia, Philippines and Costa Rica is that while most women have always injected more effort into household livelihoods than have men, there seems to be growing unevenness in gendered contributions. This strikes chords with Sassen's (2002) work on international migration, where she talks about a 'feminisation of survival' in which households, and indeed whole communities, are increasingly dependent on the labour efforts of women.

Venturing the term 'feminisation of responsibility and obligation',[1] to sum-up the patterns observed in my fieldwork, three issues transpired as particularly significant in respect of gender differences in poverty burdens.

(1) Growing gender disparities in the range and amount of labour invested in household livelihoods among the poor

Rising numbers of poor women of all ages are working outside the home, as well as continuing to perform the bulk of unpaid reproductive tasks for husbands, fathers, brothers, and sons. Men, on the other hand, seem not only to be finding it harder to be the sole or chief economic support for their households, but are not increasing their participation in reproductive work either.

This resonates with a substantial body of other research on the Global South. Despite evidence from some Latin American countries such as Chile and Mexico that men are playing a greater role in caring for children (Alméras, 2000; Gutmann, 1996; Olavarría, 2003), in the region more generally, domestic labour continues to be an almost exclusively female domain (Arriagada, 2002: 159; Lavinas and Nicoll, 2006). As summarised by ECLAC (2004b: 5): 'most men still do not share in household work or in the array of unpaid care-giving activities entailed by membership in a community or society'. In turn, men in 'male-headed households are more likely to enjoy the advantages of free domestic work by the spouse, thus avoiding expenditures otherwise associated with maintaining a household' (ibid.: 23). As echoed by UN/UNIFEM (2003: 49) in relation to the Philippines: 'Regardless of the source of care resources, whether through social services, markets, or women's own labour, women disproportionately bear the responsibility of ensuring that the household's care needs are met.' Over and above the fact that this is occurring in the context of cutbacks in state services and rising prices of basic goods which frequently imply greater investments of time in domestic labour and self-provisioning (see Chant, 1996; UNMP/TFEGE, 2005: 7), that women are also bringing more money into households through wage labour or income-generating activities raises serious concerns about inequality, exploitation and sustainability. Moreover, in some respects it could be argued that the feminisation of effort is not only increasing over time, but across generations: young women. who are potentially more likely to have employment than their older counterparts, may find themselves with even bigger burdens of labour and obligation relative to men, especially in The Gambia (see below).

(2) Persistent and/or growing disparities in women's and men's capacities to negotiate gendered obligations and entitlements in households: the unhappy marriage of tradition and transition?

Leading on from the above, although women's responsibilities for coping with poverty are growing they do not seem to be gaining any ground for negotiating greater inputs to household incomes or labour on the part of men, let alone reductions in their discretionary expenditure. Indeed, regardless of their declining shares of household effort, men continue to withhold earnings (and/or to appropriate those of their wives or other household members), to finance extra-domestic, and fundamentally compensatory and/or recreational, pursuits such as spending time with male friends, and/or indulging in drugs, drink, extramarital sex and gambling. While this by no means applies to all men, and some activities (passing time in male company, for example) may help to secure profitable contacts and resources, as well as provide solace, others add up to evasion of crucial responsibilities which women have no choice other than to assume. Underlining Whitehead's (2003: 8) observation that: 'men and women are often poor for different reasons, experience poverty differently, and have different capacities to withstand and/or escape poverty', men's extra-domestic 'indulgences' not only reinforce women's obligations, but in the process can compound them, such as when additional pressures are exerted on household resources through men becoming ill or unable to work (see also Chapter 2).

Some women faced with egoism or neglect on the part of spouses are able through design or default to set up their own households and create environments which are more personally enabling and/or enhance the well-being and prospects of their children. For the majority of women, however, the present state of affairs is arguably exposing them to risks of greater extremes of inequality and servitude.

Despite some talk of advances towards gender equality among women and men in the case study countries, just as notable is the apparent resilience of normative social and cultural ideals which reflect and condone gender injustice. Expectations of female altruism, for example, continue to be remarkably persistent and mean that women often remain resigned to assuming heavier burdens, if not without complaint then without major open confrontation. In The Gambia, for instance, rarely do women of any age expect or ask their menfolk to help out with 'female tasks', let alone get them to refrain from the exercise of male prerogatives, no matter how injurious to household welfare. In some cases, it appears that women are even redoubling their efforts to perform the roles of 'good wives' and 'dutiful daughters' as they 'encroach' on male terrain such as paid work. This not only helps to reaffirm their identities as women, but to defuse potential conflict.[2] As for men, their declining contributions to household survival may well derive from a perceived need to assert elements of 'traditional masculine behaviour' over which they still have some control – and which women may tolerate through their own perceptions of how men should be (see Chant, 2000; Chant, with Craske, 2003: ch. 1). Yet while recourse to, or intensification of, 'traditional' norms of 'masculinity' and 'femininity' may represent tactical psycho-social steps for all parties concerned, the motivations and outcomes are perniciously gender differentiated: for men this is arguably in their personal interests, but for women, mainly in the interests of others.

(3)   Increasing disarticulation between investments/responsibilities and rewards/rights

Leading on from this, a third and related element in my proposed 'feminisation of responsibility and obligation' is that while the onus of dealing with poverty is becoming progressively feminised, there is no obvious increase in women's rights and rewards – whether of a material or non-material nature. Gambian, Filipino and Costa Rican women frequently stress that they are working harder inside and outside the home. However, seldom, if ever (unless they head their own households), do they claim that this has entitled them to any benefits such as more personal over collective expenditure, more freedom, or licence to pursue goals which might be construed as individualistic or self-orientated. Indeed, in most cases I get the sense that women see no justification to ask or expect more as a result of giving more. This is even the case with young women who are undoubtedly the biggest beneficiaries of institutional attempts to level the gender playing field in such areas as education and employment. While young women's growing personal asset base might be expected to strengthen their bargaining power and aspirations, potential gains are frequently circumscribed by weighty social and familial constraints which lay them open to greater exploitation. Young women's higher earning capacity, for example, does not necessarily 'empower' or enable them to negotiate new deals within households, but simply exposes them to more demands. This undoubtedly owes in part to a seeming intransigence in traditional gender socialisation. In none of the case study countries do young women appear to be escaping housework and childcare from an early age, or from others' claims on the fruits of their enhanced capabilities and opportunities, or from the notion that part and parcel of 'being female' is to acquiesce to these expectations willingly and obligingly.

Conformity with gender-differentiated duties and privileges seems to be particularly marked in The Gambia. This is possibly because as a society in which respect, power and status increase with age, and where intergenerational family contracts remain strong in the absence of meaningful livelihood opportunities and alternative sources of welfare: 'children are likely to take the terms of the contract as given, rather than seeking to contest them or renege on them' (Kabeer, 2000: 465). Thus although education potentially offers young women a means of becoming stronger and more self-sufficient, it does not seem to be equipping them to challenge fundamental gender injustices in the home or beyond (see ECLAC, 2004b: 29).

Indeed, while some Costa Rican women profess that education and employment may even be a passport to avoiding marriage (which is often recognised as prejudicial to women), it is almost inevitable that they will spend some time in their lives cohabiting with men, and once in this situation are unlikely to be able to negotiate on the same terms. As noted by Lavinas and Nicoll (2006: 84) for Brazil, but eminently applicable to the case study contexts: 'the conjugal contract . . . places women in a relationship of subordination and dependence in the family ambit and . . . a sexual division of labour which reduces their autonomy and compromises their potential as human beings'.

Just as most women encounter major barriers to increased empowerment, men, despite their lesser inputs to household livelihoods, are managing to retain their traditional privileges, including the exercise of authority, distancing from the time and labour efforts necessary for household survival, and recourse to resource-draining 'escape routes' such as alcohol, drugs, and extramarital affairs. If this scenario is not puzzling given the perpetuation of patriarchal norms in families and in wider society, it is decidedly worrying that investments are becoming progressively detached from rights and rewards, and perceptibly evolving into a new and deeper form of female exploitation. Recognising that men's static or declining inputs to household livelihoods may owe to rising structural barriers to fulfilling the roles of 'breadwinner' and/or 'responsible father', this should not detract from the fact that this is likely to entrench, if not exacerbate, gender inequality – and at considerable financial, physical, psychological and emotional cost to their female counterparts. More disturbing still, perhaps, is that there are few signs of change across generations.

REVISITING THE 'FEMINISATION OF POVERTY': RETENTION OR REVISION?

The above findings raise important questions about how to proceed with the 'feminisation of poverty', which, in respect of its current referents, does not seem to capture the essence of where poor women's most significant contemporary privations lie. In my view the overemphasis on women's monetary poverty and on female household headship is misplaced. Gendered poverty goes well beyond the question of income, with a broader perspective on poverty also indicating that the 'feminisation' of privation may owe more to the persistence of male household headship (under patriarchal conditions) than a rise in the numbers of households headed by women.

Notwithstanding that the dearth of sex-disaggregated panel data makes it impossible to establish how many women are poorer than men or how gendered gaps in income are evolving over time, there is enough evidence of gender differences in wages, as well as of 'secondary poverty' under male household headship, to suggest that women are at greater risk of income poverty than men. However, this is not necessarily an ongoing or upward trend, added to which a possibly more significant tendency as far as women themselves are concerned, is that they are bearing an increasingly disproportionate responsibility for steering themselves and others through hardship. Indeed, following on from the observation made by UNMP/TFEGE (2005: 11), that 'Women's work, both paid and unpaid, is critical to the survival and security of poor households and an important route through which households escape poverty', the only grounds on which I feel we can sustain the idea that poverty is 'feminising' is if inputs are given as much emphasis as income, and due attention is paid to their subjective and objective corollaries (see also Chant, 2007).[3] The mounting *onus* on women to cope with household survival arises not only because they cannot necessarily rely on men and/or do not *expect* to rely on men, but because a growing number seem to be supporting men as well, whether through income or labour contributions. At the same time, this greater responsibility is not commensurately rewarded and, if anything, means more female exploitation. This underlines the argument that poverty is not just about the privation of minimum basic needs, but also 'the denial of opportunities and choices to individuals' (UN/UNIFEM, 2003: 19; see also Sané, 2005). While on one hand female household heads could conceivably be seen as an extreme case of 'choicelessness' and 'responsibility' – in having little option other than to fend for themselves and their dependents and on potentially weaker grounds given gender discrimination in society at large, this needs to be qualified: (a) because female-headed households do not necessarily lack male members; (b) free of a senior male 'patriarch', their households can become 'enabling spaces' in which there is scope to distribute household tasks and resources more equitably, and (c) women in *male*-headed households may be in the position of supporting not only children, but spouses as well, as an increasing proportion of men seem to be stepping out of the shoes of 'chief breadwinner' into those of 'chief spender'.

If classic conceptualisations of the 'feminisation of poverty' are methodologically and analytically inappropriate in depicting trends in gendered privation, then we arguably have two choices. Either the existing terminology is abandoned – and perhaps replaced with something akin to the 'feminisation of responsibility and/or obligation' or the 'feminisation of survival' (see earlier and note 1), or it is retained with the proviso that the poverty part of the construct refers not just to income but other, albeit related, privations. In my view, the latter option is preferable: first, because the 'feminisation of poverty' is succinct, well known, and has already gone some way to 'en-gender' poverty reduction strategies, and second because giving poverty a more explicit multidimensional emphasis would bring it more in line with poverty discourses in general. Provided it is made patently clear that poverty is not just about incomes, but inputs, then the 'feminisation of poverty' would have greater theoretical and empirical currency, as well as being more useful for policy.

IMPLICATIONS FOR RESEARCH AND METHODOLOGY

While the trends in gendered privation and inequality documented for The Gambia, the Philippines and Costa Rica might not apply in other countries in the Global South, it is important that future research helps to illuminate their broader relevance. This exercise would undoubtedly be aided by better sex-disaggregated data not only on incomes, but also on time-use, labour, assets and expenditure. Along the lines of proposals for improving the gender-responsiveness of MDGs and poverty assessment (Chapters 1 and 2), for example, one issue of particular importance will be to enhance the measurement and visibility of domestic labour and unpaid care work. This is not important for analysis, but is important for policy, when the idea that reproductive labour is a 'naturalised' attribute of women, is 'free', and 'limitless' in respect of supply (see Budlender, 2004; Molyneux, 2006a; 2006b), runs the risk of overburdening women, diminishing the levels and quality of care they provide, and undermining their rights to the equitable sharing of household resources (ibid.; also Folbre, 2006; UNDP, 1995: 98). An important complementary tool in determining gendered inputs to livelihoods will be to collect data not only on what women and men in poor households earn (or manage), but what they *spend* their money on, and/or the extent to which this expenditure is directed to collective household needs or to personal interests.

While household headship should definitely be retained as a criterion of differentiation in a broader but more nuanced concept of a 'feminisation of poverty', we need to know which sub-groups of female-headed households are especially prone to poverty (for example, in relation to stage in the life course, composition, marital status and so on – see Lampietti and Stalker, 2000: 25), as well as which axes of difference among women more generally, including age and ethnicity – make them particularly vulnerable to privation. As discussed earlier, age-disaggregated data is vital in respect of gaining a clearer idea of generational trends in gendered poverty.

Another crucial role for future research will be to get to grips with the elusive question of why women continue to tolerate lack of cooperation and support from men in their households, especially in light of Jackson's (2003: 476) argument that since 'Patriarchy rewards those that play by its own rules', it is likely to be 'from the women who are *not* offered much by patriarchy . . . that most gender experimentation and change will come' (emphasis in original).

A further issue is how the 'feminisation of poverty', however defined, relates to a possible 'masculinisation of wealth and privilege'. As we have seen in this book, despite some growth in women's capabilities and opportunities, men always seem to be one step ahead, possessing a seemingly infinite reservoir of props for asserting masculinity, and 're-masculinising' advantage. If there *is* a masculinisation of privilege going on, then attention needs to be focused not only on the 'female victims', but the structures which uphold gender inequality, just as more general discussions of poverty have identified the need to 'confront wealth and its privilege' (Murphy, 2001: 32; see also Chambers, 2001).

IMPLICATIONS FOR POLICY

In respect of the implications for policy, there is undoubtedly a case for challenging the current vogue for the 'feminisation' of anti-poverty programmes. As noted at various junctures in the book this has frequently not been in women's best interests when it capitalises on their 'voluntarism', reinforces or intensifies already heavy burdens of household survival, and entrenches subordinate familial roles (see Molyneux, 2006a; 2006b). As echoed by UN/UNIFEM (2003: 19): 'One might even argue that the economic and social reproductive realms which women are expected to tread, overextend the range of roles and responsibilities of women compared to men, which does not necessarily enlarge their life choices, but may even limit them.'

Although many anti-poverty programmes nominally claim to foment 'female empowerment', as Johnson (2005: 57) observes, 'more attention has usually been paid to women's poorer *condition* than to their inferior *position*, with steps taken to improve women's condition rarely challenging men's condition *or* position' (emphasis in original). As it is, a focus on practical gender needs alone may not even have that much impact on increasing women's incomes, with Sweetman (2005: 2) claiming that 'Solving material poverty is not possible for women who lack the power to challenge the discriminatory policies of social institutions ranging from the family to the state' (see also Mayoux, 2006).

Clearly much remains to be done in respect of determining different types of gendered poverty and to devise policies which are sensitive to variations among women.[4] As Gangopadhyay and Wadhwa (2003: 2–3) have argued:

If poverty incidence reflects a gender bias it is important to investigate where it originates. If it is in the workplace, such biases have to be fought differently from the case where it originates within the household. If the bias is in workplace, policy measures such as affirmative action may be a way out. On the other hand, if the bias against the girl child originates in the household, policies must aim at improving awareness within the family. To combat the first one requires a strict enforcement of laws. The second is a deeper social problem and laws alone may not help.

Recognising that ongoing attention needs to be paid to increasing women's access to employment and incomes, more dedicated attention still may have to be directed to eradicating deep-seated social and cultural norms and biases. Notwithstanding that 'changing gender cultures is a long-term process and not immediately tractable to government policies and projects' (Jackson, 2003: 476), and that home and family have nominally been regarded as 'private spheres' beyond the purview of the state, it is vital to recognise that an implicit recognition of family (and women's 'altruistic' and subordinate roles within it) drives current agendas for reducing poverty (see Molyneux, 2006a; 2006b). Building on Abeyesekera's (2004: 7) argument with respect to the MDGs that without acknowledging the family it is unlikely that any major changes in women's position will be effected, it is imperative that future attempts to reduce poverty and gender inequality tackle domestic issues in a more head-on fashion. As Jackson (2003: 477) contends: 'rather than wishing the family or household away, more detailed understanding of them is necessary'.

With this in mind, and while acknowledging the need for context-sensitive variations, one starting point might be for the current emphasis on women's 'co-responsibility' in anti-poverty programmes to stop going 'one-way' and to be matched by greater co-responsibility from those who benefit from their labour. Aside from bringing men on board to a greater extent in these initiatives, governments could do a great deal more in alleviating women's disproportionate responsibility for raising children in society at large through more flexible working hours, state-subsidised childcare and family benefits, and services to assist with household chores (ECLAC, 2004a: 38). As articulated by UN/UNIFEM (2003: 49): 'Social care generates positive externalities in that it allows individuals to enhance their capabilities, contributing to overall growth in the economy . . . Thus society in general benefits from the care an individual receives at home.' The underprovision of care is 'solved' by women, but at their expense, when ideally: 'caring labour and the costs of care should be borne equitably among women and men, as well as considered in national accounts and development plans' (ibid.).

Leading on from this, governments should probably play a more proactive role in stimulating greater and broader engagement by men in the domestic realm. Encouraging more participation by men in domestic labour and childcare, for example, would be one step towards rectifying gender imbalances not only in the home, but in the workforce, and thereby help to close gender gaps in time-use and income (see, for example, ECLAC, 2004b: 10; UNRISD, 2005: 60).

Another need is for greater monitoring and enforcement of paternal obligations. Ensuring that lone mothers receive maintenance payments, for example, could go a substantial way to reducing financial hardship. Acknowledging that it may be much more difficult to ensure men's compliance with economic obligations where households remain 'in-tact', one strategy might be to mount public information campaigns (as has been done with some success in relation to domestic violence in Nicaragua – see Solórzano et al., 2000), and/or to encourage men (with or without their spouses) to attend workshops in which they are exposed to family legislation and children's rights, and how these can (and should) be safeguarded in gender-egalitarian ways (see also Molyneux, 2006a). Such interventions may be more successful still where attempts are made to promote male participation in a portfolio of 'family' activities which extends beyond the generation of income, to emotional support and practical care (Chant, 2002b; UNICEF, 1997). As highlighted by England and Folbre (2002: 28): 'Less gender specialisation in the form of parental involvement could lead to improved outcomes for children, not only by improving mothers' economic position, but also by improving emotional connections between fathers and children', as has been demonstrated where men do play an active role in parenting (see, for example, Chant, 2000; Gutmann, 1996; 1999). On top of this, there is arguably a case for encouraging men's involvement with children who are not their biological offspring.[5] While such goals could conceivably be achieved in the context of local-level projects, broader state directives are also paramount, as noted by Corner (2002: 5):

> The experience of developed countries suggests that significant change in the sex distribution of unpaid housework and childcare requires it to be seen explicitly as a policy issue and as something that must be addressed in order to implement national and international commitments on gender equality and women's human rights.

Last but not least, and in the spirit of the BFPA, it is imperative to promote greater social acceptance, status and opportunity for female-headed households, and to treat them as a *part of* (rather than *apart from*), normative and/or legally endorsed arrangements for the rearing of children. As articulated by Baden (1999: 9):

> Legislative and policy frameworks are required which promote choice and flexibility in family arrangements (e.g. facilitating female-initiated divorce)

which recognise the wide variety of households that exist and their fluid nature, and which grant equal or parallel status to different family types, irrespective of their perceived moral legitimacy. (See also Safa, 1998; van Driel, 1994: 220.)

Although as noted for India by Gangopadhyay and Wadhwa (2003: 4) social biases against female-headed households 'may not get reflected in the incidence of (income) poverty, or for that matter, in any obvious economic outcome' (see also Mukhopadhyay, 2000), poor female heads and their children arguably have most to gain from greater support from state and society. A strengthening of women's 'fallback' position may not only lead to personal gains in bargaining power, but, as a result, ensure greater compliance from men with their familial obligations. This would help to mitigate the purported 'inter-generational transmission of disadvantage' children suffer when raised only by their mothers, lessen social stigmatisation against them, and even provide a platform from which to foment greater cooperation and equality between parents.

Nearly 3 billion of the world's population are currently estimated to receive a mere 1.2 per cent of the world's income (Sané, 2005: 6). Although it is impossible to determine how many of the latter are women, and whether their income poverty is increasing relative to that of men, the present analysis suggests that women are bearing a rising brunt of confronting poverty at the household level. Popularisation of the term the 'feminisation of poverty' has clearly raised women's visibility in poverty discourses and in anti-poverty initiatives. However, more value still could be gained by linking 'feminisation' to a multidimensional concept of poverty which addresses the myriad forms of privation and exploitation suffered by women, and which seem to be persisting, if not intensifying, across time, space, and generation.

NOTES

1. The term 'feminisation of responsibility and obligation' is more cumbersome than the 'feminisation of poverty' or the 'feminisation of survival'. However, the term is useful in respect of delineating the dimensions of poverty which appear to be affecting women most, and intensifying over time. The 'feminisation of responsibility' is intended to convey the idea that women are assuming greater liability for dealing with poverty, and the 'feminisation of obligation', that women have progressively less choice other than to do so. 'Duty' is implicated in 'obligation', with the salient aspects being that women have less scope to resist the roles and activities imposed on them structurally (for example through legal contracts or moral norms), or situationally (through the absence of spouses or male assistance), and that duty often becomes 'internalised', perceived as non-negotiable, and binding (see Chant, 2007).
2. That an ostensible reaffirmation of femininity may be a short-term strategy for women to improve their longer-term 'fallback' position has been noted by Gates (2002) in the

context of Mexico, where some women offer to do more unpaid work in the home as a means of getting their husbands' permission to take employment.

3. I am grateful to Liza Taylor, a student on my MSc course 'Gender, Development and Poverty' in 2005, for raising the very interesting question that if the 'feminisation of poverty' was to encompass the elements proposed in my construct of 'feminisation of responsibility and obligation', whether this would mean upward or downward revision of the widely circulated figure of women being 70 per cent of the world's poor. Although this cannot be determined with any precision, I anticipate on the basis of my field evidence that this may be greater.

4. Life course is a major issue here, with Agarwal (2001, cited in UN/UNIFEM, 2003: 12) suggesting that for girl children and adolescents, key interventions to reduce poverty might include nutrition, health care and education, whereas for women in their working years, assets and employment may be more relevant, and for senior women, social security.

5. In women-headed households, for example, men often perform parenting roles in their capacities as grandfathers, uncles, brothers and sons (see Fonseca, 1991).

Bibliography

Abeyesekera, Sunila (2004) 'Development and women's human rights', in Women's International Coalition for Economic Justice (WICEJ) (ed.) *Seeking Accountability on Women's Human Rights: Women Debate the UN Millennium Development Goals* (New York: WICEJ), pp. 6–9.

Acosta-Belén, Edna and Bose, Christine (1995) 'Colonialism, structural subordination and empowerment: women in the development process in Latin America and the Caribbean', in Christine Bose and Edna Acosta-Belén (eds) *Women in the Latin American Development Process* (Philadelphia, PA: Temple University Press), pp. 15–36.

Adaba, Gemma (2004) 'A view from labour', Women's International Coalition for Economic Justice (WICEJ) (ed.) *Seeking Accountability on Women's Human Rights: Women Debate the UN Millennium Development Goals* (New York: WICEJ), pp. 31–3.

Adepoju, Aderanti and Mbugua, Wariara (1997) 'The African family: an overview of changing forms', in Aderanti Adepoju (ed.) *Family, Population and Development in Africa* (London: Zed), pp. 41–59.

Adjamagbo-Johnson, Kafui (2004) 'From Beijing to Addis Ababa: what progress for African women?', *Pambazuka News*, September, pp. 1–11.

Aganon, Marie (2002a) 'Women workers and unions in the formal sector: adjusting to the crisis', in Jeanne Frances Illo and Rosalinda Pineda-Ofreneo (eds) *Carrying the Burden of the World: Women Reflecting on the Effects of the Economic Crisis on Women and Girls* (Quezon City: University of the Philippines Centre for Integrative and Development Studies), pp. 111–25.

Aganon, Marie (2002b) 'Women workers and unions in the midst of a continuing job crisis', in Jeanne Frances Illo and Rosalinda Pineda-Ofreneo (eds) *Carrying the Burden of the World: Women Reflecting on the Effects of the Economic Crisis on Women and Girls* (Quezon City: University of the Philippines Centre for Integrative and Development Studies), pp. 126–40.

Aganon, Marie (2003) 'Gender mainstreaming in the workplace in times of crisis', in Jeanne Frances Illo and Rosalinda Pineda-Ofreneo (eds) *Beyond the Crisis: Questions of Survival and Empowerment* (Quezon City: University of the Philippines Centre for Integrative and Development Studies and Centre for Women's Studies), pp. 129–48.

Agarwal, Bina (2001) *UN Expert Group Meeting on Gender and Poverty, Empowerment of Women Throughout the Life Cycle as a Transformative Strategy for Poverty Eradication: Some Issues* (New York: United Nations Division for the Advancement of Women [UNDAW]).

Aguilar, Delia (1988) *The Feminist Challenge: Initial Working Principles Towards Reconceptualising the Feminist Movement in The Philippines* (Manila: Asian Social Institute in cooperation with the World Association for Christian Communication).

Aguilar, Delia (1991) *Filipino Housewives Speak* (Manila: Rainfree Trading and Publishing).

Aikman, Sheila, Unterhalter, Elaine and Challender, Chloe (2005) 'The education MDGs: achieving gender equality through curriculum and pedagogy change', in Caroline Sweetman (ed.) *Gender and the Millennium Development Goals* (Oxford: Oxfam), pp. 44–55.

Alcid, Mary Lou (2002a) 'The impact of the Asian financial crisis on international labour migration of Filipino women', in Jeanne Frances Illo and Rosalinda Pineda-Ofreneo (eds) *Carrying the Burden of the World: Women Reflecting on the Effects of the Economic Crisis on Women and Girls* (Quezon City: University of the Philippines Centre for Integrative and Development Studies), pp. 83–96.

Alcid, Mary Lou (2002b) 'Trends in the overseas employment of Filipina workers four years after the Asian financial and economic crisis', in Jeanne Frances Illo and Rosalinda Pineda-Ofreneo (eds) *Carrying the Burden of the World: Women Reflecting on the Effects of the Economic Crisis on Women and Girls* (Quezon City: University of the Philippines Centre for Integrative and Development Studies), pp. 97–110.

Alliance for Popular Reorientation and Construction (APRC) (2001) *The APRC Education Plan and Programme*, http://www.edugambia.gm/aprc.html, accessed 28 March 2003.

Alméras, Diane (2000) 'Equitable social practices and masculine personal history: a Santiago study', *European Journal of Development Research*, 12:2, 139–52.

Anand, Sudhir and Sen, Amartya (2000) 'The income component of the Human Development Index', *Journal of Human Development*, 1:1, http://hdr.undp.org/docs/publications/background_papers/Anand_Sen_2000.pdf, accessed October 2004.

Angeles, Leonora (1990) 'Women's roles and status in the Philippines: a historical perspective', in Marjorie Evasco, Aurora Javate de Dios and Flor Caagusan (eds) *Women's Springbook: Readings on Women and Society* (Quezon City: Fresam Press), pp. 15–24.

Angeles, Leonora (2000a) 'Women, bureaucracy and the governance of poverty in Southeast Asia: integrating gender and participatory governance in poverty reduction programmes in the Philippines and Vietnam', paper presented at the DEVNET International Conference on 'Poverty, Prosperity, Progress', University of Victoria, Wellington, New Zealand, 17–19 November.

Angeles, Leonora (2000b) 'Women, bureaucracy and the governance of poverty in Southeast Asia: a preliminary study on the integration of gender and participatory governance in social service delivery in two Philippine cities', *Philippine Political Science Journal*, 20:46, 54–98.

Angeles, Leonora (2001) 'The Filipino male as "macho-machunurin": bringing men and masculinities into gender and development studies', *Kasarinlan* (Third World Studies Centre, University of The Philippines), 16:1, 9–30.

Angeles, Leonora (2003) 'Creating social spaces for transnational feminist advocacy: Canadian International Development Agency, the National Commission on the Role of Filipino Women and Philippine Women's NGOs', *The Canadian Geographer/Le Geographe Canadien*, 47:3, 283–302.

Ansell, Nicola (2001) ' "Because it's Our Culture!": (re)negotiating the meaning of lobola in Southern African secondary schools', *Journal of Southern African Studies*, 27:4, 697–716.

Ansell, Nicola (2003) 'Secondary schooling and rural youth transitions in Lesotho and Zimbabwe', paper presented at interdisciplinary research symposium 'Uncertain Transitions: Youth in a Comparative Perspective', Department of Geography, University of Edinburgh, 27 June.

Antrobus, Peggy (2004) 'MDGs – the most distracting gimmick', in Women's International Coalition for Economic Justice (WICEJ) (ed.) *Seeking Accountability on Women's Human Rights: Women Debate the UN Millennium Development Goals* (New York: WICEJ), pp. 14–16.

Antrobus, Peggy (2005) 'Critiquing the MDGs from a Caribbean perspective', in Caroline Sweetman (ed.) *Gender and the Millennium Development Goals* (Oxford: Oxfam), pp. 94–104.

Appleton, Simon (1991) 'Gender dimensions of structural adjustment: the role of economic theory and quantitative analysis', *IDS Bulletin*, 22:1, 17–22.

Appleton, Simon (1996) 'Women-headed households and household welfare: an empirical deconstruction for Uganda', *World Development*, 24:12, 1811–27.

Arias, Omar (2000) *Are All Men Benefiting from the New Economy? Male Economic Marginalisation in Argentina, Brazil and Costa Rica* (Washington DC: World Bank, LCSPR), www.worldbank.org/external/lac, accessed April 2006.

Arriagada, Irma (1998) 'Latin American families: convergences and divergences in models and policies', *CEPAL Review*, 65, 85–102.

Arriagada, Irma (2002) 'Cambios y Desigualdad en las Familias Latinoamericanas', *Revista de la CEPAL*, 77, 143–61.

Asgary, Nader and Pagán, José (2004) 'Relative employment and earnings of female household heads in Mexico, 1987–1995', *Journal of Developing Areas*, 38:1, 93–106.

Asian Development Bank (ADB) (2000) *Women in Pakistan: Country Briefing Paper* (Manila: ADB Programs Department [West] and Office of Environment and Social Development).

Asian Development Bank (ADB) (2002) *Sociolegal Status of Women in Indonesia, Malaysia, Philippines, and Thailand* (Manila: ADB).

Asian Development Bank (ADB) (2003) *Policy on Gender and Development* (Manila: ADB).

Asian Development Bank (ADB) (2004) *Country Gender Assessment: Philippines* (Manila: ADB).

Asian Development Bank (ADB) (2005a) *Country Assistance Plans – Philippines* (Manila: ADB), http://www.adb.org/Documents/CAPs/PHI/0100.asp, accessed 28 January 2005.

Asian Development Bank (ADB) (2005b) *Poverty in the Philippines*: *Income, Assets, and Access* (Manila: ADB).

Asien, Etumudon Ndidi (2003) *Helping The Gambia Out of Economic Difficulty* (Serrekunda: Ena International Enterprises).

Baden, Sally (1999) 'Gender, governance and the "feminisation of poverty"'. background paper prepared for UNDP meeting on 'Women and Political Participation: 21st Century Challenges', New Delhi, 24–26 March.

Baden, Sally, with Milward, Kirsty (1997) *Gender, Inequality and Poverty: Trends, Linkages, Analysis and Policy Implications* (Brighton: Institute of Development Studies, University of Sussex, Bridge Report No. 30).

Baden, Sally and Goetz, Anne Marie (1998) 'Who needs [sex] when you can have [gender]', in Cecile Jackson and Ruth Pearson (eds) *Feminist Visions of Development: Gender Analysis and Policy* (London: Routledge), pp. 19–38.

Badia, Monica (1999) *The Chilean 'Social Integration' Approach to Poverty Alleviation: The Case of the Programme for Female Heads of Households* (Hertford: University of Hertfordshire Business School, Employment Studies Paper No. 25).

Badilla, Ana Elena and Blanco, Lara (1996) *Código de la Mujer* (San José: Editorial Porvenir S.A./CECADE).

Badjie, Dembo (2003) *Report on Youth and Poverty for Project 552/GAM/0* (Banjul: SPACO).

Balisacan, Arsenio and Fuwa, Nobuhiko (2004) *Changes in Spatial Inequality in the Philippines*, Research Paper No. 2004/34 (Helsinki: World Institute for Development Economics Research).

Ball, Rochelle E. (2004) 'Divergent development, racialised rights: globalised labour markets and the trade of nurses – the case of the Philippines', *Women's Studies International Forum*, 27, 119–33.

Banzon-Bautista, Ma Cynthia Rose (1989) 'Studies of women in terms of socio-cultural dimensions', in Amaryllis Torres (ed.) *The Filipino Woman in Focus: A Handbook of Reading* (Bangkok: UNESCO).

Bardhan, Kalpana and Klasen, Stephan (1999) 'UNDP'S gender-related indices: a critical review', *World Development*, 27:6, 985–1010.

Barker, Gary and Knaul, Felicia, with Cassaniga, Neide and Schrader, Anita (2000) *Urban Girls: Empowerment in Especially Difficult Circumstances* (London: Intermediate Technology Publications).

Barquero, Jorge and Trejos, Juan Diego (2005) *Types of Household, Family Life Cycle and Poverty in Costa Rica*, California Center for Population Research On-Line Conference Paper Series, CCPR-CP-002-05 (Los Angeles: CCPR), http://repositories.cdlib.org/ccpr/olcp/ccpr.cp-002–05, accessed 18 May 2005.

Barrett, Hazel and Browne, Angela (1996) 'Export horticultural production in sub-Saharan Africa: the incorporation of the Gambia', *Geography*, 81:1, 47–56.

Barry, Tom (1991) *Costa Rica: A Country Guide*, 3rd edn (Albuquerque, NM: Inter-Hemispheric Education Resource Center).

Barton, Carol (2004) 'Introduction', in Women's International Coalition for Economic Justice (WICEJ) (ed.) *Seeking Accountability on Women's Human Rights: Women Debate the UN Millennium Development Goals* (New York: WICEJ), pp. 3–5.

Barton, Carol (2005) 'Where to for women's movements and the MDGs?', in Caroline Sweetman (ed.) *Gender and the Millennium Development Goals* (Oxford: Oxfam), pp. 25–35.

Bauer, Elaine and Thompson, Paul (2004) ' "She's always the person with a very global vision": the gender dynamics of migration, narrative interpretatioon, and the case of Jamaican transnational families', *Gender and History*, 16:2, 334–75.

Baulch, Bob (1996) 'Editorial. The new poverty agenda: a disputed consensus', *IDS Bulletin*, 27:1, 1–10.

Baylies, Carolyn (1996) 'Diversity in patterns of parenting and household formation', in Elizabeth Bortolaia Silva (ed.) *Good Enough Mothering? Feminist Perspectives on Lone Motherhood* (London: Routledge), pp. 76–96.

Beck, Tony (1999) *Using Gender-Sensitive Indicators* (London: Commonwealth Secretariat).

Benería, Lourdes (1991) 'Structural adjustment, the labour market and the household: the case of Mexico', in Guy Standing and Victor Tokman (eds) *Towards Social Adjustment: Labour Market Issues in Structural Adjustment* (Geneva: International Labour Organisation), pp. 161–83.

Benería, Lourdes (1999) 'The enduring debate over unpaid labour', *International Labour Review*, 138:3, 287–309.

Benería, Lourdes and Roldan, Martha (1987) *The Crossroads of Class and Gender: Industrial Homework, Subcontracting and Household Dynamics in Mexico City* (Chicago, IL: University of Chicago Press).

Bennagen, Pia C. (2000) *The Social Reform Council and National Anti-Poverty Commission, the Philippines* (Falmer: University of Sussex, Institute of Development Studies, Civil Society and Governance Programme).

Bergés, Ame R. (2005) 'Living standards and equality in Latin America over the long run', preliminary draft prepared for the ESRC Seminar Series 'Social Policy, Stability, and Exclusion in Latin America: Theories and Concepts', Institute for the Study of the Americas, University of London, 2–3 June.

Bertranou, Fabio, van Ginneken, Wouter and Solorio, Carmen (2004) 'The impact of tax-financed pensions on poverty reduction in Latin America: evidence from Argentina, Brazil, Chile, Costa Rica and Uruguay', *International Social Security Review*, 57:4, 3–18.

Bhat, Rashmi (2002) 'Feminisation of poverty and empowerment of women: an Indian perspective and experience', paper presented at Townsville International Women's Conference on 'Poverty, Violence and Women's Rights: Setting a Global Agenda', James Cook University, Townsville, Queensland, 3–7 July.

Bhavnani, Kum-Kum, Foran, John and Kurian, Priya A. (eds) (2003a) *Feminist Futures: Women, Culture and Development* (London: Zed).

Bhavnani, Kum-Kum, Foran, John and Kurian, Priya A. (2003b) 'An introduction to women, culture and development', in Kum-Kum Bhavnani, John Foran and Priya A. Kurian (eds) *Feminist Futures: Women, Culture and Development* (London: Zed), pp. 1–21.

Bibars, Iman (2001) *Victims and Heroines: Women, Welfare and the Egyptian State* (London: Zed).

Bjinsdorp, Mireille and Montgomery, Micheal (2003) *Gambia . . . The Smiling Coast: A Study of Child Sex Tourism in The Gambia and the Involvement of Dutch Tourists* (Bakau: Child Protection Alliance/The Hague: Terre des Hommes Netherlands).

Blanc-Szanton, Cristina (1990) 'Gender and inter-generational resource allocation among Thai and Sino-Thai households', in Leela Dube and Rajni Palriwala (eds) *Structures and Strategies: Women, Work and Family* (New Delhi: Sage), pp. 79–102.

Blumberg, Rae Lesser (1995) 'Introduction: engendering wealth and well-being in an era of economic transformation', in Rae Lesser Blumberg, Cathy Rakowski, Irene Tinker and Michael Monteón (eds) *Engendering Wealth and Well-Being: Empowerment for Global Change* (Boulder, CO: Westview), pp. 1–14.

Bolles, A. Lynn (1986) 'Economic crisis and female-headed households in urban Jamaica', in June Nash and Helen Safa (eds) *Women and Change in Latin America* (South Hadley, MA: Bergin and Harvey), pp. 65–83.

Bolt, Vincent and Bird, Kate (2003) *The Intrahousehold Disadvantages Framework: A Framework for the Analysis of Intra-household Difference and Inequality*, Chronic Poverty Research Centre Working Paper No. 32 (London: Overseas Development Institute).

Bongaarts, John (2001) *Household Size and Composition in the Developing World*, Working Paper No. 144 (New York: Population Council).

Borges Sugiyama, Natasja (2002) *Gendered Budget Work in the Americas: Selected Country Experiences* (Austin, TX: University of Texas at Austin).

Bortolaia Silva, Elizabeth (1996) 'Introduction', in Elizabeth Bortolaia Silva (ed.) *Good Enough Mothering? Feminist Perspectives on Lone Motherhood* (London: Routledge), pp. 1–9.

Bradshaw, Sarah (1995a) 'Women's access to employment and the formation of women-headed households in rural and urban Honduras', *Bulletin of Latin American Research*, 14:2, 143–58.

Bradshaw, Sarah (1995b) 'Female-headed households in Honduras: perspectives on rural–urban differences', *Third World Planning Review* (special issue on 'Gender and Development'), 17:2, 117–31.

Bradshaw, Sarah (1996a) 'Female-headed households in Honduras: a study of their formation and survival in low-income communities', unpublished PhD thesis (Department of Geography, London School of Economics).

Bradshaw, Sarah (1996b) 'Inequality within households: the case of Honduras', paper presented at the symposium 'Vulnerable Groups in Latin American Cities', Annual Conference of the Society of Latin American Studies, University of Leeds, 29–31 March.

Bradshaw, Sarah (2001) *Dangerous Liaisons: Women, Men and Hurricane Mitch* (Managua: Puntos de Encuentro).

Bradshaw, Sarah (2002) *Gendered Poverties and Power Relations: Looking Inside Communities and Households* (Managua: ICD, Embajada de Holanda, Puntos de Encuentro).

Bradshaw, Sarah and Linneker, Brian (2001) 'Challenging poverty, vulnerability and social exclusion in Nicaragua: some considerations for poverty reduction strategies', *The Nicaraguan Academic Journal – NAJ*, 2:2, 186–224.

Bradshaw, Sarah and Linneker, Brian (2003) *Challenging Women's Poverty: Perspectives on Gender and Poverty Reduction Strategies from Nicaragua and Honduras* (London: Catholic Institute of International Relations).

Bradshaw, Sarah, Linneker, Brian and Quirós Víquez, Ana (2002) 'Las Mujeres en Nicaragua, La Pobreza y Cómo se Pretende Reducirla', paper presented at the panel 'Reducción de la Pobreza con Enfoque de Género', Conferencia Centroamericana y del Caribe 'Reducción de la Pobreza, Gobernabilidad Democrática y Equidad de Género', Centro de Convenciones, Hotel Intercontinental Managua, 28–30 August.

Brenes Camacho, Gilbert (2005) *Left Behind in the Economic Crisis: Poverty Among the Elderly in Costa Rica*, California Center for Population Research On-Line Conference Paper Series, CCPR-CP-003-05 (Los Angeles: CCPR), http://repositories.cdlib.org/ccpr/olcp/ccpr.cp-003-05, accessed 18 May 2005.

BRIDGE (2001) Briefing paper on the 'feminisation of poverty' (prepared for the Swedish International Development Cooperation Agency), *BRIDGE Report No. 59* (Brighton: Institute of Development Studies, University of Sussex).

BRIDGE (2003) 'Gender and budgets', *Bridge Bulletin: Gender and Development in Brief*, issue 12 (Brighton: Institute of Development Studies, University of Sussex).

Brown, Suzanne Francis (2000) 'Women no cry: female-headed households in the Caribbean', in Judith Mirsky and Marty Radlett (eds) *No Paradise Yet: The World's Women Face a New Century* (London: Panos/Zed), pp. 101–18.

Bruce, Judith and Lloyd, Cynthia (1992) *Finding the Ties That Bind: Beyond Headship and the Household* (New York/Washington, DC: Population Council/International Center for Research on Women).

Brydon, Lynne and Legge, Karen (1996) *Adjusting Society: The IMF, the World Bank and Ghana* (London: I.B. Tauris).

Bucoy, Rhodora (1992) 'Some notes on the status of women in Cebu', *Review of Women's Studies* (University of the Philippines, Quezon City), 3:1, 33–50.

Budlender, Debbie (2000) *A Global Assessment of Gender Responsive Budget Initiatives* (Washington, DC: World Bank), www.worldbank.org/wbi/publicfinance/documents/gender/budlender.pdf, accessed August 2001.

Budlender, Debbie (2004) *Why Should We Care About Unpaid Care Work?* (New York: United Nations Development Fund for Women).

Budlender, Debbie and Hewitt, Guy (eds) (2002) *Gender Budgets Make More Cents: Country Studies and Good Practice* (London: Commonwealth Secretariat).

Budowski, Monica (2002) 'Lone motherhood in Costa Rica: a threat for society or a chance for change?', in Christian Giordano and Andrea Boscoboinik (eds) *Constructing Risk, Threat, Catastrophe* (Fribourg: University Press Fribourg Switzerland), pp. 121–43.

Budowski, Monica (2003) '"Yo Valgo". The importance of dignity for daily practice: lone mothers in Costa Rica' (Fribourg: University of Fribourg Switzerland, Habilitation manuscript).

Budowski, Monica and Guzmán, Laura (1998) 'Strategic gender interests in social policy: empowerment training for female heads of household in Costa Rica', paper presented at the International Sociological Association XIV World Congress of Sociology, Montreal, 26 July–1 August.

Budowski, Monica and Rosero Bixby, Luis (2003) 'Fatherless Costa Rica? Child acknowledgement and support among lone mothers', *Journal of Comparative Family Studies*, 34:2, 229–54.

Budowski, Monica, Tillman, Robin and Bergman, Manfred Max (2002) 'Poverty, stratification, and gender in Switzerland', *Swiss Journal of Sociology*, 28:2, 297–317.

Bullock, Susan (1994) *Women and Work* (London: Zed).

Bureau of Labour and Employment Statistics (BLES) (2004) *LABSTAT Updates*, 8:9 (DOLE, Manila) 'Highlights of the April 2004 Labour Force Survey'.

Bureau of Women and Young Workers (BWYW) (2002) *Eliminating the Worst Forms of Child Labour: The Philippine Time-Bound Programme* (Manila: BWYW, Department of Labour and Employment).

Bureau of Women and Young Workers (BWYW) (2003) *Republic Act No. 9321 and its Implementing Rules and Regulations* (Manila: BWYW, Department of Labour and Employment).

Buvinic, Mayra (1990) 'The vulnerability of women-headed households: policy questions and options for Latin America and the Caribbean', paper presented at the Economic Commission for Latin America and the Caribbean Meeting on 'Vulnerable Women', Vienna, 26–30 November.

Buvinic, Mayra (1995) *Investing in Women* (Washington, DC: International Center for Research on Women, Policy Series).

Buvinic, Mayra and Gupta, Geeta Rao (1993) 'Responding to insecurity in the 1990s: targeting woman-headed households and woman-maintained families in developing countries', paper presented at the International Workshop 'Insecurity in the 1990s: Gender and Social Policy in an International Perspective', London School of Economics and European Association of Development Institutes, London, 5–6 April.

Buvinic, Mayra and Gupta, Geeta Rao (1997) 'Female-headed households and female-maintained families: are they worth targeting to reduce poverty in developing countries?', *Economic Development and Cultural Change*, 45:2, 259–80.

Cagatay, Nilüfer (1998) *Gender and Poverty* (New York: United Nations Development Programme, Social Development and Poverty Elimination Division, Working Paper 5).

Caldwell, John (1976) 'Towards a restatement of demographic transition theory', *Population and Development Review*, 2:3–4, 321–65.

Caldwell, John (1977) *Population Growth and Family Change in Africa* (London: C. Hurst).

Camacho Zamora, Antonio (1985) 'En Busca del Paraíso Perdido: Ciclos Migratorios en Costa Rica, *Revista de Ciencias Sociales*, 2, 47–66.

Camara, Lamin, Njie, John C., Sowe, Falu and Peacock, Joseph Taiwo (2003) 'A country situational analysis on streetchildren in The Gambia', paper prepared for a West Africa Regional Civil Society Forum on Promoting and Protecting the Rights of Streetchildren, Accra, Ghana, 21–24 October.

Canadian International Development Agency (CIDA) (2001) *Gender Profile: The Philippines*, May 2001 (Hull, Quebec: CIDA), http://www.acdi-cida.gc.ca/cida_ind.nsf, accessed 20 May 2004.

Canadian International Development Agency (CIDA) (2002) *INC – Gender Profile: Costa Rica*, February 2002 (Hull, Quebec: CIDA), http://www.acdi-cida.gc.ca/cida_ind.nsf, accessed 13 April 2005.

Carba, Delia (2003) 'Maternal characteristics and first intercourse among Filipino adolescent girls', paper presented at 2003 Asia Pacific Conference on 'Reproductive and Sexual Health', Bangkok, Thailand, 6–10 October.

Carranza, María (2003) 'Making sense of common sense: female sterilisation in Costa Rica', unpublished PhD dissertation, Department of Social Anthropology, University of Cambridge.

Carstens, Agustín (2004) 'Twenty years without a crisis in Costa Rica: the IMF's view', speech given by Deputy Managing Director, IMF, at the Academy of Central America, 12 July, http://www.imf.org/external/np/speeches/2004, accessed 8 May 2005.

Castillo, Gelia (1991) 'Family and household: the microworld of the Filipino', in Department of Sociology-Anthropology (eds) *SA21: Selected Readings* (Quezon City: Ateneo de Manila University, Office of Research and Publications), pp. 244–50.

Castro, Carlos (2002) Informe Final de Investigación: Migración Nicaragüense en Costa Rica, mimeo (San José: Facultad Latinoamericano de Ciencias Sociales, Sede Académica Costa Rica).

Castro, Carlos (2004) 'Programas Gubernamentales Ante la Pobreza: Alcances y Limitaciones en la Ultima Década', in Proyecto Estado de la

Nación (PEN) *Décimo Informe Sobre el Estado de la Nación en Desarrollo Humano Sostenible* (San José: PEN), http://www.estadonacion.or.cr/Info2004/Paginas/ponencias.html, accessed 9 June 2005.

Central Department of Statistics (CSD) (1998) *1998 National Household Poverty Survey Report* (Banjul: CSD), http://www4.worldbank.org/afr/poverty/databank/docnav/show_doc.cfm?ID=2327, accessed 31 July 2003.

Central Department of Statistics (CSD) (2004) *Preliminary 2003 Census Results* (Banjul: CSD).

Centre for Women's Resources (CWR) (2003) 'The life and struggle of women workers under contractualisation', paper prepared for the Asia-Pacific Research Network (APRN) Conference on 'Globalisation and its Impact on Women's Labour', Bangkok, 18–20 June.

Centro Latinoamericano y Caribeño de Demografía (CELADE) (2002) *Los Adultos Mayores en América Latina y el Caribe: Datos e Indicadores* (Santiago de Chile: CELADE).

Centro Nacional para el Desarrollo de la Mujer y la Familia (CMF) (1996) *Plan Para la Igualdad de Oportunidades entre Mujeres y Hombres (PIOMH) 1996–1998* (San José: CMF).

Cerna, Madrilena de la (1992) 'Women empowering wimen: the Cebu experience', *Review of Women's Studies* (University of The Philippines, Quezon City), 3:1, 51–66.

Cerrutti, Marcela (2000) 'Economic reform, structural adjustment and female labour force participation in Buenos Aires, Argentina', *World Development*, 28:5, 879–91.

Chambers, Robert (1983) *Rural Development: Putting the Last First* (Harlow: Longman).

Chambers, Robert (1988) *Poverty in India: Concepts, Research and Reality* (Brighton: University of Sussex, Institute of Development Studies Discussion Paper No. 241).

Chambers, Robert (1989) 'Vulnerability: how the poor cope', *IDS Bulletin*, 20:2, 1–9.

Chambers, Robert (1995) 'Poverty and livelihoods: whose reality counts?', *Environment and Urbanisation*, 7:1, 173–204.

Chambers, Robert (1997) 'Vulnerability: how the poor cope', *IDS Bulletin*, 28:2, 1–19.

Chambers, Robert (2001) 'The world development report: concepts, content and a chapter 12', *Journal of International Development*, 13:3, 299–306.

Chant, Sylvia (1985) 'Single-parent families: choice or constraint? The formation of female-headed households in Mexican shanty towns', *Development and Change*, 16:4, 635–56.

Chant, Sylvia (1991a) *Women and Survival in Mexican Cities: Perspectives on Gender, Labour Markets and Low-Income Households* (Manchester: Manchester University Press).

Chant, Sylvia (1991b) 'Gender, households and seasonal migration in Guanacaste, Costa Rica', *European Review of Latin American and Caribbean Studies*, 50, 51–85.

Chant, Sylvia (1994) 'Women, work and household survival strategies in Mexico, 1982–1992', *Bulletin of Latin American Research*, 13:2, 203–33.

Chant, Sylvia (1996) *Gender, Urban Development and Housing* (New York: United Nations Development Programme, Publications Series for Habitat II, Volume 2).

Chant, Sylvia (1997a) *Women-Headed Households: Diversity and Dynamics in the Developing World* (Basingstoke: Macmillan).

Chant, Sylvia (1997b) 'Women-headed households: poorest of the poor? Perspectives from Mexico, Costa Rica and the Philippines', *IDS Bulletin*, 28:3, 26–48.

Chant, Sylvia (1999) 'Women-headed households: global orthodoxies and grassroots realities', in Haleh Afshar and Stephanie Barrientos (eds) *Women, Globalisation and Fragmentation in the Developing World* (Basingstoke: Macmillan), pp. 91–130.

Chant, Sylvia (2000) 'Men in crisis? Reflections on masculinities, work and family in north-west Costa Rica', *European Journal of Development Research*, 12:2, 199–218.

Chant, Sylvia (2002a) 'Whose crisis? Public and popular reactions to family change in Costa Rica', in Christopher Abel and Colin Lewis (eds) *Exclusion and Engagement: Social Policy in Latin America* (London: Institute of Latin American Studies), pp. 349–77.

Chant, Sylvia (2002b) 'Families on the verge of breakdown? Views on contemporary trends in family life in Guanacaste, Costa Rica', *Journal of Developing Societies*, 18:2–3, 109–48.

Chant, Sylvia (2003a) *Female Household Headship and the Feminisation of Poverty: Facts, Fictions and Forward Strategies* (London: London School of Economics, Gender Institute, New Working Paper Series, Issue 9).

Chant, Sylvia (2003b) *New Contributions to the Analysis of Poverty: Methodological and Conceptual Challenges to Understanding Poverty from a Gender Perspective* (Santiago de Chile: Comisión Económica para América Latina (CEPAL), Unidad Mujer y Desarrollo, Serie 47, www.eclac.org.

Chant, Sylvia (2006) *Revisiting the 'Feminisation of Poverty' and the UNDP Gender Indices: What Case for a Gendered Poverty Index?* LSE Gender Institute, New Series Working Paper, Issue 18, London.

Chant, Sylvia (2007) 'The "feminisation of poverty" and the "feminisation" of anti-poverty programmes: room for revision?', *Journal of Development Studies* (forthcoming).

Chant, Sylvia, with Craske, Nikki (2003) *Gender in Latin America* (London/New Brunswick, NJ: Latin America Bureau/Rutgers University Press).

Chant, Sylvia and Gutmann, Matthew (2000) *Mainstreaming Men into Gender and Development: Debates, Reflections and Experiences* (Oxford: Oxfam).

Chant, Sylvia and Jones, Gareth A (2005) 'Youth, gender and livelihoods: perspectives from Ghana and The Gambia', *Children's Geographies*, 3:2, 185–99.

Chant, Sylvia and McIlwaine, Cathy (1995) *Women of a Lesser Cost: Female Labour, Foreign Exchange and Philippine Development* (London: Pluto).

Chant, Sylvia and McIlwaine, Cathy (1998) *Three Generations, Two Genders, One World: Women and Men in a Changing Century* (London: Zed).

Charmes, Jacques and Wieringa, Saskia (2003) 'Measuring women's empowerment: an assessment of the Gender-Related Development Index and the Gender Empowerment Measure', *Journal of Human Development*, 4:3, 419–35.

Chen, Ling Ping (2005) 'Social and cultural dimensions of labour migration: a study of overseas Filipino workers', unpublished PhD dissertation, Faculty of Social and Economic Studies and Magdalene College, University of Cambridge.

Chen, Martha Alter, Vanek, Joann and Carr, Marilyn (2004) *Mainstreaming Informal Employment and Gender in Poverty Reduction: A Handbook for Policy-Makers and other Stakeholders* (London: Commonwealth Secretariat).

Chen, Marty and Drèze, Jean (1992) 'Widows and health in rural North India', paper presented at workshop on 'Health and Development in India', National Council of Applied Economic Research and the Harvard Center for Population and Development Studies, India International Center, New Delhi, 2–4 January.

Christopher, Karen, England, Paula, McLanahan, Sara, Ross, Katherin and Smeeding, Tim (2001) 'Gender inequality in affluent nations: the role of single motherhood and the state', in Koen Vleminckx and Tim Smeeding (eds) *Child Well-Being in Modern Nations* (Bristol: The Policy Press).

Cicerchia, Ricardo (1997) 'The charm of family patterns: historical and contemporary patterns in Latin America', in Elizabeth Dore (ed.)

Gender Politics in Latin America: Debates in Theory and Practice (New York: Monthly Review Press), pp. 118–33.

Clarke, Gerard and Sison, Marites (2003) 'Voices from the top of the pile: elite perceptions of poverty and the poor in the Philippines', *Development and Change*, 34:2, 215–42.

Colaboración Area Legal (CAL) (1997) 'Pulso Legislativo: Nuevos Proyectos de Ley', *Otra Mirada* (Centro Nacional para el Desarrollo de la Mujer y la Familia, San José), 1:2, 51.

Collins, Dana (2003) 'Gendered sexualities and lived experience: the case of gay sexuality in women, culture and development', in Kum-Kum Bhavnani, John Foran and Priya A. Kurian (eds) *Feminist Futures: Women, Culture and Development* (London: Zed), pp. 117–23.

Collins, Stephen (1991) 'The transition from lone-parent family to step-family', in Michael Hardey and Graham Crow (eds) *Lone-Parenthood: Coping with Constraints and Making Opportunities* (Hemel Hempstead: Harvester Wheatsheaf), pp. 156–75.

Colón-Warren, Alice (1998) 'The feminisation of poverty among women in Puerto Rico and Puerto Rican women in the Middle Atlantic Region of the United States', *The Brown Journal of World Affairs*, 5:2, 263–81.

Committee on the Elimination of Discrimination Against Women (CEDAW) (2003) *Fourth Periodic Reports of States Parties: Costa Rica* (New York: United Nations CEDAW).

Comisión Económica Para América Latina (CEPAL) (2001) *Panorama Social de América Latina 2000–2001* (Santiago: CEPAL), www.cepal.org, accessed August 2002.

Comisión Económica Para América Latina (CEPAL) (2002) *Boletín Demográfico No.70, América Latina y el Caribe: Indicadores Seleccionados con una Perspectiva de Género* (Santiago: CEPAL), www.cepal.org, accessed March 2003.

Consejo Social de Gobierno (CSG), República de Costa Rica and Sistema de las Naciones Unidas en Costa Rica (2004) *Primer Informe de Costa Rica sobre el Avance en el Cumplimiento de los Objectivos de Desarrollo del Milenio* (San José: CSG).

Consortium for Streetchildren (2003a) *Gambia Country Paper* (London: Consortium for Streetchildren).

Consortium for Streetchildren (2003b) *Painted Grey Faces: Behind the Bars and in the Streets. Philippine Report* (London: Consortium for Streetchildren).

Consortium for Streetchildren (2003c) *A Civil Society Forum for Anglophone West Africa on Promoting and Protecting the Rights of Streetchildren* (London: Consortium for Streetchildren).

Convention on the Elimination of All Forms of Discrimination Against Women (CEDAW) (2003) *Fourth Periodic Reports of States Parties: Costa Rica (CEDAW/C/CRI/4)* (New York: United Nations Division for the Advancement of Women).

Cook, Bill (ed.) (2002) *Participation: The New Tyranny* (London: Zed).

Corner, Lorraine (2002) 'Time use data for policy advocacy and analysis: a gender perspective and some international examples', paper presented at the National Seminar on Applications of Time Use Statistics, UNIFEM Asia-Pacific and Arab States, Regional Programme for Engendering Economic Governance, UNDP Conference Hall, Delhi, 8–9 October, http://www.unifem-ecogov-apas/ecogov-apas/EEGProjectsActivities/TimeUseMeeting, accessed December 2002.

Corner, Lorraine (2003) 'From margins to mainstream: from gender statistics to engendering statistical systems' (Bangkok: UNIFEM in Asia-Pacific and Arab States), http://www.unifem-ecogov-apas/ EEGKnowledgeBase/Engendering, accessed December 2003.

Cornia, Giovanni Andrea, Shorrocks, Anthony and van der Hoeven, Ralph (2004) 'WIDER perspectives on growth, inequality and poverty', *WIDER Angle* (World Institute for Development Economics Research, Helsinki), 1, 1–2.

Cornwall, Andrea (2000) 'Missing Men? Reflections on men, masculinities and gender in GAD', *IDS Bulletin*, 31:2, 18–27.

Cornwall, Andrea (2003) 'Whose voices? Whose choices? Reflections on gender and participatory development', *World Development*, 31:8, 1325–42.

Cornwall, Andrea and Lindisfarne, Nancy (1994) 'Dislocating masculinity: gender, power and anthropology', in Andrea Cornwall and Nancy Lindisfarne (eds) *Dislocating Masculinity: Comparative Ethnographies* (London: Routledge), pp. 1–47.

Cornwall, Andrea and White, Sarah (2000) 'Men, masculinities and development: politics, policies and practice', *IDS Bulletin*, 31:2, 1–6.

Costa Rica (CR) (2004) *Costa Rica: Report of Costa Rica on the Implementation of the Beijing Platform for Action and the Outcome of the Twenty-Third Special Session of the United Nations General Assembly*, http://www.cities_localgovernment.org/udg/upload/docs/COSTA_RICA _English.PDF, accessed 7 March 2006.

Council for the Welfare of Children (CWC) (2000) *Second Country Report on the Implementation of the Convention on the Rights of the Child (1995–2000)* (Manila: CWC).

Cueva Beteta, Hanny (2006) 'What is missing in measures of women's empowerment?', *Journal of Human Development*, 7:2, 221–41.

Cunningham, Wendy V. (2000) Sectoral allocation by gender in the 1990s: evidence from Argentina, Brazil and Costa Rica, mimeo, LCSPR-Gender (Washington, DC: World Bank).

Daleng, Tjabel (1998) *Costa Rica in Focus* (London/New York: Latin America Bureau/Interlink Books).

Davids, Tine and Driel, Francien van (2001) 'Globalisation and gender: beyond dichotomies', in Frans J. Schuurman (ed.) *Globalisation and Development Studies: Challenges for the 21st Century* (London: Sage), pp. 153–75.

Davids, Tine and Driel, Francien van (2005) 'Changing perspectives', in Tine Davids and Francien van Driel (eds) *The Gender Question in Globalisation: Changing Perspectives and Practices* (Aldershot: Ashgate), pp. 1–22.

Delamonica, Enrique, Donahue, Maureen and Minujin, Alberto (2004) *Children Living Only with Their Mothers. Are They Disadvantaged?* Report to UNICEF (New York: UNICEF).

Department for International Development (DFID) (2000) *Poverty Elimination and the Empowerment of Women* (London: DFID).

Department of Labour and Employment (DOLE) (1998) *Gender and Life Long Learning: Enhancing the Contributions of Women to SMEs in the Philippines for the 21st Century* (Manila: DOLE).

Department of Labour and Employment (DOLE) (2002) *Development of a Design for the Conduct of a National Migration Survey* (Manila: DOLE, Bureau of Labour and Employment Statistics).

Department of Labour and Employment (DOLE) (2003) *Final Report on the Development of Measurement Framework on Decent Work within the Philippine Context (Phase 1 of the Project on Development of the Philippine Decent Work Index)* (Manila: DOLE).

Department of Social Welfare and Development (DSWD) (2004) *Primer: Comprehensive Package of Services for Solo Parents* (Cebu City: DSWD, Field Office 7).

Department of Social Welfare and Development (DSWD)/United Nations Childrens Fund (UNICEF) (2003) *ERPAT: A Manual for Implementers and Father-Volunteers* (Manila: DSWD/UNICEF).

Department of State for Education (DOSE) (1998) Mission statement (Banjul: DOSE), http://www.edugambia.gm/Mission_Statement_And_Policy/body_mission.

Department of State for Education (DOSE) (2003) *Education Statistics* (Banjul: DOSE).

Department of State for Finance and Economic Affairs (DOSFEA) (2002) *Mainstreaming Poverty and Gender Project: Output to Purpose Review, 19–22 January 2002* (Banjul: DOSFEA).

Department of State for Finance and Economic Affairs (DOSFEA) (2004) *Progress Report on SPA II/PRSP Completion and Progress in Implementation, July 2002–December 2003* (Banjul: DOSFEA).

Department of State for Finance and Economic Affairs (DOSFEA) (2006) *Second Poverty Reduction Strategy. PRSP II:2007890–2011. A Medium Term Plan for Operationalising Vision 2020 (Cabinet Copy)* (Banjul: DOSFEA).

Dia, Ibrahima Amadou (2001) ' "Feminisation" of poverty, informal sector and masculinity in a global area: the experience of Senegalese women', paper prepared for Research Committee 19 on Poverty, Social Welfare and Social Policy, University of Oviedo, Spain, 6–9 September.

Dierckxsens, Wim (1992) 'Impacto del Ajuste Estructural Sobre la Mujer Trabajadora en Costa Rica', in Acuña-Ortega, Marvin (ed) *Cuadernos de Política Económica* (Heredia: Universidad Nacional de Costa Rica), pp. 2–59.

Dietz, Tom (2001) 'The Agenda', in Neil Middleton, Phil O'Keefe and Rob Visser (eds) *Negotiating Poverty: New Directions, Renewed Debate* (London: Pluto), pp. 19–25.

Dijkstra, A. Geske and Hanmer, Lucia (2000) 'Measuring socio-economic inequality: towards an alternative to the UNDP Gender-Related Development Index', *Feminist Economics*, 6:2, 41–75.

Dixon, John and Macarov, David (eds) (1998) *Poverty: A Persistent Global Reality* (London: Routledge).

Dore, Elizabeth (1997) 'The holy family: imagined households in Latin American history' in Elizabeth Dore (ed.) *Gender Politics in Latin America: Debates in Theory and Practice* (New York: Monthly Review Press), pp. 101–17.

Driel, Francien van (1994) *Poor and Powerful: Female-headed Households and Unmarried Motherhood in Botswana* (Saarbrücken: Verlag für Entwicklungspolitik Breitenbach GmbH, Nijmegen Studies 16).

Duclos, Jean-Yves and Wodon, Quentin (2004) 'What is pro-poor?', mimeo (Washington, DC: World Bank, LCSPR).

Dumont, Jean-Paul (1994) 'Matrons, maids and mistresses: Philippine domestic encounters', *Philippine Quarterly of Culture and Society*, 22, 174–91.

Durbin, Elizabeth (1999) 'Towards a gendered human poverty measure', *Feminist Economics*, 5:2, 105–8.

Dwyer, Daisy and Bruce, Judith (eds) (1988) *A Home Divided: Women and Income in the Third World* (Stanford, CA: Stanford University Press).

Economic Comission for Latin America and the Caribbean (ECLAC) (2004a) *Social Panorama of Latin America 2004* (Santiago de Chile: ECLAC).

Economic Commission for Latin America and the Caribbean (ECLAC) (2004b) *Roads Towards Gender Equity in Latin America and the Caribbean* (Santiago de Chile: ECLAC).

Economist Intelligence Unit (EIU) (2004a) *Country Report: Senegal, The Gambia, Mauritania* (London: EIU).

Economist Intelligence Unit (EIU) (2004b) *Country Report: Philippines* (London: EIU).

Economist Intelligence Unit (EIU) (2004c) *Country Report: Costa Rica* (London: EIU).

Economist Intelligence Unit (EIU) (2005a) *Country Report: The Gambia, Mauritania* (London: EIU).

Economist Intelligence Unit (EIU) (2005b) *Country Report: Philippines* (London: EIU).

Economist Intelligence Unit (EIU) (2005c) *Country Report: Costa Rica* (London: EIU).

Economist Intelligence Unit (EIU) (2006a) *Country Report: Mauritania, The Gambia* (London: EIU).

Economist Intelligence Unit (EIU) (2006b) *Country Report: Philippines* (London: EIU).

Economist Intelligence Unit (EIU) (2006c) *Country Report: Costa Rica* (London: EIU).

Edwards, Rosalind and Duncan, Simon (1996) 'Lone mothers and economic activity', in Fiona Williams (ed.) *Social Policy: A Reader* (Cambridge: Polity Press).

Elder, Sara and Schmidt, Dorothea (2004) *Global Employment Trends for Women, 2004* (Geneva: International Labour Organisation).

Elson, Diane (1989) 'The impact of structural adjustment on women: concepts and issues', in Bade Onimode (ed.) *The IMF, the World Bank and the African Debt Vol 2: The Social and Political Impact* (London: Zed), pp. 55–74.

Elson, Diane (1991) 'Structural adjustment: its effects on women', in Tina Wallace, with Candida March (eds) *Changing Perceptions: Writings on Gender and Development* (Oxfam: Oxford), pp. 39–53.

Elson, Diane (1992) 'From survival strategies to transformation strategies: women's needs and structural adjustment' in Lourdes Benería and Shelley Feldman (eds) *Unequal Burden: Economic Crisis, Persistent Poverty and Women's Work* (Boulder, CO: Westview), pp. 26–48.

Elson, Diane (1995) 'Gender awareness in modelling structural adjustment', *World Development*, 32:11, 1851–68.

Elson, Diane (1998) 'Integrating gender issues into national budgetary policies and procedures: some policy options', *Journal of International Development*, 10, 929–41.

Elson, Diane (1999a) 'Labour markets as gendered institutions: equality, efficiency and empowerment issues', *World Development*, 27:3, 611–27.

Elson, Diane (1999b) *Gender Budget Initiatives*, background paper (London: Commonwealth Secretariat).

Elson, Diane (2002) 'Gender justice, human rights and neo-liberal economic policies', in Maxine Molyneux and Shahra Razavi (eds) *Gender Justice, Development and Rights* (Oxford: Oxford University Press), pp. 78–114.

Elson, Diane (2004) 'Engendering government budgets in the context of globalisation(s)', *International Feminist Journal of Politics*, 6:4, 623–42.

England, Paula and Folbre, Nancy (2002) 'Involving dads: parental bargaining and family well-being', in Catherine Tamis-LeMonda and Natasha Cabrera (eds) *Handbook of Father Involvement: Multidisciplinary Perspectives* (Mahwah, NJ: Lawrence Erlbaum Associates).

Engle, Patrice L. (1995) 'Father's money, mother's money, and parental commitment: Guatemala and Nicaragua' in Rae Lesser Blumberg, Cathy Rakowski, Irene Tinker and Michael Monteón (eds) *Engendering Wealth and Well-Being: Empowerment for Global Change* (Boulder, CO: Westview), pp. 155–79.

Enriquez, Virgilio (1991) 'Kapwa: a core concept in Filipino social psychology', in Department of Sociology-Anthropology (eds) *SA21: Selected Readings* (Quezon City: Ateneo de Manila University, Office of Research and Publications), pp. 98–105.

Enríquez Rosas, Recío (2002) 'Women and survival strategies in poor urban contexts: a case study from Guadalajara, Mexico', *Journal of Developing Societies*, 18:2–3, 81–108.

Equal Opportunities Commission (EOC) (2003) *Gender and Poverty in Britain* (Manchester: EOC).

Escobar Latapí, Agustín (1998) 'Los Hombres y Sus Historias: Reestructuración y Masculinidad en México', *La Ventana* (Universidad de Guadalajara), pp. 122–73.

Escobar Latapí, Agustín (2003) 'Men and their histories: restructuring, gender inequality and life transitions in urban Mexico', in Matthew Gutmann (ed.) *Changing Men and Masculinities in Latin America* (Durham, NC: Duke University Press), pp. 84–114.

Etemadi, Felisa (2004) 'The politics of engagement: gains and challenges of the NGO coalition in Cebu City', *Environment and Urbanisation*, 16:1, 79–93.

Eviota, Elizabeth (1992) *The Political Economy of Gender: Women and the Sexual Division of Labour in the Philippines* (London: Zed).

Fashoyin, Tayo (2003) *Social Dialogue and Labour Market Performance in the Philippines*, InFocus Programme on Social Dialogue, Labour Law and Labour Administration, Working Paper 14 (Geneva: International Labour Organisation).

Fauné, María Angélica (1997) 'Costa Rica: Las Inequidades de Género en el Marco de la Apertura Comercial y la Reestructuración Productiva: Análsis a Nivel Macro, Meso, Micro', in Diane Elson, María Angélica Fauné, Jasmine Gideon, Maribel Gutiérrez, Armida López de Mazier and Eduardo Sacayón (eds) *Crecer con la Mujer: Oportunidades para el Desarrollo Económico Centroamericano* (San José: Embajada Real de los Países Bajos), pp. 51–126.

Feijoó, María del Carmen (1999) 'De Pobres Mujeres a Mujeres Pobres', in Mercedes González de la Rocha (ed.) *Divergencias del Modelo Tradicional: Hogares de Jefatura Femenina en América Latina* (México DF: Centro de Investigaciones y Estudios Superiores en Antropología Social), pp. 155–62.

Fernández-Kelly, María Patricia (1983) 'Mexican border industrialisation, female labour force participation and migration', in June Nash and María Patricia Fernández-Kelly (eds) *Women, Men and the International Division of Labour* (Albany, NY: State University of New York Press), pp. 205–23.

Fight Against Social and Economic Exclusion Programme (FASE) (2001) *Micro-Enterprise Development Training Manual* (Banjul: FASE).

Fight Against Social Exclusion (FASE) (2003) *Mid-Term Evaluation Report* (Bakau: FASE).

Finne, Giselle (2001) 'Feminisation of poverty' (Geneva: World Alliance of YMCAs, Global Programmes and Issues), http://www.ymca.int/programs.

Flor, Celia and Lizares-Si, Andrea (2002) 'The Philippines: getting smart with local budgets', in Debbie Budlender and Guy Hewitt (eds) *Gender Budgets Make More Cents* (London: Commonwealth Secretariat), pp. 98–116.

Floro, Maria Sagrario (1995) 'Women's well-being, poverty and work intensity', *Feminist Economics*, 1:3, 1–25.

Folbre, Nancy (1991) 'Women on their own: global patterns of female headship', in Rita S. Gallin and Ann Ferguson (eds) *The Women and International Development Annual Vol. 2* (Boulder, CO: Westview), pp. 69–126.

Folbre, Nancy (1994) *Who Pays for the Kids? Gender and the Structures of Constraint* (London: Routledge).

Folbre, Nancy (2006) 'Gender, empowerment, and the care economy', *Journal of Human Development*, 7:2, 183–99.

Fonseca, Claudia (1991) 'Spouses, siblings and sex-linked bonding: a look at kinship organisation in a Brazilian slum', in Elizabeth Jelin (ed.)

Family, Household and Gender Relations in Latin America (London: Kegan Paul International/Paris: UNESCO), pp. 133–60.

Fonseca, Claudia (2003) 'Philanderers, cuckolds and wily women: reexamining gender relations in a Brazilian working class neighbourhood', in Matthew Gutmann (ed.) *Changing Men and Masculinities in Latin America* (Durham, NC: Duke University Press), pp. 61–83.

Ford, Reuben (1996) *Childcare in the Balance: How Lone Parents Make Decisions About Work* (London: Policy Studies Institute).

Franco, Susana (2003) 'Different concepts of poverty: an empirical investigation and policy implications', paper prepared for Conference on Inequality, Poverty and Human Well-Being, World Institute for Development Economics Research, United Nations University, Helsinki, 30–31 May.

Fraser, Arabella (2005) 'Approaches to reducing maternal mortality: Oxfam and the MDGs', in Caroline Sweetman (ed.) *Gender and the Millennium Development Goals* (Oxford: Oxfam), pp. 36–43.

Freedman, Lynn (2004) 'Health as a human right: maternal mortality and the MDGs', in Women's International Coalition for Economic Justice (WICEJ) (ed.) *Seeking Accountability on Women's Human Rights: Women Debate the UN Millennium Development Goals* (New York: WICEJ), pp. 36–8.

Fukuda-Parr, Sakiko (1999) 'What does feminisation of poverty mean? It isn't just lack of income', *Feminist Economics*, 5:2, 99–103.

Fuller, Norma (2000) 'Work and masculinity among Peruvian urban men', *European Journal of Development Research*, 12:2, 93–114.

Funkhouser, Edward (1996) 'The urban informal sector in Central America: household survey evidence', *World Development*, 12:11, 1737–51.

Fuwa, Nobuhiko (2000) 'The poverty and heterogeneity among female-headed households revisited: the case of Panama', *World Development*, 28:8, 1515–42.

Fuwa, Nobuhiko (2001) 'A note on the analysis of female-headed households in developing countries', mimeo, Agricultural Economics Department, Faculty of Horticulture, Chiba University, Japan.

Fyvie, Claire and Ager, Alistair (1999) NGOs and innovation: organisational characteristics and constraints in development assistance work: The Gambia, *World Development*, 27:8, 1383–95.

Gafar, John (1998) 'Growth, inequality and poverty in selected Caribbean and Latin American countries, with emphasis on Guyana', *Journal of Latin American Studies*, 30:3, 591–617.

Gambia Committee on Traditional Practices Affecting the Health of Women and Children (GAMCOTRAP) (1999) *Reaching Adolescents with Messages of Reproductive Health* (Bakau: GAMCOTRAP).

Gambia National Youth Service Scheme (GNYSS) (2001) *The Gambia National Youth Service Scheme* (Fajara: The Observer Press).

Gangopadhyay, Shubhashis and Wadhwa, Wilima (2003) 'Are Indian female-headed households more vulnerable to poverty?', mimeo (Delhi: Indian Development Foundation).

Gates, Leslie C. (2002) 'The strategic uses of gender in household negotiations: women workers on Mexico's northern border', *Bulletin of Latin American Research*, 21:4, 507–26.

Gaudart, Dorothea (2002) 'Charter-based activities regarding women's rights in the United Nations and specialised agencies', in Wolfgang Benedek, Esther M. Kisaakye and Gerd Oberleitner (eds) *Human Rights of Women: International Instruments and African Experiences* (London: Zed), pp. 50–104.

Geldstein, Rosa (1994) 'Working class mothers as economic providers and heads of families in Buenos Aires', *Reproductive Health Matters*, 4, 55–64.

Geldstein, Rosa (1997) *Mujeres Jefas de Hogar: Familia, Pobreza y Género* (Buenos Aires: UNICEF-Argentina).

Gibson-Graham, J.K. (2005) 'Surplus possibilities: post development and community economies', *Singapore Journal of Tropical Geography*, 16:1, 4–26.

Gindling, T.H. and Terrell, Katherine (2004) *Legal Minimum Wages and the Wages of Formal and Informal Sector Workers in Costa Rica* (Baltimore, MD: University of Maryland Baltimore County, Department of Economics Working Paper No. 04-102).

Gobierno de Costa Rica (GCR) (2005) *Un Año Crucial para Costa Rica: Anexo a; Discurso del Presidente de la República, Doctor Abel Pacheco de Espriella, ante la Asemblea Legislativa*, 1 May 2005, http://216.239.59.104/search?q=cache:PS-SWxfFL8c.J:www.asamblea. go.cr/actual/bolet, accessed 18 May 2005.

Goldberg, Gertrude (1998) 'The feminisation of poverty: here to stay?', *The Brown Journal of World Affairs*, 5:2, 161–86.

Goldberg, Gertrude and Kremen, Eleanor (1987) 'The feminisation of poverty: only in America', *Social Policy*, 17, 3–14.

Goldenburg, Olga (1994) 'En Clave de Género', in Olga Goldenburg and Victor Hugo Acuña (eds) *Género y la Informalidad* (San José: FLACSO), pp. 185–233.

Goldstein, Markus (2003) 'Intra-household efficiency and individual insurance in Ghana', paper in preparation, DESTIN, London School of Economics.

Goldstein, Markus, de Janvry, Alain and Sadoulet, Elisabeth (2001) 'Is a friend in need a friend indeed? Inclusion and exclusion in mutual insurance networks in southern Ghana', paper prepared for 'Insurance Against Poverty' programme, World Institute for Development Economics Research (WIDER), United Nations University, Helsinki.

Gomáriz, Enrique (1997) *Introducción a los Estudios Sobre la Masculinidad* (San José: Centro Nacional para el Desarrollo de la Mujer y Familia).

Gonzales, Ernesto (2003) 'Editorial summary', in Ernesto Gonzales (ed.) *Globalisation and the Asian Family. Volume 1: The Filipino Family Survey 2003* (Manila: University of Santo Tomas Social Research Centre), pp. 1–13.

González de la Rocha, Mercedes (1988a) 'Economic crisis, domestic reorganisation and women's work in Guadalajara, Mexico', *Bulletin of Latin American Research*, 7:2, 207–23.

González de la Rocha, Mercedes (1988b) 'De Por Qué las Mujeres Aguantan Golpes y Cuernos: Un Análsis de Hogares sin Varón en Guadalajara', in Luisa Gabayet, Patricia García, Mercedes González de la Rocha, Sylvia Lailson and Agustín Escobar (eds) *Mujeres y Sociedad: Salario, Hogar y Acción Social en el Occidente de México* (Guadalajara: El Colegio de Jalisco/CIESAS del Occidente), pp. 205–27.

González de la Rocha, Mercedes (1994a) *The Resources of Poverty: Women and Survival in a Mexican City* (Oxford: Blackwell).

González de la Rocha, Mercedes (1994b) 'Household headship and occupational position in Mexico', in Eileen Kennedy and Mercedes González de la Rocha, *Poverty and Well-Being in the Household: Case Studies of the Developing World* (San Diego, CA: Center for Iberian and Latin American Studies, University of California San Diego), pp. 1–24.

González de la Rocha, Mercedes (1999) 'A Manera de Introducción: Cambio Social, Transformación de la Familia y Divergencias del Modelo Tradicional', in Mercedes González de la Rocha (ed.) *Divergencias del Modelo Tradicional: Hogares de Jefatura Femenina en América Latina* (México DF: Centro de Investigaciones y Estudios Superiores en Antropología Social/Plaza y Valdés Editores), pp. 19–36.

González de la Rocha, Mercedes (2001) 'From the resources of poverty to the poverty of resources: the erosion of a survival model', *Latin American Perspectives*, 28:4, 72–100.

González de la Rocha, Mercedes (2002) 'The urban family and poverty in Latin America', in Jennifer Abassi and Sheryl L. Lutjens (eds) *Rereading Women in Latin America and the Caribbean: The Political Economy of Gender* (Lanham, MD: Rowman and Littlefield), pp. 61–77.

González de la Rocha, Mercedes (2003a) 'The construction of the myth of survival', paper prepared for International Workshop: 'Feminist Fables and Gender Myths: Repositioning Gender in Development Policy and

Practice', Institute of Development Studies, University of Sussex, 2–4 July.

González de la Rocha, Mercedes (2003b) 'Oportunidades y Capital Social', paper presented at the conference/workshop 'Capital Social y programas de Superación de la Pobreza: Lecciones para la Acción', Comisión Económica para América Latina, Santiago de Chile, 10–11 November.

González de la Rocha, Mercedes and Grinspun, Alejandro (2001) 'Private adjustments: households, crisis and work', in Alejandro Grinspun (ed.) *Choices for the Poor: Lessons from National Poverty Strategies* (New York: UNDP), pp. 55–87.

Goodno, James (1991) *The Philippines: Land of Broken Promises* (London: Zed).

Government of The Gambia (GOTG) (1998) *Initial Report of The Gambia on the UN Convention on the Rights of the Child* (Banjul: GOTG).

Government of the Gambia (GOTG) (2000) *1998 National Household Poverty Survey Report* (Banjul: Department of State for Finance and Economic Affairs).

Government of The Gambia/Department for International Development (GOTG/DFID) (1998) *Programme Strategy Reviews 25–30 April* (London: DFID).

Government of The Gambia (GOTG) in collaboration with UNICEF (2000) *The Gambia Multiple Indicator Cluster Survey Report, 2000* (Banjul: GOTG/UNICEF).

Graham, Carol (1996) *Gender Issues in Poverty Alleviation: Recent Experiences with Demand-Based Programmes in Latin America, Africa and Eastern Europe*, Issues in Development Discussion Paper (Geneva: International Labour Organisation).

Graham, Hilary (1987) 'Being poor: perceptions and coping strategies of lone mothers', in Julia Brannen and Gail Wilson (eds) *Give and Take in Families: Studies in Resource Distribution* (London: Allen and Unwin), pp. 56–74.

Graham, Wendy (2004) 'Exploring the links between maternal death and poverty', *In Focus* (UNDP International Poverty Centre), 3: May, 6–8, http://www.undp.org/povercentre/newsletters/infocus 3May04eng.pdf, accessed May 2004.

Greeley, Martin (2001) 'Pro-poor growth: a review of three issues informing the current policy agenda', in Neil Middleton, Phil O'Keefe and Rob Visser (eds) *Negotiating Poverty: New Directions, Renewed Debate* (London: Pluto), pp. 54–73.

Green, Duncan (1995) *Silent Revolution: The Rise of Market Economics in Latin America* (London: Cassell/Latin America Bureau).

Grinspun, Alejandro (2004) 'Defining pro-poor growth: a response to Kakwani', *One Pager* (IPC, United Nations Development Programme, Brasilia), 4: November.

Grosh, Margaret (1994) *Administering Targeted Social Programs in Latin America: From Platitudes to Practice* (Washington, DC: World Bank).

Grown, Caren and Rao Gupta, Geeta (2004) 'An agenda for engendering: the Millennium Project Task Force on Education and Gender Equality', in Women's International Coalition for Economic Justice (WICEJ) (ed.) *Seeking Accountability on Women's Human Rights: Women Debate the UN Millennium Development Goals* (New York: WICEJ), pp. 42–3.

Guardian, E.A. (2003) 'Impact of access to land on food security and poverty: the case of Philippine agrarian reform', *Land Reform* (FAO, Rome), 2003/2, 70–83.

Gudmundson, Lowell (1986) *Costa Rica Before Coffee: Society and Economy on the Eve of the Export Boom* (Baton Rouge, LA: Louisiana State University Press).

Gutmann, Matthew (1996) *The Meanings of Macho: Being a Man in Mexico City* (Berkeley, CA: University of California Press).

Gutmann, Matthew (1999) 'A Manera de Conclusión: Solteras y Hombres. Cambio e Historia', in Mercedes González de la Rocha (ed.) *Divergencias del Modelo Tradicional: Hogares de Jefatura Femenina en América Latina* (México DF: Centro de Investigaciones y Estudios Superiores en Antropología Social), pp. 163–72.

Guzman, Odine de (2003) 'Overseas Filipino workers, labour circulation in Southeast Asia, and the (mis)management of overseas migration programmes, *Kyoto Review of Southeast Asia*, 4, http://kyotoreview.cseas.kyoto-u.ac.jp/issue/issue3/index.html, accessed September 2004.

Hackenberg, Robert, Murphy, Arthur and Selby, Henry (1981) 'The household in the secondary cities of the Third World', paper prepared in advance for the Wenner-Gren Foundation Symposium 'Households: Changing Form and Function', New York, 8–15 October.

Haddad, Lawrence (1991) 'Gender and poverty in Ghana: a descriptive analysis of selected outcomes', *IDS Bulletin*, 22:1, 5–16.

Hall, Carolyn (1985) *Costa Rica: A Geographical Interpretation in Historical Perspective* (Boulder, CO: Westview).

Hardey, Michael and Glover, Judith (1991) 'Income, employment, daycare and lone parenthood', in Michael Hardey and Graham Crow (eds) *Lone Parenthood: Coping with Constraints and Making Opportunities* (Hemel Hempstead: Harvester Wheatsheaf), pp. 88–109.

Harper, Caroline (2004) 'Escaping poverty cycles', *In Focus* (UNDP International Poverty Centre, Brasilia), March, 3–4.

Harris, Olivia (1981) 'Households as natural units' in Kate Young, Carol Wolkowitz and Roslyn McCullogh (eds) *Of Marriage and the Market* (London: CSE Books), pp. 48–67.

Hart, Gillian (1997) 'From "rotten wives" to "good mothers": household models and the limits of economism', *IDS Bulletin*, 28:3, 14–25.

Hayes, Ceri (2005) 'Out of the margins: the MDGs through a CEDAW lens', in Caroline Sweetman (ed.) *Gender and the Millennium Development Goals* (Oxford: Oxfam), pp. 67–78.

Herrin, Alejandro, Orbeta Jr, Aniceto, Acejo, Iris, Cuenca, Janet and del Prado, Fatima (2003) *An Evaluation of the Philippine Population Management Programme (PPMP)*, Discussion Paper Series No. 2003-18 (Makati City: Philippine Institute for Development Studies).

Hewitt, Patricia and Leach, Penelope (1993) *Social Justice, Children and Families* (London: Institute for Public Policy Research).

Heyzer, Noeleen (2005) 'Making the links: women's rights and empowerment are key to achieving the Millennium Development Goals', in Caroline Sweetman (ed.) *Gender and the Millennium Development Goals* (Oxford: Oxfam), pp. 9–12.

Hindin, Michelle and Adair, Linda (2002) 'Who's at risk? Factors associated with intimate partner violence in the Philippines', *Social Science and Medicine*, 55, 1385–99.

Hirsch, Jennifer (2003) *A Courtship After Marriage: Sexuality and Love in Mexican Transnational Families* (Berkeley, CA: University of California Press).

Hobson, Barbara (1994) 'Solo mothers, social policy regimes and the logics of gender', in Diane Sainsbury (ed.) *Gendering Welfare States* (London: Sage), pp. 170–88.

Hoddinott, John and Haddad, Lawrence (1991) *Household Expenditures, Child Anthropomorphic Status and the Intra-Household Division of Income: Evidence from the Côte d'Ivoire* (Oxford: University of Oxford, Unit for the Study of African Economics).

Hollnsteiner, Mary (1991a) 'The wife', in Department of Sociology-Anthropology (ed.) *SA21: Selected Readings* (Quezon City: Ateneo de Manila University, Office of Research and Publications), pp. 251–75.

Hollnsteiner, Mary (1991b) 'The husband', in Department of Sociology-Anthropology (ed.) *SA21: Selected Readings* (Quezon City: Ateneo de Manila University, Office of Research and Publications), pp. 276–84.

Hornilla, Patricia (1995) 'Terms and conditions of homework', paper presented at the 6th National Statistical Convention, Manila, 4–5 December.

Illo, Jeanne Frances (1989) 'Who heads the household? Women in households in the Philippines', in Amaryllis Torres (ed.) *The Filipino Woman in Focus: A Handbook of Reading* (Bangkok: UNESCO), pp. 245–66.

Illo, Jeanne Frances (2002a) 'Gender and markets: a framework for analysing the effects of the economic crisis on women', in Jeanne Frances Illo and Rosalinda Pineda-Ofreneo (eds) *Carrying the Burden of the World: Women Reflecting on the Effects of the Economic Crisis on Women and Girls* (Quezon City: University of the Philippines Centre for Integrative and Development Studies), pp. 1–19.

Illo, Jeanne Frances (2002b) 'Life three years after the 1997–98 crisis', in Jeanne Frances Illo and Rosalinda Pineda-Ofreneo (eds) *Carrying the Burden of the World: Women Reflecting on the Effects of the Economic Crisis on Women and Girls* (Quezon City: University of the Philippines Centre for Integrative and Development Studies), pp. 20–28.

Illo, Jeanne Frances (2003a) 'Surviving the crisis: women's groups and "safety nets"', in Jeanne Frances Illo and Rosalinda Pineda-Ofreneo (eds) *Beyond the Crisis: Questions of Survival and Empowerment* (Quezon City: University of the Philippines Centre for Integrative and Development Studies and Centre for Women's Studies), pp. 23–40.

Illo, Jeanne Frances (2003b) 'Crisis, survival and empowerment: reflections on the case studies', in Jeanne Frances Illo and Rosalinda Pineda-Ofreneo (eds) *Beyond the Crisis: Questions of Survival and Empowerment* (Quezon City: University of the Philippines Centre for Integrative and Development Studies and Centre for Women's Studies), pp. 149–58.

Illo, Jeanne Frances and Polo, Jaime B. (1990) *Fishers, Traders, Farmers, Wives* (Quezon City: Institute of Philippine Culture, Ateneo de Manila University).

Illo, Jeanne Frances and Veneracion, Cynthia (1988) *Women and Men in Rainfed Farming Systems: Case Studies of Households in the Bicol Region* (Quezon City: Institute of Philippine Culture, Ateneo de Manila University).

Instituto de Fomento y Asesoría Municipal (IFAM) (2003) *Regiones y Cantones de Costa Rica* (San José: IFAM).

Instituto Mixto de Ayuda Social (IMAS) (1998) *Ley No. 7769 Atención a las Mujeres en Condiciones de Pobreza* (San José: IMAS).

Instituto Mixto de Ayuda Social (IMAS) (1999a) *Programa: Atención a las Mujeres en Condiciones de Pobreza* (San José: IMAS).

Instituto Mixto de Ayuda Social (IMAS) (1999b) *Programa Construyendo Oportunidades* (San José: IMAS).

Instituto Mixto de Ayuda Social (IMAS) (1999c) *Plan Anual Operativo 1999* (San José: IMAS).

Instituto Mixto de Ayuda Social (IMAS) (2001) *Area Atención Integral para el Desarrollo de las Mujeres. Programas: Creciendo Juntas, Construyendo Oportunidades* (San José: IMAS).

Instituto Nacional de Estadísticas y Censos (INEC) (2000) *Manual para el Empadronamiento: Censos Nacionales IX de Población y V de Vivienda, Censo 2000* (San José: INEC).

Instituto Nacional de Estadísticas y Censos (INEC) (2001) *IX Censo Nacional de Población y V de Vivienda del 2000: Resultados Generales* (San José: INEC), http://www.inec.go.cr.

Instituto Nacional de Estadísticas y Censos (INEC) (2003a) *Encuesta Hogares de Propósitos Múltiples* (San José: INEC), http://www.inec.go.cr.

Instituto Nacional de Estadísticas y Censos (INEC) (2003b) *Encuesta Hogares de Propósitos Múltiples: Cifras Básicas sobre Pobreza e Ingresos, Julio 2003* (San José: INEC), http://www.inec.go.cr.

Instituto Nacional de Estadísticas y Censos (INEC) (2004a) *Encuesta Hogares de Propósitos Múltiples: Cifras Básicas sobre Pobreza e Ingresos, Julio 2004* (San José: INEC), http://www.inec.go.cr.

Instituto Nacional de Estadísticas y Censos (INEC) (2004b) *Encuesta de Hogares de Propósitos Múltiples* (San José: INEC), http://www.inec.go.cr.

Instituto Nacional de Estadísticas y Censos (INEC) (2005a) *Encuesta Hogares de Propósitos Múltiples: Cifras Básicas sobre Pobrez e Ingresos, Julio 2005* (San José: INEC), http://www.inec.go.cr.

Instituto Nacional de Estadísticas y Censos (INEC) (2005b) *Encuesta de Hogares de Propósitos Múltiples* (San José: INEC), http://www.inec.go.cr.

Instituto Nacional de la Mujeres (INAMU) (2001) *Responsible Paternity Law* (San José: INAMU).

Instituto Nacional de la Mujeres (INAMU) (2005) *Mujeres y Pobreza* (San José: INAMU), http://www.inamu.go.cr/Acciones/DerechosPobreza.html, accessed 18 May 2005.

International Fund for Agricultural Development (IFAD) (1999) *The Issue of Poverty Among Female-headed Households in Africa* (Rome: IFAD), http://www.ifad.org/gender/learning/challenges/women/60.htm, accessed June 2003.

International Labour Organisation (ILO) (1996) 'All women are working women: the feminisation of poverty' (Geneva: ILO), http://www.ilo-mirror.cornell.edu, accessed May 2002.

International Labour Organisation (ILO) (2001) *Action Programme for Decent Work: Philippines* (Geneva: ILO).

International Labour Organisation (ILO) (2002) *Women and Men in the Informal Economy: A Statistical Picture* (Geneva: ILO).

International Labour Organisation (ILO) (2003a) *Investing in Every Child: An Economic Study of the Costs and Benefits of Eliminating Child Labour* (Geneva: ILO).

International Labour Organisation (ILO) (2003b) *Working Out of Poverty*, report of the Director-General, International Labour Conference, 91st session (Geneva: ILO).

International Labour Organisation (ILO) (2004a) 'The economic returns from eliminating child labour', *In Focus* (UNDP International Poverty Centre, Brasilia), March, 14–15.

International Labour Organisation (ILO) (2004b) *Gender Dimensions of Patterns and Characteristics of Poverty in the Islamic Republic of Iran* (Geneva: ILO).

International Labour Organisation (ILO) (2004c) *A Current Affair: Current Issues and Developments on Gender Equality and Mainstreaming in the ILO* (Geneva: ILO).

International Labour Organisation (ILO) (2004d) *Global Employment Trends for Women, 2004* Employment Strategy Papers (Geneva: ILO).

International Labour Organisation (ILO) (2005) *Decent Work Indicators Database* (San José: ILO Sub-regional Office for Central America, Haiti, Panama and the Dominican Republic), http://www.oitsial.org.pa/td. paise, accessed 29 May 2005.

International Monetary Fund (IMF)/International Development Association (IDA) (2002) *Poverty Reduction Strategy Paper: Joint Assessment* (Washington, DC: IMF/IDA).

International Organisation for Migration (IOM) (2001) *Binational Study: The State of Migration Flows between Costa Rica and Nicaragua* (San José: IOM).

International Organisation for Migration (IOM) (2005) *World Migration 2005: Costs and Benefits of International Migration* (Geneva: IOM).

International Poverty Centre (IPC) (2004a) 'Pro-poor growth: what is it?', *One Pager* (IPC, United Nations Development Programme, Brasilia), 1.

International Poverty Centre (IPC) (2004b) 'Poverty Measurement Matters: An Indian Story?', *One Pager* (IPC, United Nations Development Programme, Brasilia), 2.

International Poverty Centre (IPC) (2004c) *Country Estimates of Poverty Based on Three International Poverty Lines* (Brasilia: IPC, United Nations Development Programme).

International Trade Centre (ITC) (2001) *Product Profile: Tourism* (Geneva: ITC, UNCTAD).

Investigaciones Jurídicas S.A. (IJSA) (1990) *Ley de Promoción de la Igualdad de la Mujer* (San José: IJSA).

Isis International (II)/Asia-Pacific Women's Watch (APWW) (2004) *Big Purple Book: Draft Compilation of the Asia-Pacific Regional Assessment of the Implementation of the Beijing Platform for Action* (Manila: Isis International).

Israel-Sobritchea, Carolyn (1991) 'Gender ideology and the status of women in a Philippine rural community', in Sister Mary John Mananzan (ed.) *Essays on Women*, revd edn (Manila: Institute of Women's Studies, St Scholastica's College), pp. 90–103.

Itzigsohn, José (2000) *Developing Poverty: The State, Labour Market Deregulation, and the Informal Economy in Costa Rica and the Dominican Republic* (Philadelphia, PA: Pennsylvania State University Press).

Jackson, Cecile (1996) 'Rescuing gender from the poverty trap', *World Development*, 24:3, 489–504.

Jackson, Cecile (1997) 'Post poverty, gender and development', *IDS Bulletin*, 28:3, 145–55.

Jackson, Cecile (1998) 'Rescuing gender from the poverty trap', in Cecile Jackson and Ruth Pearson (eds) *Feminist Visions of Development: Gender Analysis and Policy* (London: Routledge), pp. 39–64.

Jackson, Cecile (2003) 'Gender analysis of land: beyond land rights for women?', *Journal of Agrarian Change*, 3:4, 453–80.

Jackson, Cecile and Palmer-Jones, Richard (1999) 'Rethinking gendered poverty and work', *Development and Change*, 30:3, 557–83.

Japan Bank for International Cooperation (JBIC) (2001) *Poverty Profile: Executive Summary, Republic of the Philippines* (Manila: JBIC).

Jassey, Katja (2002) 'Active, visible women in poverty discourses – an impossibility?', paper presented at workshop 'Agency, Power Relations and Globalisation', Institute for Peace and Development Research, Gothenberg University, 29 August.

Javate de Dios, Aurora (2003) 'Progress towards the elimination of violence against women and remaining challenges: the Philippine experience', paper presented at the conference 'Empowered Women: Breaking the Chains of Poverty and Gender Inequality', Westin Philippine Plaza, Manila, 2–3 October.

Jiménez, Erika (2002) *Informe Comparativo. Formación Integral para Mujeres Jefas de Hogar (Asignación Familiar Temporal) 1994–1998 y Atención a Mujeres en Condiciones de Pobreza (Creciendo Juntas) 1998–2002* (San José: Secretaría Técnica Programa Creciendo Juntas).

Jobarteh, Satang (2001) *The Socio-Political Strides of Gambian Women* (Serrekunda: SIMMA Vocational Training Institute).

Johnson, Robert (2005) 'Not a sufficient condition: the limited relevance of the gender MDG to women's progress', in Caroline Sweetman (ed.) *Gender and the Millennium Development Goals* (Oxford: Oxfam), pp. 56–66.

Johnsson-Latham, Gerd (2004a) ' "Ecce Homo"? A gender reading of the World Bank study "Voices of the Poor"', in Gerd Johnsson-Latham (ed.)

Power and Privileges: Gender Discrimination and Poverty (Stockholm: Regerinskanliet), pp. 6–15.

Johnsson-Latham, Gerd (2004b) 'Understanding female and male poverty and deprivation', in Gerd Johnsson-Latham (ed.) *Power and Privileges: Gender Discrimination and Poverty* (Stockholm: Regerinskanliet), pp. 16–45.

Johnsson-Latham, Gerd (2004c) 'Masculinities: a threat of development?', in Gerd Johnsson-Latham (ed.) *Power and Privileges: Gender Discrimination and Poverty* (Stockholm: Regerinskanliet), pp. 74–81.

Jones, Mark P. (2004) 'Quota legislation and the election of women: learning from the Costa Rican experience', *Journal of Politics*, 66:4, 1203–23.

Kabeer, Naila (1994) *Reversed Realities: Gender Hierarchies in Development Thought* (London: Verso).

Kabeer, Naila (1996) 'Agency, well-being and inequality: reflections on the gender dimensions of poverty', *IDS Bulletin*, 27:1, 11–21.

Kabeer, Naila (1997) 'Editorial. Tactics and trade-offs: revisiting the links between gender and poverty', *IDS Bulletin*, 28:3, 1–25.

Kabeer, Naila (1999) 'Resources, agency, achievements: reflections on the measurement of women's empowerment', *Development and Change*, 30:3, 435–64.

Kabeer, Naila (2000) 'Inter-generational contracts, demographic transitions and the 'quantity–quality' tradeoff: parents, children and investing in the future', *Journal of International Development*, 12, 463–82.

Kabeer, Naila (2003) *Gender Mainstreaming in Poverty Eradication and the Millennium Development Goals: A Handbook for Policy-Makers and Other Stakeholders* (London: Commonwealth Secretariat).

Kabeer, Naila (2005) 'Gender equality and women's empowerment: a critical analysis of the third Millennium Development Goal', in Caroline Sweetman (ed.) *Gender and the Millennium Development Goals* (Oxford: Oxfam), pp. 13–24.

Kakwani, Nanak (2004a) 'Pro-poor growth in Asia', *In Focus* (UNDP Centre for Policies Against Poverty), January, 5–6.

Kakwani, Nanak (2004b) 'New global poverty counts', *In Focus* (UNDP International Poverty Centre), 4: September, 9–11, http://www.undp.org/povertycentre/newsletters/infocus 4Sep 04eng.pdf, accessed September 2004.

Kakwani, Nanak, Soares, Fábio Veras and Son, Hyun H. (2005) *Conditional Cash Transfers in African Countries*, Working Paper No. 9 (Brasilia: International Poverty Centre).

Kakwani, Nanak and Son, Hyun H. (2005) *On Assessing Pro-Poorness of Government Programmes: International Comparisons*, Working Paper No. 6 (Brasilia: International Poverty Centre).

Kakwani, Nanak and Subbarao, Kalanhidhi (2005) *Ageing and Poverty in Africa and the Role of Social Pensions*, Working Paper 8 (Brasilia: International Poverty Centre, United Nations Development Programme).

Kanbur, Ravi (2003) 'Conceptual challenges in poverty and inequality: one development economist's perspective', paper prepared for Conference on Inequality, Poverty and Human Well-Being, World Institute for Development Economics Research, United Nations University, Helsinki, 30–31 May.

Kanji, Nazneen (1991) 'Structural adjustment policies: shifting the social costs of reproduction to women', *Critical Health*, 34, 61–7.

Karshenas, Massoud (2003) 'Global poverty: national accounts versus survey-based estimates', *Development and Change*, 34:4, 683–712.

Kaztman, Rubén (1992) 'Por Qué Los Hombres son Tan Irresponsables?', *Revista de la CEPAL*, 46, 1–9.

Kennedy, Eileen (1994) 'Development policy, gender of head of household, and nutrition', in Eileen Kennedy and Mercedes González de la Rocha, *Poverty and Well-Being in the Household: Case Studies of the Developing World* (San Diego, CA: Center for Iberian and Latin American Studies, University of California San Diego), pp. 25–42.

Khundker, Nasreen (2004) 'A gentle touch? Gender and the World Bank: a critical assessment', paper prepared for the event 'Reforming the World Bank: Will the Gender Mainstreaming Strategy Make a Difference?', hosted by the Neirich Boell Foundation, Gender Action and Bank Information Centre, Washington, DC, http://www.genderaction.org/images/Khundker_GentleTouch.pdf, accessed September 2004.

Klasen, Stephan (2004) *Gender-Related Indicators of Well-Being*, Discussion Paper No. 102 (Goettingen: Georg-August Universität, Ibero-Amerika Institüt für Wirtschaftsforschung), http://www.iai.wiwi. uni-goettingen.de, accessed September 2005.

Klasen, Stephan (2006) 'Guest editor's introduction', *Journal of Human Development*, 7:2, 145–59.

Klouzal, Linda (2003) 'The subjective side of development: sources of well-being, resources for struggle', in Kum-Kum Bhavnani, John Foran and Priya A. Kurian (eds) *Feminist Futures: Women, Culture and Development* (London: Zed), pp. 256–62.

Kothari, Rajni (1993) *Poverty, Human Consciousness and the Amnesia of Development* (London: Zed).

Krauskopf, Dina (1998) 'The rights and reproductive health of urban adolescents' in UNICEF (ed.) *Adolescence, Child Rights and Urban Poverty in Costa Rica* (San José: UNICEF/HABITAT), pp. 101–12.

Kumari, Ranjana (1989) *Women-Headed Households in Rural India* (New Delhi: Radiant).

Kusakabe, Kyoko (2002) 'Vulnerability of female-headed households in Cambodia', paper presented at workshop 'Family, Gender and Health', Centre for Family and Women's Studies, Hanoi, 11–13 December.

Kuznesof, Elizabeth (1980) 'Household composition and headship as related to changes in modes of production: São Paolo 1765–1836', *Comparative Studies in Society and History*, 22:1, 78–108.

Lakshminarayanan, Rama (2003) 'Decentralisation and its implications for reproductive health: the Philippines experience', *Reproductive Health Matters*, 11:21, 96–107.

Lamberte, Mario and Manlagñit, Ma Chelo V. (2003) 'Household poverty: addressing the cores of microfinance', *PIDS Policy Notes*, No. 2002-15 (Philippine Institute for Development Studies, Makati City).

Lampietti, Julian and Stalker, Linda (2000) *Consumption Expenditure and Female Poverty: A Review of the Evidence*. Policy Research Report on Gender and Development, Working Paper Series No. 11 (Washington, DC: World Bank, Development Research Group/Poverty Reduction and Economic Management Network).

Lancaster, Roger (1992) *Life is Hard: Machismo, Danger and the Intimacy of Power in Nicaragua* (Berkeley, CA: University of California Press).

Langer, Ana, Lozano, Rafael and Bobadilla, José Luis (1991) 'Effects of Mexico's economic crisis on the health of women and children' in Mercedes González de la Rocha and Agustín Escobar (eds) *Social Responses to Mexico's Crisis of the 1980s* (San Diego, CA: Center for US–Mexican Studies), pp. 195–219.

Laopao, Manuel (1998) 'Statistics from administrative records: an alternative approach in monitoring labour market response to economic crisis', paper presented at the 7th National Convention on Statistics, Shangri-la EDSA Plaza Hotel, Manila, 2–4 December.

Lara, Silvia, with Barry, Tom and Simonson, Peter (1995) *Inside Costa Rica* (Albuquerque, NM: Resource Center Press).

Lavinas, Lena and Nicoll, Marcelo (2006) 'Atividade e Vulnerabilidade: Quais os Arranjos Familiares em Risco?', *Dados: Revista de Ciências Sociais*, 9:2, 67–97.

Laws, Sophie (1996) 'The single mothers debate: a children's rights perspective', in Janet Holland and Lisa Adkins (eds) *Sex, Sensibility and the Gendered Body* (Basingstoke: Macmillan), pp. 60–77.

Leach, Fiona (1999) 'Women in the informal sector: the contribution of education and training', in Oxfam (ed.) *Development for Women* (Oxford: Oxfam), pp. 46–62.

Lewis, David (1993) 'Going it alone: female-headed households, rights and resources in rural Bangladesh', *European Journal of Development Research*, 5:2, 23–42.

Lewis, Jane (1989) 'Lone parent families: politics and economics', *Journal of Social Policy*, 18:4, 595–600.

Licuanan, Patricia (1991) 'A situation analysis of women in the Philippines', in Jeanne Frances Illo (ed.) *Gender Analysis and Planning: The 1990 IPC-CIDA Workshop* (Quezon City: Institute of Philippine Culture, Ateneo de Manila University Press), pp. 15–28.

Lim, Joseph and Bautista, Carlos (2002) 'External liberalisation, growth and distribution in the Philippines', paper presented at the international conference 'External Liberalisation, Growth, Development and Social Policy', Melia Hotel, Hanoi, 18–20 January.

Lind, Amy (1997) 'Gender, development and urban social change: women's community action in global cities', *World Development*, 25:8, 1187–203.

Linneker, Brian (2003) 'Gender comparisons of capital influences on the well-being of women and households experiencing poverty in Nicaragua', Working Draft Report, Coordinadora Civil – Nicaragua (CCER), Managua.

Lipton, Michael (2001) 'Poverty concepts, policies, partnerships and practice: a plea for simplicity', in Neil Middleton, Phil O'Keefe and Rob Visser (eds) *Negotiating Poverty: New Directions, Renewed Debate* (London: Pluto), pp. 41–53.

Lisulo, Angela (2003) *Costa Rica: Health Policies* (Washington, DC: World Bank, Working Paper 28007), http://www.wds.worldbank.org/servlet; WDS_Ibank_servelet, accessed December 2004.

Lloyd, Cynthia and Gage-Brandon, Anastasia (1993) 'Women's role in maintaining households: family welfare and sexual inequality in Ghana', *Population Studies*, 47, 115–31.

Lloyd-Evans, Sally (2002) 'Child labour', in Vandana Desai and Robert Potter (eds) *The Companion to Development Studies* (London: Arnold), pp. 215–19.

Loáiciga Guillén, María Elena (1999) 'Acerca de la Educación Superior Pública en Guanacaste', *Ciencias Sociales*, 66, 7–20.

Londoño, Juan Luis and Frenk, Julio (2000) 'Structured pluralism: towards an innovative model for health system reform in Latin America', in Peter Lloyd-Sherlock (ed.) *Healthcare Reform and Poverty in Latin America* (London: Institute of Latin American Studies), pp. 21–56.

Longwe, Sara Hlupekile (1995) 'A development agency as a patriarchal cooking pot: the evaporation of policies for women's advancement', in Mandy MacDonald (compiler) *Women's Rights and Development*, Working Paper (Oxfam: Oxford), pp. 18–29.

López de Mazier, Armida (1997) 'La Mujer, Principal Sostén del Modelo Económico de Honduras: Un Análisis de Género de la Economía Hondureña', in Diane Elson, María Angélica Fauné, Jasmine Gideon, Maribel Gutiérrez, Armida López de Mazier and Eduardo Sacayón (eds) *Crecer con la Mujer: Oportunidades para el Desarrollo Ecónomico Centroamericano* (San José: Embajada Real de los Países Bajos), pp. 215–52.

Lopez-Claros, Augusto and Zahidi, Saadia (2005) *Women's Empowerment: Measuring the Global Gender Gap* (Geneva: World Economic Forum), www.weforum.org, accessed 18 May 2005.

Lumsden, Ian (1996) *Machos, Maricones and Gays: Cuba and Homosexuality* (Philadelphia/London: Temple University Press/Latin America Bureau).

Lutz, Helma (2002) ' "At your service madam!" The globalisation of domestic service', *Feminist Review*, 70, 89–104.

Mädge, E. and Neusüss, C. (1994) 'Lone mothers on welfare in West Berlin: disadvantaged citizens or women avoiding patriarchy?', *Environment and Planning, A*, 26, 1419–33.

Madrigal Pana, Johnny (2002) *Estratificación de Hogares y Segmentos por Niveles de Ingreso en el Censo 2000*, Serie Censal No. 6 (San José: Instituto Nacional de Estadísticas y Censos).

Marchand, Marianne and Parpart, Jane (eds) (1995) *Feminism/Postmodernism/Development* (London: Routledge).

Marcoux, Alain (1997) *The Feminisation of Poverty: Facts, Hypotheses and the Art of Advocacy* (Rome: Food and Agriculture Organisation, Population Programme Service, Women and Population Division).

Marcoux, Alain (1998a) 'How much do we really know about the feminisation of poverty?', *The Brown Journal of World Affairs*, 5:2, 187–94.

Marcoux, Alain (1998b) 'The feminisation of poverty: claims, facts and data needs', *Population and Development Review*, 24:1, 131–9.

Marenco, Leda, Trejos, Ana María, Trejos, Juan Diego and Vargas, Marienela (1998) *Del Silencio a la Palabra: Un Modelo de Trabajo con las Mujeres Jefas del Hogar* (San José: Segunda Vicepresidencia).

Martin, Tracey (2003) 'Gambian Schools and the UN Convention on the Rights of the Child', unpublished dissertation submitted in part requirement for MEd in Inclusive Education, University of Sheffield.

Maxwell, Simon (2001) 'WDR 2000: is there a "new poverty agenda" ', *Development Policy Review*, 19:1, 143–9.

May, Julian (2001) 'An elusive consensus: definitions, measurement and the analysis of poverty', in Alejandro Grinspun (ed.) *Choices for the Poor: Lessons from National Poverty Strategies* (New York: UNDP), pp. 23–54.

May, Julian (2004) 'Accumulation failures and poverty traps in South Africa', *In Focus* (UNDP International Poverty Centre), 3: May, 9–11, http://www.undp.org/povertycentre/newsletters/infocus 3May04eng.pdf, accessed May 2004.

Mayoux, Linda (2002) 'Women's empowerment or the feminisation of debt? Towards a new agenda in African microfinance', paper given at One World Action Conference, London, 21–22 March, http://www.oneworldaction.org/Background.htm, accessed November 2002.

Mayoux, Linda (2006) 'Women's empowerment through sustainable micro-finance: rethinking "best practice"', Discussion Paper, Gender and Micro-finance website, http://www.genfinance.net, accessed 2 July 2006.

Mbilinyi, Marjorie (2004) 'Lessons of civil society engagement', in Women's International Coalition for Economic Justice (WICEJ) (ed.) *Seeking Accountability on Women's Human Rights: Women Debate the UN Millennium Development Goals* (New York: WICEJ), pp. 10–12.

Mboup, Gora and Amunyunzo-Nyamongo, Mary (2005) 'Getting the right data – helping municipalities help women', *Habitat Debate*, 11:1, http://www.unhabitat.org/hd/hdv11na/9.asp, accessed May 2005.

McClenaghan, Sharon (1997) 'Women, work and empowerment: romanticising the reality', in Elizabeth Dore (ed.) *Gender Politics in Latin America: Debates in Theory and Practice* (New York: Monthly Review Press), pp. 19–35.

McIlwaine, Cathy (1993) 'Gender, ethnicity and the local labour market in Limón, Costa Rica', unpublished PhD thesis, Department of Geography, London School of Economics.

McIlwaine, Cathy (1997) 'Vulnerable or poor? A study of ethnic and gender disadvantage among Afro-Caribbeans in Limón, Costa Rica', *European Journal of Development Research*, 9:2, 35–61.

McIlwaine, Cathy (2002) 'Perspectives on poverty, vulnerability and exclusion', in Cathy McIlwaine and Katie Willis (eds) *Challenges and Change in Middle America: Perspectives on Mexico, Central America and the Caribbean* (Harlow: Pearson Education), pp. 82–109.

McIlwaine, Cathy and Datta, Kavita (2003) 'From feminising to engendering development', *Gender, Place and Culture*, 10:4, 369–82.

McLanahan, Sara (n.d.) 'Father absence and the welfare of children', MacArthur Research Network on the Family and the Economy, working paper, http://www.olin.wustl.edu/macarthur.

McLanahan, Sara and Kelly, Erin (n.d.) 'The feminisation of poverty: past and future', MacArthur Research Network on the Family and the Economy, working paper, http://www.olin.wustl.edu/macarthur.

McNay, Kirsty (2005) 'The implications of the demographic transition for women, girls and gender equality: a review of developing country evidence', *Progress in Development Studies*, 5:2, 115–34.

Medeiros, Marcelo and Costa, Joana (2006) *Poverty Among Women in Latin America: Feminisation or Over-representation?* Working Paper No. 20 (Brasilia: International Poverty Centre).

Medina, Belen (1991) *The Filipino Family: A Text with Selected Readings* (Quezon City: University of the Philippines Press).

Mehra, Rekha, Esim, Simel and Simms, Margaret (2000) *Fulfilling the Beijing Commitment: Reducing Poverty, Enhancing Women's Economic Options* (Washington, DC: International Center for Research on Women).

Mendoza, Lorelei (2000) 'Gender, households, and markets: inherited land and labour force participation of rural households in the Cordillera region, Philippines: a critique of the unitary view of the household in the Philippines', Global Development Network: www.gnet.org, accessed 16 July 2004.

Menjívar, Rafael and Trejos, Juan Diego (1992) *La Pobreza en América Central*, 2nd edn (San José: FLACSO).

Menjívar Ochoa, Mauricio (2003) *Actitudes Masculinas Hacia la Paternidad: Entre las Contradicciones del Mandato y el Involucramiento* (San José: Instituto Nacional de las Mujeres, Colección Teórica 2).

Merrick, Thomas and Schmink, Marianne (1983) 'Households headed by women and urban poverty in Brazil', in Mayra Buvinic, Margaret Lycette and William McGreevey (eds) *Women and Poverty in the Third World* (Baltimore, MD: Johns Hopkins University Press), pp. 244–71.

Middleton, Neil, O'Keefe, Phil and Visser, Rob (2001) 'Introduction', in Neil Middleton, Phil O'Keefe and Rob Visser (eds) *Negotiating Poverty: New Directions, Renewed Debate* (London: Pluto), pp. 1–18.

Milagros, Maruja B. Asis, Huang, Shirlena and Yeoh, Brenda (2004) 'When the light of the home is abroad: unskilled female migration and the Filipino family', *Singapore Journal of Tropical Geography*, 25:2, 198–215.

Millar, Jane (1992) 'Lone mothers and poverty', in Caroline Glendinning and Jane Millar (eds) *Women and Poverty in Britain in the 1990s* (Hemel Hempstead: Harvester Wheatsheaf), pp. 149–61.

Millar, Jane (1996) 'Mothers, workers, wives: comparing policy approaches to supporting lone mothers', in Elizabeth Bortolaia Silva (ed.) *Good Enough Mothering? Feminist Perspectives on Lone Motherhood* (London: Routledge), pp. 97–113.

Ministerio de Planificación Nacional y Política Económica (MIDEPLAN) (1995) *Estadísticas Sociodemográficas y Económicas Desagregadas por Sexo, Costa Rica, 1980–1994* (San José: MIDEPLAN).

Ministerio de Planificación Nacional y Política Económica (MIDEPLAN) (1998) *Plan Nacional de Desarrollo Humano 1998–2002* (San José: MIDEPLAN).

Ministerio de Planificación Nacional y Política Económica (MIDEPLAN) (2002) *Plan Nacional de Desarrollo Humano 2002–2006* (San José: MIDEPLAN).

Ministerio de Planificación Nacional y Política Económica (MIDEPLAN) (2005) *Evolución de la Pobreza a Partir de Estimaciones de Encuesta de Hogares* (San José: MIDEPLAN), http://www.mideplan.go.cr/sides/social/09-01.htm, accessed 3 July 2005.

Ministerio de Trabajo (MT) (2002) *Resúmen de Encuesta del Trabajo Infantil y Adolescente en Costa Rica* (San José: Ministerio de Trabajo).

Ministry of Education, The Gambia (METG) (1997) *Population and Family Life Education, Pupil's Book Grades 7–9* (London and Oxford: Macmillan Education).

Mission, Gina (1998) 'The breadwinners: female migrant workers', *WIN: Women's International Net*, November, http://www.geocities.com/wellesley/3321/win15a.htm, accessed June 2005.

Moghadam, Valentine (1997) *The Feminisation of Poverty: Notes on a Concept and Trend*, Women's Studies Occasional Paper No. 2 (Normal, IL: Illinois State University).

Moghadam, Valentine (1998) 'The feminisation of poverty in international perspective', *The Brown Journal of World Affairs*, 5:2, 225–48.

Moghadam, Valentine (2005) *The 'Feminisation of Poverty' and Women's Human Rights*, Social and Human Sciences Papers in Women's Studies/Gender Research, No. 2 (Paris: UNESCO).

Mojico Mendieta, Francisco (2004) *Inmigración Nicaragüense en Costa Rica y Cooperación Internacional en Salud, Educación y Vivienda* (Heredia: Universidad Nacional, Instituto de Estudios Sociales en Población).

Molyneux, Maxine (2001) *Women's Movements in International Perspective: Latin America and Beyond* (Basingstoke: Palgrave).

Molyneux, Maxine (2002) 'Gender and the silences of social capital: lessons from Latin America', *Development and Change*, 33, 167–88.

Molyneux, Maxine (2006a) *Poverty Relief and the New Social Policy in Latin America: Mothers at the Service of the State? Research Paper* (Geneva: United Nations Research Institute for Social Development).

Molyneux, Maxine (2006b) 'Mothers at the service of the new poverty agenda: Progresa/Oportunidades, Mexico's conditional transfer programme', *Journal of Social Policy and Administration*, 40:4, 425–49.

Molyneux, Maxine and Razavi, Shahra (2002) 'Introduction', in Maxine Molyneux and Shahra Razavi (eds) *Gender Justice, Development and Rights* (Oxford: Oxford University Press), pp. 1–42.

Monge, Guillermo and González, Gladys (2005) *Igualdad de Género, Pobreza, Políticas de Conciliación entre los Ambitos Productivo y Reproductivo y Presupuestos Públicos: En Estudio de Caso sobre Costa Rica*, Fondo de Población de las Naciones Unidas, Proyecto Regional 'Política Fiscal con Enfoque de Género' de GTZ (San José: PROCESOS).

Monk, Sue (1993) *From the Margins to the Mainstream: An Employment Strategy for Lone Parents* (London: National Council for One-Parent Families).

Montero, Sary and Barahona, Manuel (2003) *La Estrategia de Lucha Contra la Pobreza en Costa Rica: Institucionalidad, Financiamento Políticas, Programas*, Serie Políticas Sociales 77 (Santiago de Chile: CEPAL).

Mookodi, Godisang (2000) 'The complexities of female household headship in Botswana', *Pula: Botswana Journal of African Studies*, 14:2, http://www.thuto.org/pula.html/sample-articles.htm, accessed 18 July 2005.

Moore, Henrietta (1988) *Feminism and Anthropology* (Cambridge: Polity).

Moore, Henrietta (1994) *Is There a Crisis in the Family?* (Geneva: World Summit for Social Development, Occasional Paper No. 3).

Moore, Henrietta (1996) 'Mothering and social responsibilities in a cross-cultural perspective', in Elizabeth Bortolaia Silva (ed.) *Good Enough Mothering? Feminist Perspectives on Lone Motherhood* (London: Routledge), pp. 58–75.

Moore, Henrietta and Vaughan, Megan (1994) *Cutting Down Trees: Gender, Nutrition and Agricultural Change in the Northern Province of Zambia, 1890–1990* (Portsmouth, NH: Heinemann).

Morada, Hector (2001) 'Left-behind households of overseas Filipino workers', paper presented at the Asian Population Network Workshop on 'Migration and the "Asian Family" in a Globalising World', River View Hotel, Singapore, 16–18 April.

Morada, Hector and Llaneta, Mylene (2000) 'Working couples in the Philippines', paper presented at the 13th SRTC Annual Conference, Sulo Hotel, Quezon City, 6 October.

Morada, Hector and Manzala, Teresita (2001) 'Mismatches in the Philippine labour market', paper presented at the Symposium on 'Mismatch in the Labour Market', EDSA-Shangri-La Hotel, Manila, 11–13 July.

Morada, Hector and Santos, Lani Q. (1998) 'Pre-employment sex discrimination: a three-period comparison', paper presented at the 7th National Convention on Statistics, Shangrila EDSA Plaza Hotel, Manila, 2–4 December.

Morada, Hector, Llaneta, Mylene, Pangan, Theresita and Pomentil, Christopher (2001) 'Female-headed households in the Philippines', paper presented at the Department of Labour and Employment First Research Conference, Occupation Safety and Health Centre, Quezon City, 5 December.

Moreno, Wagner (1997) 'Cambios Sociales y el Rol del Adolescente en la Estructura Familiar', *Ciencias Sociales* (Universidad de Costa Rica), 75, 95–101.

Morley, Samuel (2004) 'Cash for education', *In Focus* (UNDP Centre for Policies Against Poverty) January, 7–9.

Morrisson, Christian and Jütting, Johannes (2004) *The Impact of Social Institutions on the Economic Role of Women in Developing Countries*, Working Paper No. 234, DEV/DOC (2004)03 (Paris: OECD).

Moser, Caroline (1989) 'The impact of structural adjustment at the micro-level: low-income women, time and the triple role in Guayaquil, Ecuador', in UNICEF (ed.), *Invisible Adjustment Vol. 2* (New York: UNICEF, Americas and Caribbean Office), pp. 137–62.

Moser, Caroline (1993) *Gender Planning and Development: Theory, Practice and Training* (London: Routledge).

Moser, Caroline (1996) *Confronting Crisis: A Comparative Study of Household Responses to Poverty in Four Poor Urban Communities* (Washington, DC: Environmentally Sustainable Development Studies and Monographs Series No. 8).

Moser, Caroline (1998) 'The asset vulnerability framework: reassessing urban poverty reduction strategies', *World Development*, 26:1, 1–19.

Moser, Caroline and McIlwaine, Cathy (1997) *Household Responses to Poverty and Vulnerability, Volume 3: Confronting Crisis in Commonwealth, Metro Manila, Philippines* (Washington, DC: World Bank, Urban Management Programme).

Moser, Caroline and McIlwaine, Cathy (2000a) *Urban Poor Perceptions of Violence in Colombia.* (Washington, DC: World Bank).

Moser, Caroline and McIlwaine, Cathy (2000b) *Violence in a Post-Conflict Context: Urban Poor Perceptions from Guatemala* (Washington, DC: World Bank).

Moser, Caroline and Rodgers, Dennis (2005) *Change, Violence and Insecurity in Non-Conflict Situations*, Working Paper 245 (London: Overseas Development Institute).

Moser, Caroline, Gatehouse, Michael and Garcia, Helen (1996a) *Urban Poverty Research Sourcebook. Module I: Sub-City Level Household Survey* (Washington, DC: UNDP/UNCHS/World Bank – Urban Management Program, Working Paper Series 5).

Moser, Caroline, Gatehouse, Michael and Garcia, Helen (1996b) *Urban Poverty Research Sourcebook. Module II: Indicators of Urban Poverty* (Washington, DC: UNDP/UNCHS/World Bank – Urban Management Program, Working Paper Series 5).

Movimiento Familiar Cristiano (MFC) (1997) *Reseña Histórica del MFC en Costa Rica* (San José, Costa Rica: MFC).

Mukhopadhyay, Tanni (2000) 'Gender, work and familial ideology: women workers in the garment export industry, Delhi, India, 1995–99', unpublished PhD thesis, Department of Sociology, Faculty of Social and Political Sciences, University of Cambridge.

Mundlak, Yair, Larson, Donald and Butzer, Rita (2004) 'Agricultural dynamics in Thailand, Indonesia and the Philippines', *The Australian Journal of Agricultural and Resource Economics*, 48:1, 95–126.

Muñoz, Cristina (1998) 'The feminisation of poverty in developing countries', *The Brown Journal of World Affairs*, 5:2, 283–8.

Muñoz, Eduardo (1997) 'Madres Adolescentes: Una Realidad Negada', *Otra Mirada* (Centro Nacional para el Desarrollo de la Mujer y la Familia, San José), 1:3, 43–5.

Murphy, Brian (2001) 'Thinking in the active voice: macropolicy and the individual', in Neil Middleton, Phil O'Keefe and Rob Visser (eds) *Negotiating Poverty: New Directions, Renewed Debate* (London: Pluto), pp. 26–40.

Muthwa, Sibongile (1993) 'Household survival, urban poverty and female household headship in Soweto: some key issues for further policy research', paper presented in seminar series 'The Societies of Southern Africa in the 19th and 20th Centuries: Women, Colonialism and Commonwealth', Institute of Commonwealth Studies, University of London, 19 November.

N'jie, Makaireh and Loum, Abdoulie with Benett, Yves (2003) 'A study of parent–teacher associations at lower basic schools in The Gambia', mimeo (Bakau: Educational Research Network for West and Central Africa, The Gambia Chapter).

Nagot, Ma Cristina D. (1991) 'Preliminary investigation on domestic violence against women', in Sister Mary John Mananzan (ed.) *Essays on Women*, revd edn (Manila: Institute of Women's Studies, St Scholastica's College), pp. 113–28.

National Anti-Poverty Commission (NAPC) (2003) *Ulat NAPC*, 30 June 2001–30 June 2003 (Quezon City: NAPC).

National Commission on the Role of Filipino Women (NCRFW) (2001) *The GAD Budget* (Manila: NCRFW).

National Commission on the Role of Filipino Women (NCRFW) (2002a) *Framework Plan for Women* (Manila: NCRFW).

National Commission on the Role of Filipino Women (NCRFW) (2002b) *Making LGUs Gender-Responsive: A Primer for Local Chief Executives* (Manila: NCRFW).

National Commission on the Role of Filipino Women (NCRFW) (2003) *Directory of Non-Government Organisations Working on Women* (Manila: NCRFW).

National Commission on the Role of Filipino Women (NCRFW) (2004a) *Philippine Progress Report (2001–2003) on the Implementation of the Beijing Platform for Action and Outcome of the 23rd Special Session of the General Assembly* (Manila: NCRFW).

National Commission on the Role of Filipino Women (NCRFW) (2004b) *Republic Act 9262: Anti-Violence Against Women and their Children Act of 2004* (Manila: NCRFW).

National Commission on the Role of Filipino Women (NCRFW) (2004c) *Gender and Development Budgeting in the Philippines: Issues, Challenges and Imperatives* (Manila: NCRFW).

National Commission on the Role of Filipino Women (NCRFW) (2004d) *Report on the State of Filipino Women 2001–2003* (Manila: NCRFW).

National Economic and Development Authority (NEDA) Region 7 (2002) *Central Visayas Socio-Economic Profile* (Cebu City: NEDA Regional Office 7).

National Economic and Development Authority (NEDA) (2001) *The Medium-Term Philippine Development Plan 2001–2004 – Philippines* (Manila: NEDA).

National Economic and Development Authority (NEDA) (2004) *The Medium-Term Philippine Development Plan 2004–2010 – Philippines* (Manila: NEDA).

National Statistics Office (NSO) (2003) *The Philippines in Figures 2003* (Manila: NSO).

National Women's Bureau (NWB) (2002) *2003–2007 Strategic Plan* (Banjul: NWB).

Nauckhoff, Eva (2004) 'Poverty without poor', in Gerd Johnsson-Latham (ed.) *Power and Privileges: Gender Discrimination and Poverty* (Stockholm: Regerinskanliet), pp. 46–83.

Neumayer, Eric and de Soysa, Indra (2005) 'Globalisation, women's economic rights and forced labour', mimeo, London School of Economics, Department of Geography and Environment.

Nitsch, Manfred and Schwarzer, Helmut (1996) *Recent Developments in Financing Social Security in Latin America*, Discussion Paper No. 1, Issues in Social Protection (Geneva: ILO).

Njie-Saidy, Isatou (2000) Speech at special session of the UN General Assembly, Women 2000: Equality, Development and Peace for the 21st

Century, http://www.un.org/womenwatch/daw/follow-up/beijing+5stat/statements/gambia5.htm, accessed 31 July 2003.

NORFIL (2004) *Situation of Filipino Children* (Lapu-Lapu City: NORFIL).

Oduber Quirós, Daniel (1987) 'Consideraciones Generales sobre Ocupación de Baldios y Tenencia de la Tierra en los Ultimos Decadas', *Revista ABRA*, 7–8, 35–41.

Oficina de la Primera Dama (OPD), Consejo Interinstitucional de Atención a la Madre Adolescente, and Instituto Nacional de la Mujeres (INAMU) (1999) *Construyendo Oportunidades: Un Programa de Apoyo para Abrir Caminosa las Adolescentes Embarazadas y Madres* (San José: INAMU).

Ofstedal, Mary Beth, Reidy, Erin and Knodel, John (2004) 'Gender differences in economic support and well-being of older Asians', *Journal of Cross-Cultural Gerontology*, 19, 165–201.

Olavarría, José (2003) 'Men at home? Child rearing and housekeeping among Chilean working-class fathers', in Matthew Gutmann (ed.) *Changing Men and Masculinities in Latin America* (Durham, NC: Duke University Press), pp. 333–50.

Oliver, Chloe (2002) 'Female-headed households: diverse and disadvantaged? An investigation into households headed by women in low-income neighbourhoods of Montevideo, Uruguay', unpublished BA dissertation, Department of Geography, University College London.

Olsen de Figueres, Karen (2002) *The Road to Equality – Women in Parliament in Costa Rica* International IDEA: Stockholm, http://www.idea.int, accessed May 2005.

Oppong, Christine (1997) 'African family systems and socio-economic crisis', in Aderanti Adepoju (ed.) *Family, Population and Deveolpment in Africa* (London: Zed), pp. 158–82.

Orbeta, Aniceto (2002) *Population and Poverty: A Review of the Links, Evidence and Implications for the Philippines*, Discussion Paper Series No. 2002-21 (Makati City: Philippine Institute for Development Studies).

Orbeta, Aniceto (2003) 'Population and the fight against poverty', *PIDS Policy Notes*, No. 2004-04 (Philippine Institute for Development Studies, Makati City).

Organisation for Economic Co-operation and Development (OECD) (2004) *OECD Investment Policy Review, Caribbean Rim: Costa Rica, Dominican Republic, Jamaica* (Paris: OECD).

Oxaal, Zöe, with Baden, Sally (1997) *Gender and Empowerment: Definitions, Approaches and Implications for Policy* (Brighton: Institute of Development Studies, University of Sussex, BRIDGE Report No. 40).

Pacheco de la Espriella, Abel (2005) 'Un Año Crucial para Costa Rica' (San José: Legislative Assembly), http://www.asamblea.go.cr/actual/boletin/2005/may05/discurso_pacheco/, accessed 18 May 2005.

Painter, Genevieve (2004) *Gender, the Millennium Development Goals, and Human Rights in the Context of the 2005 Review Processes*, Report for the Gender and Development Network (London: GADN).

Painter, Genevieve Renard (2005) 'Linking women's human rights and the MDGs: an agenda for 2005 from the UK Gender and Development Network', in Caroline Sweetman (ed.) *Gender and the Millennium Development Goals* (Oxford: Oxfam), pp. 79–93.

Palmer, Ingrid (1992) 'Gender, equity and economic efficiency in adjustment programmes', in Haleh Afshar and Carolyne Dennis (eds) *Women and Adjustment Policies in the Third World* (Basingstoke: Macmillan), pp. 69–83.

Palmer, Steven and Molina, Iván (2004) 'Costa Rica: a millennial profile', in Steven Palmer and Iván Molina (eds) *The Costa Rica Reader: History, Culture and Politics* (Durham, NC: Duke University Press), pp. 361–3.

Pan American Health Organization (PAHO) (2002) *Costa Rica: Core Health Data Selected Indicators* (Washington, DC: PAHO).

Pan American Health Organization (PAHO) (2003) *Gender and Health in the Americas* (Washington, DC: PAHO).

Pan American Health Organization (PAHO) and Merck Institute of Aging and Health (MIAH) (2004) *The State of Aging and Health in Latin America and the Caribbean* (Washington, DC: PAHO/MIAH).

Panda, Pradeep Kumar (1997) 'Female headship, poverty and child welfare: a study of rural Orissa', *Economic and Political Weekly*, 25 October, 73–82.

Pankhurst, Helen (2002) 'Passing the buck? Money literacy and alternatives to savings and credit schemes', *Gender and Development*, 10:3, 10–21.

Paolisso, Michael and Gammage, Sarah (1996) *Women's Responses to Environmental Degradation: Case Studies From Latin America* (Washington, DC: International Center for Research on Women).

Parpart, Jane (2002) 'Gender and empowerment: new thoughts, new approaches', in Vandana Desai and Robert Potter (eds) *The Companion to Development Studies* (London: Edward Arnold), pp. 338–42.

Parreñas, Rhacel Salazar (2001) *Servants of Globalisation: Women, Migration and Domestic Work* (Stanford, CA: Stanford University Press).

Pascua, Melissa (2003) 'Some notes on the questions asked in the family incomes and expenditures surveys', *Notes on the Official Poverty Statistics in the Philippines*, Series TN 200307-SS1-02 (Manila: National Statistical Coordination Board).

Pavia-Ticzon, Lucia (1990) 'A feminist reflection on organisation development', in Marjorie Evasco, Aurora Javate de Dios, and Flor Caagusan (eds) *Women's Springbook: Readings on Women and Society* (Quezon City: Fresam Press), pp. 115–20.

Pearce, Diana (1978) 'The feminisation of poverty: women, work and welfare', *The Urban and Social Change Review*, 11, 23–36.

Pearson, Ruth (1998) ' "Nimble fingers" revisited: reflections on women and Third World industrialisation in the late twentieth century', in Cecile Jackson and Ruth Pearson (eds) *Feminist Visions of Development: Gender Analysis and Policy* (London: Routledge), pp. 171–88.

Pedro, Amor B. (2003) 'A profile of the Filipino family 2003', in Ernesto Gonzales (ed.) *Globalisation and the Asian Family. Volume 1: The Filipino Family Survey 2003* (Manila: University of Santo Tomas Social Research Centre), pp. 16–47.

Pereira García, María Teresa (1998) *Orientación Educativa* (San José, Costa Rica: Editorial Universidad Estatal a Distancia).

Pérez Echeverría, Laura (2005) *Las Mujeres en la Agenda Económica y la Apertura Comercial: El Caso de Costa Rica* (San José: Programa de las Naciones Unidas para el Desarrollo).

Perez-Corral, Violeta (2002a) 'Women's lives at stake', in Jeanne Frances Illo and Rosalinda Pineda-Ofreneo (eds) *Carrying the Burden of the World: Women Reflecting on the Effects of the Economic Crisis on Women and Girls* (Quezon City: University of the Philippines Centre for Integrative and Development Studies), pp. 191–216.

Perez-Corral, Violeta (2002b) 'Women, water and power: a continuing privatisation saga', in Jeanne Frances Illo and Rosalinda Pineda-Ofreneo (eds) *Carrying the Burden of the World: Women Reflecting on the Effects of the Economic Crisis on Women and Girls* (Quezon City: University of the Philippines Centre for Integrative and Development Studies), pp. 217–28.

Perrons, Diane (1999) 'Flexible working patterns and equal opportunities in the European Union: conflict or compatibility?', *European Journal of Women's Studies*, 6:4, 391–418.

Perrons, Diane (2004) *Globalisation and Social Change: People and Places in a Divided World* (London: Routledge).

Pertierra, Raul (1991) 'Viscera suckers and female sociality: the Philippine Asuang', in Department of Sociology-Anthropology (eds) *SA21: Selected Readings* (Quezon City: Ateneo de Manila University, Office of Research and Publications), pp. 184–201.

Peterson, Jean Treloggen (1993) 'Generalised extended family exchange: a case from the Philippines', *Journal of Marriage and the Family*, 55, 570–84.

Phoenix, Ann (1996) 'Social constructions of lone motherhood: a case of competing discourses', in Elizabeth Bortolaia Silva (ed.) *Good Enough Mothering? Feminist Perspectives on Lone Motherhood* (London: Routledge), pp. 175–90.

Pietila, Hilkka (2004) 'We can take over the MDGs', in Women's International Coalition for Economic Justice (WICEJ) (ed.) *Seeking Accountability on Women's Human Rights: Women Debate the UN Millennium Development Goals* (New York: WICEJ), pp. 35–6.

Pineda-Ofreneo, Rosalinda (1999) 'Filipino women remain poor', *PBSB Bulletin* (Manila), 2, 1–3, http://www.philwomenh.net/pbsb/bulletin/2nd-issue/wmnpoor.htm, accessed 14 September 2004.

Pineda-Ofreneo, Rosalinda (2002a) 'Confronting the crisis: women in the informal sector', in Jeanne Frances Illo and Rosalinda Pineda-Ofreneo (eds) *Carrying the Burden of the World: Women Reflecting on the Effects of the Economic Crisis on Women and Girls* (Quezon City: University of the Philippines Centre for Integrative and Development Studies), pp. 51–70.

Pineda-Ofreneo, Rosalinda (2002b) 'The informal sector four years later', in Jeanne Frances Illo and Rosalinda Pineda-Ofreneo (eds) *Carrying the Burden of the World: Women Reflecting on the Effects of the Economic Crisis on Women and Girls* (Quezon City: University of the Philippines Centre for Integrative and Development Studies), pp. 71–82.

Pineda-Ofreneo, Rosalinda (2002c) 'Some light, but not yet at the end of the tunnel', in Jeanne Frances Illo and Rosalinda Pineda-Ofreneo (eds), *Carrying the Burden of the World: Women Reflecting on the Effects of the Economic Crisis on Women and Girls* (Quezon City: University of the Philippines Centre for Integrative and Development Studies), pp. 235–9.

Pineda-Ofreneo, Rosalinda (2003) 'Women's empowerment in the light of poverty and continuing crisis', in Jeanne Frances Illo and Rosalinda Pineda-Ofreneo (eds) *Beyond the Crisis: Questions of Survival and Empowerment* (Quezon City: University of the Philippines Centre for Integrative and Development Studies and Centre for Women's Studies), pp. 1–21.

Pineda-Ofreneo, Rosalinda and Acosta, Ma Lourdes (2001) 'Integrating gender concerns in anti-poverty strategies', *Public Policy* (University of the Philippines), 5:2, 1–41.

Pineda-Ofreneo, Rosalinda and Cabanilla, Phoebe (2003) 'Empowerment amidst crisis: the experience of subcontracted embroidery workers in three communities', in Jeanne Frances Illo and Rosalinda Pineda-Ofreneo (eds), *Beyond the Crisis: Questions of Survival and Empowerment* (Quezon City: University of the Philippines Centre for Integrative and Development Studies and Centre for Women's Studies), pp. 41–78.

Porter, Gina and Blaufuss, Kathrin (2002) 'Children, transport and traffic in southern Ghana', paper presented at the International Workshop on Children and Traffic, Copenhagen, 2–3 May.

Presidencia de la República, Consejo Social (PRCS) (2003) *Plan Nacional para la Superación de la Pobreza y Desarrollo de Capacidades Humjanas 'Vida Nueva' Período 2002–2006* (San José: PRCS).

Primera Dama de la República (PDR) (2001) *Programas: Amor Jóven y Construyendo Oportunidades* (San José: PDR).

PROCESS (1993) *Gender Needs Assessment in PROCESS-supported Areas in Panay, Bohol and Northern Luzon* (Iloilo City: PROCESS).

Proctor, Sharon (2003) 'Gender, livelihoods and labour in rural Mexican households: the impact of neoliberal reform upon the farm and non-farm economy', unpublished PhD dissertation, Department of Agricultural and Food Economics, University of Reading.

Programa de las Naciones Unidas para el Desarrollo (PNUD), Costa Rica (2004) *Estrategia 2005–2006* (San José: PNUD, Costa Rica).

Programa de las Naciones Unidas para el Desarrollo (PNUD), Costa Rica (2005) *Comunicado de Prensa: Matrícula Educativa y Poder Adquisitivo Profundizan Brechas Cantonales* (San José: PNUD, Costa Rica).

Pro-Poor Advocacy Group (PROPAG) (2003) *Strategic Plan 2003 to 2005* (Bakau New Town: PROPAG).

Pro-Poor Tourism Partnership (PPTP) (2004) *Pro-Poor Tourism Info-Sheet No. 7: Economic Data on the Importance of Tourism in the Poorest Countries* (London: Pro-Poor Tourism Organisation).

Proyecto Estado de la Nación (PEN) (1998) *Estado de la Nación en Desarrollo Humano Sostenible* (San José: PEN).

Proyecto Estado de la Nación (PEN) (2002) *Octavo Informe sobre el Estado de la Nación, 2002* (San José: PEN).

Proyecto Estado de la Nación (PEN) (2005) *Undécimo Informe sobre el Estado de la Nación, 2004: Resumen* (San José: PEN).

Punch, Samantha (2001) 'Household division of labour: generation, gender, age, birth order and sibling composition', *Work, Employment and Society*, 15:4, 803–23.

Punch, Samantha (2002) 'Youth transitions and interdependent adult–child relations in rural Bolivia', *Journal of Rural Studies*, 18, 123–33.

Punch, Samantha (2003) 'Childhoods in the majority world: miniature adults or tribal children?', *Sociology*, 37:2, 277–95.

Quisumbing, Agnes (2003) 'What have we learned from research on intra-household allocation?', in Agnes Quisumbing (ed.) *Household Decisions, Gender, and Development: A Synthesis of Recent Research* (Washington, DC: International Food Policy Research Institute), pp. 1–16.

Quisumbing, Agnes, Estudillo, Jonna and Otsuka, Keijiro (2004) *Land and Schooling: Transferring Wealth Across Generations* (Baltimore, MD: Johns Hopkins for the International Food Policy Research Institute).

Quisumbing, Agnes, Haddad, Lawrence and Peña, Christine (1995) *Gender and Poverty: New Evidence from Ten Developing Countries* (Washington, DC: International Food Policy Research Institute, Food Consumption and Nutrition Division, Discussion Paper No. 9).

Quisumbing, Agnes and Maluccio, John (2003) 'Intrahousehold allocation and gender relations: new empirical evidence from four developing countries', in Agnes Quisumbing (ed.) *Household Decisions, Gender, and Development: A Synthesis of Recent Research* (Washington, DC: International Food Policy Research Institute), pp. 23–8.

Racelis, Mary (2005) 'Recasting urban power relations', *In Focus*, 7 (International Poverty Centre, Brasilia), 3–5.

Ragragio, Junio (2003) 'The case of Metro Manila', in UN Habitat (ed.) *Understanding Slums: Case Studies for the Global Report on Human Settlements 2003* (London: Development Planning Unit, University College London, http://www.ucl.ac.uk/dpu-projects/Global_Report/cities/manila.htm, accessed May 2004.

Rahnema, Majid (1993) 'Poverty', in Wolfgang Sachs (ed.) *The Development Dictionary* (London: Zed), 158–76.

Rai, Shirin (2002) *Gender and the Political Economy of Development* (Cambridge: Polity).

Rakodi, Carole (1999) 'A capital assets framework for analysing household livelihood strategies: implications for policy', *Development Policy Review*, 17, 315–42.

Rakodi, Carole with Lloyd-Jones, Tony (eds) (2002) *Urban Livelihoods: A People-Centred Approach to Reducing Poverty* (London: Earthscan).

Ramirez, Mina (1984) *Understanding Philippine Social Realities Through the Filipino Family: A Phenomenological Approach* (Manila: Asian Social Institute Communication Centre).

Ramos, Pilar (2001) *Revisión para Costa Rica: Propuesta de Indicaores de la CEPAL para el Seguimieno de la Plataforma de Acción de Beijing* (San José: INAMU/State of the Nation Project/UNDP).

Ravallion, Martin (2004a) 'Monitoring progress against global poverty', *In Focus* (UNDP International Poverty Centre), 4 September, 12–15, http://www.undp.org/povertycentre/newsletters/infocus4Sep04 eng.pdf.

Ravallion, Martin (2004b) *Pro-Poor Growth: A Primer*, World Bank Policy Research Working Paper 3242 (Washington, DC: World Bank), accessed September 2004.

Ravallion, Martin and Chen, Shaohua (2004) *China's (Uneven) Progress Against Poverty* World Bank Policy Research Working Paper 3408 (Washington, DC: World Bank), accessed September 2004.

Razavi, Shahra (1999) 'Gendered poverty and well-being: introduction', *Development and Change*, 30:3, 409–33.

Reddy, Sanjay (2004) 'A capability-based approach to estimating global poverty', *In Focus* (UNDP International Poverty Centre), 4 September, 6–8, http://www.undp.org/povertycentre/newsletters/infocus4Sep04eng.pdf.

Reddy, Sanjay and Heuty, Antoine (2005a) 'Peer and partner review: a practical approach to achieving the MDGs', mimeo, Department of Economics, Barnard College, Columbia University, New York.

Reddy, Sanjay and Heuty, Antoine (2005b) 'Achieving the Millennium Development Goals: what's wrong with existing analytical models?', mimeo, Department of Economics, Barnard College, Columbia University, New York.

Republic of The Gambia (RTG) (1993) *Population and Housing Census 1993 Vol. 7* (Banjul: Central Statistics Department).

Republic of The Gambia (RTG) (2002) *Strategy for Poverty Alleviation (SPA II) (PRSP)* (Banjul: Department of State for Finance and Economic Affairs [DOSFEA], Strategy for Poverty Alleviation Coordinating Office [SPACO]).

Republic of The Gambia (RTG) (2003a) *Annual Progress Report on SPAII/PRSP Completion and Progress in Implementation* (Banjul: Strategy for Poverty Alleviation Coordinating Office [SPACO]/ Department of State for Finance and Economic Affairs [DOSFEA]).

Republic of The Gambia (RTG) (2003b) *First National Millennium Development Goals Report* (Banjul: Statehouse).

Republic of the Philippines (RTP) (2000) *Republic Act 8972* (Manila: RTP).

Reyes, Cecila (2002) *The Poverty Fight: Have We Made an Impact?* Discussion Paper Series No. 2002-20 (Makati City: Philippine Institute for Development Studies).

Rico de Alonso, Ana and López Téllez, Nadia (1998) 'Informalidad, Jefatura Femenina y Supervivencia', *Revista Javeriana*, September, 193–7.

Robertson, Claire C. (1998) 'The feminisation of poverty in Africa: roots and branches', *The Brown Journal of World Affairs*, 5:2, 195–201.

Robson, Elspeth (1996) 'Working girls and boys: children's contributions to household survival in West Africa', *Geography*, 81:4, 403–7.

Rodenberg, Birte (2004) *Gender and Poverty Reduction: New Conceptual Approaches in International Development Cooperation*, Reports and Working Papers 4/2004 (Bonn: German Development Institute).

Rodgers, Dennis (2006) 'Living in the shadow of death: gangs, violence and social order in urban Nicaragua, 1996–2002', *Journal of Latin American Studies*, 38, 267–92.

Rodríguez, Eugenia (1999) 'La Redefinición de los Discursos sobre la Familia y el Género en Costa Rica (1890–1930)', *Populaçao e Familia*, July–December, 147–82.

Rodríguez, Eugenia (2000) *Hijas, Novias y Esposas: Familia, Matrimonio y Violencia Doméstica en el Valle Central de Costa Rica (1750–1850)* (Heredia, Costa Rica: Editorial Universidad Nacional).

Rodríguez Cháves, Bach Guiselle (1999) *Diocésis de Tilarán: Análsis del Quehacer Pastoral con Enfasis en la Diocésis de Tilarán* (Tilarán, Costa Rica: Diocésis de Tilarán).

Rodríguez Rodríguez, Geovanni (2000) *Guanacaste: Recursos Naturales, Empleo, Actividades Económicas y Desarrollo Local* (San José: Centro de Documentación e Investigación Legislativa), http://www.asamblea. go.cr/biblio/cedil/estudios/desarrollo%20ProvGuanacaste.htm, accessed September 2004.

Rodríguez Vignoli, Jorge (2004) 'La Fecundidad Alta en el Istmo Centroamericano: Un Riesgo en Transición', *Población y Salud en Mesoamérica*, 2:1 (Centro Centroamericano de Población, San José), http://www.ccp.ucr.ac.cr/revista.

Roe, Dilys, Goodwin, Harold and Ashley, Caroline (2002) 'The tourism industry and poverty reduction: a business primer, *Pro-Poor Tourism Briefing No. 2* (London: Pro-Poor Tourism Organisation).

Rogers, Beatrice (1995) 'Alternative definitions of female headship in the Dominican Republic', *World Development*, 23:12, 2033–9.

Rojas, Mariano (2003) 'The multidimensionality of poverty: a subjective well-being approach', paper prepared for Conference on Inequality, Poverty and Human Well-Being, World Institute for Development Economics Research, United Nations University, Helsinki, 30–31 May.

Rosario, Rosario S. Del (2002a) 'Girl child workers', in Jeanne Frances Illo and Rosalinda Pineda-Ofreneo (eds) *Carrying the Burden of the World: Women Reflecting on the Effects of the Economic Crisis on Women and Girls* (Quezon City: University of the Philippines Centre for Integrative and Development Studies), pp. 165–80.

Rosario, Rosario S. Del (2002b) 'Girls working in the street and in the home', in Jeanne Frances Illo and Rosalinda Pineda-Ofreneo (eds) *Carrying the Burden of the World: Women Reflecting on the Effects of the Economic Crisis on Women and Girls* (Quezon City: University of the Philippines Centre for Integrative and Development Studies), pp. 181–90.

Roseneil, Sasha and Mann, Kirk (1996) 'Unpalatable choices and inadequate families: lone mothers and the underclass debate', in Elizabeth

Bortolaia Silva (ed.) *Good Enough Mothering? Feminist Perspectives on Lone Motherhood* (London: Routledge), pp. 191–210.

Rosenhouse, Sandra (1989) *Identifying the Poor: Is 'Headship' a Useful Concept?* World Bank Living Standards Mesaurement Survey Working Paper No. 58 (Washington, DC: World Bank).

Rowlands, J. (1996) 'Empowerment examined', in Oxfam (ed.) *Development and Social Diversity* (Oxford: Oxfam), pp. 86–92.

Ruggeri Laderchi, Caterina, Saith, Ruhi and Stewart, Frances (2003) 'Everyone agrees we need poverty reduction, but not what this means', paper prepared for Conference on Inequality, Poverty and Human Well-Being, World Institute for Development Economics Research, United Nations University, Helsinki, 30–31 May.

Safa, Helen (1990) 'Women and industrialisation in the Caribbean', in Sharon Stichter and Jane Parpart (eds) *Women, Employment and the Family in the International Division of Labour* (Basingstoke: Macmillan), pp. 72–97.

Safa, Helen (1995) *The Myth of the Male Breadwinner: Women and Industrialisation in the Caribbean* (Boulder, CO: Westview).

Safa, Helen (1998) 'Female-headed households in the Caribbean: sign of pathology or alternative form of family organisation?', *The Brown Journal of World Affairs*, 5:2, 203–14.

Safa, Helen (2002) 'Questioning globalisation: gender and export processing in the Dominican Republic', *Journal of Developing Societies*, 18:2–3, 11–31.

Safa, Helen and Antrobus, Peggy (1992) 'Women and the economic crisis in the Caribbean', in Lourdes Benería and Shelley Feldman (eds) *Unequal Burden: Economic Crises, Persistent Poverty and Women's Work* (Boulder, CO: Westview Press), pp. 49–82.

Sagot, Monsterrat (ed.) (1999) *Analysis Situacional de los Derechos de las Niñas y las Adolescentes en Costa Rica* (San José: United Nations Children's Fund (UNICEF)/Universidad de Costa Rica, Maestría Regional en Estudios de la Mujer).

Saint Joseph's Adult Education Centre (SJAEC) (2003) *A Selection of Students' Writings* (Banjul: SJAEC).

Sajor, Edsel (2003) 'Globalisation and the urban property boom in Metro Cebu, Philippines', *Development and Change*, 34:4, 713–41.

Sánchez-Ancochea, Diego (2005) 'Domestic capital, civil servants and the state: Costa Rica and the Dominican Republic under globalisation', *Journal of Latin American Studies*, 37:4, 693–726.

Sancho Montero, Silvia María (1995) *El Programa Hogares Comunitarios en Costa Rica, Sus Primeros Pasos: Primera Parte* (San José: Institute Mixto de Ayuda Social, Dirección Hogares Comunitarios).

Sande, Marianne A.B. van der, Inskip, Hazel, Jaiteh, Kebba O., Maine, Nicholas P., Walraven, Gijs E.L., Hall, Andrew and McAdam, Keith P.W.J. (2001) 'Changing causes of death in the West African town of Banjul, 1942–97', *Bulletin of the World Health Organization*, 79:2, 133–41.

Sandoval, Irma and González, Lidia (2000) 'La Composición de los Hogares Costarricenses en los Censos de 1984 y 2000: Un Análisis desde las Jefaturas Femeninas y Masculinas', paper given at Simposio 'Costa Rica a la Luz del Censo 2000', www.inec.co.gr, accessed May 2005.

Sandoval-García, Carlos (1997) *Sueños y Sudores en la Vida Cotidiana: Trabajadores y Trabajadoras de la Maquila y la Construcción en Costa Rica* (San José: Universidad de Costa Rica, Colección Instituto de Investigaciones Sociales).

Sandoval-García, Carlos (2004a) *Threatening Others: Nicaraguans and the Formation of National Identities in Costa Rica* (Athens, OH: Ohio University Press).

Sandoval-García, Carlos (2004b) 'Contested discourses on national identity: representing Nicaraguan immigration to Costa Rica', *Bulletin of Latin American Research*, 23:4, 434–45.

Sané, Pierre (2005) 'Reducing poverty: how human rights can help', paper presented at the Centre for the Study of Human Rights, London School of Economics, January 2005.

Sanneh, Faal (2003) *Report on the Theme of Youth, Environment, Eco-Tourism and Poverty Reduction in The Gambia* (Banjul: SPACO).

Sassen, Saskia (2002) 'Counter-geographies of globalisation: feminisation of survival', in Kreimild Saunders (ed.) *Feminist Post-Development Thought* (London: Zed), pp. 89–104.

Satterthwaite, David (2003) 'The Millennium Development Goals and poverty reduction', in David Satterthwaite (ed.) *The Millennium Development Goals and Local Processes: Hitting the Target or Missing the Point?* (London: International Institute for Environment and Development), 7–46.

Satterthwaite, David (2005) 'Under-counting the urban poor', *In Focus*, (International Poverty Centre, Brasilia), 7 (September), 3–5.

Sauma, Pablo (2004) 'Distribución del ingreso, pobreza, y vulnerabilidad social en Costa Rica', in PEN (ed.) *Décimo Informe sobre el Estado de la Nación en Desarrollo Humano Sostenible* (San José: PEN).

Save the Children Sweden (SCS) (2005) *Female Genital Mutilation: Save the Children Sweden's Activities in West Africa and at the Global Level* (Stockholm: SCS).

Schifter, Jacobo and Madrigal, Johnny (1996) *Las Gavetas Sexuales del Costarricense y el Riesgo de la Infección con el VIH* (San José: Editorial IMEDIEX).

Scott, Alison MacEwen (1994) *Divisions and Solidarities: Gender, Class and Employment in Latin America* (London: Routledge).

Scott, Steffanie (2003) 'Gender, household headship and entitlements to land: new vulnerabilities in Vietnam's decollectivisation', *Gender, Technology and Development*, 7:2, 233–63.

Sear, Rebecca, Allal, Nadine and Mace, Ruth (2007) 'Family matters: kin, demography and child health in a rural Gambian population', in Gillian Bentley and Ruth Mace (eds), *Substitute Parents: Alloparenting in Human Societies* (Oxford: Bergahn) (forthcoming).

Sear, Rebecca, Mace, Ruth and McGregor, Ian (2000) 'Maternal grandmothers improve nutritional status and survival of children in rural Gambia', *Proceedings of the Royal Society, Series B, Biological Sciences*, 267, 1641–7.

Secretaría de Gobernación (1996) *Alianza para la Igualdad: Programa Nacional de la Mujer, 1995–2000* (México DF: Secretaría de Gobernación).

Selby, Henry, Murphy, Arthur and Lorenzen, Stephen (1990) *The Mexican Urban Household: Organising for Self-Defence* (Austin, TX: University of Texas Press).

Sen, Amartya K. (1981) *Poverty and Famines* (Oxford: Clarendon Press).

Sen, Amartya K. (1985) *Commodities and Capabilities* (Helsinki: United Nations University, World Institute for Development Economics Research).

Sen, Amartya K. (1987a) *Hunger and Entitlements* (Amsterdam: North Holland Press).

Sen, Amartya K. (1987b) *Gender and Cooperative Conflicts* (Helsinki: World Institute for Development Economics Research, Working Paper No. 18).

Sen, Amartya K. (1990) 'Gender and cooperative conflicts', in Irene Tinker (ed.) *Persistent Inequalities: Women and World Development* (New York: Oxford University Press), pp. 123–49.

Sen, Amartya K. (1999) *Development as Freedom* (Oxford: Oxford University Press).

Sen, Gita (1999) 'Engendering poverty alleviation: challenges and opportunities', *Development and Change*, 30:3, 685–92.

Senate Economic Planning Office (SEPO) (2005) *Philippine Poverty at a Glance* (Manila: SEPO).

Sethuraman, S.V. (1998) *Gender, Informality and Poverty: A Global Review. Gender Bias in Female Informal Employment and Incomes in Developing Countries* (Geneva/Cambridge, MA/Washington, DC: Women in Informal Employment Globalising and Organising [WIEGO]/World Bank).

Shanthi, K. (1994) 'Growing incidence of female household headship: causes and cure', *Social Action* (New Delhi) 44, 17–33.

Shaw, Matthew and Jawo, Michelle (2000) 'Gambian experiences with stepping stones: 1996–99', in *Participatory Leaning and Action (PLA) Notes: Sexual and Reproductive Health* (International Institute of Environment and Development, London), 37, 73–8.

Shimuzu, Hiromu (1991) 'Filipino children in the family and society: growing up in a many people environment', in Department of Sociology-Anthropology (eds) *SA21: Selected Readings* (Quezon City: Ateneo de Manila University, Office of Research and Publications), pp. 106–25.

Shire, Amy and Pesso, Lauren (2003) 'Changing policies and attitudes: postabortion care in the Philippines', *Compass* (Engender Health, New York) 1, 1–4.

Silberschmidt, Margrethe (1999) *'Women Forget that Men are the Masters': Gender Antagonism and Socio-Economic Change in Kisii District, Kenya* (Uppsala: Nordiska Afrikainstitute).

Singh, Susheela, Cabgon, Josefina, Hossain, Altaf, Khamal, Haidary and Perez, Aurora (1997) 'Estimating the level of abortion in the Philippines and Bangladesh', *International Family Planning Perspectives*, 23:3, 100–107 and 144.

Slon Montero, Pablo and Zúñiga Rojas, Edwin (2005) 'Dinámica de la Pobreza en Costa Rica en el Período 2002–2004', in Proyecto Estado de la Nación, *Undécimo Informe Sobre el Estado de la Nación en el Desarrollo Humano Sostenible* (San José: PEN), http://www.estadonacion.or.cr/Info2005, accessed May 2005.

Smith, Harry (2004) 'Costa Rica's triangle of solidarity: can government-led spaces for negotiation enhance the involvement of civil society in governance', *Environment and Urbanisation*, 16:1, 63–77.

Social Weather Stations (SWS) (2001) Media release, 'SWS survey: poverty rise but hunger declines' (Quezon City: Social Weather Stations), http://www.sws.org/ph, accessed 28 January 2005.

Solórzano, Irela, Abaunza, Humberto and Bradshaw, Sarah (2000) 'Evaluación de la Campaña "Violencia Contra las Mujeres: Un Desastre que los Hombres Sí Podemos Evitar"', mimeo (Managua: Puntos de Encuentro).

Sosseh-Gaye, Adelaide (2001) 'Civil society in the new millennium: The Gambia national report. A critique', mimeo, Educational Research Network of West and Central Africa [ERNWACA], Bakau.

Srinivasan, T.N. (2004) 'The unsatisfactory state of global poverty estimation', *In Focus* (UNDP International Poverty Centre), 4: September, 3–5, http://www.undp.org/povertycentre/newsletters/infocus4Sep04eng.pdf, accessed September 2004.

Stacey, Judith (1997) 'The neo-family-values campaign', in Roger Lancaster and Michaela di Leonardo (eds) *The Gender/Sexuality Reader* (New York: Routledge), pp. 432–70.

Standing, Guy (1999) 'Global feminisation through flexible labour: a theme revisited', *World Development*, 27:3, 583–602.

Statehouse, Gambia (SG) (2002) 'Budget speech 2002', http://www.statehouse.gm/budget2002.6htm, accessed 31 July 2003.

Statehouse, Gambia (SG) (2005) 'Budget speech 2005', http://www.statehouse.gm/bdgtspeech2005/section6.htm, accessed 5 July 2005.

Staudt, Kathleen (1998) 'The feminisation of poverty: global perspectives', *The Brown Journal of World Affairs*, 5:2, 215–24.

Strategy for Poverty Coordinating Office (SPACO)/Central Statistics Department (CSD)/ActionAid The Gambia/Support to Decentralised Rural Development (2002a) *Participatory Poverty Assessment: Banjul/KMC Synthesis, 1999–2002* (Banjul: SPACO).

Strategy for Poverty Coordinating Office (SPACO)/Central Statistics Department (CSD)/ActionAid The Gambia/Support to Decentralised Rural Development (2002b) *Participatory Poverty Assessment: Greater Banjul Synthesis, 1999–2002* (Banjul: SPACO).

Strategy for Poverty Coordinating Office (SPACO)/Central Statistics Department (CSD)/ActionAid The Gambia/Support to Decentralised Rural Development (2002c) *Participatory Poverty Assessment: Western Division Synthesis, 1999–2002* (Banjul: SPACO).

Strategy for Poverty Coordinating Office (SPACO) (2003a) *Strategy for Poverty Alleviation II, Volume I: Poverty in The Gambia* (Banjul: SPACO).

Strategy for Poverty Coordinating Office (SPACO) (2003b) *Strategy for Poverty Alleviation II, Volume II: SPA II Goals and Objectives* (Banjul: SPACO).

Strategy for Poverty Coordinating Office (SPACO) (2003c) *Strategy for Poverty Alleviation II, Volume III: SPA II Priority Poverty Reducing Actions* (Banjul: SPACO).

Strategy for Poverty Coordinating Office (SPACO) (2003d) *Strategy for Poverty Alleviation II, Volume IV: Policy Planning and Budgeting Framework* (Banjul: SPACO).

Strategy for Poverty Coordinating Office (SPACO) (2003e) *Strategy for Poverty Alleviation II, Volume V: Partnership Arrangements for Implementing SPA II* (Banjul: SPACO).

Strategy for Poverty Coordinating Office (SPACO) (2004) *Participatory Poverty Assessment 2003: National Report on the Health Sector PPA* (Banjul: SPACO).

Stryker, J. Dirck (2001) 'Common diagnostic framework for poverty reduction', in Neil Middleton, Phil O'Keefe and Rob Visser (eds) *Negotiating Poverty: New Directions, Renewed Debate* (London: Pluto), pp. 74–88.

Subrahmanian, Ramya (2002) 'Children's work and schooling: a review of the debates', in Vandana Desai and Robert Potter (eds) *The Companion to Development Studies* (London: Arnold), pp. 400–405.

Subramanian, S. (2005) 'Headcount poverty comparisons', *One Pager* (IPC, United Nations Development Programme, Brasilia), November, 18.

Sweetman, Caroline (2002) 'Editorial', *Gender and Development*, 10:3, 2–9.

Sweetman, Caroline (2005) 'Editorial', in Caroline Sweetman (ed.) *Gender and the Millennium Development Goals* (Oxford: Oxfam), pp. 2–8.

Taal, A.B.S. (2003) *Youth Culture Tackling Poverty and Promoting Sustainable Development Through Multi-Sectoral Approach in The Gambia* (Banjul: SPACO).

Tacoli, Cecilia (2002) *Changing Rural–Urban Interactions in Sub-Saharan Africa and their Impact on Livelihoods: A Summary* (London: International Institute for Environment and Development).

Tasies Castro, Esperanza (1996) 'Mujer, Pobreza y Conflicto Social', *Ciencias Sociales* (FLACSO, San José) 71, 39–32.

Thayer, Millie (1997) 'Identity, revolution and democracy: lesbian movements in Central America', *Social Problems*, 44:3, 386–407.

The Association of Non-Governmental Organisations (TANGO) (1999) Report of TANGO Sub-regional Workshop on Gender, Peace and Social Justice, 7–9 July (Bakau: TANGO).

The Association of Non-Governmental Organisations (TANGO) (2000a) *The Gambia National Report: Civil Society in the New Millennium Project of the Commonwealth Foundation* (Bakau: TANGO).

The Association of Non-Governmental Organisations (TANGO) (2000b) *NGOs' Assessment of the Government's Strategy for Poverty Alleviation* (Bakau: TANGO).

The Association of Non-Governmental Organisations (TANGO) (2001) *Report on Divisional Consultation Workshops on SPA II* (Bakau: TANGO).

The Gambia Social Development Fund (TGSDF) (2002a) *Social Services Interventions* (Bakau New Town: SDF).

The Gambia Social Development Fund (TGSDF) (2002b) *Micro-Credit Interventions* (Bakau New Town: SDF).

Thomas, J.J. (1995) *Surviving in the City: The Urban Informal Sector in Latin America* (London: Pluto).

Thomas, Susan (1994) 'From the culture of poverty to the culture of single motherhood: the new poverty paradigm', *Women and Politics*, 14:2, 65–97.

Tiano, Susan (2001) 'From victims to agents: a new generation of literature on women in Latin America', *Latin American Research Review*, 36:3, 183–203.

Tidalgo, Hilda (2004) *What is the ILO? A Backgrounder* (Manila: ILO Sub-Regional Office).

Tiffer, Carlos (1998) 'Status of adolescents in conflict with the criminal law: the new model for juvenile criminal justice in Costa Rica', in UNICEF (ed.) *Adolescence, Child Rights and Urban Poverty in Costa Rica* (San José: UNICEF/HABITAT), pp. 115–26.

Tinker, Irene (1990) 'A context for the field and for the book', in Irene Tinker (ed.) *Persistent Inequalities: Women and World Development* (Oxford: Oxford University Press), pp. 3–13.

Tinker, Irene (1997) *Street Foods: Urban Food and Employment in Developing Countries* (New York: Oxford University Press).

Todes, Alison and Walker, Norah (1993) 'Women and housing policy in South Africa: a discussion of Durban case studies', in Hemalata Dandekar (ed.) *Women, Shelter and Development: First and Third World Perspectives* (Ann Arbor, MI: George Wahr), pp. 41–53.

Tokman, Victor (1989) 'Policies for a heterogeneous informal sector in Latin America', *World Development*, 17:7, 1067–76.

Toulmin, Camilla and Guèye, Bara (2003) 'How will West African countries meet the MDGs?' in David Satterthwaite (ed.) *The Millennium Development Goals and Local Processes: Hitting the Target or Missing the Point?* (London: International Institute for Environment and Development), pp. 107–33.

Townsend, Janet, Zapata, Emma, Rowlands, Jo, Alberti, Pilar and Mercado, Marta (1999) *Women and Power: Fighting Patriarchies and Poverty* (London: Zed).

Townsend, Peter (2004) 'Fighting child poverty through direct policies', *In Focus* (UNDP International Poverty Centre, Brasilia), March, 9–11.

Trejos, Juan Diego (1995) 'Costa Rica: La Respuesta Estatal Frente a la Pobreza – Instituciones, Programas y Recursos', in Dagmar Raczynski (ed.) *Estrategias para Combatir Pobreza en América Latina: Programas, Instituciones y Recursos* (Santiago de Chile: CIEPLAN/IADB), pp. 163–215.

Trejos, Juan Diego and Montiel, Nancy (1999) *El Capital de los Pobres en Costa Rica: Acceso, Utilización y Rendimiento* (Washington, DC: IADB).

Tuoane, Malatela, Malatjane, Tiisetso and Ntsoaki, Mapetla (2001) 'Gender differentials and their socio-economic implications on household headship in Lesotho', paper presented at the International Colloquium on Gender, Population and Development in Africa, Abidjan, 16–21 July.

Uchida, Masako and Ogawa, Keiichi (2002) 'Education For All (EFA)–Fast Track Initiative (FTI)', paper prepared for Washington, DC, Development Forum, 19 December.

Ulate, Annabelle (1992) 'Aumento de las Exportaciones: Obsesión del Ajuste Estructural', in Juan Manuel Villasuso (ed.) *El Nuevo Rostro de Costa Rica* (Heredia: Centro de Estudios Democráticos de América Latina), pp. 471–92.

UNDP (1990) *Human Development Report 1990* (Oxford: Oxford University Press).

United Nations (UN) (1996) *Food Security for All, Food Security for Rural Women* (Geneva: International Steering Committee on the Economic Advancement of Rural Women).

United Nations (UN) (2000) *The World's Women 2000: Trends and Statistics* (New York: United Nations).

United Nations (UN) (2001) *The Gambia: Country Paper and Action Programme 2001–2010* (New York: UN).

United Nations (UN) (2003) *Millennium Indicators* (New York: UN Statistics Division), http://millenniumindicators.un.org/unsd/mi.mi.asp, accessed 9 March 2004.

United Nations Children's Fund (UNICEF) (1997) *Role of Men in the Lives of Children: A Study of How Improving Knowledge about Men in Families Helps Strengthen Programming for Children and Women* (New York: UNICEF).

United Nations Children's Fund The Gambia (UNICEF The Gambia) (1999) *Major Issues Affecting Children and Women: Programme Cycle 1999–2003* (Banjul: UNICEF The Gambia), http://www.un.gam/unicef.profile.htm, accessed 31 July 2003.

United Nations (UN) Country Team/United Nations Fund for Women (UNIFEM) (2003) *To Produce and to Care: How do Women and Men Fare in Securing Well-Being and Human Freedoms?* (Manila: UN Country Team/UNIFEM).

United Nations Department of Public Information (UNDPI) (2000) 'Women 2000: the feminisation of poverty – fact sheet no. 1', http://www.un.org/womenwatch/daw/followup, accessed May 2003.

United Nations Development Fund for Women (UNIFEM) (1995) *The Human Cost of Women's Poverty: Perspectives from Latin America and the Caribbean* (Mexico City: UNIFEM).

United Nations Development Fund for Women (UNIFEM) (2000) *Progress of the World's Women 2000* (New York: UNIFEM, Biennial Report).

United Nations Development Fund for Women (UNIFEM) (2002) *Progress of the World's Women 2002, Volume 2* (New York: UNIFEM).

United Nations Development Programme (UNDP) (1990) *Human Development Report 1990* (Oxford: Oxford University Press).

United Nations Development Programme (UNDP) (1994) *Human Development Report 1994* (Oxford: Oxford University Press).

United Nations Development Programme (UNDP) (1995) *Human Development Report 1995* (Oxford: Oxford University Press).

United Nations Development Programme (UNDP) (1996) *Human Development Report 1996* (Oxford: Oxford University Press).

United Nations Development Programme (UNDP) (1997) *Human Development Report 1997* (Oxford: Oxford University Press).

United Nations Development Programme (UNDP) (1998) *Human Development Report 1998* (Oxford: Oxford University Press).

United Nations Development Programme (UNDP) (1999) *Human Development Report 1999* (Oxford: Oxford University Press).

United Nations Development Programme (UNDP) (2000a) *The Gambia Report* (Banjul: UNDP), http://www.ungambia.gm/undp/publications/gamreport.htm, accessed 31 July 2003.

United Nations Development Programme (UNDP) (2000b) *Overcoming Human Poverty: UNDP Poverty Report 2000* (New York: UNDP), http://www.undp.org/povertyreport/Chapters/chap 9.html, accessed 31 July 2003.

United Nations Development Programme (UNDP) (2000c) *Philippines Country Assessment* (New York: UNDP), http://www.undp.org/povertyreport/countryprofiles/phillip1.html, accessed 30 May 2004.

United Nations Development Programme (UNDP) (2001a) *Human Development Report 2001* (Oxford: Oxford University Press).

United Nations Development Programme (UNDP) (2001b) *UNDP Thematic Trust Fund Gender* (New York: UNDP).

United Nations Development Programme (UNDP) (2002) *Human Development Report 2002* (Oxford: Oxford University Press).

United Nations Development Programme (UNDP) (2003a) *Human Development Report 2003* (Oxford: Oxford University Press).

United Nations Development Programme (UNDP) (2003b) *Millennium Development Goals: National Reports Through a Gender Lens* (New York: UNDP).

United Nations Development Programme (UNDP) (2004) *Human Development Report 2004* (Oxford: Oxford University Press).

United Nations Development Programme (UNDP) (2005) *En Route to Equality: A Gender Review of National MDG Reports 2005* (New York: UNDP).

United Nations Development Programme (UNDP) Philippines (2004) *Common Country Assessment: Philippines* (Manila: UNDP Philippines).

United Nations Development Programme (UNDP) and United Nations Population Fund (UNFPA) (2001) *Second Country Cooperation Framework for the Philippines (2002–2004)* (New York: UNDP/UNFPA).

United Nations Development Programme (UNDP) and United Nations Population Fund (UNFPA) (2004) *UNDP: Country Programming and Related Matters. Draft Country Programme Document for the Republic of the Philippines (2005–2009)* (Geneva: United Nations).

United Nations Development Programme (UNDP), Southern Africa – Sub-Regional Resource Facility (SURF) and United Nations Fund for Women (UNIFEM) Regional Office for Southern Africa (2003) *Proceedings: Experts Meeting on Gender Mainstreaming of Poverty Reduction Strategy Papers in Selected African Countries* (Pretoria: UNDP/SURF/UNIFEM).

United Nations Division for the Advancement of Women (UNDAW) (1991) 'Women and Households in a Changing World', in Eleanora Barbieri Masini and Susan Stratigos (eds) *Women, Households and Change* (Tokyo: United Nations University Press), pp. 30–52.

United Nations Division for the Advancement of Women (UNDAW) (2000) *Women 2000: Gender Equality, Development and Peace for the 21st Century* (New York: UNDAW).

United Nations Division for the Advancement of Women (UNDAW) (2005) *The Role of National Mechanisms in Promoting Gender Equality and the Empowerment of Women*, report of the Expert Group meeting (New York: UNDAW).

United Nations Economic and Social Commission for Western Asia (UNESCWA) (2003) *Female-Headed Households in Selected Conflict-Stricken ESCWA Areas: An Exploratory Survey for Formulating Poverty Alleviation Policies* (New York: UN).

United Nations Educational, Scientific and Cultural Organisation (UNESCO) (1997) *Male Roles and Masculinities in the Perspective of a Culture of Peace*, report, Expert Group meeting, Oslo, Norway, 24–28 September (Paris: UNESCO).

United Nations Fund for Population Activities (UNFPA) (2002) *State of World Population 2002: People, Poverty and Possibilities*, http://www.unfpa.org/swp/2002, accessed May 2003.

United Nations Fund for Population Activities The Gambia (UNFPA The Gambia) (2003) *UNFPA Mandate and Focus Area* (Banjul: UNFPA).

United Nations Millennium Project (UNMP), Task Force on Education and Gender Equality (TFEGE) (2005) *Taking Action: Achieving Gender Equality and Empowering Women* (London: Earthscan).

United Nations Research Institute for Social Development (UNRISD)

(2005) *Gender Equality: Striving for Justice in an Unequal World* (Geneva: UNRISD).

United Nations Statistics Division (UNSD) (2005) *Special Report of the World's Women 2005: Progress in Statistics. Focusing on Sex-Disaggregated Statistics on Population, Births and Deaths* (New York: UNSD, Department of Social and Economic Affairs).

United States Department of State (USDS) (2004) 'Background note: Costa Rica' (Washington, DC: USDS, Bureau of Western Hemisphere Affairs), http://www.state.gov.r/pa/ei/bgn, accessed 7 May 2005.

United States Department of State (USDS) (2005) 'Background note: The Gambia' (Washington, DC: USDS, Bureau of African Affairs), http://www.state.gov.r/pa/ei/bgn, accessed 5 July 2005.

Universidad de Costa Rica (UCR), Observatorio de Desarrollo (OdD) (2004) Indicadores de Hoy (San José: UCR, OdD), http://www.odd.ucr/ ac.cr/vistazo/indicadores/hoy/pobreza.htm, accessed 3 July 2005.

Vargas, Claudia María (2002) 'Women in sustainable development: empowerment through partnerships for healthy living', *World Development*, 30:9, 1539–60.

Varley, Ann (1996) 'Women-headed households: some more equal than others?', *World Development*, 24:3, 505–20.

Varley, Ann (2002) 'Gender, families and households', in Vandana Desai and Robert Potter (eds) *The Companion to Development Studies* (London: Edward Arnold), pp. 329–34.

Varley, Ann and Blasco, Maribel (2000) 'Exiled to the home: masculinity and ageing in urban Mexico', *European Journal of Development Research*, 12:2, 115–38.

Varua, Ma Estela A (1999) 'Women's invisible work: the case of the Philippines', paper presented to the Seventh International Interdisciplinary Congress on Women, University of Tromsø, Tromsø, Norway, 20–26 June.

Vera-Sanso, Penny (2006) 'Defining the neighbourhood in South India', in Geer de Neve and Henrike Donner (eds) *The Meaning of the Local: Revisiting the Urban Neighbourhood in South India* (London: UCL/Routledge).

Vice President and Secretary of State for Women's Affairs (VPSSWA) (1999) *National Policy for the Advancement of Gambian Women 1999–2009* (Banjul: Office of the Vice President).

Villariba, Mariya (1993) 'Canvasses of women in the Philippines', *International Reports, Women and Society*, No. 7 (London: Change).

Vincenzi, Atilio (1991) *Código Civil y Código de la Familia* (San José: Lehmann Editores).

Virola, Romulo A. (2002) 'Statistical challenges on poverty reduction in the

Philippines', paper prepared for the Regional Seminar for Asian Managers on Monitoring and Evaluation of Poverty Reduction Programmes, sponsored by the World Bank Institute (WBI), Bangkok, 9–11 October.

Vuuren, Anke van (2003) *Women Striving for Self-Reliance: The Diversity of Female-Headed Households in Tanzania and the Livelihood Strategies they Employ* (Leiden: African Studies Centre).

Vylder, Stefan de (2004) 'Gender in poverty reduction strategies', in Gerd Johnsson-Latham (ed.) *Power and Privileges: Gender Discrimination and Poverty* (Stockholm: Regerinskanliet), pp. 82–107.

Wadda, Rohey (2000) 'Brain drain and capacity building in Africa: the Gambian experience', contribution to the Joint ECA/IOM/IDRC Regional Conference on 'The Brain Drain and Capacity Building in Africa', Addis Ababa, 22–24 February.

Waldfogel, Jane (1996) *What Do We Expect Lone Mothers to Do? Competing Agendas for Welfare Reform in the United States* (London: London School of Economics, Suntory Toyota International Centre for Economics and Related Disciplines, Welfare State Programme, Discussion Paper No. 124).

Wartenburg, Lucy (1999) 'Vulnerabilidad y Jefatura en los Hogares Urbanos Colombianos', in Mercedes González de la Rocha (ed.) *Divergencias del Modelo Tradicional: Hogares de Jefatura Femenina en América Latina* (México DF: Centro de Investigaciones y Estudios Superiores en Antropología Social/Plaza y Valdés Editores), pp. 77–96.

Weekes-Vagliani, Winifred (1992) 'Structural adjustment and gender in the Côte d'Ivoire', in Haleh Afshar and Carolyne Dennis (eds) *Women and Adjustment Policies in the Third World* (Basingstoke: Macmillan), pp. 117–49.

Wennerholm, Carolina Johansson (2002) *The 'Feminisation of Poverty': The Use of a Concept* (Stockholm: Swedish International Development Cooperation Agency).

Westwood, Sallie (1996) ' "Feckless fathers": masculinities and the British state', in Maírtín Mac An Ghaill (ed.) *Understanding Masculinities: Social Relations and Cultural Arenas* (Buckingham: Open University Press), pp. 21–34.

Whitehead, Ann (2003) *Failing Women, Sustaining Poverty: Gender in Poverty Reduction Strategy Papers: Report for the UK Gender and Development Network* (London: GADN/Christian Aid).

Whitehead, Ann and Lockwood, Matthew (1999) 'Gendering poverty: a review of six World Bank African poverty assessments', *Development and Change*, 30:3, 525–55.

Wichterich, Christa (2004) 'Food for thought from yesterday's discussion: women's human rights as terms of reference for women's struggles for social and gender justice', in Mandy MacDonald (ed.) *Globalising Women's Rights: Confronting Unequal Development Between the UN Rights Framework and the WTO Trade Agreements* (Bonn: Network Women in Development Europe [WIDE]), 62–6.

Williams, Chris and Lee-Smith, Diana (2000) 'Feminisation of poverty: re-thinking poverty reduction from a gender perspective', *Habitat Debate*, 6:4, 1–5, http://www.unhabitat.org/HD, accessed February 2003.

Williams, Mariama (2004) 'The MDGs in the context of gender and trade', in Women's International Coalition for Economic Justice (WICEJ) (ed.) *Seeking Accountability on Women's Human Rights: Women Debate the UN Millennium Development Goals* (New York: WICEJ), p. 17.

Willis, Katie (1993) 'Women's work and social network use in Oaxaca City, Mexico', *Bulletin of Latin American Research*, 12:1, 65–82.

Willis, Katie (1994) 'Women's work and social network use in Oaxaca City, Mexico', unpublished DPhil dissertation, Nuffield College, Oxford.

Willis, Katie (2000) 'No es fácil, pero es posible: the maintenance of middle-class women-headed households in Mexico', *European Review of Latin American and Caribbean Studies*, 69, 29–45.

Willis, Katie (2005) *Theories and Practices of Development* (London: Routledge).

Winchester, Hilary (1990) 'Women and children last: the poverty and marginalisation of one-parent families', *Transactions, Institute of British Geographers*, NS, 15:1, 70–86.

Womenaid International (1996) 'Capability poverty measure', http://www.womenaid.org/press/info/poverty.cpm.html, accessed October 2002.

Women's Environment and Development Organisation (WEDO) (2005) *Beijing Betrayed: Women Worldwide Report that Governments Have Failed to Turn the Platform into Action* (New York: WEDO).

World Bank (1994) *Enhancing Women's Participation in Economic Development* (Washington, DC: World Bank).

World Bank (1996) *A Strategy to Fight Poverty: Philippines* (Washington, DC: World Bank, Country Operations Division, East Asia and Pacific Region).

World Bank (1997) *Costa Rica: Identifying the Social Needs of the Poor: An Update* (Washington, DC: World Bank, Central American Department, Latin America and Caribbean Region).

World Bank (2000) *World Development Report 2000/2001: Attacking Poverty* (New York: Oxford University Press).

World Bank (2002a) *Integrating Gender into the World Bank's Work* (Washington, DC: World Bank).

World Bank (2002b) *World Development Indicators 2002* (Washington, DC: World Bank).

World Bank (2003a) *Global Economic Prospects 2003* (Washington, DC: World Bank).

World Bank (2003b) *World Development Indicators 2003* (Washington, DC: World Bank).

World Bank (2003c) *The PRSP Process in The Gambia* (Washington, DC: World Bank).

World Bank (2003d) *Costa Rica: Social Spending and the Poor* (Washington, DC: World Bank).

World Bank (2003e) *Challenges and Opportunities for Gender Equality in Latin America and the Caribbean* (Washington, DC: World Bank, Gender Unit, Latin America and the Caribbean Division).

World Bank (2004a) *Global Economic Prospects 2004* (Washington, DC: World Bank).

World Bank (2004b) *World Development Indicators* (Washington, DC: World Bank).

World Bank (2004c) *Memorandum of the President of the International Bank for Reconstruction and Development to the Executive Directors on a Country Partnership Strategy for the Republic of Costa Rica. Report No. 28570* (Washington, DC: World Bank, Central America Country Management Unit).

World Bank Gender and Development Group (World Bank GDG) (2003) *Proceedings of the International Workshop on Gender Equality and the Millennium Development Goals, 19–23 November 2003* (Washington, DC: World Bank, GDG).

World Bank Group (2003) *Millennium Development Goals* (Washington, DC: World Bank), http://www.developmentgoals.org/index.html, accessed 10 March 2004.

World Health Organization (WHO) (2000) *World Health Report 2000: Health Systems, Improving Perfomance* (Geneva: WHO).

World Health Organization (WHO) (2004) *World Health Report 2004: Changing History* (Geneva: WHO).

World Health Organization (WHO) (2005a) *World Health Report 2005: Make Every Mother and Child Count* (Geneva: WHO).

World Health Organization (WHO) (2005b) 'Country statistics' (Geneva: WHO), http://www.who.int/countries, accessed 11 May 2005.

World Tourism Organisation (WTO) (2005) *Tourism Market Trends* (Madrid: WTO), http://www.world-tourism.org/facts/trends/market_trends.htm, accessed 16 May 2005.

World Vision Costa Rica (WVCR) (2004) 'Public services and the girl-child in Costa Rica', in Alan Whaites (ed.) *The Girl-Child and Government*

Service Provision (Monrovia, CA: World Vision International), pp. 55–69.

Wratten, Ellen (1995) 'Conceptualising urban poverty', *Environment and Urbanisation*, 7:1, 11–36.

Yates, Rachel (1997) 'Literacy, gender and vulnerability: donor discourses and local realities', *IDS Bulletin*, 28:3, 112–21.

Yeandle, Sue, Escott, Karen, Grant, Linda and Batty, Elaine (2003) *Women and Men Talking About Poverty*, Working Paper Series No. 7, Manchester: Equal Opportunities Commission.

Yea, Sallie (2004) 'Runaway brides: anxieties of identity among trafficked Filipina entertainers in South Korea', *Singapore Journal of Tropical Geography*, 25:2, 180–97.

Young, Kate (1992) 'Household resource management', in Lise Østergaard (ed.) *Gender and Development: A Practical Guide* (London: Routledge), pp. 135–64.

Ypeij, Annelou and Steenbeek, Gerdien (2001) 'Poor single mothers and cultural meanings of social support', *Focaal – European Journal of Anthropology*, 38, 71–82.

Yu, Sandra and Karaos, Anna Marie (2004) 'Establishing the role of communities in governance: the experience of the Homeless People's Federation Philippines', *Environment and Urbanisation*, 16:1, 107–19.

Zaoude, Aster (2002) 'The hard path to equality' (Women's Human Rights Net), http://www.whrnet.org/docs/perspective-zaoude-0205.html, accessed 9 March 2004.

Zlotnik, Hanna (1995) 'Migration and the family: the female perspective', *Asian and Pacific Migration Journal*, 4:2–3, 253–71.

Zuckerman, Elaine (2003) 'Engendering PRSPs: conceptual and policy issues', paraphrased in UNDP/SURF, *Proceedings: Experts Meeting on Gender Mainstreaming of Poverty Reduction Strategy Papers in Selected African Countries* (Pretoria: UNDP/SURF/UNIFEM), p. 10.

Index